Issued under the authority of the

HOME OFFICE (FIRE DEPARTMENT)

MANUAL OF FIREMANSHIP

A Survey of the Science of Firefighting

Part 6B

Practical Firemanship—II

LONDON

HER MAJESTY'S STATIONERY OFFICE

ISBN 0 11 340567 7

Introduction to the Second Edition

THIS Part of the *Manual* was first issued in 1946. Since then there have been so many changes in the industries which are dealt with in this book that the fire-fighting methods used by fire brigades have had to be radically amended.

Until the 1950's town gas was produced by the carbonisation of coal, but at the beginning of the fifties the gas industry began to produce gas from oil (naphtha) and to import liquid natural gas (methane) from Algeria to assist in the manufacture of town gas. Then the first major strike of North Sea natural gas was made in 1965 and so the gas industry had to make another change; the gigantic scheme to convert to natural gas is now well under way.

Oil refining, too, is a development of the post-war era. Instead of petrol, lubricating oils, etc. being imported as finished products, crude oil is now shipped in bulk in giant tankers and brought to this country to be refined here. Consequently major refineries are opening up and expanding, producing even more problems for the fire service—those of tackling fires in refineries or giant tankers requiring the use of thousands of gallons of foam. A further subsidiary is the manufacture of chemicals and their by-products.

Civil aviation is another industry which has developed enormously in the last decade, and the problems of the fire service attending an aircraft accident are different from any other major civil disaster by the combination of high life and fire risk, varying in magnitude with the size of aircraft and the location of the accident. The very infrequency of aircraft accidents adds to the operational difficulties because it is almost impossible for one officer to accumulate experience which he can later employ to advantage.

It has been necessary, therefore, to re-write these three chapters in their entirety, and the two remaining chapters on rural fire fighting and electricity have also been completely revised and brought up to date. The Home Office would like to place on record its appreciation of the considerable efforts of the many people within the fire service and in the industries concerned to make this volume of the *Manual* as complete and informative as possible.

HOME OFFICE
June, 1972.

iii

Editorial Note

WHEN the *Manual of Firemanship* was originally planned in 1942, the chapters were to be numbered consecutively throughout the nine Parts. Since 1960 many revisions have taken place, but the system of chapter numbering has prevented any possibility of chapters being added or deleted without breaking the sequence. It has now been decided that more flexibility will be achieved if the numbering of chapters of each Part commences at No. 1. This change has now started, but until all Parts are either reprinted or revised, some confusion will exist in the numbering of chapters and in the cross-reference to them. In order to enable readers to check on chapter numbers, the following shows the old and new chapter numbers.

	Chapter numbers	
Part 1—Theory of fire-fighting and equipment	*Old*	*New*
Physics and chemistry of combustion	1	1
Extinguishing fire	2	2
Methods used by the fire service	3	3
Hose	4	4
Hose fittings	5	5
Ladders	6	6
Ropes and lines	7	7
Hand and stirrup pumps	8	8
Portable chemical fire extinguishers	9	9
Foam and foam-making equipment	10	10
Breathing apparatus	11	11
Resuscitation	12	12
Small gear	13	13
Part 2—Appliances		
Pumps, primers and pumping appliances	14	1
Practical pump operation	15	2
Wheeled escapes	16	3
Turntable ladders	17	4
Hydraulic platforms	—	5
Special appliances	18	6
Part 3—Hydraulics and water supplies		
Hydraulics	19	1
Waterworks, mains water supplies and fire hydrants	20	2
Emergency water supplies (deleted in 1968)	21	—
Water relaying (formerly chapter 22, but renumbered in 1968)	21	3

Editorial Note

vii

Metrication

List of S.I. units for use in the fire service.

Quantity and basic or derived S.I. unit and symbol	Approved unit of measurement	Conversion factor
Length metre (m)	kilometre (km) metre (m) millimetre (mm)	1 mile = 1·609 km 1 yard = 0·914 m 1 foot = 0·305 m 1 inch = 25·4 mm
Area square metre (m²)	square kilometre (km²) square metre (m²) square millimetre (mm²)	1 mile² = 2·590 km² 1 yard² = 0·836 m² 1 foot² = 0·093 m² 1 inch² = 645·2 mm²
Volume cubic metre (m³)	cubic metre (m³) litre (l) (10⁻³ m³)	1 cubic foot = 0·028 m³ 1 gallon = 4·546 litres
Volume Flow cubic metre per second (m³/s)	cubic metre per second (m³/s) litres per minute (l/min = 10⁻³m³/min)	1 foot³/s = 0·028 m³/s 1 gall/min. = 4·546 l/min
Mass kilogramme (kg)	kilogramme (kg) tonne (t) = (10³ kg)	1 lb. = 0·454 kg 1 ton = 1·016 t
Velocity metre per second (m/s)	metre/second (m/s) International knot (kn) kilometre/hour (km/h)	1 foot/second = 0·305 m/s 1 UK knot = 1·853 km/h 1 Int. knot = 1·852 km/h 1 mile/hour = 1·61 km/h
Acceleration metre per second² (m/s²)	metre/second² (m/s²)	1 foot/second² = 0·305 m/s² 'g' = 9·81 m/s²
Force newton (N)	kilonewton (kN) newton (N)	1 ton force = 9·964 kN 1 lb force = 4·448 N
Energy Work joule (J) (= 1 Nm)	joule (J) kilojoule (kJ) kilowatt-hour (kW h)	1 British thermal unit = 1·055 kJ 1 foot lb force = 1·356 J

Quantity and basic or derived S.I. unit and symbol	Approved unit of measurement	Conversion factor
Power watt (W) ($=1$ J/s$=1$ Nm/s)	kilowatt (kW) watt (W)	1 horsepower$=0\cdot746$ kW 1 foot lb force/second$=$ $\qquad 1\cdot356$ W
Pressure newton/metre^2 (N/m^2)	bar$=10^5$ N/m^2 millibar (m bar) ($=10^2$ N/m^2) metrehead	1 atmosphere$=$ $101\cdot325$ kN/m$^2=1\cdot013$ bar 1 lb force/in$^2=$ $6894\cdot76$ N/m$^2=0\cdot069$ bar 1 inch Hg$=33\cdot86$ m bar 1 metrehead$=0\cdot0981$ bar 1 foot head$=0\cdot305$ $\qquad$ metrehead
Heat, Quantity of Heat joule (J)	joule (J) kilojoule (kJ)	1 British thermal unit $\qquad =1\cdot055$ kJ
Heat Flow Rate watt (W)	watt (W) kilowatt (kW)	1 British thermal unit/ $\qquad$ hour$=0\cdot293$ W 1 British thermal unit/ $\qquad$ second$=1\cdot055$ kW
Specific Energy, Calorific Value, Specific Latent Heat joule/kilogramme (J/kg) joule/m^3 (J/m^3)	kilojoule/kilogramme $\qquad$ (kJ/kg) kilojoule/m^3 (kJ/m^3) megajoule/m^3 (MJ/m^3)	1 British thermal unit/ lb$=2\cdot326$ kJ/kg 1 British thermal unit/ft$^3=37\cdot26$ kJ/m^3
Temperature degree Celsius (°C)	degree Celsius (°C)	1 degree centigrade$=$ 1 degree Celsius

Contents of Part 6B

Chapter 3—Electricity and the Fire Service

SECTION V—FIRE-FIGHTING PROCEDURE

Chapter 4—Fires in aircraft

SECTION I—CIVIL AIRCRAFT

SECTION II—MILITARY AIRCRAFT

SECTION III—ROTARY WING AIRCRAFT

SECTION IV—AERODROME EQUIPMENT AND FACILITIES

Part 6B   Chapter 1

Fires in Rural Areas

THE technique of country fire fighting is very different from that necessary in the town. The distance appliances have to travel, the possibility of delayed calls, the scarcity of water and the dependence of the fire service upon retained fire brigade cover with its delayed response and probable longer distances to travel, provide the background against which such fires are fought. Small quantities of water must be made to do the utmost amount of work and the use of nozzle sizes exactly appropriate to the situation is important. In many cases, fires have to be extinguished or confined not by water but partly or entirely by beating, trenching, pulling down or covering with earth; these are methods which involve firemen in arduous work for long periods, whilst in others fires are rightly and properly allowed to burn out under supervision.

Yet another feature is that machinery or implements used in agriculture can, when they are available, often be put to good use and may on occasion prove more effective than the equipment of the fire brigade itself. This chapter refers in a number of places to such use of agricultural implements and to the assistance which can be given by persons not in the fire service, but it must be understood that the chapter deals only with the technique of fire fighting and has no concern with the means by which agricultural implements and persons to use them may be made available, nor with any administrative or financial questions that may arise.

The important place farming occupies in the national life and the increasing mechanisation of agriculture, particularly in the harvesting of grain and crops, together with a tendency on the part of the general public, following upon the development of transport facilities, to seek out open spaces—a practice which may involve the lighting of picnic fires and the dropping of cigarette ends—has greatly increased the chances of fires occurring in rural areas. The use of mechanised machinery has also resulted in the storage of flammable liquids, and there is the additional danger of fires resulting from hot exhaust pipes in cornfields, etc. It is increasingly important that the technique of fighting the commoner types of rural fire should be familiar to all firemen.

Apart from the fires which are caused by carelessness, the incidence of fires in the country varies greatly with the time of the year.

1

Thus forest, heath and grass fires are in general most prevalent either in the early spring before the sap has fully risen, and when the winds are keen and drying, or during hot spells at the height of summer when the vegetation has been dried out by the heat. Crop fires only occur during a short period after the grain is ripe or nearly so and before it is cut. Perhaps the most vulnerable period is during the actual harvest operations. The making of silage from grass crops has lessened the number of haystacks, and consequently fires due to spontaneous combustion in such stacks are no longer as frequent as in the past. However, the new hazard of fires caused by spontaneous combustion of silage presents a much more difficult problem for the fireman and special attention is devoted to such fires in par. 6 (h).

The weather has its greatest effect, of course, upon the state of water supplies and also of the ground. Within a few days, water in streams and ponds may increase or decrease greatly, while a field which is inaccessible to a water tender one week, may be passable the next. The influence of rain upon fire fighting itself should not be forgotten, for many large grass or heath fires are only finally extinguished by rain, and the officer who sees or is told that rain is probable should not fail to take that fact into account. It should, therefore, be one of the first tasks of an urban fireman stationed in a country area to understand how the countryside is affected by the changing seasons and the weather that they bring, and to relate this knowledge to his fire-fighting technique.

1. FIRES ON HEATHS, MOORS AND PEAT-LANDS

Heather, moor and other lands of this type (Plates 1 and 2) are covered with low growing vegetation which is wiry and tends to burn readily in dry weather. Water is generally scarce and the ground is often covered by a layer, a foot (305 mm) or more in thickness, of dry peat-like matter which is very open in texture, and in which fire can travel readily.

Fires on these lands are of frequent occurrence, especially during the dry weather, being caused by owners burning off old vegetation and allowing the fire to get out of hand; by picnic parties, or by cigarette ends being thrown carelessly away. The passing of the steam locomotive has removed the hazard of sparks igniting standing crops and heath land, but diesel locomotives have been known to produce sparks due to carbon building up in the exhaust system. Whilst most are of small extent, large fires covering an area of 10 to 20 square miles (26 to 52 km^2) of moorland are not unknown.

(a) General

Unless military or similar assistance is available or considerable civilian help can be obtained, fire brigades will generally be unable, because of insufficiency of numbers, to extinguish a large heath fire. Such fires usually occur in areas supplied with little water, where the nature and accessibility of the country make it difficult to use water tenders, while the provision of water relays is often impracticable because of the amount of equipment and numbers of men required.

In general, therefore, the efforts of fire brigades are devoted to the protection of adjoining property, such as woodlands, farms and houses, by diverting the fire and allowing it to burn out against a natural fire break, the available manpower being used to prevent the fire passing the break. The course to be taken at any particular fire will be dictated by circumstances, which will include the number of men and appliances which can be called upon, the amount of water and its distance from the fire area, the nature of access, prevailing weather conditions, and the proximity of other fire risks.

The following paragraphs contain a number of general suggestions to be borne in mind where it is necessary to extinguish rather than control a fire, while points which relate particularly to special types of land are grouped in the remainder of the section.

(i) At large heath and moorland fires there is great value in a thorough preliminary reconnaissance. The first step is to determine what buildings, plantations, overhead power lines or other properties are likely to be endangered. For this purpose large scale maps are generally carried on appliances or in fire officers' cars, so that they are available at the fireground. Maps, together with information from local workers, provide the quickest method of sizing up the situation, since in many cases it is impossible to see across the fire area on account of the flames and smoke, while it might take several hours, especially in mountainous districts, to make a circuit of the fire. Upon the completion of this preliminary survey, the officer in charge should make his initial disposition and send back his request for assistance. If beating is to be employed, he should know whether local equipment is available and, if not, give instructions for beaters to be obtained and sent on. (The design of beaters is described on pages 64/66.)

The officer in charge should then make a detailed survey of the fire area. Two or more persons should complete a circuit, each taking a portion, and should note:

A.   The direction and rate of spread of the fire in various directions;

3

B. Wind direction and velocity (in mountainous districts the wind may blow in different directions on different parts of the fire area);

C. Natural breaks such as roads, watercourses, strips of green vegetation or cultivated land likely to check the course of the fire. (Tarred roads are not always a perfect fire break, since the surface of the road itself may take fire.)

D. Any change in the character of the ground or vegetation, *e.g.*, from earth to peat or from heather to bracken or gorse.

It should be emphasised that deliberation and thorough investigation at the beginning may, in the end, save much labour, time and damage, so that when reinforcements arrive, they can be deployed to the best advantage.

(ii) Military personnel and civilians can be of great assistance in beating so long as their efforts are co-ordinated and properly controlled. Groups of such helpers should be placed in the charge of a fireman and stationed in the least dangerous positions.

(iii) Firemen should be sent to the natural fire breaks with spades and beaters to deal with small fires caused by sparks blowing across the breaks or through openings in dry stone walls. Such sparks can sometimes be carried long distances and patrols should therefore operate in depth. When molinia grass* (Plate 3) especially is affected, wisps of burning grass which become detached are easily carried long distances by a light breeze and are capable of remaining alight for a long time and of starting new fires. Gorse is also liable to cast showers of sparks which may be carried long distances and may continue to burn for some time.

(iv) At heath fires, unlined hose, if available, is useful, since its damp outer surface prevents scorching of the fabric, but as many brigades no longer carry unlined hose, extreme care should be taken when using non-percolating hose. The danger of a change of wind causing hose lines to become involved in the fire should be borne in mind.

(v) Where a bulldozer can be made available, its use for clearing a track along and as near as possible to the fire front is the most effective and least exhausting method of fighting all types of fire on open heaths and moors, where the fire is not likely to burn deeply into peat and where there is no risk of the bulldozer becoming bogged.

* Molinia grass, also known as purple melic grass, has a flat leaf with a rough edge, and grows in tussocks. It is purplish in colour when growing, turning to grey–yellow or bleached colour during fire danger periods. It is a natural weed found on wet moorlands or badly drained hard woodland areas.

4

(vi) Communications at large heath or moorland fires are often difficult owing to lack of roads. Most appliances and staff cars are equipped with radio and this can be used effectively to collate information where large areas are involved. Radio pack or hand sets and loud hailers may also be of considerable value in maintaining communications with crews engaged in the operations.

(vii) In order to avoid damage to the tyres, appliances should not be taken over land which has been burning until the ground is cool, or parked where there is a danger of the vehicle being involved in rapid fire spread. Drivers should also remember that if a vehicle is parked on soft ground it may sink slowly in and be impossible to move in an emergency.

(viii) This type of fire throws up large quantities of carbonised dust, and personnel should therefore beware of this getting into their eyes. If eyeshields are available, they should be worn. Since burning moorland holds the heat for a considerable time, leather boots can quickly be ruined. Those of rubber are preferable, though rubber absorbs heat and can in time burn the feet and make the boots difficult to remove. Leather insoles to rubber boots have proved satisfactory.

(ix) Upon high moors the temperature drops considerably at night, and hoar frost is not uncommon even in the middle of summer. A fire, therefore, tends to die down towards nightfall and to burn up again the next morning. Patrols left on the fireground overnight should be reinforced early in the morning.

(x) Large fires in open country—especially in times of drought— may travel in any direction, irrespective of the wind, because of radiant heat and the formation of air eddies.

(xi) In areas where open heath, forest and similar fires are of frequent occurrence, the fire brigade officer will be wise to arrange in advance, as far as possible, for the use of tractors, ploughs, rollers, etc.

(b) Heath and grass fires in non-peaty soil

This type of heath fire usually occurs in very dry weather and is comparatively easy to fight, since the fire only travels through the surface growth and does not affect the sub-surface. Grassland of this type is shown in Plate 2. When appliances arrive in good time, it is usually preferable to attack the fire at once by beating rather than to let it burn while water is being obtained, unless a source of supply is close to the fire area.

If beating is decided on, it is advisable to attack the fire with small parties of beaters working on the flanks and attempting to drive the fire to a point, or to confine it against a natural fire break such as a road or stone wall. On windless days a fire extending outwards from a central point can be attacked in several places by concentrating parties of beaters and, after it has been split up, by dealing with each section individually. It is not advisable to disperse the force of the beaters; instead they should be set to work in groups where concentrated effort can best be brought to bear. It will sometimes be found practicable to attack the fire from inside as well as from outside the burnt area, a position which protects the beaters from the worst effects of heat, smoke and dust.

When natural fire breaks are absent, it is not generally practicable to attempt to make a fire break, as it often requires a large number of men and heavy equipment, and so every effort should be made to utilise such natural fire breaks as may be available.

If water is available, jets are effective; they should have a good throw and are best held about 3 ft (1 m) above the ground and directed with a swivelling movement. Variable branches can be used so long as they are adjusted to the pressure at the nozzle. The edge of the fire can often be extinguished by branches from a water tender, gradually moving the tender along the edge; in other cases a hand pump working from a bucket can have considerable effect if used for damping down in advance of the fire and for extinguishing 'bulls-eyes'. When appliances and staff cars are used on rough grass or heath-land, care must be taken to see that the hot exhaust system does not start a fire under the appliance or car.

Even after beating has been successful, small quantities of water are usually required to deal with tree roots and patches of peaty sub-soil, and a strip some 20 ft (6 m) wide of unburnt ground should be damped in order to extinguish any sparks that may have been raised during beating operations.

In some instances, a combination of beating and the application of water has met with success, a small quantity of water available at one side of the fire being used to extinguish that side, whilst beating takes place upon the other. Eventually the two parties drive the fire to a single point where it can finally be extinguished with water. Beating is seldom effective upon couch grass (quitch), the matted condition of which produces a bellows effect, and water will generally be needed to extinguish a fire in such grass.

(c) Heath fires on peaty soil

In many cases, heather, gorse, bracken or scattered trees or under-growth may be found growing on a thick layer of leaf mould, the first stage in the formation of a peat bed. When the surface vegetation of such an area catches fire (Plate 16) the ground will burn itself to a depth which depends upon the heat generated, but which usually reaches 12 to 18 in. (305 to 457 mm). The drier the surface, the deeper the burning will go. Fire is able to travel underground, and the smoke is almost invisible.

The surface fire can be extinguished as described in par. 1(b) above; the spread must be checked not only on the surface but also beneath it. The most efficient way of doing this is trenching, preferably by mechanical means such as a bulldozer or a tractor pulling a plough, since by employing this method a break is made in the burning sub-surface, while at the same time the trench forms a suitable line upon which to make a surface stop. The trench should be wide enough to prevent the fire jumping it, extra width being necessary if a strong wind is blowing, and should extend through the leaf mould to the soil beneath. Vegetation dug from the trench should be thrown to the rear, but earth banked upon the side which is towards the fire. When large areas of fire are involved, it may not be possible to dig enough trenches, and efforts should then be devoted to connecting up existing breaks, such as streams or moorland tracks.

Should adequate supplies of water be available, the fire should be surrounded, using jets at good pressure (Plate 17) since spray will not penetrate the surface. Men should work slowly in front of the perimeter covering the whole of the affected area, and they should beware of the danger of receiving burns from embers thrown up by steam when high pressure jets reach patches of fire. Burning tree roots, ground behind trees that may have been screened from a jet by the trees themselves, and any other specially hot patches should be damped, and where appropriate, turned over and damped again, an axe being used to cut out smouldering wood. At the same time the trench should be flooded (unless it has filled itself, as may happen on peaty soil) and the ground in advance of it given a thorough wetting.

When water is scarce, surface extinction should be attempted, either by beating, pressing glowing pockets of embers downwards with a spade, or digging out burning patches until the non-peaty sub-soil is encountered and then putting the burning peat, top downwards, into the hole so made.

(d) Gorse, bracken and undergrowth fires

Bracken (fern) is usually found growing tall and thick on poor stony ground; gorse (furze, whins) on poor grassland. Fires in gorse or bracken, together with those in areas of shrubs and thick undergrowth, cannot satisfactorily be dealt with by beating, as the height of the flames (some 6 ft—1·8 m) and the intense heat and smoke make such work impossible (Plate 4).

The solution is to cut a fire break at a sufficient distance from the fire to make sure that it will be completed in time, and then to have water available along the line of the break, using small high-pressure jets applied with a sweeping motion which can penetrate to the roots of the gorse or bracken. These breaks can be cut with axes or long-handled billhooks (slashers) (*see* Fig. 1-14) or made by a tractor, if possible pulling a grubber or, where the ground is suitable, a plough. Where sufficient water is available, a break can be made by thoroughly wetting a strip of bracken and then holding this line with jets. When the wind is suitable, controlled counterfiring (which consists in starting a controlled fire the position and travel of which forms a break to check the spread of the fire it is desired to extinguish) may also be attempted by those with experience of the results to be obtained, but *this method should never be used except by those thoroughly conversant with it.* Counterfiring should be started at a point of vantage, such as a narrow footpath or a place where the growth is less thick. The fire once started, burns quietly, since it is sheltered from the wind by the growth not yet affected, and will burn slowly towards the oncoming fire. The counterfire should be extended along the required line and carefully controlled by beating or by the application of water, so that it burns in the desired direction.

Fires in cut brushwood are difficult to extinguish and are best left to burn, surrounding risks being protected. The practice of covering brushwood with earth is not usually satisfactory. In some parts of the country, plantations of rhododendron bushes which may reach a height of 20 ft (6 m) will be found. Such plantations may be almost impenetrable, and a fire in them evolves intense heat and choking fumes. Fire fighting is best limited to damping the edge of the plantation to form a break where any fire not arrested by the water may be beaten out. Any available natural fire break, such as a track, should be used as a stop.

The anthills, up to 4 ft (1·2 m) high, sometimes found in thickets, etc., burn with an intense white heat and should be thoroughly flooded, for, if left, they are liable to cause a fresh outbreak.

(e) Marsh fires

In winter, rush-bearing marshland often becomes flooded and when the water freezes, the dry projecting rushes are very susceptible to fire. Such fires, which travel above the ice at great speed, are capable of spreading to adjoining property and are difficult to handle. It is necessary to operate on dry ground well ahead of the fire front and, if there is combustible material such as frosted grass or a forest

plantation within range, to watch for sparks well in advance of the
fire.

(f) Fires in peat moss and peat stacks

Peat moss is formed in the same way as coal, and comprises dead
vegetation which has been acted upon by climatic conditions and
decay for hundreds of years. It is occasionally found extending to a
depth of over 40 ft (12 m) from the surface, but usually the beds are
only a few feet (a metre or so) thick.

Peat is very spongy and absorbent, and presents a boggy appearance once the surface layer is disturbed. As a result of dry weather
and strong winds, however, the top layer, extending from 2 to 18 in.
(51–457 mm) from the surface, will dry out, while below this the peat
remains moist. In some districts, a wiry type of low vegetation is
found growing on the peat, and occasionally a poor type of tree,
about 20 ft (6 m) in height, grows in groups to form a small wood.

Owing to the absorbent nature of peat, though small springs and
water pockets do occur, good natural supplies of water, such as ponds
and streams, are seldom found, and the absence of such supplies
makes the task of extinguishing a peat fire difficult. A large hole dug
down below the dry layer will, however, tend to drain the sub-surface
moisture and may provide a useful quantity of water, sufficient to
extinguish small pockets of fire on the surface.

Fires in peat generally begin as scrub fires, which attack the surface
to a depth of 1 or 2 in. (25–51 mm), tending to burn quietly in a
circle, but if a strong wind should develop, fire travels moderately
fast in line and extends over such a wide area that manpower is
generally not available in sufficient quantity to check its progress at
all points. Quick action is then called for, especially if the fire is
heading towards adjoining woods, crops or property.

One method of attack is shallow trenching, necessary since the fire
will be affecting the dry surface of the peat, or the digging out of the
burning material. Should digging take place in peat which is burning,
it should be thrown upon the burnt surface and broken up. Men
should not be allowed to trample or stamp upon glowing peat with
the idea of extinguishing it, as such efforts will not be successful.
In some places, drainage trenches are to be found, generally 4 to 5 ft
(1·2–1·5 m) deep at the bottom of which there is a quantity of sludge,
which can be successfully used to stop the travel of small fires (Plate
17) but the filling and carrying of buckets of such material is labor-
ious work. The sludge is placed in line in front of the fire and will
usually retain its moist condition long enough to prevent the progress
of the fire. These trenches are a danger at night, for it is extremely

9

difficult for a person who has fallen into one of them to get out un-aided. Plenty of light should, therefore, always be used to mark routes across the peat beds.

When the fire leaves the scrub and the upper layer of peat and works down into the peat bed itself, it becomes extremely difficult to extinguish. The peat beds will smoulder indefinitely at red heat, or will flame in a good wind, and even if signs of burning do not show on the surface, the fire may persist underground, or in rare cases may even travel under a road and appear at the other side. Deep trenching will confine the fire, but in order to extinguish it water must be used in considerable quantities.

A small fire can be dealt with by removing the surface peat to a depth of about 1 ft (305 mm) and then filling the hollow with water which is allowed to work down into the peat. If the fire is larger, small diameter nozzles at a fairly high pressure should be pressed or forced into the ground, the affected area being worked over in a methodical way. This procedure can be rendered easier if holes are first made with a crowbar or if an extended branch (see Part 1 of the *Manual*, Chapter 5, 'Hose Fittings') is used. It will be necessary to arrange for adequate water supplies if this method is to be employed, the whole area inside the trenching being so treated.

Instead of trenching, a break can be made by using high-pressure jets in the manner described above. If the branch is held a few degrees from the vertical, the jet will rip the peat and loosen the fibres, leaving a groove which allows the peat beneath to become thoroughly saturated for long enough for the fire to burn out against it. This method has the advantage over trenching of being far less exhausting.

In some districts peat is cut in blocks which are built up into 'hogs' to be dried by sun and wind before being used a fuel. These 'hogs', some 30 ft by 8 ft (9 × 2·5 m) are constructed like a honeycomb with spaces between the blocks to allow air to enter, and are built some 250 ft (76 m) apart, a large area of peat containing as many as 400 hogs. When ignited, the blocks burn quickly with intense heat, combustion ensuing throughout the hog almost at once and the whole being consumed in approximately two hours. The smoke given off is not dense, but it has a pungent smell which clings to clothing and causes slight irritation to the eyes.

A fire in a peat bog can be extinguished by a large jet used at moderate pressure to prevent sparks flying too severely. Embers of red hot peat are very light and will quickly set fire to the dry peat of adjacent hogs unless the latter are protected. When turning over, the remains of the hog can be thrown into a drainage trench and so extinguished. Before direct attack on a burning hog is begun, however, the surrounding peat should be saturated and neighbouring hogs, especially those downwind, should be protected.

The use of heavy pumps on peat moss is quite impossible, and even portable pumps, which may have to be manhandled a considerable distance, will soon get bogged down as a result of the vibration caused by pumping unless planks or faggots can be found on which to stand the pump, while the use of towing vehicles is out of the question. In some places where hogs may be encountered, there may be a light railway to carry the peat blocks away, and in that case trucks can be used to transport portable pumps and provide a platform upon which they can work.

Men working on peat fires rapidly become fatigued owing to the fact that at every step taken the feet sink into the ground. When the fire is in the peat moss itself and not in the hogs, it is advisable to tread carefully, for the top layer may have burned away and will crumble when weight it put upon it; there is then a danger of falling into holes where the peat is burning.

Unlined hose should be used where possible, since the exterior of non-percolating hose may be burnt by a sudden outbreak beneath and around the hose.

(g) Fires in reclaimed peat-lands used for farming (Fens)

For centuries the fen lands have provided some of the richest farmland in the country. The rich, dark peat-land laced with waterways, is particularly suitable for such crops as potatoes, carrots and celery, and whilst the crops themselves present no fire hazard, the land itself does. Once ignited, fen soil, which is practically pure peat, will burn until extinguished either by prolonged natural wet weather, or by fire-fighting operations. Such fires give very little indication of their presence. The wisps of smoke are barely visible but there is a characteristic smell of burning peat which can always be detected.

The fires are usually started by farmers burning rubbish, or by so-called controlled burning of rough growth on the banks of the ditches, dykes and drains. Extinguishing these fires is an arduous and lengthy task since the burning is slow and persistent. The most practical method is by the use of strong jets and digging out. Some fire brigades have developed special probe jets for this work to save the digging otherwise involved. These probe jets are similar to those used for haylage silos (*see* Fig. 1-7).

One of the additional hazards met with when dealing with such fires is the presence of bog oaks. These are oak trees which formed parts of the ancient forests and which have lain buried in the peat for sometimes thousands of years.

To extinguish fen soil fires, a large quantity of water is required. Fortunately, the fen lands are well supplied with ditches, dykes and drains, but the fields are very large and operations usually call for portable pumps and large quantities of hose. A danger to both personnel and appliances are the pitted areas where the fire is burning deep underground and may not be visible to the unwary. Spraying the top with water, even trenching and filling with water (as for irrigation) will seldom prove effective against soil fires. Usually fire brigade personnel stationed in these parts of the country are only too familiar with this type of fire and its attendant problems.

During very dry seasons, water—even in the fens—may be scarce and often the farmer will use water from the dykes for vegetable washing; he may therefore be reluctant to see it used for fighting land fires. In such cases, priorities must be established since the land will burn away to valueless ash unless extinguished.

Driving appliances over peat-lands can be precarious and although in some brigades four-wheel-drive appliances are used especially for this purpose, caution must be observed when leaving the hard tracks or 'droves' as they are locally named.

Distinct from the fens, during the past century much rough woodland and scrub growing on a peat surface has been cleared for agricultural purposes and such land may now often produce large crops. Farmhouses and buildings are sometimes erected upon hard clay patches in the peat land and, in these areas, there may be a danger of a fire spreading to buildings and crops from adjoining heath or peat moss or from peat bogs.

Trenching, preferably by mechanical means, is the best method of confining the main body of fire. There are usually drains beneath the surface of the land and if these can be opened up, they provide ready-made trenches. This method does not, however, prevent the spread of flying embers. On reclaimed land, these are light in weight and so small as to be almost invisible, the only sign of their having landed being wisps of smoke. If a large area is involved and there is a wind, the only practicable method of extinction is for parties with hand pumps and buckets of water to attack all places where wisps of smoke can be seen.

Water supply to these farms is always difficult; it is, therefore, desirable to avoid using for fire-fighting purposes, supplies upon which the farmer depends and as soon as possible after fire-fighting operations are begun, arrangements should be made to use water tenders or to institute a relay.

2. FIRES IN FORESTS AND WOODLANDS

(a) General

Though a forest fire starts in a small way, it soon gains in momentum, the rate of travel being sometimes faster than a man can run, and in a short time great destruction may be done. These fires are potentially the most serious rural risk a fireman has to face. Once a fire has developed to a large size it produces eddies above the fire area sufficient to nullify the effect of the prevailing wind; spread may then be in any direction, and it is therefore always necessary to keep open a line of retreat for men and appliances. Forestry Commission plantations often cover vast areas and fires can result in huge financial loss and serious unemployment for personnel employed on them.

It is generally the case that a small wood or plantation consists of hardwood trees such as oak, beech and birch, which do not burn easily, though ash and to a lesser extent sycamore, are dangerous when the sap is up, between May and October. In a tree of this latter type on fire this sap expands and with explosive force blows burning pieces up to 50 ft (15 m) away. The larger forests, however, which are in most cases administered by the Forestry Commission, usually consist of plantations of Scots pine (Plate 6), Corsican pine, Douglas fir, larch and spruce. Of these, Scots pine, Corsican pine, and Douglas fir have a high resin content at all times of the year and burn furiously. Spruce (Plate 8) is highly flammable before it sheds its needles, but at other times is not difficult to deal with. There are two varieties of larch, European and Japanese, both of which lose their needles in winter like hardwood trees. Fires spread rapidly through European larch plantations, but Japanese larch (Plate 7) is much less flammable and has a retarding influence on fire, sometimes being grown in belts to serve this purpose.

When the trees are first planted they are spaced 4 ft 6 in. (1·37 m) apart, giving 2,000 trees to the acre (approximately 5,000 trees to the hectare), their height being from 12 to 18 in. (305 to 457 mm). Fires in plantations of trees up to 4 ft (1·2 m) in height are comparatively easy to extinguish. The burning trees can be beaten out without undue trouble and can be cut off at ground level by one or two strokes of a sharp billhook, slasher or even a spade, if it is necessary to create a fire break. The fire may spread rapidly, but the direction and rate of advance of the fire can easily be seen when standing upright, movement through the trees is easy, and appliances can be driven without damage through a plantation not exceeding 3 ft (914 mm) in height (Plate 3). These factors simplify the co-ordination of fire-fighting

13

squads and speed the attack. Dispositions can then be made without the delay which is unavoidable when it is necessary to range round a burning area because the trees are too high to see over it.

When the trees are approximately 4 ft (1·2 m) in height however, plantations present a special hazard, for the trees themselves are not old enough to permit clearing of the undergrowth that has grown up between their lower branches, and there is frequently an accumulation of dried, combustible needles suspended on the undergrowth which acts as a connecting link for fire to travel between the ground and the branches of the trees. Fires in this undergrowth are difficult to control, especially if they spread to the tops of the young trees, and in this case the flames are likely to travel to any quarter irrespective of the direction of the wind.

Trees which have grown 12 to 15 ft (3·5 to 4·5 m) high are still at the original spacing and the branches are alive down to ground level. The fire risk is high, and there is considerable danger to firemen, since they cannot see more than 2 to 3 yards (metres) and movement is restricted. To avoid the danger of being cut off, men moving in such forests should do so in couples and keep within earshot of one another (by voice or by means of radio) while a chain of men also within earshot connects them with the outside of the danger area.

When the trees reach a height of 15 ft (4·5 m) the lower branches die away, and those above form a canopy which kills the undergrowth round the trees (Plate 9), the fire risk then being increased by the dead lower branches and the accumulation of dead needles upon the ground. Movement is still difficult, but visibility is 30 to 40 yards (27 to 37 m) and there is not the same danger of being cut off. When the lower branches of the trees have been removed (or brashed as it is called in forestry), the danger is still further decreased, movement being easier and the fire hazard from the trees less. The brashing is left in the alleyways between the trees, but each third alleyway is kept clear.

(b) Fire breaks and fire belts

In general forests under the control of the Crown are divided by rides (Plate 14) into blocks which may be from 5 to 30 acres (2 to 12 hectares) in extent, but in other plantations blocks up to 60 acres (24 hectares) may still be found. The taller the trees the more valuable they are, and if a decision has to be made as to relative priorities, the taller trees should be protected first. Serious scorching will kill a tree, the vulnerability depending upon the thinness of the bark.

14

(c) Fire plans

There should be a fire plan for every woodland area where fire danger is serious because of size, access or other special considerations. With the co-operation of neighbouring owners a number of small estates are sometimes protected by a group plan.

The purpose of a fire plan is to set down the arrangements which are designed to lessen the risk or consequence of woodland fires. It should deal fully with the action to be taken in the event of an outbreak. The chief fire officer for the area should be consulted during the preparation of the fire plan.

Generally the fire plan should cover the following points:

(i) *Area.* The area of plantation with a description of those sections of special value.

(ii) *Special danger area.* Areas where there is a high degree of danger because of the flammable nature of the vegetation or the probability of an outbreak.

(iii) *Danger period.* The danger periods in the year.

(iv) *Fire protection.* The form of protection reckoned as most adequate to deal with the type of woodland.

(v) *Natural firebreaks.* Existing natural barriers where a fire may be stopped.

(vi) *Prepared firebreaks.* Any cleared or cultivated traces, mown strips, controlled burning areas and brashed belts.

(vii) *Firebelts.* Protective belts of larch or hardwood.

(viii) *Equipment and water supplies.* Locations and method of transport.

(ix) *Rendezvous points.* Locations and arrangements for a man to direct fire appliances.

(x) *Communications and alarm methods.* Public roads, forest roads, telephones, etc.

(xi) *Firewatchers and patrols.* Details.

(xii) *Assistance.* Details of employees and outside assistance.

(xiii) *Alarm action.* How the alarm is raised.

(xiv) *Mobilisation.* Details.

(xv) *Action at fires.* Details of special consideration.

It is recommended that a forest fire map with a scale of 1 : 50,000 (1 mm = 50 m) (6 in. to the mile) should accompany the fire plan and should show the following:

Forest boundary   Yellow wash

Estate roads passable to all vehicles   Solid dark brown line

Estate roads or tracks passable to   Broken dark brown line
  4 wheel drive vehicles

Firebreaks

                                         Hatched
                                         (green)

Larch or Hardwood Belts   Dotted
                                         (green) band   ✳✳✳✳

Hydrant   single

                                              double

Open water with access point

Static water supply, surface tank   50,000
  (with capacity in gallons—litres)

Static water supply, underground   50,000
  tank (with capacity in gallons—
  litres)

Perennial streams
  (indicating direction of flow)
                                              (pale blue)

Telephones   Red 'T' in ¼-in. (6mm.) green circle

Fire towers and look-outs   Red triangle with ½-in. (13 mm.) base

Danger areas   Red or Orange wash

Depots   ½-in. (13 mm.) circle hatched (purple)

Rendezvous (R.V.) points   ¼-in. (6 mm.) solid red circle with
                                           black arrow and number or name
                                           at sides.

Plate 1. Heather and gorse covered ground merging into sparse forest.

Plate 2. Open rough countryside covered with rh?ola grass.

Plate 3. Molinia grass growing in a plantation of young trees. When the grass is dry it is in its most dangerous condition until the new growth appears about May.

Plate 4. A gorse fire which is involving bushes, trees and other vegetation.

Plate 5. A Forestry Commission fire lookout tower.

Plate 6. A forest of 25 years old Scots pine prior to brashing.

Plate 7. Japanese larch growing on the sides of a steep slope. Note the density of the overwood.

Plate 8. A dense forest of Sitka spruce. Note how the trees have overgrown the road running through the forest.

Plate 9. Men in the process of brashing a forest of Sitka spruce.

Plate 10. Fire in undergrowth which has not yet involved the upper parts of the trees.

Plate 11. A forest fire which has involved the crowns of the trees.

Plate 12. *Liaison between the fire service and Forestry Commission officials. Note the store of beaters for fire fighting.*

Plate 13. *An army cadet forestry patrol in Rhondda, South Wales.*

Plate 14. A forest ride being used as a dump for pit props.

Plate 15. Damage to trees resulting from fire.

(d) Liaison with the Forestry Commission

The technique of forest fire fighting is specialised and can be acquired only by considerable experience. For this reason the officer in charge of fire brigade appliances attending a forest fire should always seek the guidance of Forestry Commission officials on the spot as to the measures to be used for attacking the fire, since these men are fully trained in forest fire-fighting. Fire calls will often be sent to the fire brigade from one of the control points which have been established by the Commission. These control points are in touch with the patrols (Plate 13) and, in large forests, with the watch towers (Plate 5) maintained by the Commission's staff. Calls will state the rendezvous point (see paragraph (m)) to which the appliances are to proceed, whence they will be guided by a Forestry Commission official. Forestry Commission staff on duty are distinguished by yellow armlets bearing the initials FC. The various grades are indicated on the armlets as follows:

Workmen	No bars
Foreman	One bar
Forester	Two bars (one on each side of the letters FC)
District Officer	Three bars (two on one side of the letters FC and one on the other)
Divisional Officer	Four bars (two on each side of the letters FC)

(e) Causes of fire and fire spread

As with moorlands, forest fires are caused by the careless cigarette end, broken bottles, camp fires of walkers and picnickers, by the burning of brashings or loppings getting out of control, or by the 'burning off' of adjacent moorland. In addition lightning provides an occasional natural cause of an outbreak of fire. The speed and extent of fire spread depends upon several factors. The most dangerous fires occur either early in the year when there is little sap in the trees, the undergrowth being in a flammable condition because the grass has been killed by frost and there is much dead bracken and leaves, or in the summer and early autumn after periods of drought. A high wind greatly increases the speed with which a fire spreads, and also creates eddies which may cause the fire to travel against the wind, especially when the trees are tall. The degree of flammability plays an important part in the rate of spread, particularly in crown fires (i.e. when the fire travels from the top of one tree to the top of the next) (Plate 11). In pine and fir trees especially, the hot air moving in front of the fire may raise the temperature of the resinous oils in the unburnt trees to near their ignition point, with the consequence

17

that one spark alighting on a tree will set the whole tree almost instantly ablaze.

Sparks from a forest fire can fly a considerable distance, and the danger they represent cannot be over-emphasised. Up to 800 yards (731 m) in front of a fire or behind any fire break must be considered as a danger area, in which small fires may occur and rapidly develop, if not sought out and immediately extinguished. It is possible to be unaware of a second fire until the two blazes coalesce, and thus run the risk of finding that men and appliances have been cut off. A change in the direction of the wind should be watched for, since it may necessitate rapid alterations in the position of appliances and men.

As in the case of heath fires on peaty soil, it should be remembered that where pine needles are thick, or in hardwood forests where a deep layer of decayed vegetation has been formed, the fire may spread in the surface of the ground and a stop in the trees alone is not sufficient. In smaller woods the presence of drainage ditches which have become filled with leaves may lead to undetected spread, since the fire will travel through the combustible matter often against the wind.

(f) Fires in felled timber

Fires often occur in an area where the trees have been felled and are still lying upon the ground. The branches are lopped and burned and outbreaks of this type are usually caused by these fires getting out of hand.

The felled trees make it impossible to drive vehicles nearer than the edge of such an area, and difficult quickly to lay lines of hose. There is some danger to personnel from such lopped trunks, since on uneven ground a comparatively small application of force may make them roll. Resin which has flowed on to the ground causes persistent fires close to the trunks of felled trees; it is particularly important therefore that search should be made beneath such trees for signs of fire. The same remarks as were made above in the last section regarding the layer of surface material also apply.

(g) Fires on steep slopes or on steep-sided valleys

These fires are difficult, since vehicles cannot usually be used and areas where they might occur demand previous inspection and planning to determine how portable pumps could best be used and how water supplies should be made available (Plate 8 shows a typical example of a forest on a steep slope). Points to notice are:

(i) the value of tractors for hauling pumps, including any arrangements that can be made with neighbouring farmers to supply them;

(ii) the necessity for careful pump spacing in relay work;

(iii) the tendency of fire to travel up a steep mountain side much more quickly than it would on level ground, and the ease with which it can jump from one side to the other of a steep and narrow valley;

(iv) working on a steep slope is extremely strenuous and it may be advantageous to lay a line of hose from the top to the bottom of the slope which men can use to pull themselves upwards and so conserve their energies;

(v) men should be divided into groups so that adequate rest periods may be given.

(h) Creation of fire breaks

While a fire involving a few trees can be directly attacked, one that has already spread must be methodically dealt with. The first necessity is to decide the line upon which the fire must be held; this will usually be an existing ride in the case of a Forestry Commission forest, but may be a natural open space or a track in the case of natural planted woodlands. The fire plan should give details of this. In some forests, conifers are interspersed with belts of hardwoods or larch, since it has been found that a change in the type of tree may help to check the fire. Where there is such a dividing line it may be desirable to attempt to stop the fire along it. Undergrowth should be cut away or trampled down and, where necessary and possible, a farmer should be asked to plough up a break or have a tractor driven up and down a chosen line to tear up the undergrowth, which can then be trampled and beaten down. Army tanks have sometimes been used to create a break in forest areas. It may be necessary to cut away branches and undergrowth on the line of the fire break with axes and billhooks, or even to fell certain trees which might carry fire over the break, especially when water is not available to keep them wet. Where a sub-surface fire is occurring, trenching will also have to be carried out, the trench being carried down to below the surface of the earth under the top fibrous stratum and made as wide as possible with the available manpower.

(j) Beating

Beating is most effective upon fires in very young trees, when the top of the tree can be reached by the beaters, or when undergrowth as well as trees are involved. Grown trees are much less easily dealt with by this method, since the great heat which is given off may not allow sufficiently close approach and the height of the trees themselves makes it impossible to reach the burning material. Circumstances may, however, be such that there is no alternative method of dealing with the fire, and in this case every advantage should be taken of any momentary lull in intensity which permits sufficiently close approach to be made, and of any local characteristic of the plantation or site which brings down the fire from the tops of the trees to a lower level.

Beating is a very exhausting operation and men should therefore be divided into groups so that they work in relays, the off-duty group providing a reserve which can be sent to another spot in case of emergency. In making the attack, men should be placed along the flanks of the approaching fire in order that they may drive it into an ever-narrowing wedge; frontal attacks should not be attempted unless absolutely unavoidable, because of the effects of heat and smoke and the danger involved. In forests administered by the Forestry Commission, stocks of beaters are kept in huts placed at intervals and their position should be indicated upon the fire plan.

(k) Counterfiring

If a counterfire is to be used it should be started at some considerable distance from the main conflagration, at a position as free as possible from timber or thick undergrowth. It is best done in a direction almost at right angles to the fire rather than from the front, where burning molinia is liable to be carried ahead by the wind and so start a fresh fire. It is always best if possible to choose an open space or one with sparse undergrowth where the counterfire can easily be controlled with the number of men available. The whole line of counterfire must be continually manned to prevent it spreading in the same direction as the main conflagration. It is obvious that this method can only be used when it can be controlled and, generally speaking, when there is only a slight wind, otherwise it can easily get out of hand and cause more damage than the fire which it is intended to extinguish.

This method should never be employed in forests administered by the Crown without the concurrence of the senior Forestry Commission official present who will in such cases almost invariably arrange for it to be carried out under his own supervision.

In other woodlands, where little or no water supplies are available, however, it is sometimes the only method of attack available to the fire brigade officer.

(l) Use of water

When the fire is chiefly in undergrowth (Plate 10) it may be possible to use spray branches with effect, but it will be found that the lower branches of the trees are very quickly dried by a crown fire (Plate 11), so that the whole tree becomes involved and scatters sparks into the air, to be blown to other parts of the forest. Jets of small diameter are generally preferred, since they have better carrying power than spray. When it has been decided to stop the fire on a certain line and water is available the supply should be well distributed behind the chosen line by means of hose and dividing breechings. It is then advisable to saturate the ground, undergrowth and trees as thoroughly as possible, so that advantage can be taken of the check the fire will receive to attack it directly.

It will be realised that moving hose and pumps, even portable pumps, about a forest is a matter of considerable difficulty, and the planning of the attack must take this into account. The close spacing of the trees, combined with the rapidly changing fire situation, renders it difficult to make up equipment and get it to work again in new positions. Where ample manpower is available (for instance when service personnel have been called in) hose can be more rapidly moved if it is carried on men's shoulders.

Water tenders are of the greatest value in any forest area in which they can move about. Rides which appear rough can generally be negotiated by vehicles driven carefully, but the passage is sometimes limited by numerous and large protruding stumps, boulders, bogs and the fact that the ride often follows a contour without being levelled.

Wherever water tenders can move about they should be used, while a shuttle service of water tenders is often preferable to a relay, principally owing to the ease with which it is possible to alter the delivery point. Where suitable tracks are not available all the way to the fire area, water tenders should be used to bring water to the nearest point, from which it could be pumped through hose lines to where it is required.

In Crown forests, the Forestry Commission has erected a number of static water tanks together with signs indicating both these and natural supplies, all of which should, of course, be marked upon the fire maps kept at fire controls. The Commission also possesses a number of 15/20 gallons (68/90 litres) per minute pumps mounted on dam-carrying lorries of 500 gallons (2273 litres) capacity.

(m) Control and communications

Most of the larger forests have rendezvous points for the assembly of fire brigade vehicles. A control unit (or radio-equipped car taking its place) carrying the fire plan and map of the forest, should be stationed at the rendezvous point, and here, in the case of a large fire, the officers responsible for communications, transport, catering and other necessary administrative sections should be found. A canteen van should provide men working at the fire with refreshments, and adequate personnel to do this must be provided, since the conditions at a forest fire usually make it necessary to take food and drink to the men rather than allow them to visit the van.

Fire towers are used by the Forestry Commission, but often these are only manned during high fire risk seasons.

A standard route sign (Fig. 1-1) for directing fire brigade crews to forest fires has been adopted by the Forestry Commission. The sign has red fluorescent lettering on a black background with a red

Fig. 1–1. Forestry Commission standard sign for directing fire brigade crews to forest fires.

fluorescent outer circle, the reverse side being painted white. The pointer, red fluorescent on the front and white on the reverse, is designed to fit into a slot at the back of the sign, so that the pointer can be set to indicate to the left or to the right. The sign is mounted on a white post.

It is intended that forestry staff will erect the signs at the time of any outbreak of fire to indicate, at the roadside and other suitable points, the approach to the area involved. This sign will supplement and not supersede the use of rendezvous points.

The problems of control and communications at a large forest fire are very similar to those which have already been outlined for a large heath fire. It is usually necessary to have an officer in charge on each side of the fire, the more so because communications in forest areas are always difficult, though the use of wireless cars or radio pack sets can ease matters. Care should be taken to park vehicles so that they do not obstruct roads or tracks and, as far as possible, one way traffic should be maintained.

(n) After the fire

During dry periods especially, it is unsafe to leave a fire for some time after it has been extinguished; damping down should therefore be thorough and a patrol should be maintained. The men forming this patrol should be reasonably fresh and should be equipped with adequate fire-fighting gear. Where possible dams should be left at strategic points with a central relay from a good water supply, which is capable of being switched to any point where fire may break out. Once the major fire is under control, a search for further outbreaks should be made, especially down-wind. This is often best done by pairs of men, one carrying a spade and the other buckets of water, who together can dig out and damp down dangerous spots.

When extinguishing the ground over which the fire has passed, a special note should be made of hollows and sunken road tracks as the wind in sweeping over the burning ground picks up small pieces of charcoal and deposits them in the hollows to varying depths, in the same way as snow is piled up in drifts. Outward appearance by day gives no evidence of fire, since charcoal burns without smoke, but charcoal may be found at red heat a little way below the surface. It is often only at night that it is possible to verify that all traces of fire have been extinguished. Even where the charcoal is allowed to burn out, there may be a danger from a shift or increase of wind, which might disturb the drifts and result in glowing particles being picked up and carried to other parts of the forest.

Tree stumps and roots must also be carefully inspected for latent fire. When water is not available in quantities sufficient for damping down, it may be necessary to isolate the smaller areas of burning by digging an encircling trench.

3. SINGLE TREE FIRES

These fires usually occur in hollow trees, the interior of which contains highly combustible touchwood. Once the main body of fire has been dealt with, every trace of fire should be cut away, for a spark remaining in touchwood will in time cause a fresh fire. Alternatively, the base of the tree should be filled with earth and a hole cut high in the trunk, through which a branch can be inserted so that the trunk can be filled with water. This is often necessary when the touchwood cannot be reached with a jet and when it is impracticable to cut down the tree. If the tree can be cut down, regard should be paid to the possible spread of fire due to sparks.

External fires can usually be extinguished by means of a spray, or if they are of considerable size, with a jet. It is important to guard against the burning embers being carried by the force of the jet on to other combustible material. Should the tree be unsafe, or near a road or public footpath, arrangements should be made to inform the owner and the police.

4. HARVESTING FIRES

The suitability of the land and the profitability of the crops have resulted in an increase in the acreage of cereal crops in this country, especially barley. The increased production has brought with it the need for more efficient harvesting methods and the pattern set by the grain harvesters in America has now become the accepted method in this country.

It means using the maximum concentration of effort in the shortest possible time and involves the use of the now familiar combine harvesting machine. These implements combine the jobs of cutting and threshing and include their own motive power. They are large and cumbersome machines and can be used most efficiently and economically on large undivided fields. In the grain growing areas of this country, preparations for harvest are almost in the order of battle preparations, with half a dozen combine harvesters, a fleet of grain trucks and tractors and, in some cases, lorries and land-rover type vehicles fitted with radio communications. The aim is to harvest the crop in a continuous effort with an unbroken flow of the threshed grain to the drying plant or store.

With such a concentration of machinery and the vulnerability of the vast areas of grain crop, this is when fires are most likely to occur and when the damage from fire can be at its greatest.

(a) Combine harvesters

The machines (Plate 19), although cumbersome and ponderous, are most effective in use. In essentials, they comprise a prime mover, a cutter for mowing the crop, a thresher for separating the ears of grain from the stalks, a conveyor for disposing of (i) the grain and (ii) the straw. The combine harvester is usually under the control of the driver, whose position is placed high up on the machine in order to give him a good view of clearances all round, and especially where the cutting tool comes into contact with the standing crop. The design of these machines varies with the manufacture but apart from slight differences in the method of disposing of the grain, they are essentially alike.

Harvesting is normally carried out when the weather is hot and is a very dusty operation. A great deal of finely divided dust from the cutting and threshing covers all parts of the machine during the operation, and it is the collection of this dust on the hot surfaces of the engine and exhaust system which causes most fires. The most vulnerable time is when the machine is halted for a short while during working and is enclosed on two sides by the standing crop and on the other two by loose straw deposited on the ground.

(b) Fire fighting in growing crops

Growing crops (Fig. 1-2) may be a fire risk for a short period immediately before harvest, especially if there have been several consecutive days of hot weather. This is especially so in certain crops,

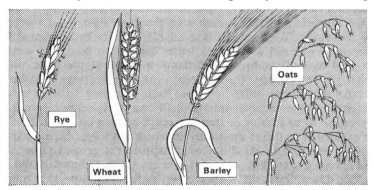

Fig. 1–2. Four of the most commonly grown cereals.

when a fast-spreading and destructive fire can occur. Corn becomes flammable when the water content in the upper portion of the plant falls below 30 per cent of the fresh weight. Dew and heavy rain sharply increase the water content, though a light shower has a negligible effect; in both cases if sunshine follows it will evaporate the water rapidly. The margin of safety in a ripe crop may be small (a few per cent of water content) even in an abnormally wet season.

A rough sign of flammability in crops is the drooping of the ears. A flammable condition is reached in barley and wheat in normal seasons shortly before harvest when nearly all the plants in the crop have lost their green colour, except perhaps in some of the small shoots. Oats, on the other hand, is normally harvested in a slightly immature condition and before reaching a flammable stage. Ripe barley generally attains the lower water content, whilst wheat sometimes remains above the critical point, even when fully ripe, especially in a wet season. In fact, barley accounts for the majority of crop fires.

The first necessity when fighting fires in growing crops is to prevent spread by creating a break. It is fatal to attempt to fight the fire before making provision for a definite line on which to stop it. The break can be made in many ways: by driving a tractor or fire brigade vehicle backwards and forwards; by flattening the crop for a width of some 4 yards (4 m) at an angle across the line of fire, using wet sacks or beaters; by towing a barred gate or a ladder behind a vehicle; by cutting with a scythe; or by asking the farmer to use his reaping machine or a plough. Such a break will cause a check in the progress of the fire, which can then be attacked with water if it is available, but otherwise with beaters, which should not be swept about but should be used to press down and crush the burning stems to the ground, a method which is at the same time more effective and less tiring. Where water is available, the fire break should be thoroughly damped down, or a water tender can be driven across the field to make a break and damp it down at the same time. Driving a water tender through crops can be precarious as there is considerable danger of the appliance itself becoming involved in fire due either to the accumulation of chaff and straw being blown into the engine, or to stubble or standing crops coming into contact with the exhaust. The driver must also take care not to get his appliance stuck in soft ground. If this should happen, the ground under the appliance where the hot exhaust is in contact with the crop should be damped down. Generally, if the crop is ripe for harvesting, the ground will take the weight of a fire appliance.

After the fire is out, water from a water tender may be usefully employed in damping down the edges of the burnt area and making sure that no heated spots remain.

Where a fire break has not been made, it is inadvisable to make a frontal attack on a fast-moving fire. Where beaters must be used, separate parties should work inwards from each flank in order to corner the fire, which should be driven towards any ditch, road, hedge, wall or other feature which will act as a fire break. To control the upwind spread, one person to approximately 25 yards (25 m) is enough, but downwind on the flanks, one person to each 10 yards (10 m) of fire front is desirable.

In addition to the direct attack upon this type of fire, patrols should watch for sparks carried from the flaming corn over the break into

26

the unburnt crop. Any spare water can usefully be employed in heavily spraying through diffuser branches the corn on the unburnt side of the break.

(c) Fire fighting in stooked corn and stubble

In some parts of the country, the older method of harvesting is still used (Plate 18). A fire in a field of stooked corn is really a stubble fire, with the stooks providing an additional hazard. However, the difference lies in the value, since the stooks contain unthreshed grain.

Where a field has been cut by combine harvesters, the stubble is much longer than that in the stooked fields and, moreover, the straw from the threshing process in the combine is deposited on to the stubble in the wake of the combine. The straw may be left for some while after cutting depending upon the manpower available and whether it is to be collected and baled or burned in situ. Burning the straw is a popular method of disposal since the ash forms a valuable fertiliser for the soil. If it is to be baled, then the baler machine may follow immediately behind the combine, thus completing the operating all at once.

The burning off of the combine straw presents several hazards, not the least being the number of false alarm calls to the fire brigade which are made by well-intentioned strangers. Another serious hazard is that of smoke blowing across busy roads. The heat raised by a field of combine straw on fire can cause convected currents to carry hot embers high into the air and these can then be carried on the wind and settle on nearby uncut crops.

The burning of straw should be undertaken with caution. Co-operation between the fire brigade and the farmer is essential. Publicity in farming journals, talks and lectures to 'Young Farmers' Clubs' and visits to the farms are some of the ways to tackle the problem. The 'Straw Burning Code'* is issued by the National Farmers' Union, but if this is to be distributed or published in the press, timing is important so that the advice may be incorporated in the harvesting plan.

A break should be created either by ploughing or by thoroughly soaking a wide strip across the path of the fire, which can most easily be done by a water tender. A ploughed strip 6 ft (1·8 m) wide will normally suffice to check the spread of a fire in stubble. If sufficient water is not available, beating can be employed as before in order to stop the fire at the break. Stubble and any stooks behind the break

---

* The following is the leaflet which has been produced by the National Farmers Union in consultation with the Ministry of Agriculture, Fisheries and Food and the Home Office, on straw and stubble burning.

THE STRAW BURNING CODE—1972

A. NEVER BURN:

1. *When the fire may get out of control:*
   in strong winds;
   in exceptionally dry conditions.
2. *In the vicinity of:*
   thatched cottages or residential areas;
   farm buildings;
   hay or straw stacks;
   any other concentrations of flammable material;
   standing straw crops;
   any industrial buildings or plant.
3. *Without adequate firebreaks to protect, in particular:*
   woodland, hedgerows or any wildlife habitat;
   trees growing in fields;
   electricity or telegraph poles;
   any other public utility installations.
4. Near roads where drifting smoke could be a serious traffic hazard.
5. At night. This is dangerous and may alarm the public.
6. On peaty soil which may catch fire.

B. SPECIAL CARE IS NEEDED

1. In the vicinity of aerodromes.
2. Near oil gas pipeline installations.
3. When burning extra large fields.

C. BEFORE YOU START BURNING

1. Make firebreaks at least 20 ft (6 m) wide. This may be done by removing straw and ploughing or by cultivating around the boundary and between swathes and then burning straw in from the perimeter one swath at a time. This should preferably be done in the early morning when the dew is still on the ground.
   N.B. Wider firebreaks may well be needed to protect trees and hedgerows from scorching.
2. Consult you local fire brigade well in advance and prepare directions to locate the site of burning in case of emergency.
3. Notify your neighbours in order to prevent unnecessary alarm when burning starts.

D. WHEN BURNING

1. Start early in the day.
2. Burn into the wind rather than downwind.
3. *Put an experienced person in charge* and never leave the fire unattended.
4. Have plenty of fire beaters available for use and know where you can get helpers to use them in an emergency.
5. Ensure that the fire is completely out before leaving the field. Return later in order to make doubly sure.
6. *Should the fire get out of control, call the fire brigade immediately.* Meet the fire brigade at the roadside and show them the best way to reach the fire.

*** FOR SAFETY'S SAKE FOLLOW THIS SIMPLE CODE ***

should also be watched and damped down. After the fire is out, a wide band round the edge of the burnt area should be thoroughly damped. Burnt stooks should be pulled apart, beaten out or wetted.

5. FIRES IN STORED CROPS

(a) Ricks and stacks

The changes in methods of harvesting cereal crops and the making of silage from grass crops have brought about corresponding changes in the methods of crop storage. Ricks (stacks) are still used, but much less so than was the case with the older methods. Except on the smaller farms, the corn rick has disappeared and hay is now more frequently stored in barns than in ricks in the open. Where ricks are in use, they may be for temporary or long period storage of such commodities as unthreshed grain crops, hay (including clover), beans and peas, bracken and ferns and, most common of all today, baled straw.

(b) Unthreshed grain ricks

These, although less common now, are still the most valuable of ricks and the loss by fire is greater than for comparable ricks of other commodities since their purpose is to store the grain until such time as it can be threshed. They are often built close together in order to facilitate easy threshing operations and for the same reason, if not built in a rick-yard, they are placed near to a roadway, making them vulnerable to the dropped cigarette end or discarded lighted match.

The ricks are built by placing the sheaves of corn in courses with the grain heads inwards. When such ricks are fired and it is decided to pull them apart, this may best be done by taking each layer or course of sheaves off before attempting to remove those lower down.

Since corn is rarely allowed to remain in the stack for any considerable time, the sheaves do not have time to bed down and the spaces between them allow fire to penetrate quickly to the interior, a tendency which is increased by the air spaces in the stalks themselves. For the same reason, water is able to penetrate through the rick more easily than is the case with a densely packed commodity. Any unburnt ricks likely to be involved should be protected if possible.

It is usually impossible to remove the burnt portion of a corn rick; occasionally when a prompt call has been received and the rick has not been burning long, it may be possible for a corner to be cut away, but in most cases the whole rick must be pulled down. The flames should be doused with a spray branch (using the minimum quantity of water to avoid damage to the corn), after which firemen should

29

climb on top of the rick and fork the sheaves off, while a man stands by with a spray branch. Burnt corn should be separated during this process from unburnt and the latter put direct into a wagon or taken to dry ground away from the rick. The burnt corn should be spread out and turned over, water being applied when necessary. It is not usual to pull a corn rick over with hawser and tractor because of the solidity with which it is constructed.

(c) Straw stacks

Although it is possible to find a few straw stacks constructed in a similar way to the unthreshed corn, this is only done where the long straw is required for roof thatching. The use of the combine harvester (*see* par. 4(a) above) has meant that the straw is now baled in the fields and then removed to the storage area to be built into stacks. The convenient nature, shape and size of the bales has, unfortunately, encouraged the building of huge stacks without fire breaks. Bales may be bound with wire or string. So long as the binding holds, the bales are relatively easy to manhandle but when the string or wire burns through or breaks, the freed straw is much more difficult to handle.

Baled straw burns fairly slowly, due to the compression of the straw when being made up into bales, but because of the air spaces between the individual bales in the stack, the fire will penetrate rapidly. Spray branches should be used in order to minimise the use of water, but jets may sometimes be used to advantage where the fire has penetrated between bales.

(d) Haystacks

Hay consists of grass which is cut and then dried by leaving it out in the fields exposed to the sun. Grass may very occasionally be dried artificially in grass driers. The dried grass, or hay as it then becomes, is generally stored in stacks which may be built in the open or under cover in a Dutch barn, although haylage silos (*see* par. 6(h)) are now becoming increasingly popular. Haystacks are now invariably made by baling the hay by means of a combine harvester, and then building the bales into a stack in the same way as for straw. In one or two isolated cases, haystacks may be found composed of hay which has been pitched, or raised by an elevator.

A haystack may fire internally through spontaneous combustion, although fires resulting from internal firing of baled haystacks are a rarity, or the stack may be ignited by external means. The action to be taken at a haystack fire depends chiefly upon the position of the stack. Where surrounding property is endangered, the hay must be promptly extinguished, or the fire prevented from spreading; in other cases the officer in charge should contact the farmer and obtain his advice as to whether an attempt should be made to put the fire out, or whether the stack should be allowed to burn out under control, its rate of burning being accelerated by loosening the material. It is necessary to explain to the farmer the reasons for and possible advantages of allowing the fire to burn out, and he should be consulted at all stages of fire-fighting operations. It has been found that a number of farmers do not possess suitable mechanical equipment or an adequate quantity of hand implements and may not be able to call upon an adequate labour force to assist. As mentioned in the introduction to this chapter, the officer in charge should be aware of the possible financial implications when requesting assistance from farmers which may mean using neighbouring farmers' appliances. Except for a haystack which has been built for a considerable time and in which the hay is solid enough to resist penetration by smoke, the travel of smoke through the stack normally makes the hay unfit for cattle food or bedding, and the material is therefore useless to the farmer and better disposed of.

Whilst burning is taking place, fire brigade personnel should maintain control at all times, and should take care to see that other structures, overhead cables, etc., do not become involved, or that smoke from the fire does not affect traffic on nearby roads. It is a sound policy to notify the police of such controlled burning and to maintain liaison with them throughout.

The production of good hay depends on the fact that a certain amount of heat is generated in the interior of all haystacks. Hay cut early in the season and particularly that cut late in the year as a second crop is, however, liable to overheat, since the sap will not have dried out completely, and certain stacks may therefore be found with a central vertical vent, consisting either of a metal or wooden shaft pierced with holes or of an unlined shaft constructed by raising a chaff-filled sack on a rope as the stack is built. In addition, horizontal shafts leading into the central vent or running through the stack are occasionally encountered, or layers of pea haulms (the stems of the plant) may be laid between the layers of hay with the same purpose. It is not, however, usual to incorporate any type of vent.

Some farmers use preservatives to reduce the spoilage of hay due to heat and oxidation. These preservatives usually contain a number of acids, solvents and sweeteners to prevent the formation of bacterial agents and to keep the hay sweet. If the moisture content of the hay is initially too high (it should be less than 30 per cent), the preservatives will not prevent rapid chemical curing occurring which will result in heating of the hay. None of these substances used in the preservatives is likely to increase the fire hazard, but it is possible that in a fire involving treated hay the fumes and increased smoke would appear to be more unpleasant with a vinegary pungent smell. The use of preservatives may be a nuisance from a fire-fighting point of view, but the fumes are not a danger to firemen.

If a farmer is in any doubt as to the probable behaviour of a hay-stack, he will test it for heat at regular intervals. Testing is carried out in many ways: by an iron rod approximately ¾-in. (20 mm) in diameter and about 12 ft (3·5 m) long; by a testing rod which withdraws a sample of hay from the centre of the stack (black or dark brown hay shows the existence of fire), or which is fitted with a thermometer at its end (Fig. 1-3); by a boring iron, or by a temperature probe (*see* Fig. 1-6), which locates the point of greatest heat.

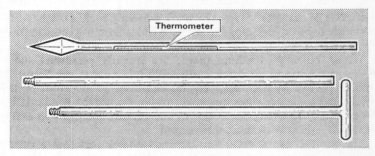

Fig. 1–3. A testing rod which consists of a series of sections, screwed at one end. One section is shaped as a handle, and another with a spearhead to facilitate driving it into the stack. A thermometer is inserted in the rod immediately above the spearhead. The spearhead is thrust into the stack, left there for a few minutes and then withdrawn, and the temperature registered by the thermometer is noted.

As a result of these tests, should the farmer find signs of overheating, he will tunnel a shaft through the stack to allow the heat to escape, or he will cut away the hottest part. If, however, the temperature has risen above about 70°C, he will generally call the fire brigade because once that temperature has been reached the hay is almost certain to fire spontaneously when air reaches it on cutting away. Alternatively, it is not unknown for an internal fire to start and subsequently smother itself, its existence not being discovered until the hay comes to be used. (For spontaneous heating, see Part 1 of the *Manual*, Chapter 1, 'Physics and Chemistry of Combustion'.)

(i) *Internally-fired haystacks.* Ricks of baled hay do not usually fire as a result of spontaneous heating because the air spaces between the bales act as ventilation. Ricks of unbaled hay may, in certain circumstances, heat up spontaneously. Due to the characteristic smell, the overheating of hay is usually detected by the farmer before destruction occurs. In the event, however, of a rick actually firing, the officer in charge should consult with the owner as to whether the remainder of the rick is worth saving, since it may not be suitable for fodder. Then, provided the fire does not endanger any other ricks or property, it may be allowed to burn under supervision.

Officers should be careful not to return the cause of fire in a haystack as 'spontaneous combustion' unless they are quite certain that this is the true cause, (see Part 6A of the *Manual*, Chapter 3, Section II, 'The Investigation of Fires'), since some insurance policies exclude the payment of claims for losses caused by spontaneous combustion. Internal firing seldom takes place more than three months after a haystack is built, and it is therefore most unusual for a stack built in June to fire after early October, or for a stack built in September to fire after Christmas. While it is often difficult when the fire is burning to be sure whether a stack has been fired internally or not, it is usually possible after it has been extinguished to obtain samples of hay from the interior by means of a pricker bar, and these will indicate what was the condition of the hay in the centre of the stack.

(ii) *Externally-fired haystacks.* Upon reaching a haystack which is on fire externally, the first task is to douse the flames. A considerable amount of fire will be showing, but this can usually be extinguished quite soon with a couple of spray branches applied first to the roof and then to the sides. When a last year's stack has not been burning long, much of the labour of pulling away can sometimes be saved by using a jet and, commencing at the base of the stack on the windward side, working along the side, thoroughly soaking the hay in layers a foot or so thick at a time.

Once the external fire on the roof and sides of the stack has been extinguished, a stack of recently mown hay must usually be completely pulled down, since it will not have become consolidated and fire penetrates quickly into the interior. For baled stacks, a satisfactory method of extinguishment is a systematic removal of undamaged bales, utilising such labour as is available. In these circumstances, careful and minimal use of water is important to avoid saturating the bales and thus increasing their weight. It is also important not to waste time by trying to manhandle bales with broken ties.

Before deciding to cut or pull apart a damaged hayrick, the owner should be consulted as to the use of the 'saved portion'. Often the conclusion will be that it is not worth saving because of the reluctance of animals to eat it.

The old method of cutting away an unbaled stack was by means of hayknives, which were used to cut into the stack so that portions could be removed. Hayknives, however, are extremely dangerous tools in inexperienced hands and generally can only be used competently by a few farm workers. Most brigades in rural areas who used to carry hayknives have dispensed with them, and so if they are available and it is suggested that they should be used, the handling of them should be confined to such farm workers who are competent to use them. Power saws (specifically for use on thatched roofs) are now carried by many rural fire brigades.

With haystacks, as with other types of rick, the minimum quantity of water necessary to keep down flame should be used. As has already been said, any additional water is absorbed by the material and merely serves to make it heavier when it has to be pulled or lifted down by firemen. It is especially important to keep water off the unaffected portion of the stack to avoid spoiling the hay.

(e) Clover

Clover (Fig. 1-4, left) ricks are liable to fire internally and should be treated in all respects in the same way as haystacks. Cutting, however, is more difficult because of the increased thickness of the material.

(f) Beans and peas

Bean (Fig. 1-4, right) ricks, which are not liable to fire internally, may be found either threshed or unthreshed; both types burn very

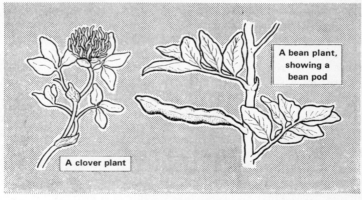

A bean plant, showing a bean pod

A clover plant

Fig. 1–4. Left: a clover plant. Right: a bean plant.

quickly, giving off considerable heat and thick acrid smoke. Un-threshed beans are generally bundled with twine and the whole rick thatched with straw. After the flame has been controlled, the whole of the rick must usually be pulled down, though it is occasionally possible to cut away a small portion.

Pea ricks are very similar to bean ricks, and should be dealt with in precisely the same way.

(g) Bracken and fern

Bracken ricks are found in areas where the bracken is used as bedding for cattle. The material is thick and heavy, and in most cases the best method is to pull the rick down.

(h) Grain storage

The economics of farming prove that it is more profitable to dry and store grain so as to market it at its highest value than to dispose of it fresh from the harvester without further artificial drying. This has resulted in an increase in the numbers of grain dryers (Plate 26) and stores (Plates 24 and 25). These modern granaries contain expensive machinery and plant and the quantity of grain stored in bulk can run into thousands of tons (tonnes). The methods used for artificial drying are discussed in section 6(g) on grain drying. Where-ever possible, the drying and storing is done in the same building, since this ensures good weather-proof storage and no open air transportation after drying.

Sometimes, existing barns are used to house the drying machines and storage hoppers, but since these buildings, particularly if built of stone, are difficult to keep free from damp, it is more usual to erect purpose-built buildings. In such buildings the 'wet' grain is carried in bulk from the harvester and tipped into a pit. From the pit, a conveyor takes the grain to the dryer and from there it is finally conveyed to the hoppers or silos. These latter vary in design; the self-emptying type must, of necessity, be elevated and with a 45° angle base to the emptying pipe so that the grain runs down freely into either sacks or whatever type of transporting container is used. The other types rely upon mechanical emptiers and these can rest upon the floor and, in some cases, be sunken partly in the ground. The hoppers or silos may be constructed of almost any material, but are usually bound round with steel bands to hold the sides in position. In some cases, grain may be stored in sacks but only where humidity is controlled, since under warm damp conditions the grain will start to 'sprout'.

Fires in grain stores are usually caused by overheating of the drying plant and sometimes burning grain is conveyed into hoppers or silos containing large quantities of dried grain. When this occurs, if the hoppers are bottom emptying type, the best plan is to remove the unburnt grain. With other types of storage, it may be very difficult to separate the burning grain but if soaking is resorted to, it must be remembered that the dried grain will absorb a great deal of water, thus adding to the weight and size of the contents of the store, with the possible result that the expanding force may cause the hoppers or silos to disintegrate. If it is decided to remove grain, the advice of the farmer is necessary. He should be able to provide suitable transport and, equally important, alternative storage for the grain.

Occasions have occurred when rescues have had to be made of persons who have fallen into a bin full of grain. The chief danger is that the loose surface will not bear the weight of anyone entering on it, and they will sink down into the grain; there is also the possibility of carbon dioxide gas being present where grain is stored.

The attention of the reader is also drawn to Part 6C of the *Manual*, Chapter 6, 'Fires in grain, hops and their derivatives', where the subject of grain storage and silos is also dealt with in detail.

(j) Fruit cold storage

Fruit growers who grow specialised crops such as dessert apples, have found that the best demand and price can be commanded during winter and at Christmas; consequently, the use of cold storage for such fruit is now common. The apples are normally graded and packed into cardboard containers, usually 10 lb (4·5 kg) in each, ready for dispatch and sale. These containers are then placed in the cold store, where they remain until the appropriate sale time.

Cold stores are often built into ordinary barns and frequently are housed in pre-fabricated buildings, usually near to a roadway in order to facilitate loading and transport. They usually employ the cold dry air system in order to maintain the fruit in non-ripening condition.

The subject of refrigeration plant is dealt with in Part 6C of the *Manual*, Chapter 12, and the fire officer is advised to familiarise himself with such plant if on his fireground. This is particularly important where these apple stores exist in remote rural areas.

6. FIRES IN BARNS AND FARM BUILDINGS

(a) Dutch barns

A Dutch barn (Plate 20) consists of an open-sided or part open-sided barn made from a metal, wood or pre-stressed concrete frame, or a combination of these, with a corrugated, asbestos or metal roofing. Its main use is to hold such crops as hay, straw or wheat to save thatching and yet to protect them from the weather. The barns consist of a number of bays. Dependant upon the acreage of a farm and other storage facilities, it is customary today to build very large units, thus creating a concentration of storage. Whilst this is good from the farm manager's point of view, it increases the vulnerability to fire and adds greatly to the problems of the fireman when a fire occurs.

When fires occur in a Dutch barn, the closeness of the stacks and the trapping of heat and smoke under the roof make fire fighting more difficult than in stacks in the open. When quantities of water have to be used, the area around soon becomes a quagmire. If it is decided, therefore, to remove the fired portion or, alternatively, to leave the fired portion in situ and remove the remainder, the use of water must be kept to a minimum.

(i) The first consideration must be to prevent the spread of the fire. The unaffected ricks should be sheeted and protected with spray branches, passages between the ricks being cut or widened if necessary. Care should be taken to see that the fire does not creep along the spaces between the stacks. It will be found that the spaces round the supports of the barn are usually filled with loose hay and are especially liable to burn freely. Where one side or end is enclosed with galvanised iron, it is sometimes advisable to remove this to prevent the fire working between it and the rick.

(ii) Tractors, agricultural machinery or implements and grain sacks should be removed from the barn and placed where water damage cannot occur. Tractors should be driven out or towed by a fire brigade appliance.

(iii) If the fire is hot and likely to distort the steelwork, the supports and framing should be cooled by jets or spray as appropriate. In addition to the monetary loss involved, collapse of the barn will make fire fighting more difficult.

(iv) When surrounding ricks have been protected, firemen should work towards the fire along the sides and top of the ricks, damping and possibly sheeting as they go. Water directed against the underside of the roof will help to clear the smoke and make it easier to find the seat of the fire. Before any pulling away of a hot or burning stack can be undertaken, it is necessary to pull down or cut away portions of the ricks on each side, in order to leave a clear space on to which burnt material can be thrown down.

(v) The top of the stack is often only a few feet from the roof, and heat and smoke are driven downwards. As soon as possible, therefore, the fire at the top and sides of the stack should be doused in order that loose hay may be pulled from the top until a man can ascend and start removing bales. Men should take care when working in smoke at the top of a rick that they do not slip into any vent hole there may be, into the narrow space between one rick and the next, or between the rick and the side wall. Should a vent hole have been built in the stack, the fire may also have spread up through the centre, thus adding to the heat and smoke present beneath the roof.

(vi) When working on the top of a rick in a barn, the danger of carbon monoxide poisoning should not be overlooked, and adequate ventilation should be provided. Where a man cannot be sent to the top of a rick, it may be possible to remove bales from the side, whilst the use of a grapnel to pull away the top part is often practicable.

(vii) It may be possible to get some of the galvanised or asbestos sheets off the roof in order to ventilate the fire, but the heat is usually too great for this to be done. If the roof is galvanised iron, it may be possible to work from the ends and to use a crowbar to remove the bolts, or working conditions may be materially improved if the roof is cooled by means of a spray. Where the roof is of corrugated asbestos, this presents no difficulty and it may already have disintegrated with the heat.

(viii) Should the roof already have collapsed before the arrival of the brigade, it should be pulled clear by stack drags or similar method.

(b) Stone and brick-built barns

These barns are very solidly built of stone or brick (Plate 22), usually with a heavy slate or tile roof supported on wooden timbering. As mentioned previously, these barns, which were originally built to store grain and other crops as well as wagons and implements, may now house expensive plant and machinery (Plate 23), and if used as a cover for implements, these may comprise combined harvesters, tractors, spraying machines—all of which are valuable pieces of mobile equipment. Barns may be grouped with other buildings, such as stables, cattle-pens and even the farmhouse. The first problem when a fire spreads is to ensure the safety of any occupants and to prevent spread.

Where the whole barn is given over to storage it usually has double doors as the only means of access, the wagons or other equipment being driven into a central standing place (usually about the middle of the long wall) which is enclosed on each side by boarding behind which hay may be stacked.

There is one particular danger in this type of barn. When a fire occurs, the loose hay between the boards and the stack burns away; firemen, after having extinguished the surface fire, may begin to remove hay from the top of the stack and throw it down on to carts or the ground of the central standing place for removal outside. In so doing the cavity between stack and boards tends to become covered over, and men who may come up afterwards and start work should be warned of its presence, as they might otherwise slip into the space and might sometimes be very difficult to rescue.

In some parts of the country, cattle are housed on the ground floor, and hay, etc., is stored on a wooden first floor, which is reached by means of a loading bay door at first floor height, and by an internal ladder from the ground floor. This practice, however, is strongly deprecated owing to the danger to cattle in case of fire and is now dying out.

The principal characteristic of a barn fire is the smoke, since it is almost impossible to ventilate the building. The first task is to carry out any necessary rescue of animals (see Part 6A of the *Manual*, Chapter 5, 'Rescue'), and then to cool the timbers of the roof to prevent its collapse. The next step should be to extinguish the surface flame in order to reduce the smoke and the danger to the roof, which may be considerable in those cases where hay is stacked to the full height of the barn. Since the floor is often weak with age and decay it is always wise early in the operations to try to prevent the fire spreading to the floor and possibly bringing about the total collapse of the building. Where fire has started on the ground floor, it is extremely difficult to prevent it involving the floor above, and the risk of spread is great. In such a case, the contents of the upper floor must always be worked out.

(c) Cob-built barns

Cob walls are built from clay and straw, and whilst they will resist the weather for long periods, they are very vulnerable to fire, and will collapse suddenly without warning or show signs of cracks when seriously affected by heat or by the application of water. Cob-built barns are often thatched, but may also be tiled or slated. The hay inside is often built up from floor to roof timbers, occupying the whole of the interior space, and generally the only course possible is to work out the contents of the rick through the door. Unless the roof can be saved, there is usually little that can be done at such a fire once it has obtained a good hold.

(d) Farm buildings

As has been mentioned earlier, the term 'farm buildings' now has a much wider meaning than used to be the case. There is a tendency today to erect a pre-fabricated shell which can house many variations within. Progressive farmers have learned that flexibility is important and that the type of farming which proves most profitable today may well change in the course of a few years. Thus, when investing capital in buildings, the object is to make them all-purpose and this usually results in large single storey buildings similar to factory buildings. Construction varies but many of them have metal or pre-stressed concrete frames clad in corrugated asbestos sheet. Such buildings easily become smoke-logged but where the fire is intense or localised, the asbestos cladding will quickly shatter, giving ventilation for the heat and smoke.

(e) Machines and implements in buildings

These have already been mentioned in par. 6(c) above on farm buildings. However, where a fire occurs in buildings used to house farm implements, it must be realised that the money value involved is similar to that of a well-equipped factory. Fortunately, the implements are usually mobile, since they are intended for work in the fields. When a fire occurs, therefore, it should be possible unless the call is delayed, to remove some of the machinery. Tractors and harvesters usually have pneumatic tyres, but many of the other implements may have ordinary metal wheels.

Removal of implements from buildings on fire will naturally depend upon the circumstances and the judgment of the officer in charge, but where there is a danger of spread, evacuation is to be recommended. Alternatively, in well-constructed buildings, sheeting over the implements and damping with water spray may be sufficient, but in this latter case, account should be taken of the quantity of fuel in the tanks of tractors, etc.

(f) Brooder and intensive stock farms

Intensive rearing of poultry and animals for food purposes has developed into a specialised form of farming. Because of its special requirements, this type of farming is not often found on ordinary type mixed farms. A typical intensive poultry farm is to be seen on

Plate 30. Such buildings house thousands of heads of poultry and differ only in purpose, *i.e.*, egg producing or poultry for table. For economic reasons, the greater the number of birds that can be kept in a given sized building, the better since they can be more easily fed, watered and kept warm. In fact, the warmth factor is less of a problem when the maximum numbers are housed in the minimum space.

Heating is often by means of liquefied petroleum gas and, in such cases, the modern installations are equipped with safety devices, with the main LPG supply cylinders being stored in reasonable isolation to each building. Food is mechanically fed from large hoppers and the 'farm' tends to look and operate as a factory.

A fire occurring in any of the buildings housing birds will inevitably result in the destruction of the occupants and the work of the fire brigade is confined to the prevention of spread and to the protection of the LPG tanks.

Due to the emphasis on fire prevention and, perhaps, to the disastrous results of fires in some of the earlier timber-type buildings, the intensive poultry or egg farm is usually constructed so as to enable the movement of fire appliances and the task of fire fighting to be reasonable. Separation between the buildings, concrete roads and pathways are to be advised whenever new buildings for this purpose are being erected.

Intensive stock breeding does not present the same hazard as poultry houses. There is less need for heating and, because of the size of the animal as compared with poultry, the buildings and stalls are of a more substantial character. However the advice to fire officers who have such farms on their ground is to visit and ensure familiarity with the premises and to agree an evacuation plan with the owners. Since, as with most farms, they are in positions of relative isolation, the time taken to get the first appliances there in the event of a call will mean that the farmer and his staff will need to deal with the evacuation of the animals whenever possible. Drivers of appliances approaching a fire in such premises should be wary of straying animals, since cattle reared under intensive conditions are not used to freedom; this advice, however, is applicable to all farm fires and is usually well appreciated by fire brigade personnel stationed in rural areas.

(g) Piggeries

There are many places where pig rearing is carried on on the intensive plan similar to poultry and stock farms. However, because of the habits of pigs, isolation into small groups is usually maintained even under intensive production conditions. Also, because of the strength of this animal and its natural curiosity and routing tendency, the structures housing them need to be of a robust character.

However, the danger of fire is much less in the large piggeries than in the smaller units found on mixed farms. These so-called smaller units can often house up to 200 pigs at a time. The main cause of fire in these is the infra-red heating equipment used during the winter months when young piglets are being raised (Plate 31). Properly installed, these systems present no unusual hazard, but, as with the amateur electrician in the household, so with piggeries; it is easy to obtain equipment and to make extensions to the systems. This, coupled with the use of plenty of straw for warm bedding, adds to the fire hazard in such buildings.

(h) Grain and grass drying plant

Grain drying and grass drying plants are similar in one respect only, *i.e.* the processing of a combustible substance and for which purpose each uses a heating element.

Grain dryers are in more common use and even small farms are often equipped with one. The system of agricultural building grants encouraged the extensive use of this type of equipment. The dryers may be housed in either existing barns or in purpose-built buildings, but in all cases they contain the same principal parts: (i) an intake or feed where the 'wet' grain is deposited, (ii) a conveyor by which the grain is passed to the drying units, (iii) a heated oven in which the grain is dried, and (iv) a final conveyor to the storage bins or despatching areas (Plate 26).

The main fire risk is in the oven-heating element. This may be electrical, oil-fired, gas-fired, and still, in some cases, solid fuel fired; the most common are electrical or oil fired. The risk of fire is similar to that associated with any drying plant concerned with a combustible product. The risk will be low if the plant is properly maintained and cleaned.

When fighting a fire in a grain dryer, water should be used sparingly unless the fire has attained the proportions when jets have to be used. The dried grain in the hoppers or bins will absorb a large quantity of water with consequent swelling and possible eventual bursting of the walls. If the fire starts in the drying area, it may be possible to stop the movement of the charred grain before it is deposited in the hopper or bin. Hot spots in the trunking will indicate where the burning grain is and these may be dealt with by using a spray branch after having taken precautions to ensure that neither the burning grain or the water can pass into the storage area.

Grass drying plants vary in type but the most common is where the grass is loaded on to a metal grid through which is forced a hot dry air current. This latter is produced by a fan blowing air over a heater element which may be heated in similar fashion as those described above for grain dryers.

Fires in such plants are best fought by removing the hay from the drying plant and treating it in the same manner as a haystack fire. Where it is necessary to use water inside the dryer, it will be found that some of the water will have drained into the air chamber beneath the grill and this will need to be cleared before the plant can be brought back into operation.

(j) Fires in agricultural silos

The storage of green forage or haylage in silos, forage or haylage towers as they are variously described, is extensively established in the United States of America. It is increasingly gaining favour in this country because mechanisation of farming with the consequent reduction in the number of farm workers favours the adoption of silo storage and so the number of silos being erected is rapidly growing. Because the nature of the process requires limited fermentation of the raw material, hazards can be introduced unless the appropriate safeguards are adopted. One of these is that fire can result from the overheating of the silage if air gains access to it, and fermentation is allowed to proceed beyond a safe limit. Another is the risk to firemen of exposure to toxic gases if they enter the silo.

Research carried out in 1969 by the University of Wisconsin showed that the number of fires in silos in the USA was causing concern and it was found that although the annual damage to farm crops arising from spontaneous ignition was considerable, spontaneous ignition in silos was of recent origin and increasing in frequency. An additional hazard was the danger of explosion due to accumulation of flammable gases.

In 1967 there were about 500 to 600 silos in use in the United Kingdom but an estimate made in 1970 suggested that the number was then nearer 1,600 and although the number of fires compared with the number of silos is small, such fires pose difficult problems for fire brigade personnel.

(i) *Principle of silo storage.* The principle of silo storage is based on cutting green forage, which consists mainly of grasses but which may also contain alfalfa, lucerne and similar materials and storing it in a silo until required for animal feedstuff. The green material is fed into the top of the silo, usually by a blower system, as soon as possible after cutting; it then settles into a compact and dense mass and may be subsequently removed by a rotating cutter and conveyor system.

To preserve the forage and ensure the maximum nutritive value, limited fermentation is necessary. After the silo is charged, respiration of oxygen from the air within the compacted material occurs and starts a microbiological action in the forage which is accompanied by the evolution of a relatively small amount of heat. If, however, the moisture content of the silage material is initially lower than the recommended minimum and the silage is insufficiently compacted, entry of oxygen due to inadequate sealing of the silo will permit more vigorous heating which will raise the temperature to a point where microbiological action ceases (said to be about 75°C), and heating continues by chemical oxidation alone. If oxygen continues to be available the action continues and ignition will eventually occur. The temperature to which fermentation is normally allowed to reach is between 27 and 49°C. A temperature in excess of 60°C indicates the onset of dangerous heating.

(ii) *Spontaneous heating*. There are three major controllable factors which influence spontaneous heating of the silage. These are the size of cut or chop of the material fed into the silo, the moisture content of the material and the accessibility of oxygen (air) to the stored material. If the cut of the material is too long or varies in length the silage will not become adequately compacted and air will be occluded within it. The moisture content is vitally important. A number of American farmers who had fires in silos were interviewed in the course of research referred to earlier and in each case it was estimated that part or all the material put into their silos had a moisture content of 40 per cent or less, most less than 30 per cent.

It is possible to assess the moisture content of the cut material with the use of instruments but an experienced farmer can tell by squeezing the forage in his hand whether the moisture content is about right. The time of day and weather conditions when the crop is cut can have an influence on the moisture content and needs to be taken into account. Ideally the crop should be cut and loaded into the silo without delay. It should be fed in continuously in such a way that a minimum depth of 10 ft (3 m) is achieved at one loading. If there is delay the unloaded material may become partially dry. Sometimes water is sprinkled on to the top of the silo during loading but this is not generally a very satisfactory way of making up for loss of moisture prior to loading. It has been suggested that additives or 'improvers' which can be put into the silage may have some influence on the possibility of spontaneous heating. No data is at present available on this.

(iii) *Silo construction.* Forage silos (Fig. 1-5) are vertical cylinders about 20 to 25 ft (6 to 7·6 m) in diameter and up to 70 ft (21·4 m) in height. A 65 ft (20 m) silo with a diameter of 25 ft (7·6 m) may contain up to 500 tons (508 tonnes) of silage based on a 50 per cent moisture content. There are two basic forms of construction:

A. Precast concrete blocks interlocked both horizontally and vertically, restrained at each course by steel hoops or bands (*see* Plate 28), or

B. steel plated sections bolted together (*see* Plate 29).

In either construction, the base of the silo is set in concrete. To prevent corrosion both forms of shell usually have an internal lining of vitreous or other protective material.

The top or cap of the silo is usually dome-shaped and is constructed with sheet steel, aluminium or glass-reinforced polyester. A door or hatch in the dome gives access to the interior for the assembly, maintenance and removal of cutting and elevating machinery. A series of hatchways is provided vertically up the side of the silo; these are closed on the inner side by doors, either of wood or steel plate, which are secured in position by latches or bolts. Rubber gaskets ensure a gastight seal between the hatchway and the door. A metal ladder, protected by safety rails or a ladder cage, gives access to all the hatchways and to the top of the silo.

(iv) *Use.* The cut forage is loaded into the top of the silo by a blower system terminating in a goose-neck shaped head which is traversed to ensure even disposition. The silage is subsequently removed from the silo by an electrically-driven rotating cutter and conveyor system which is lowered on to the surface of the silage by a winch (Fig. 1-5, rear), and control device at the base of the silo. The cut silage falls to the base of the silo via a chute either at the centre or the perimeter of the silo. Chutes at the side of silos are usually V-shaped and are formed by hinged plates fitted to the access hatches. After the silo is unloaded and before any recharging can commence the cutting machinery has to be dismantled and removed.

In one type of silo which is designed for maximum sealing against any air intake, a heavy gauge plastic bag communicating with the outside atmosphere is fitted inside the top of the silo (Fig. 1–5, front). Pressure changes within the silo, due to atmospheric and temperature differentials, cause the bag to breathe and compensate for the ingress and egress of air to the silage which would otherwise occur. In this type of silo the cutter and conveyor device for unloading is permanently fitted in the base.

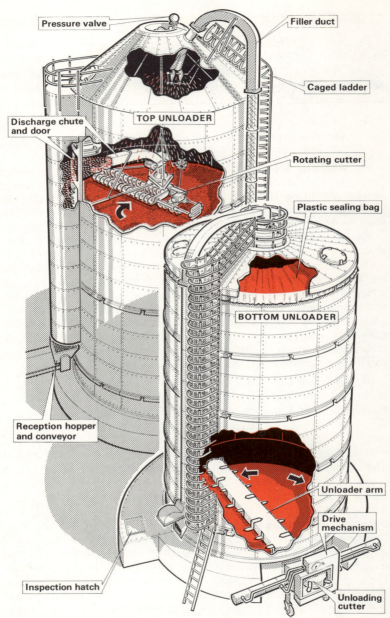

Fig. 1–5. Diagram showing two types of haylage silo (which should not be confused with a grain silo—see Part 6C of the Manual, *Chapter 6). At the rear is shown a 'top unloader' and in front is a 'bottom unloader'.*

46

(v) *Fire fighting*. Before tackling a fire in an agricultural silo, the officer in charge will find it useful to have some knowledge of the design of the silo and its ability to withstand reasonable internal pressure as the result of the introduction of water. The availability of water supplies and hardstanding for appliances will be known, and in many cases brigades may find it advantageous to have an arrangement for the provision of some type of scaffolding and platform from which the fire can be fought. Details of availability of water probes and temperature recording probes will also be useful.

As with any fire situation the first essential, apart from rescue work, is to locate the seat of the fire and time spent on this aspect can be rewarding. If flames are showing from the top of the silo, the possibility is that the fire is not deep-seated and can probably be dealt with by a reasonable application of water to the top crust, but no attempt should be made to enter the silo as there may be cavities under the crust into which a fireman could fall.

If the fire is deep-seated, its location then becomes a question of elimination. A metal temperature probe (Fig. 1-6) inserted through selected hatch doors should be used to gauge the intensity and depth

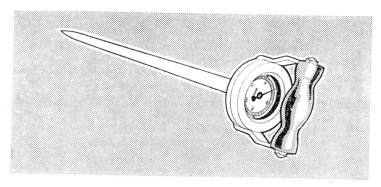

Fig. 1–6. A probe type silage thermometer which is normally in lengths up to 5 ft (1·5 m).

of the fire. The design of the internal chute behind the doors has an important bearing on the penetration problem, but practical fire experience indicates that in spite of structural difficulties, probe penetration can be made. Access to the hatch doors can be gained from the vertical metal ladder, but care should be taken when working on the ladder as the protective shield could retain dangerous gases, and there could be a build up of heat. Experience has proved that it is usually necessary to remove a section of the plating of the protective shield to disperse the heat and gases. The initial penetration work could prove to be so difficult that it may be necessary to make use of a hydraulic platform or some suitable scaffolding (as mentioned above).

Whilst at the time of writing an explosion in these types of silo has not occurred in the United Kingdom the possibility is always present. With a deep-seated spontaneous fire care should be taken in the disposition of personnel. Men should not be permitted to go on to the roof of the structure because of the evolution of dangerous vapours. It is also advisable for personnel to be withdrawn from the fixed external platform giving access to the dome hatch whilst water is being injected using water probes at lower levels.

At the same time as an attempt is being made to determine the seat and extent of the fire, every effort must be made to retard the heating by sealing all apertures where air could enter the silo. A thorough inspection of the silo should be made to see if there is any ingress of air and wet clay or any suitable (mastic) sealing material can be used for sealing apertures. The sealing process may give the impression to on-lookers that little is being done to extinguish the fire and officers may well find themselves under pressure from the farmer to take more positive action, but such pressure should be resisted in the knowledge that the sealing of apertures is a prerequisite to successful fire extinction.

As soon as the seat and extent of the fire have been located, an attack should be made on the fire. On two fires in silos, high expansion foam was used without success in an attempt to control the fire, and the use of 'dry ice' was also abortive. There is no reason to believe that low or medium expansion foam would have proved any more successful. Consideration was given to the use of bulk carbon dioxide, but difficulties of injection were such that its use was rejected. The possibility of using 'wet' water was also considered but present experience indicates that any advantages gained would be minimal.

The silage is packed so tightly that high pressure water jets applied to the exterior of the silage are quite incapable of penetrating the mass, and flooding of the upper crust is not likely to be effective; further, the increased weight of water could bring about the collapse of the silo structure.

When the main body of fire has been located, the most satisfactory method of attack appears to be by the use of a water probe, fed by a line of 1¾ in. (45 mm) hose (Fig. 1-7, above) or by hose reel tubing (Fig. 1-7, below). It will be found, however, that the injection of the

Plate 16. Fire in reclaimed peat-land. The whole length of the dyke bank is burning and pitted ash can be seen in the foreground.

Plate 17. The result of fire-fighting operations in the peat-land fire shown in Plate 16. Loose peat ash is being washed into the dyke.

Plate 18. The older method of stooking cereals. This type of harvesting has now almost completely been replaced by combine harvesting.

Plate 19. A combine harvester at work. The cereal is delivered direct into the grain truck.

Plate 20. A typical 5-bay Dutch barn used for storing baled hay or straw.

Plate 21. A fine example of thatching on a farm cottage.

Plate 22. External view of a typical brick built barn, with a high central loading door. This type of barn has largely been replaced by that shown in Plate 23.

Plate 23. An example of a concrete-trussed farm building used for storing agricultural machinery.

Plate 24. A typical large grain store.

Plate 25. Another method of storing grain in bulk.

Plate 26. The equipment for grain drying is shown in the front of the picture. At the back is a grain elevator.

Plate 27. This mass of smoke and flame was caused when a tank of creosote exploded. The creosote was being heated for dipping fencing spiles when it boiled over and caught fire. It was another drum of creosote lying alongside which exploded.

Plate 28. Two examples of concrete haylage silos, 65ft. (20 m) high and 20 ft. (6·1 m) in diameter.

Plate 29. Another example of a haylage silo, constructed of steel plates.

Plate 30. A typical intensive breeder poultry battery house.

Plate 31. The type of heating and lighting used for rearing young piglets can be a source of danger from fire.

probe into the tightly packed silage through a hole made by a cutter
or drilling in the hatch door nearest to the seat of the fire is a labori-
ous task. To force the probe into the mass, it is often necessary to
use a sledge hammer while radial movement pressure is applied to
the probe and a modification to the probe shown in Fig. 1-7 (above)
would be to have a side entry for the hose coupling with the existing
coupling removed and the end blanked off by a heavy cap. This

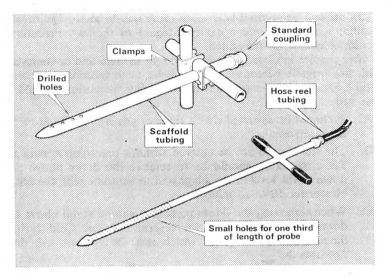

Fig. 1–7. Diagram showing two types of probe used to get water into the heart of a fire in a haylage silo.

would enable a sledge hammer to be used if necessary. Experience
shows that if the insertion of the probe cannot be carried out from
a hydraulic platform an alternative is to use scaffolding embodying a
suitable working platform. Firemen should wear protective gloves
as a precaution against heat blast from the hole when the probe is
being inserted into the silage, and goggles to give eye protection from
chips of the vitreous lining or other protective material used in the
construction of the silo.

Application of water through the probe is best carried out in
stages and the effect of each application carefully observed, as flooding must be avoided for structural stability reasons (as mentioned
above). It must be stressed that no attempt should be made to enter
the silo for 'working-out' purposes. After each application of water

the fire area should be tested for heat reduction by means of the metal probe and as the temperature is reduced, it may be possible to make use of a temperature probe without damage to the instrument.

When the fire is known to be under control and working out by mechanical cutter is considered to be expedient, it may, under certain circumstances, be necessary for firemen to enter the silo to free the internal chute from wet haylage. Such men must wear breathing apparatus and be secured with a lowering line to guard against the possibility of falling into a cavity. Stage 1 of the 'BA Procedure' should, of course, be instigated.

After the fire has been extinguished and the silo and contents are cold, fire brigade personnel should make an inspection from time to time. During such inspections the following precautions should be observed:

A. It should be assumed that a layer of gas is present above the silage material.

B. The silo should not be entered without breathing apparatus. The first action should be to remove the doors above and down to the level of the silage and to ventilate with the filling blower for 10 to 15 minutes.

C. When removing the doors personnel should stand above the doors and remain there for several minutes. Cold carbon dioxide and other gases which may be present will drift downwards.

(k) Fires involving fertilisers

Fertilisers will be found, often in large quantities, stored in plastic or paper sacks on farms, although they may also be found in towns and in the holds of ships. Those in current production are quite stable under normal conditions of handling and transport; indeed some fertilisers are unaffected by fire or would tend to damp out a fire rather than sustain it. Most fertilisers, however, contain ammonium nitrate and their properties and the special problems which arise if they are involved in fire, together with the measures to be adopted in these circumstances, are described in the following paragraphs.

(i) *Properties.* All fertilisers contain one or more of the essential plant nutrients—nitrogen, phosphate and potash—and these are referred to on the bags as N, P_2O_5 and K_2O respectively. In many instances the nitrogen is derived from ammonium nitrate which, in its almost pure state, is made in granular form for use as a fertiliser. Ammonium nitrate does not itself burn, but is classified as a rather

50

weak oxidising agent, and if involved in fire it may enable combustible material to continue to burn even when all air has been excluded. If heated sufficiently it will melt, so to keep the fertiliser cool, it may be advantageous to encourage free circulation of air. Moreover, confinement of any kind is to be avoided as it promotes decomposition of the ammonium nitrate and indeed strong confinement may lead to explosion.

(ii) *Effect of heat or fire.* When ammonium nitrate is mixed with other materials, such as chalk, phosphates or potassium salts (as in fertilisers), the properties of ammonium nitrate are modified. The oxidising capacity of the mixture is reduced, so that few commercial mixed fertilisers which contain ammonium nitrate are, in fact, supporters of combustion. The effect of strong heat, however, on any fertiliser mixture will cause some decomposition. If the fertiliser contains ammonium nitrate (or other nitrates), this decomposition may produce oxides of nitrogen which are insidiously toxic and call for special care.

Such a decomposition may be recognised by the presence of copious white or brown fumes with a pungent odour. The fumes themselves do not generally assist combustion; in a great many cases, decomposition and fume evolution will stop when the source of heat is removed or extinguished, but there are some fertilisers in which decomposition may continue progressively throughout the whole mass. This phenomenon is not the same as normal combustion and is sometimes referred to as 'self-sustaining decomposition', since it is independent of the presence (or absence) of air. This type of decomposition has been known to begin after sustained heating from a relatively small heat source such as, for example, a buried electric lamp.

The officer in charge of a fire in which fertilisers are involved should assume that at least some of them will contain ammonium nitrate, and he should be prepared for the evolution of toxic fumes.

(iii) *Fire-fighting principles.* In the event of fire in combustible substances adjoining stored fertilisers, the primary objective must be to extinguish the fire as quickly as possible while keeping the fertiliser cool. If the fertiliser becomes directly involved, it will be important to disperse the heat and products of decomposition quickly. This means that as much ventilation as possible must be provided from then onwards, even though this is contrary to advice normally applied to combustible materials.

Decomposition of the fertiliser may be accompanied by the evolution of toxic fumes including nitrous gases, so all personnel who may be exposed to the fumes should wear breathing apparatus. The emission of a large volume of toxic fumes in a built-up area could cause injury to the general public. Where this danger might arise, the officer in charge should warn the police of the dangers and should maintain liaison with them. He should, if possible, contact the fertiliser manufacturers for technical advice or assistance.

(iv) *Fire-fighting procedure.* Where an outbreak of fire has actually involved fertilisers which may contain ammonium nitrate and where heat has initiated decomposition, the following procedure is recommended:

A. As much water as possible should be applied to the hot zone (*see* B below). Sea water may be used if there is no other adequate water supply. Foam or chemical extinguishers should not be used; they will certainly prove inadequate. The fire should not be smothered by covering the hot area with more fertiliser or other substances because decomposition will proceed all the faster underneath. Steam should not be used (*e.g.* if aboard ship) as this will only accelerate decomposition and retard heat dispersal.

B. If the fire is severe, the application of water spray may result in sudden eruptions of steam and molten fertiliser which may be violent. Firemen should take whatever cover may be provided by walls and bulkheads. However, the more quickly the temperature is lowered at the seat of the fire, the less likely will there be any sudden eruptions of steam and the smaller will be the quantity of toxic fumes generated.

C. Nearby fertiliser should be cooled with water. In the early stages water spray is effective.

D. Copious supplies of water should be used to control self-sustaining decomposition in that part of bulk fertiliser which is decomposing. A hard crust will probably form on the surface of the heap and means will be needed to penetrate it.

E. Maximum ventilation should be provided by opening doors, windows, ventilators and hatches, or by making holes in the roof. This will assist in keeping down the temperature, minimising the evolution of dangerous fumes and avoiding any build up of pressure which could be dangerous. In addition, a high level escape for the gases evolved will reduce the danger of toxicity to personnel. Nitrous fumes are heavier than air at the same temperature, but when heated will rise in cooler surrounding air.

F. If, as a result of the outbreak, progressive self-sustaining
    decomposition through the fertiliser is suspected, the part
    involved should be isolated from the rest. When the fertiliser
    is in sacks this may mean manhandling or mechanical
    removal of fairly large quantities to a safe place. A break may
    be created in bulk storages by digging out a clear space, or by
    carefully removing the fertiliser with a jet of water.

G. Precautions should be taken to avoid inhaling the fumes;
    breathing apparatus should be worn. Nitrous fumes are very
    poisonous and their effect may be delayed for some hours
    after inhalation. Any person exposed to the fumes should
    have complete rest and prompt medical attention (see (vi)
    below). Care should also be taken to guard against injuries
    to firemen's feet as a result of contact with molten fertiliser
    salts.

H. Molten fertiliser should not be allowed to accumulate in the
    fire area, to come into contact with combustible materials or
    to run into a drain. It should be dispersed as quickly as pos-
    sible with adequate quantities of water. This is particularly
    important since an explosion might be possible. If molten
    fertiliser does enter any drain, the appropriate department of
    the local authority, the River Board and water undertaking
    for the area should be informed as soon as possible.

J. All possible precautions should be taken to prevent contamina-
    tion of the fertiliser during the fire by oil or other combustible
    materials which may be in the vicinity. Such contamination
    would be likely to encourage the fire, to produce more fumes
    and may lead to violent reaction or explosion.

(v) *After the fire.* When the fire has been extinguished, the area
involved should be thoroughly cleared. Undamaged bags should be
separated from the damaged ones and removed to a place of safety.
Spilled, wet or contaminated fertiliser should not be removed from
the store until it has been examined and disposal instructions given
by a competent authority.

Ammonium nitrate is soluble in water and unless the store is
thoroughly cleaned, a solution of ammonium nitrate may dry out on
the floor or walls. If this should come into direct contact with straw
or other organic matter, it could give rise to spontaneous heating,
especially if there is any oily waste contaminating the area.

(vi) *Medical treatment.* Nitrous fumes which may be generated in a
fire involving ammonium nitrate are very poisonous and their effects
may be delayed for as much as forty-eight hours. It is imperative

therefore that any person without adequate protection who has been exposed to these fumes should be given early medical attention, even if he protests that he feels no serious ill effects.

An ambulance should be called immediately, and before the patient is taken to hospital, he should have a label attached to him marked 'nitrous fumes'. The ambulance attendants should also be informed of the kind of poisoning which may be involved. Whilst awaiting the ambulance, the person should be removed to fresh air, kept warm and at absolute rest (lying down). Oxygen should be given but not artificial respiration.

Because the effects of the fumes may be delayed, any person who has been exposed to them should be kept under medical supervision for at least forty-eight hours.

(l) Petrol, oil and LPG storage

The increase in the use of mechanisation on farms has led to a need for the storage of larger quantities of fuel.

The Ministry of Agriculture, Fish and Food and other bodies have produced advisory leaflets on the methods of storage and these are readily available to farmers. Probably the most hazardous conditions apply on smaller farms where the quantities stored do not require a petroleum licence or where liquefied petroleum gas is used direct from cylinders. However, whether it is this type of hazard or that of very large quantities of fuel being stored, the officer in charge of the fire station covering such farms should visit and familiarise himself with the risk.

Where the fuel is stored for a specific use, such as for heating or drying plant, the storage tanks will be little different from those used for domestic and industrial storage. They will be near enough to the plant to obviate long runs of pipe and in a position convenient for the supply tankers to stand whilst re-filling the store. Consequently, in the event of the plant or nearby hazards being involved in a fire, the isolation and cooling of the tanks will form part of the fire-fighting plan.

Part 6C of the *Manual*, Chapter 5, deals at length with petrol, fuel oil and LPG, and the Fire Protection Association offers guidance in F.P.A. Technical Booklet No. 32, 'Storage of petroleum spirit and petroleum mixture'. In addition the Home Office have issued a Code of Practice for the storage of small LPG containers.

7. FIRES IN THATCH

Thatch is a method of roofing a house or farm building by laying upon the roof framing layers of straw, hay, reeds or heather, until the whole forms a solid and watertight mass. Occasionally the roof is close boarded, but generally the thatch is laid on battens and the underside can be seen from the roof space. Since straw thatch is the most common, the following section will deal principally with that material. In the case of reed thatching, the spread of fire will usually be more rapid.

The thatching (Fig. 1-8) consists of bundles of straw about 2 ft 6 in. (760 mm) long, laid vertically upon the battens, those higher

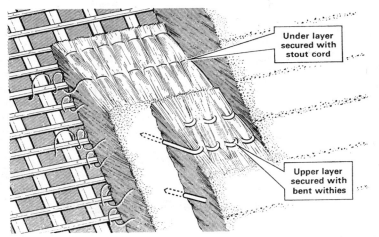

Under layer
secured with
stout cord

Upper layer
secured with
bent withies

Fig. 1–8. Sketch showing the method of securing the lower bundles of thatch to the roof timbers.

up the roof overlapping those below. Each bundle of the topmost layer is secured by twine, wire, strips of willow or a twisted length of straw to wooden pegs thrust into the thatch upon each side of the bundle. The roof is completed with a ridge which may be of thatch or of other materials. In some cases, in order to protect the thatch from birds, it is entirely covered with wire netting, which is secured to the ridging and beneath the eaves by staples.

In old houses, it is the usual practice to lay a new layer of thatch from time to time over the top of that already in place. It is not unknown, therefore, to find thatched roofs from 9 in. (230 mm) to as much as 4 ft (1·2 m) thick, with two or more pegged layers. The thicker the roof, the greater the compression of the bottom layer, and it will be found that the straw deep in the roof has become so dry that it tends to powder and is likely to cause rapid fire spread. Sometimes, however, when property is re-thatched, the old material is thrown into the roof void for insulation, thus adding to the fire load of the building. Normally, however, thatch burns slowly, steadily and with much smoke, though holes made by birds or rats may increase the amount of air which reaches the interior and allow the fire to spread more rapidly.

Where a fire, due perhaps to a spark from a chimney, has caught the outside of a roof, it will tend to burn downwards into the thatch. Water spray should be applied, after which firemen must get on to the roof and pull away the burning thatch with ceiling hooks or other implements, water spray being applied when necessary. A hook or special roof ladder can be used to give men a foothold. The bundles of thatch can be freed by inserting the point of a fireman's axe under the binding and giving a sharp tug, after which the bundles can be pulled away, preferably starting at the top of the roof. Every piece of burning thatch must be removed and care must be taken that no sparks are left. Thatch thrown to the ground should be pulled clear, damped and spread out. Wire netting (Fig. 1-9) presents a considerable problem, since it must be removed before the thatch can be

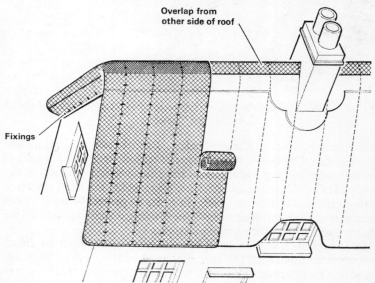

Fig. 1–9. Sketch showing how wire netting which is fixed over thatch to prevent the access of birds and small rodents is secured to the eaves and ridge. It is laid in strips from eaves to ridge and tied together every 12 in. (305 mm). It is fixed by staples at the gable ends and under the eaves.

pulled away. It can often be ripped off, using the point of an axe or a ceiling hook, or, in exceptional cases, it can be pulled away by means of a grapnel attached to a vehicle. Alternatively it can be cut with shears.

Early consideration should be given to salvage operations in order to prevent damage that otherwise might be caused to the upper rooms of the building by water and pieces of burning thatch or other debris.

It is useless to fight a fire in thatch by playing jets from the ground on to the surface, since a thatched roof is constructed so as to be waterproof. Such jets may cut off surface flame, but will not stop burning into the thatch. In addition, the use of a strong jet from within will result in extensive water damage inside the building. Hose reel jets are generally the most suitable as water conservation is a top priority. It is sometimes possible to pull off the top surface of burnt straw and get jets into the roof itself, but usually pulling away is preferable. It may be possible using a spade to make a cut through the thatch which, if kept wet, will act as a fire break, at any rate until a true break has been stripped, as described later. It should be remembered that too much water in the thatch greatly increases the weight upon rafters and may cause collapse of the whole roof. The thickness of old beams is not necessarily an indication of their strength for they may have been weakened by internal decay.

Fire may also start on the underside of the thatch or may reach it by burning through from the top, or by reaching the end of the roof and burning downwards. The spread can often be traced by noticing the discoloration of the ceilings. In barns and buildings without ceilings, it may be practicable to fight the fire from the inside, simultaneously with the work outside of clearing the top thatch, and then cutting a break to prevent side travel. In old cottages, however, access to the roof space is often difficult, since the closeness of the beams and the thickness of the ceiling make it difficult to get to work.

Less final damage will be caused if a quick cut is made through a ceiling to reach the underside of a roof and prevent the spread of fire, than if a fire gets a good hold and flaming thatch and loosened timbers fall through a ceiling into the upper rooms. A hose reel branch, or even a hand pump, can do good work within the roof space upon the timbers and the thatch. When the fire has a good hold, all thatch will have to be removed as quickly as possible.

In the case of a long thatched roof, such as that on a barn or a row of cottages, where the fire has a good hold and also where there is an acute shortage of water, it is essential to make fire breaks to limit the possible spread by choosing two points on the roof well clear of the fire (the distance will depend upon the strength of the wind and the rate of burning), and to strip the thatch completely for a distance of some 4 ft (1·2 m) (Fig. 1-10).

Power-driven chain saws are an extremely useful tool for cutting through thatch, but their use should be confined to personnel who are specially trained to operate them. It is essential that the operator

Fig. 1–10. Sketch showing a suggested method of making fire breaks in a thatched roof. Note that the break in the leeward side should be made farther from the fire than that on the windward side.

chooses a firm footing when using the saw so that balance is easily maintained. If working from a ladder, the man should remain on the ladder all the time. The cuts should be made downwards from the ridge to the eaves, and before men are sent aloft to clear the channel, the saw should be switched off and returned to the ground. The thatch should be removed from the ridge downwards to the eaves. It may be necessary, depending on the thickness of the thatch, to repeat the operation. Both sides of the roof at the point selected will require similar treatment.

The far edge of the breaks should then, if possible, be sheeted to prevent sparks lodging in the sides of the cuts, or alternatively should be well damped or protected with spray. In old houses, on account of the age of the thatch, the shrinkage of timbers in the ridge and, in some cases, the absence of separating walls extending to the ridge, cavities are formed which will allow the fire to spread along the whole length of the building with considerable speed.

In some parts of the country a thatched roof may be covered with galvanised iron or asbestos sheeting carried on a timber framework.

It is not always easy to recognise at once that a thatched roof is involved in a fire. In such cases the smoke from the burning thatch will travel along the spaces between the covering and the thatch and often emerge some distance from the seat of the burning. The first step is to get the covering off, generally sheet by sheet, cooling with spray branches during the removal operation. Once the iron has been removed, the fire in the thatch can be attacked as before.

After the fire, all thatch, whether on or off the roof, should be examined carefully for latent fire, and all charred wood from the roof timbers should be completely cut away.

8. WATER IN RURAL FIRE FIGHTING

Water supply is the basic problem in rural fire fighting. It is, therefore, essential that the fireman should have a good knowledge of the supplies in his area, especially those near villages and farm houses, and of the likely state of such supplies at different times of the year. The Ordnance Survey maps carried on appliances invariably have water supplies indicated on them, and use can also be made of the reports from inspection under Section 1 (I)(d) of the *Fire Services Act*.

It will be found, however, that most rural fire fighting demands comparatively small quantities of water, supplemented by considerable manual labour in beating, digging, pulling down, carting and turning over. The rural fireman does not, therefore, despise very small sources of water, but is prepared to take his pump to the water by one means or another, and then to employ possibly lengthy lines of hose to carry this water to the fire, although the use of water tenders has made it possible to get water to a fire without long relays.

(a) Water tenders

These appliances have become generally accepted as the most suitable for dealing with fires in rural areas and the requirement specifications are contained in Specification No. JCDD/3/1 (see Part 2 of the *Manual*, Chapter 1, 'Pumps, etc.'). Water tenders are nearly all of type 'B' with built-in pump, and carry additionally a portable pump. The tank has a capacity of not less than 400 gallons (1818 litres) of water.

For heath, crop and forest fires, the water carried on the appliance is a great advantage and permits fire fighting to be carried out expeditiously. The portable pump can be used either for direct fire fighting in places inaccessible to the appliance, or to keep the appliance supplied with water from a distant source.

(b) Portable pumps

The portable pump is basic to rural work, either when carried on a water tender, or, exceptionally, when towed. There are many occasions when it is essential to remove the pump and carry it to the water supply. Often a farm tractor or cart can be used to transport the pump over rough ground. In the case of pumps with open-circuit cooling in which the cooling water runs to waste, care should be taken to see that the pump does not get bogged down owing to the state of the ground. Sheep hurdles, planks or corrugated iron placed beneath the pump will prevent it sinking.

(c) Hose

Since rural fire fighting often involves the use of very long lines of hose, water tenders generally carry a greater quantity of hose than appliances used for suburban fire fighting, and as a further means of conserving water supplies, $1\frac{3}{4}$ in. (45 mm) hose is also carried to an increasing extent instead of, or in addition to, standard $2\frac{3}{4}$ in. (70 mm) hose. It is also the practice in some areas for a number of lengths of $3\frac{1}{2}$ in. (90 mm) hose to be stowed (often flaked) on a water tender for relaying water from a distance.

In the past it has been the practice to carry unlined hose because of its lightness and because it was less bulky than non-percolating hose, but with the development of lightweight hose, there is now a tendency to carry mostly non-percolating hose, with its lower frictional loss when long hose lines are required.

Since the first essential is to get *some* water on to the fire as soon as possible, the full length of one hose line should be laid followed, if practicable, by a second. These lines can afterwards be broken and pumps inserted as they become available. As friction loss is the factor governing long hose lines, it is obviously desirable that hose lines should be twinned as soon as possible, unless $3\frac{1}{2}$ in. (90 mm) hose is available, when it will usually not be necessary to lay more than one line. On the delivery side $1\frac{3}{4}$ in. (45 mm) hose will be found useful when laid either direct from the pump or from dividing breeches, as appropriate.

(d) Branches

The relative value of jets and spray for use on rural fires has been discussed in previous paragraphs. Where a jet is required, the nozzle should be as small as possible consistent with efficiency, and some brigades carry variable branches so that the jets can be quickly adapted to available water supplies. The judicious use of a hose reel jet will also help to prolong the water supply in the tank of a water tender. It should be remembered that a $\frac{1}{4}$ in. (6·4 mm) nozzle at 25 lbf/in² (1·7 bars) pressure at the branch uses about 8 gallons (36 litres) per minute whereas a $\frac{1}{2}$ in. (12.8 mm) nozzle at the same pressure uses about four times as much, *i.e.*, 31 gallons (141 litres) per minute, and a diffuser branch at 40 lbf/in² (2·8 bars) (the lowest pressure which will give an effective spray) uses 65 gallons (296 litres) per minute. Small nozzles use far less water than a diffuser branch at comparable pressures. Graphs showing the consumption of water at various pressures by small nozzles are shown in Fig. 1–11.

Where supplies are scarce and where dividing the line would not yield two jets of any value, it is sometimes possible to have the final length of hose carried on the shoulders of firemen. It is thus relatively easy to move the position of the branch and a much greater area of ground can be brought within range of the jet, which can thus to some extent be made to do the work of two.

There are many occasions on which diffuser or hand-controlled branches are valuable, not so much for the water spray produced as because the water can be shut off when it is not needed. For damping down hay thrown off a stack, for instance, this method is ideal and most economical with water.

(e) Use of water supplies

The following are a few hints which may help the officer in charge of a rural area to make the best use of the available water supplies.

(i) The position of all water supplies of value for fire fighting should be noted in book or card index form in the station watchroom, in order that the officer in charge of the first appliance can take the appropriate particulars with him. Since, however, the level of ponds and streams varies greatly at different times of the year or even from day to day, he should note the state of water supplies on his way to the fire. A fireman should always investigate the water supply and choose a standing place; information given by bystanders should not be relied upon.

(ii) It is usually a good policy to take a self-propelled appliance and crew direct to the fire, even if the source of supply is passed on the way, because property can sometimes be saved by quick use of hose reel equipment, or of hand pumps. It may also be possible to give advice to the farmer and his workers, to unship ladders and other gear and drop off lengths of hose at intervals on the run back to the source. It may be possible to drive the pumping appliance back to the fire while the hose is being laid from the source of supply, provided there is sufficient pressure available at the source.

(iii) Water should be used as economically as possible and all sources of even a small supply should be explored. Quite good stops

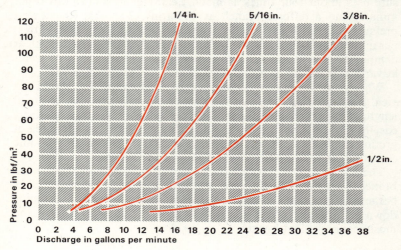

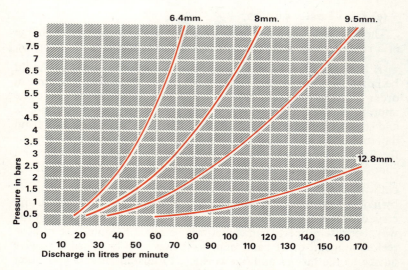

Fig. 1–11. Graphs showing the output in gallons (above) and litres (below) per minute of small diameter nozzles used in rural fire fighting.

62

have been obtained by using water tenders filled from small ditches or ponds and employing a portable pump with the smallest possible nozzle, whilst hand pumps have also done good work. The use of 1¾ in. (45 mm) hose or hose reel tubing will also help to conserve water. Where hose lines can be divided, control dividing breechings should preferably be used in order to facilitate the moving of hose lines, and to make it easier to reach all sides of the fireground. It may also be possible to divert water from a hydrant into a stream possibly at a considerable distance from the pumping position to augment supplies.

(iv) Should a reasonable supply be available, *e.g.* from a pond, the officer should estimate how long it is likely to last in relation to the size of the fire, and make provision for its replenishment by relaying from another supply or by using water tenders, if practicable. It should be remembered that country supplies, such as ponds, are often large in area but shallow and contain less water than appears to be the case. Adaptors to enable hose reel hose to connect up to the suction inlet of the pump can be used to collect water from small tanks.

(v) Should the first supply be likely to prove inadequate, a search for alternative sources should be started at once, and it may be useful to place a water tender or a portable dam into which water from different sources can be collected. Alternatively, if the sources are at some distance, it may be best to erect a portable dam at the fireground and use available water tenders for fetching water and emptying it into the dam, the aim being always to keep a supply in reserve sufficient to preserve continuity in fire fighting. In rural areas, sufficient pumps are seldom immediately available to enable a long relay to be established, and the general practice is to employ a water tender where it would be necessary for a single pump to work over a distance exceeding about half a mile (800 m) on level ground or its equivalent.

(vi) Streams are often too shallow to be used and must be dammed with sheets of galvanised iron, or earth and brushwood, or turf sods cut with a spade and well trodden down, if necessary being supported by wooden battens or fence rails. Some brigades carry empty sandbags which can be filled with earth for this purpose. Alternatively, a sump may be dug to collect the water, and in a weedy pond, it is often useful to sink an old pail or bucket and to place the strainer of the suction in it to prevent its being choked.

Where the flow in a stream is very small, it is wise to make two dams, one below the other, since a certain amount of water will always escape from the one upstream. A pump can then be operated first from one and then from the other. Firemen not used to rural water supplies do not always realise the value of small streams or that, for instance, a stream 2 ft (610 mm) wide with an average depth of 1 in. (25 mm) and a flow of 2 ft (610 mm) per second will yield as much as 125 gallons (568 litres) per minute.

(vii) Water escaping from the fireground, *e.g.* from a haystack, can often be collected by digging a sump and then directing the water into it by means of rolls of wet hay, ridges of earth or shallow trenches, or by using salvage sheets as a water trough (see Part 6A of the *Manual*, Chapter 7, 'Salvage').

(viii) When buckets are in use for damping down pockets of burning peat for instance, and a water tender is available, the pump should be primed, after which it can be shut off, the water being siphoned from the tender and drawn off from the delivery as required as from a tap.

(ix) When using the hose reel jet from a water tender, it should be remembered that the tank of the appliance can in instances where water supplies are short be replenished by buckets from a well or other domestic supply.

(x) It should be remembered that water in farm ponds is often vital to the farmer for watering his livestock, especially in times of drought, and arrangements should therefore be made, if necessary, to replenish, as soon as possible, any supplies which have been drawn on during operations.

9. GEAR USED FOR RURAL FIRE FIGHTING

Appliances in rural areas often carry special items of gear and certain agricultural implements for dealing with the problems encountered at country fires. Of those whose use has been discussed in this chapter, the following are the most commonly found.

(a) Beaters, brooms or fire bats

These (Fig. 1-12) have usually been improvised and very many patterns will be found.

(i) Green branches of hazel, elder, birch or almost any tree can be used to make a satisfactory fire beater (Fig. 1-12 (1)). They should be about 8 to 12 ft (2·5–3·5 m) long, and should be cut in early spring when the sap is rising; this gives them longer life, greater flexibility and makes them easier to handle. If possible about 3 or

4 ft (1–1·2 m) of the bough ends should be trimmed to form a handle when bound together. A convenient way of binding is to pile the trimmed branches in the crotch of a sawing horse, pull the trimmed ends together with a bavin binder and bind them with wire at two .points, at least 1 ft (305 mm) apart. If a handle which can be bound in, is available, the length of the trimmed ends can be reduced accordingly.

Fig. 1–12. Various types of beater: (1) beater made of green branches; (2) beater made of wire netting on a metal frame; (3) beater made of canvas strips; (4) beater made from a sack passed over a framework of wire or stout withy.

A bavin binder can be improvised by joining two stout 4 ft (1·2 m) sticks with a length of rope or wire about 15 in. (380 mm) from one end of each stick. The rope is then passed round the bundles as they rest in the sawing horse and two men tighten it by pulling the sticks against the leverage of the short ends, while a third binds the bundle with a separate lashing.

In cases of emergency, small young trees can be cut or leafy branches from shrubs or bigger trees can be used as beaters.

Many other types of beater have been improvised of which the following are typical:

(ii) Wire netting is laid over a metal or withy frame of some 12 in. (305 mm) diameter and the whole is then attached to a handle (Fig. 1-12 (2)).

(iii) A piece of canvas about 18 to 30 in. (457–762 mm) long and 9 to 18 in. (229–457 mm) wide is riveted down the centre and attached to a wooden shaft 3 to 4 ft (914–1,220 mm) long (Fig. 1-12 (3)). In some cases the last 6 in. (152 mm) are divided into three strips.

(iv) A sack is passed over a framework made from wire or stout withy, the neck of the sack is then tied round the handle (Fig. 1-12 (4)). This type should be stored in water and kept wet when in use.

Wet sacks are useful as beaters, especially for molinia grass, while a long handled, light, broad shovel can be used to iron out fire in vegetation which is more or less even and free from tufts.

When using a beater it should not be raised above shoulder level, both to avoid unnecessary effort and to prevent sparks flying about. A sweeping motion is best in a direction which will tend to drive the sparks raised back into the fire, the aim being directed near the base of the vegetation. Where possible, the fire should be rubbed out rather than beaten out. It is often an advantage at heath fires for men who are beating to work in threes in staggered positions so that any embers left by the first man are extinguished by the other two.

(b) Forks

Forks are used extensively, especially at rick fires, but are fast disappearing from farms because of mechanisation and baling. Fire brigades generally either carry them, or maintain a supply at strategic key stations. They are of two principal types—drag hooks (Fig. 1-13 (1)), usually with four straight tines or prongs at right angles to the handle, which are used for pulling down and dragging away; and pitchforks (Fig. 1-13 (2)) with two upcurving tines used for lifting. These implements are of many patterns and are known by different names in different parts of the country. At a fire, all forks when not in use should have the prongs driven into the ground to avoid accident.

(c) Stack drag (fire pole)

This instrument (Fig. 1-13 (3)) consists of one or two large hooks fitted to a stout pole approximately 15 ft (4·5 m) in length. It may occasionally be found useful for pulling down a stack or dragging thatch from a roof. The stack drag is rather an unwieldy instrument as it requires several men to use it and is generally considered obsolescent as an item of fire gear.

(d) Shovels or spades

Long-handled shovels are useful for many purposes. They are used to smother fires in thick undergrowth when beating would be ineffective, and for digging out burning patches of leaf mould and peat. They are necessary for all trenching operations and for damming streams to increase water supplies.

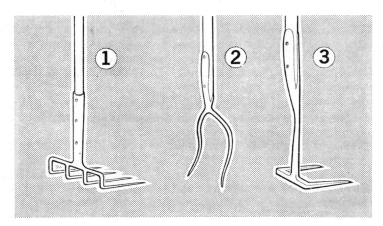

Fig. 1–13. Implements used for moving or pulling away hay, straw, etc.: (1) drag hook; (2) pitchfork; (3) stack drag.

(e) Billhooks or slashers

These tools (Fig. 1-14) may have either a long or a short handle and a curved or straight blade. They are useful for cutting hedges or small trees.

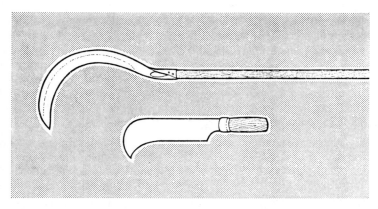

Fig. 1–14. Implements used for cutting or slashing undergrowth, hedges, etc.

10. MISCELLANEOUS SUGGESTIONS TO FIRE OFFICERS

The following general suggestions may be of value to officers whose stations cover rural areas.

(i) Since, in the country, the ground covered by one station may extend over a large area, it is impossible to expect an officer to be familiar with every detail, so it is wise for him to work out a system for identifying rural place names so as to prevent confusion and delay when answering a fire call.

One plan is to list in alphabetical order every name on the Ordnance Survey map that comes within the station's ground, together with the appropriate map reference. In this way, when a call is received it is easy to find the exact location, and if it is possible to refer to the list while the caller is on the telephone, delays may be prevented if there are several places of the same name, since the duplicates will appear on the list and the caller can then be asked for further details. Another plan is to prepare a series of cards covering the more important risks, such as farms, upon which all details of risk, water supply, access, etc., are entered. One copy is given to the farmer, who is asked to keep it in a prominent place and hand it to the crew in case of fire, while the other is available at the local station. This is only practical if fire brigade personnel are available to make frequent visits to keep such information up to date. Farmers should be strongly urged to provide a sign at the entrance to the farm which would clearly identify the name of the farm. Lists of isolated hamlets, farms and other localities should be kept with map references for the benefit of reinforcing appliances.

(ii) At all fires in rural areas it is just as necessary for the fire brigade officer to get in touch with the gamekeeper, farmer, Forestry Commission official, etc., responsible for the land upon which the fire has occurred, as it would be for him in a town to contact the manager of a factory on fire. In this way, he will receive much valuable information and advice. Gamekeepers' houses or lodges should be marked on fire brigade maps, while in strange country it may be possible to locate them by the run of telephone lines.

(iii) The man on the spot will very often have specialised knowledge, and in no type of fire fighting is detailed local knowledge of risks, water supplies, road and tracks, vegetation, soil, rick construction and availability of civilian labour and vehicles of more value.

(iv) When the fire is not accessible by road, a man should be stationed at the nearest access point to give instructions to following appliances, but if manpower is short, a piece of equipment, such as a rolled length of hose, can often be used to indicate the direction to supporting appliances at road junctions.

Should a fire be down a cul-de-sac, a man should be detailed to keep the entrance clear so that the exit of appliances is not obstructed by other vehicles. This is particularly important when water tenders are being used to maintain the water supply.

(v) At fires of considerable extent, such as heath and moor fires, the control point should be set up in as high an elevation as possible where it can be easily seen, and a sign indicating its whereabouts should be placed at the nearest point of access by road. At night it may be necessary to mark the way to it by means of white flags or lamps.

(vi) When travelling over a field, appliances should normally keep to the ground near a hedge, where it is usually harder and where less damage will be done to crops.

(vii) Since so much rural fire fighting consists of manual work, it is essential that ways of preventing unnecessary effort should always be considered. A little thought given to the organisation of the job in hand is well worth while.

(viii) When pulling down a stack, it is wise to set aside a place where all items of gear and clothing can be put, in order that nothing shall get buried by hay or straw and that each item can be quickly found. A salvage sheet should be laid on the ground in a suitable place and all gear sent to the fireground and not in actual use should be placed on it.

(ix) At a farm fire, the first requirement is the prevention of fire spread, and for this purpose a stack should be considered as less important than a building. Owing to the high value of the contents of farm buildings, salvage is always of major importance, and firemen should give what help they can in removing horses and cattle and saving agricultural machinery.

(x) The best use possible should be made of any skilled farm labour which is available, especially in handling agricultural implements, driving tractors and in similar jobs.

(xi) It should be remembered when fire fighting that various special risks may be met on a small scale. Electrical apparatus in the form of electric milking machines and battery charging plants, petrol, kerosene and oil supplies for tractors, chicken brooders, etc., liquefied petroleum gases for heating, stacks of oil cake, quicklime and fertilisers, or of commodities such as hops or unthreshed grain, may be involved in a fire. The treatment of some of these risks is covered in this Part, and others in Part 6C, 'Special and Unusual Risks'.

(xii) Most rural fires require strenuous effort by firemen in considerable heat and smoke, and early arrangements should be made for providing refreshments. There should also be plenty of drinking water available, as well as water to cool faces and hands. Arrangements for reliefs should receive special attention and the officer in charge should also use his discretion in allowing personnel to discard belts, axes, leggings and tunics when conditions make it reasonable for this concession to be granted.

(xiii) Estimating the weights of agricultural commodities involved in a fire may present some difficulties to the fire brigade officer who is not country born and bred. Variations in the yield of crops with the season will be considerable and may affect the estimate to a marked degree. In general, therefore, he will be wise to consult the farmer before finally committing himself to a statement of the quantity of the commodities involved.

As a very rough generalisation, however, from 10 to 13 cubic yards (7·6–10 m³) of hay, and from 9 to 11 cubic yards (6·8–8·4 m³) of clover, may be assumed to weigh 1 ton (1 tonne). The cubic capacity of a stack is easily calculated; for a stack with a pitched roof, the height is obtained by adding together the height from the ground to the eaves and half the height from the eaves to the ridge.

It is, however, common practice for farmers to calculate the estimated contents of a barn or rick containing baled products by the number of bales stored. Where this applies, the fire brigade officer should make a similar calculation when making an assessment.

Part 6B Chapter 2

The Gas Industry and Fires in Gasworks

Section I—Introduction

JUST as today's motor car bears little resemblance to the vintage cars of the 'twenties', so has the gas industry similarly changed. Until the 'fifties' all gasmaking was an elaboration of the well-known school experiment of heating coal in the clay-covered bowl of a clay pipe so that the gas produced could be burned at the mouthpiece. In the time-honoured system of gasmaking, the pipe bowl becomes the retort and the gas is purified by being passed through a series of processes before it is piped to the consumer.

Today, less and less gas used in this country is made by heating or 'carbonising' coal, a process which remained fundamentally unaltered for 150 years. However, at the beginning of the 1950's, the gas industry began to change from an industry based almost entirely on coal to one increasingly based on oil, making gas by processes developed some internally and some in the chemical industry. Then came the importation of liquid natural gas from Algeria, followed by the discovery of natural gas under the North Sea, and the gas industry quickly adapted itself to use natural gas as an alternative feedstock to oil in order to produce a towns gas. Some idea of the rate at which this change has occurred is given by the fact that in 1960, 90 per cent of the total gas supplied in Great Britain was made from coal; now, just over ten years later, only a very small percentage is made from coal. This move away from the traditional feedstock would have continued at an increased rate even without the discovery of natural gas under the North Sea. These discoveries have now faced the gas industry with another, and far greater, technological revolution.

NOTE: Just as this edition of the Manual closed for press, it was learnt that as from 1 *January* 1973 *the Gas Council will be known as the British Gas Corporation, and Area Gas Boards will become Regions.*

1. TOWN GAS

Town gas is a gaseous fuel which is distributed in pipes to domestic, commercial and industrial consumers. Whether derived from natural sources or manufactured, town gas consists mainly of hydrogen with smaller quantities of ethylene, benzene, carbon monoxide, butane/propane and methane (marsh gas). It falls into two major categories:

(i) *High flame speed town gas*, with a calorific value range between 450–550 BTu/ft³ (16·766–20·492 MJ/m³). All coal-gas based town gas and some oil gas supplies come within this category.

(ii) *Low flame speed town gas*, with a calorific value in the region of 1,000 BTu/ft³ (37·259 MJ/m³). This covers natural gas.

2. GASMAKING PROCESSES

The traditional gasmaking process of coal carbonisation produced a town gas containing about 50 per cent of hydrogen and having a calorific value of about 500 BTu/ft³ (18·629 MJ/m³). In order to make the gas from the new oil-based processes interchangeable with coal gas, the processes have been designed to produce a gas also containing 50 per cent or so of hydrogen and with the same calorific value. Two main types of gas are made: a 'lean' gas with a calorific value of about 340 BTu/ft³ (12·668 MJ/m³) is made by a continuous catalytic reforming process (Fig. 2-1(a)) using steam and naphtha (a light distillate fraction from crude oil) or natural gas, or a 'rich' gas of about 650 BTu/ft³ (24·218 MJ/m³) which is made in one of two ways.

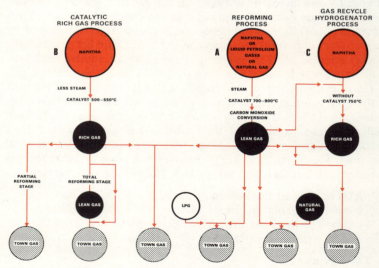

Fig. 2–1. Flow diagram showing the various ways in which the three basic gasmaking processes can be combined to produce towns gas.

In one process, naphtha is again reacted with steam over a catalyst, but at a lower temperature and with less steam in relation to the quantity of naphtha. In this 'catalytic rich gas' process (Fig. 2-1(b)) the rich gas produced consists largely of hydrocarbons with relatively small amounts of hydrogen. The other process (Fig. 2-1(c)) does not need a catalyst and simply consists of reacting naphtha with hydrogen to produce a rich gas (the 'gas recycle hydrogenator' process). The 'lean' gas process of steam reforming produces a mixture of hydrogen and carbon monoxide, and a second stage converts the poisonous monoxide into carbon dioxide and hydrogen, so that the resulting lean gas consists mainly of hydrogen. It can then be used as the source of hydrogen for the second 'rich' gas process.

Town gas is produced from these three processes in a number of ways (Fig. 2-1). The 'lean' gas can be enriched directly by admixture with the right proportion of either the manufactured 'rich' gas, or with natural gas (calorific value about 1,000 BTu/ft^3 (37·259 MJ/m^3)), or with liquid petroleum gases (butane/propane). Also the 'catalytic rich gas' process can be operated with a second stage to produce town gas direct.

3. NATURAL GAS

(a) Algerian natural gas

Natural gas (which consists chiefly of methane) is playing an important part in these new methods of gas production. Liquid natural gas at a temperature of $-160°C$ is imported in special ships designed (at the moment) to carry 12,000 tons (12 193 tonnes) of liquid gas. The natural gas is pumped from the large natural gas fields in Algeria to the Mediterranean port of Arzew where it is liquefied and loaded on to the ships for transporting to a special storage terminal at Canvey Island. Here the liquid gas is stored and re-gasified to be transmitted through the Gas Council's natural gas grid which now supplies all Area Gas Boards. This quantity of Algerian natural gas represents, at the moment, about 10 per cent of the current needs for gas in the United Kingdom.

(b) North Sea natural gas

In July 1964, the Continental Shelf Act, ratified by twenty-two countries, came into force. This defined the territorial areas of the North Sea for the seven nations bordering it and an orderly system of licensing and control started. The first major strike of North Sea natural gas was made by British Petroleum late in 1965 in the Rotliegendes sandstone some 42 miles (67 km) off the Humber estuary, and by the end of December 1965, it was known that this gas would be available in quantity. A 50 mile (80 km) pipeline under the sea brought the first experimental quantities of gas to Easington on the Yorkshire coast early in 1967. The Gas Council has constructed a 24 in. (610 mm) diameter feeder main 80 miles (128 km) long from Easington, across the Humber to feed into the national grid already carrying the Algerian gas, at a point near Sheffield. By May 1967, fifty odd wells had been drilled, sixteen of which showed significant amounts of gas. The Gas Council now plans on the assumption that there is at the very minimum enough gas to supply the United Kingdom with two thousand million cubic feet (57 million cubic metres) a day, equivalent to twice the total output of the whole British gas industry at present. It is reasonable to expect that in fact three thousand million cubic feet (85 million cubic metres) of gas per day could eventually be available for up to thirty years.

4. THE EFFECT ON THE GAS INDUSTRY

The Gas Council has decided that there would be at least sufficient gas to create a natural gas industry in Britain, and so a policy of conversion of the existing towns gas systems to natural gas has already been started. North Sea gas cannot just be fed into the existing town gas pipeline systems and distributed direct to the consumer without this 'conversion' process, because of the combustion characteristics of gas. The two properties of major importance are the calorific value and burning velocity.

If natural gas were put straight on to an existing town gas burner and at the same pressure, it would only entrain the *same* amount of air as the town gas, but since it needs twice as much, the gas would not burn completely and would give a floppy, smoky flame. So the burners have to be converted by fitting a smaller injector (or in some cases the burner has to be replaced), and the gas pressure has to be raised so that the correct amount of air is provided for complete combustion. A further modification has to be made to the burner to render the gas flame from the natural gas as stable as that from town gas.

This process of conversion to natural gas is now well under way and will involve some thirteen million consumers as well as eighty thousand industrial users. If the North Sea gas lives up to its promise, gas could provide about 20 per cent of the total national energy requirements by 1980 compared with about 6 per cent in 1967.

Section II—Gas producing plant

ALTHOUGH huge gasholders are still a familiar sight on gasworks, the general aspect has now changed. At almost all gasworks, the dust and smoke of giant coal carbonising retort houses has been replaced by the cleaner oil gasification plant and one would be forgiven for thinking that one had entered an oil refinery instead of a gasworks. Indeed at a number of refineries, some of the plant is used for reforming light fractions into gas for transmission to the Area Gas Boards. Even now, the oil reforming plant is becoming obsolescent as more and more natural gas is being used.

1. COAL GAS PLANT

Only a very small percentage of gas is now produced by coal carbonisation and at most Gas Board premises the coal and coke plants have been dismantled or removed. However, some plants carbonising coal are still being operated by the National Coal Board, the Steel Industry, etc. for the production of coke or smokeless fuels. The gas produced is mostly used as a fuel in the works themselves.

2. OIL GASIFICATION PLANT

Hydrocarbon reforming plants are designed to produce from petroleum naphtha, liquefied petroleum gas (butane/propane) or natural gas, a gas that may be burnt in equipment originally developed for coal gas burning. This means that the gas must not only have the same calorific value, but also the same density and approximately the same hydrogen content. The highly toxic carbon monoxide content is kept to a minimum. There are no by-products as found with coal carbonisation, but this does not mean that there will be fewer of the valuable products obtained from coal tar, since the chemical industry is making more and more of them from oil.

Oil refinery products are supplied to gasworks either as liquids or gases. Increasing quantities of LPG are now being used, but the oil refinery product which has been most readily available is light distillate, also known as naphtha. When mixed with steam and passed over a heated catalyst, a gas suitable for use as towns gas is produced. This process is called reforming.

There are two basic types of reforming plant: cyclic and continuous. The former are low pressure plants only, whilst the latter work at high pressure and can be divided into two types, as some produce a 'lean' gas and others a 'rich' gas. The lean gas has a lower calorific value than that required for towns gas and therefore this value has to be increased, usually by the addition of butane vapour, methane or rich gas.

(a) Cyclic reforming plants

These plants (Fig. 2-2) can reform a variety of feedstocks from naphtha to heavy fuel oil. They consist of a reactor containing a single bed of catalyst and, dependent on design, one or two adjoining vessels for preheating steam and air.

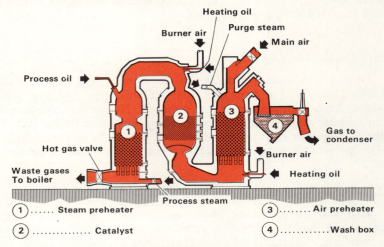

Fig. 2–2. The SEGAS cyclic reforming plant.

The cycle is usually in two parts, a 'blow' and a 'run'. On the 'blow', preheated air is passed through the catalyst bed to heat it to a temperature in the region of 900°C. On the 'run', vaporised feedstock and steam are passed through the catalyst producing a gas with a calorific value of 475–500 BTu/ft³ (17·698–18·629 MJ/m³). With the heavier feedstocks, some carbon is deposited on the catalyst during the 'run'. This burns off during the 'blow' and assists in heating the catalyst.

(b) Continuous 'lean' gas reforming plants

The lean gas plant (Fig. 2-3 and Plate 32) comprises a furnace in which stainless steel tubes containing a catalyst are heated by burners fired by naphtha or natural gas. When processing naphtha, the feedstock is first vaporised in a tubular vaporiser fired by naphtha or natural gas, before passing the de-sulphurising section. This consists of three vertical cylindrical steel vessels containing materials such as zinc oxide which remove the sulphur impurities from the feedstock.

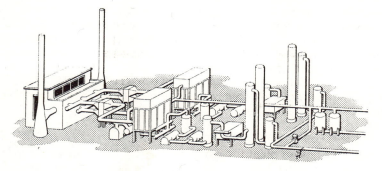

Fig. 2–3. Sketch showing the layout of reforming plant producing 'lean' gas by the continuous reforming process.

Vaporised feedstock then mixes with steam before passing through the furnace tubes, where the feedstock is reformed at a temperature of about 700°C, to a lean gas containing approximately 60 per cent of hydrogen and 11 per cent of carbon monoxide, together with some carbon dioxide and methane. The calorific value is in the region of 320 BTu/ft³ (11·923 MJ/m³). The lean gas then passes through a boiler to a vertical cylindrical steel vessel containing a bed of catalyst which converts most of the carbon monoxide to carbon dioxide.

The remaining parts of the plant consist of a carbon dioxide removal plant and heat exchangers which take the heat from the produced gas to preheat the incoming feedstock and water for the boiler feed. In the carbon dioxide removal plant the lean gas passes up a tall cylindrical vessel some 100 ft (30 m) high and is washed by a solution which can absorb carbon dioxide. This solution is then pumped to the top of an adjoining vessel some 120 ft (36 m) high, where the carbon dioxide is driven off by ascending steam and escapes with the steam through an atmospheric vent at the top of the vessel. After the carbon dioxide removal and cooling, the lean gas is enriched by either natural gas or butane vapour to a towns gas suitable for passing direct to consumers.

As an alternative to naphtha, natural gas can be used as a feedstock.

(c) Continuous 'rich' gas reforming plants

The rich gas plant (Plate 34) is similar to the lean gas plant except that the catalyst is contained in a bed in a single vessel called a reactor. Vaporised feedstock, which is either naphtha or natural gas, mixes with steam before passing through the catalyst, but the amount of steam in the naphtha/steam mixture reformed is approximately half that used in the lean gas process, whilst the reaction takes place at a lower temperature (about 500–550°C). The carbon dioxide removal plant is included as for the lean gas plants.

Rich gas with a calorific value of about 650 BTu/ft³ (24·218 MJ/m³) is used as an enricher for lean gas in place of butane vapour or natural gas.

(d) Gas recycle hydrogenator

Another type of plant for producing a 'rich' gas is the gas recycle hydrogenator (Fig. 2-4), which works by heating a mixture of hydrogen gas with different oil fractions in the form of vapour in

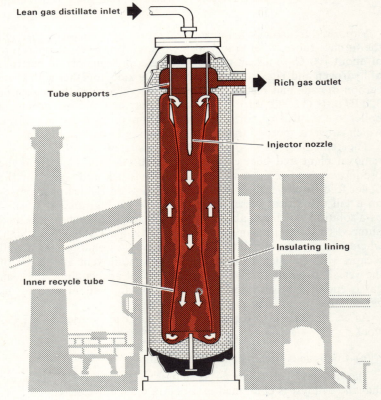

Fig. 2–4. Diagrammatic arrangement of a gas recycle hydrogenator.

steel tubes at high pressure. This plant is another source of rich gas and consists of a single vertical cylindrical brick-lined steel vessel containing a central tube. The mixture is pre-heated to 400–500°C and the hydrogen-rich lean gas vaporises in an exothermic reaction, the resulting rich gas leaving the vessel at about 750°C.

If the inlet gas contained approximately 87 per cent of hydrogen, the final gas would contain 45 per cent of hydrogen, 30 per cent of methane and would have a calorific value in the region of 750 BTu/ft³ (27·994 MJ/m³).

(e) Plant control

Not all of the above types of gasmaking plant will be found at one Gas Board premises, but as modernisation takes place, the old type of equipment is rapidly being replaced. Automation is also being introduced in the control of processes, and it will be found that the latest type of oil gasification plant is controlled from a central control room. The system is such that it will automatically shut down completely or partially and make safe the plant if conditions become potentially dangerous.

3. OIL STORAGE TANKS

Various highly flammable materials are to be found at Gas Board premises where there is oil gasification plant, and these may be in liquid or gaseous form. Butane is stored in high-pressure vessels at ambient temperatures or, if at a temperature below its boiling point (−0·6°C), it is stored in fixed roof tanks similar to those used for the storage of petroleum (see Chapter 5), but encased in some form of insulation.

Petroleum naphtha may be found in considerable quantities, together with smaller quantities of methanol, gas oil, etc. These liquids are normally stored in tanks similar to those used for normal petroleum products. Methane gas is not normally stored at gasworks, but there may be exceptions in isolated instances. Liquefied methane, or as it is now more commonly known, liquefied natural gas (LNG) can be found in either underground or surface storage. At atmospheric pressure LNG liquefies at −162°C and to maintain it at a temperature below this, considerable insulation of the tank has to be provided. With the underground tank, insulation is provided by the ground itself; prior to the construction of the tank, the periphery is frozen, the centre excavated and the frozen ground thus left is maintained in a frozen state by the temperature of the LNG itself. The surface form of storage may consist of a double skin metal tank with an insulating material between the two skins. The tank is located within a bund of sufficient capacity to accommodate the entire contents in the event of a significant leak of LNG.

4. GASHOLDERS

Gasholders are still being used for the storage of town gas, but at some Gas Board premises high-pressure vessels will be found for the storage of town gas or natural gas. When gas leaves the production units, it may go direct into the distribution mains or into gasholders. The latter may be located either on the site where the gas is produced, or at the main centres of population; one gas-producing works may in fact feed three or four gasholder stations, from each of which the gas will be distributed to the surrounding district.

A gasholder is a container in which town gas is stored prior to distribution; there are two principal types: (a) water seal and (b) waterless, both of which are shown in Plate 36.

(a) Water seal gasholders

Water seal gasholders are either column-guided (Fig. 2-5) or spiral-guided (Fig. 2-6). Both are cylindrical in shape and are constructed of riveted iron plates, closed at the top and open at the bottom, with the lower part immersed in a tank of water of such a depth that the holder can be almost completely submerged when it is empty; the internal space is then occupied by the water. Sizes range from 50,000 to 10 million cubic feet (1416 to 283 168 m³) capacity.

Gasholders consist of two or more annular sleeves, known as lifts, the upper one of which is roofed with light gauge steel plates to form the crown of the holder. The remaining lifts are, of course, open at both ends and move telescopically one within the other with the variations in the quantity of gas in the holder.

The tank in which the gasholder floats is a circular brick, concrete, steel or cast-iron water reservoir, slightly larger in diameter than the gasholders. It is often built below ground level (Fig. 2-5), but where the considerable amount of excavation required is not possible, and for some of the smaller gasholders, the water tank is built up of steel plates above ground level (Fig. 2-6). The capacity of the tanks ranges from one-half to twelve million gallons (2¼ to 54½ million litres) of water, according to the size of the holder.

The gas is fed into the holder through an inlet pipe, the mouth of which is above the level of the water in the tank. The pressure of the

Plate 32. *Hydrocarbon reforming plant producing 'lean' gas at one of the works of the South Eastern Gas Board. Note the similarity with plant in oil refineries.*

Plate 33. A 'rich' gas reforming plant showing the two reactors.

Plate 34. A continuous 'rich' gas reforming plant of the Eastern Gas Board.

Plate 35. Tower purifiers which may be found at older gasworks.

Plate 36. Three types of gasholder. A spiral-guided water-seal gasholder is on the extreme left with column-guided water-seal gasholders in the foreground. On the right is a waterless gasholder.

Plate 37. The interior of a gasholder which has grounded showing the king post and interior trussing.

Plate 38. Underground high-pressure gas storage pipe clusters in the course of construction. These can be up to 500 ft. (152 m) in length.

Plate 39. *Above-ground high-pressure gas storage vessels in the Midlands.*

Plate 40. *The Gas Council's section of the installation at Bacton, Norfolk for the reception of natural gas from the North Sea.*

Plate 41. *A section of the Control Room at the Gas Council's installation at Bacton for the reception of North Sea natural gas.*

Plate 42. *Orifice plates and gas heaters at the Gas Council's Bacton works.*

Plate 43. Gas burning from a damaged gas main.

Plate 44. A gasholder being kept cool by jets. A leakage of natural gas from an overhead pipe line also involved the gasholder, causing the plates to buckle.

gas acts on the crown of the top lift and causes it to rise as the quantity introduced increases. When it has moved to its full height, an annular ring around the bottom periphery engages a ring on the next lift, which in turn rises and engages a further lift until the full height of the holder has been reached. The function of the water in the tank is to act as a seal and prevent the gas from escaping from

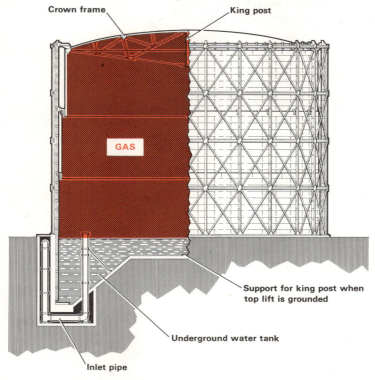

Fig. 2–5. Diagram showing a column-guided gasholder with the water tank below ground level.

the bottom of the holder. The joints between the various lifts are rendered gas-tight by means of a water seal (Fig. 2-7) in the annular channel at the bottom of each lift. The gas is expelled from the holder through an outlet pipe, also above the water level.

The crown of the top lift is carried by steel trussing which, when the lift is grounded, is normally supported by a king post (Plate 37), since the trussing does not require to be of great strength owing to the

81

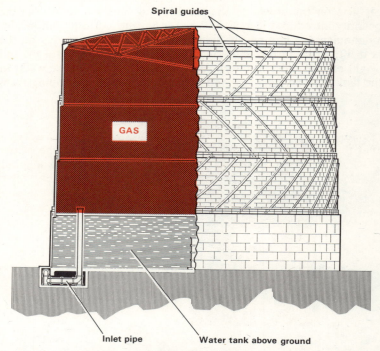

Fig. 2–6. Diagram showing a spiral-guided gasholder with the water tank built up above ground level.

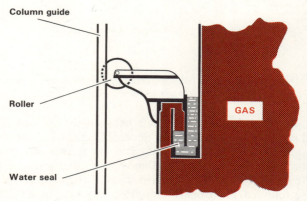

Fig. 2–7. Diagram showing the construction of the water seal.

fact that the contained gas takes all the weight when the lifts are off the ground. The pressure at which the gas is stored is relatively small (of the order of a few ounces per square inch (a few mm head)) and depends on the number of lifts in use, that is, a full holder creates a greater pressure than one which is nearly empty, owing to the extra sections whose weight is taken by the gas. Since such fluctuations in the distribution pressure are undesirable, it is usual to pass the gas, after it has left the holder, through a station governor, which maintains a steady and constant pressure in the mains.

In order to permit the lifts in the holder to move freely, it is essential that they should be suitably guided. This is effected in one of two ways, and holders are known respectively as column-guided or spiral-guided. The column-guided type (Fig. 2-5) is guided by rollers which are attached to the upper part of each lift and work against guides fitted into a series of vertical columns spaced round the periphery of the holder. These columns may be made of cast-iron or of steel lattice girder construction, and are normally mutually strengthened and braced by wrought-iron tie rods.

The spiral-guided type of holder (Fig. 2-6) is also telescopic and works on exactly the same principles as the column-guided holder, but requires no columns for its support. The several lifts are maintained in their correct relative position by a series of guides attached spirally to the sides of the individual lifts and so cause each section of the holder to rise and fall with a screw-like action.

(b) Waterless gasholders

The waterless type of gasholder (Fig. 2-8), which is widely used on the Continent, is now used to some extent in this country by Area Gas Boards on account of its cheaper cost and the fact that it does not require such a substantial foundation as the water seal type. It consists of a cylindrical steel shell, which may be up to 200 ft (61 m) in diameter and 300 ft (91 m) high, holding about 8 million cubic feet (226 535 m³) of gas, in which slides a piston making close contact with the internal walls of the shell. Gas under pressure is introduced below the piston, which rises and falls according to the quantity of gas in storage. Special types of sealing mechanism are used to maintain a relatively gas-tight joint between the piston and the walls of the holder. With the older seal (Fig. 2-9), tar of a fairly fluid consistency is pumped to the top of the holder and allowed to run down the inside walls to assist in making the seal. With the later fabric seal (Fig. 2-10), a telescoping fender is used as an abutment surface for the synthetic rubber-coated fabric seal. The great advantage of this type of gasholder is that the piston maintains a steady pressure on the

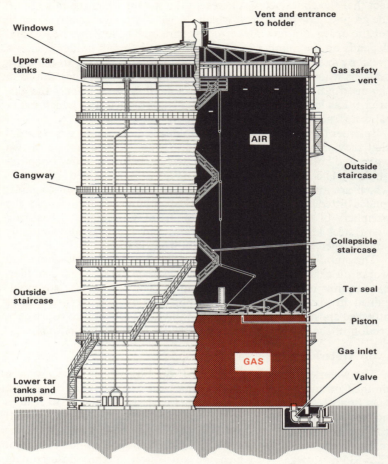

Fig. 2–8. Diagram showing a typical waterless gasholder with a tar seal.

gas, irrespective of the quantity being stored and the total contents of the holder can be effectively utilised.

The space in the holder above the piston is in communication with the atmosphere through a vent in the roof and, of course, contains air which enters or leaves as the piston moves. This space is, or should be if the seal is working properly, free of gas, but a leak at the seal would allow the gas from below the piston to mix with the air in the space above, where it might form an explosive mixture. It was on this account that all waterless gasholders were withdrawn from service during the Second World War, but with proper maintenance the seal should remain effective. In some instances gas detectors may be fitted in the space above the piston.

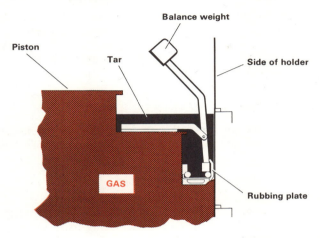

Fig. 2–9. Detail of the tar sealing mechanism between the piston and the wall of a waterless gasholder.

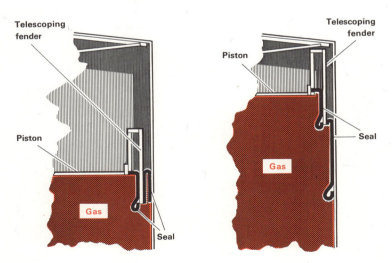

Fig. 2–10. The fabric sealing mechanism for a waterless gasholder.

85

Gasholders of the tar seal type are sometimes fitted with a fixed foam installation designed to protect the tar seal. A riser, with suitable connections for the attachment of a foam-making pump, runs up the outside of the holder to the crown and from there a flexible pipe (usually running on the collapsible staircase (Fig. 2-8) used to gain access to the piston) conveys the foam to a ring main, fitted at intervals with pourers, which runs round the circumference of the piston. In the event of a fire in the tar seal, therefore, it is only necessary to get the foam-making pump to work when foam will be automatically applied through the ring main on to the seal.

5. HIGH PRESSURE GAS STORAGE

In addition to the low-pressure gasholders, storage systems operating at high pressure are to be found. These are of various types, as follows:

(a) Large cylinders erected above ground

These cylinders (Fig. 2-11) normally have a maximum size of 14 ft (4·27 m) diameter and are 90 ft (27 m) in length. They are mounted on two supports, one end of the cylinder being fixed and the other being mounted on a roller support to allow for expansion.

Normally the maximum operating pressure is 350 lbf/in² (24 bars), but pressures up to 450 lbf/in² (31 bars) may be found. The cylinders are generally constructed in single tiers (Plate 39), but in congested areas where land is at a premium, two-tier construction may be used.

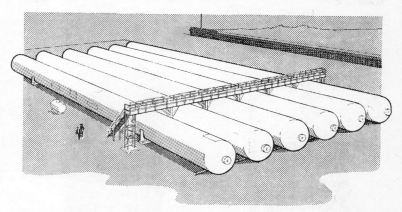

Fig. 2–11. High pressure gas storage. Typical arrangement of horizontal pressure cylinders.

(b) Arrays of pipes above ground

A typical example of this type of storage (Fig. 2-12) consists of 32 pipes, each 6 ft (1·83 m) in diameter and 260 ft (79 m) in length. These are arranged in four groups of eight pipes in two tiers. They are constructed on six supports, again one end being fixed and the other end of the support being of a roller type to allow for expansion. The normal operating pressure is 350 lbf/in² (24 bars), but pressures as high as 600 lbf/in² (41 bars) may be found.

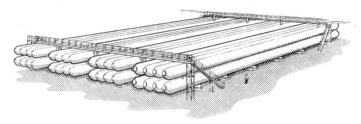

Fig. 2–12. Diagram showing the arrangement of high pressure gas storage pipes above ground.

(c) Arrays of pipes underground

These installations (Plate 38) are similar to those found in (b) above, but are arranged in single tier with sizes up to 5 ft (1·52 m) diameter and 500 ft (152 m) long. The normal maximum operating pressures may be up to 600 lbf/in² (41 bars).

(d) Pipe-lines underground used for storage and transmission

Underground pipe-lines, which are similar to the normal type of gas transmission mains, are also used for high pressure storage. The maximum diameter recommended is 24 in. (610 mm), but the pipe-lines may be many miles in length and may form part of the area grid system. The pressures found in this type of storage may be up to 900 lbf/in² (62 bars). This system is also known as 'line packing'.

The operation of these high pressure storage systems consists mainly of charging the system during periods of low demand for gas and releasing this stored gas into the consumer's system during the period of high demand. With normal towns gas, the high pressures are obtained by means of compressors, but if natural gas is being dealt with, advantage is taken of the high pressures at which the gas is available, *i.e.*, 550 to 1,000 lbf/in² (38 to 69 bars), in order to charge the storage systems.

The discharge from the high pressure storage system can be either volumetric or pressure-controlled. Before being passed into the transmission mains, the gas is scrubbed, filtered and heated. This latter operation is necessary due to the fall in temperature of the gas brought about by its release from high to low pressure.

(e) Other types of bulk storage

These are two other methods of storing gas in bulk. Part II of the *Gas Act, 1965* provided for the development and control of gas storage in natural rock strata underground, but although considerable research has been carried out into possible sites, particularly in the Winchester area, there are as yet no definite plans to go ahead with porous rock storage. The other type of underground storage is in salt cavities, although only one such storage exists at the moment, at Seal Sand in the Northern Gas Board's area. The salt, which is practicably impermeable to gas, is washed out under controlled conditions by carefully manipulated water jets and the brine is brought to the surface leaving a cavity into which the gas is pumped. The salt cavity at Seal Sand contains about 28 million cubic feet (about 0·75 million cubic metres) of gas at a pressure of 435 lbf/in^2. (30 bars).

5. FIRE, EXPLOSION AND TOXIC HAZARDS

(a) Explosion and fire

With the increasing use of highly flammable liquids and gases other than the normal town gas, the risk of fire and explosion on Gas Board premises has changed in recent years. The risk of explosion as far as gas is concerned is minimal as long as the following conditions apply:

(i) when gas is completely absent;

(ii) when any space contains gas only;

(iii) when gas is burning in a state of controlled combustion.

Hazardous conditions, *i.e.*, conditions which although not safe are not necessarily fraught with danger, obtain:

(iv) in the case of uncontrolled combustion; *e.g.* a blazing gas main in the open air away from process plants;

(v) when a mixture of gas and air is unfired and is in an enclosed and unventilated space.

Conditions are dangerous where there are explosive mixtures of gas and air in places exposed to the risk of being fired; where there are escapes of gas into confined spaces; and escapes of gas in premises which may contain naked lights. The strength of the smell of the gas/air mixture is no indication of its liability to explode. The presence of a slight smell of gas may quite well mean that the risk of explosion is higher than when it is strong. Unignited escaping gas should never be lit in order to render it safe, for this may well lead to a serious explosion. Where the presence of free gas is suspected, naked lights of any type should not be used, and no attempt should be made to operate electric switches which might spark and so cause an explosion. It will be found that where there is the possibility of a leakage of gases or flammable liquid occurring, flameproof electrical equipment is installed. However, under abnormal conditions such a leak may occur in an area not so fitted and it is therefore recommended that the precautions referred to previously should apply in all circumstances where there is a suspected leak. These restrictions should also apply to fire and other vehicles and they should be prohibited, where possible, from entering an area where there is a likelihood of an explosion being caused by electrical or other means of ignition on the vehicle. If it is absolutely essential that a vehicle approach a high risk area where there is free gas or flammable vapour, the approach should only be done downwind and a careful check maintained for wind changes. Any operation of switches should be carried out before entering the area and after leaving. This also applies to electric, hand or other lamps which are not of the sparkproof variety.

The explosive limits of manufactured town gas vary to some extent with its composition, but for the proportions of its constituents in general use the lower limit in air is normally considered to be about 5 per cent and the upper limit about 30 per cent. The ignition temperature is in the vicinity of 538°C. Similar details for methane and butane can be found in Chapter 16 of Part 6C of the *Manual*.

The explosion and fire risks of the flammable liquids found on Gas Board premises are similar to those found on oil refineries, and these are dealt with in Chapter 5.

(b) Toxic hazards

Apart from explosion and fire risks, certain toxic hazards may also be found, and these may arise from both gas and liquids. Although the use of non-toxic natural gas is rapidly on the increase, there may still be some areas where manufactured town gas containing carbon monoxide is to be encountered. It is, of course, well known that the inhalation of carbon monoxide in sufficient concentration for any length of time may cause collapse and subsequent death, and breathing apparatus should invariably be used if the presence of gas in the atmosphere is suspected. Persons suffering from gas poisoning should be kept warm and given immediate artificial respiration, preferably in conjunction with the use of resuscitation apparatus. This latter equipment is normally to be found on Gas Board premises, but if it is not available, oxygen should be administered from a breathing apparatus cylinder. Advice should be sought from Gas Board officials as to the presence of any toxic hazards.

6. FIXED FIRE PROTECTION EQUIPMENT

(a) Gas or fire detection devices

Varying types of gas and fire detection device are to be found on Gas Board premises. These may be designed merely to give warning, either locally or to a central control point, or they may also bring into operation fire-fighting equipment. An example of this latter type of equipment is the fixed carbon dioxide installation (see Part 4 of the *Manual*), which is normally found in electrical sub-stations. There may be a number of these electrical sub-stations on a gas-works, as considerable amounts of electricity are used in the operation of a modern gas production plant.

Fixed gas detectors are to be found at various points throughout the works, such as in storage or metering areas where town gas, liquefied petroleum gas, etc. are contained.

(b) Fixed fire-fighting equipment

Fixed fire-fighting equipment includes foam and water drencher systems on oil tanks, and water spray systems on LPG vessels, all of which may be either manual or automatic in operation. Fixed water monitors are also to be found at strategic points around plants, and these are normally set to give large quantities of water in the form of spray (see par. 7 (a) below).

Steam lances (see Chapter 5) on fixed hose reel equipment may be found on some Gas Board premises. These are coupled directly to high pressure steam lines, and are distributed around the plant.

Because of the highly sophisticated plant used for processing the large amount of extremely flammable liquids, vast quantities of water will be required in the event of a serious fire situation, and so provision is generally made for water storage. This may be either in the form of large capacity water mains supplied by static pumps, and/or static water tanks sited in strategic positions. In some instances, advantage has been taken to use the water tanks left by the demolition of gasholders. These of course will vary both in capacity and number, and may also be used as the source of water supply to charge the works fire-fighting mains.

7. FIRE FIGHTING AT GAS BOARD PREMISES

(a) Fire in hydrocarbon reforming plant

Fires in these plants can involve either flammable liquid, vapour, gas or all three. It must be pointed out that one of the biggest problems facing the fireman when hydrocarbon reforming plants are involved in serious fires is that, as they are constructed mainly of unprotected steelwork, there is the strong possibility of collapse of the structure if early cooling operations are not carried out. When applying water, spray nozzles should be used, wherever possible; if open nozzles have to be used, the jets from these should be arranged so that they impinge upon one another so that no solid jet strikes the heated steelwork or vessels causing them to rupture.

Fires involving flammable liquids are best dealt with using foam, but if flammable vapour or gas only is involved, the technique is different. Should the fire be of a small nature, it is most likely that it can be extinguished by the use of portable fire extinguishers of either the dry powder or carbon dioxide type, and/or shutting off the supply by the closure of the appropriate valves. This would apply generally on small fires involving pipework, flanges, valves, etc. Where, however, the fire is of large dimensions and/or the leakage of the vapour or gas cannot immediately be controlled, the fire should be allowed to burn. Adjacent vessels, pipework, structures, etc. should be kept cool by the application of copious quantities of water applied in the form of spray until the flow of vapour or gas ceases. This may be brought about by the closure of valves or plant, by the pipework or vessel being completely discharged, or by the injection of an inert gas such as nitrogen into the equipment involved in order to reduce the flammability of the material involved in the fire.

Because of the similarity of fire fighting in oil gasification plants and oil refineries, the reader is referred to Chapter 5, 'Fires in Oil Refineries' where the subject has been dealt with in greater depth.

(b) Fires in gasholders

The risk of a fire occurring in a gasholder is extremely remote. Naked lights are prohibited within a considerable distance of a holder, and all Gas Board employees are full acquainted with the dangers which their use would involve. Fires are only likely to occur as a result of negligence when repairs are being carried out, or through spread of fire from some other part of the undertaking involved in an outbreak (Plate 44).

Because it is safe whilst the gas is burning, but dangerous conditions may arise after it has been extinguished, the extinction of a burning holder should, as far as possible, be carried out by the employees of the Gas Board, the local authority fire brigade providing any assistance asked for by the management. The fire service may, however, be called upon to guard against the spread of fire by cooling neighbouring holders or by protecting adjoining buildings. In particular, every effort should be made to prevent the guides and columns from overheating, because this might result in their becoming distorted so that the lifts cannot telescope correctly, and therefore jam. Repairs to the plates of a holder are relatively easy, but the amount of metal and the labour involved in repairing the guides and columns is very considerable. For cooling, a spray is to be preferred to a jet, and every effort should be made to avoid distorting the plates or framing by too local an application of water.

Care must be taken to distinguish between cast-iron and steel or wrought iron columns because of their different behaviour in a fire. If cast-iron columns which have become heated are suddenly cooled, they are liable to crack and fail, and water should not, therefore, be applied to them in such circumstances. On the other hand, columns which are cool but which might become heated through the spread of the fire should be kept cool by means of a jet or spray as appropriate. Wrought iron columns, though liable to distortion by heat, are unlikely to fail suddenly, and they may be cooled by the application of water at any time, if care is taken to avoid too sudden and too localised effects.

The two types of column may be readily distinguished by their appearance. Cast-iron columns (Plate 44) are usually round, of very solid construction and are often ornate, the various sections being joined together by means of box-like flanges. Wrought iron columns are usually built up on the principle of a lattice girder (Plate 36).

Methods of extinction will to some extent depend on the location of the fire. If it is in the crown, then it will generally be fairly accessible by way of the steps which are always provided on a gasholder. If the hole is small and not irregular, tapered wooden plugs will probably be driven in to close it. If it is larger, a mat formed of clay, supported on expanded metal or on a wooden backing will generally give better results.

If, however, the fire is high up on the side of the holder, it may be very difficult to reach, although it may be possible to use a line to lower a clay mat from the crown to blanket the hole and thus extinguish the fire. If this cannot be done, it will not, in general, be feasible to extinguish the flame with water in the form either of a jet or of spray, and it will then be necessary to wait for the lift to telescope. It will be appreciated that, as the gas is consumed, the lifts will descend until, when sufficient gas has been removed, the hole will become submerged in the water in the tank and the fire will automatically be extinguished. Since the holder is in the open air the gas which continues to escape by rising through the water can diffuse rapidly and explosive concentrations are not likely to be reached. As the holder sinks still farther into the tank, hydrostatic pressure will prevent the further escape of gas.

Although the tank of a gasholder contains considerable quantities of water, *this supply must never be used by the fire brigade* except with the specific permission of a responsible officer of the Gas Board, as the water is essential to maintain the seal, and if water is drawn off this might break the seal and set up dangerous conditions in the holder. For the same reason, the fire brigade officer should always take any practicable steps to assist in maintaining the water level in as gasholder if there should be any risk of the seal being rendered inoperative.

To prevent gas from absorbing moisture from the large area of water exposed in the tank, many gas undertakings introduce a quantity of sealing oil on top of the water. Although the thickness of the oil film is kept to a minimum, it may, when fired, be extremely difficult to extinguish. In such cases the value of foam is unquestionable, but the method of applying it is not easy, and the advice of a Gas Board official should be sought. It is not often possible to tackle a fire of this nature until the holder has grounded.

Section III—Distribution systems

WHEN the gas industry was nationalised in 1949 there were approximately 1,000 individual production stations, each producing town gas for supply in its immediate locality. At that time, very few distribution systems operated at pressures higher than 30 lbf/in² (2 bars). The first high-pressure networks, designed principally for working at pressures up to 300 lbf/in² (21 bars) were constructed in connection with high pressure gasification plants; in the first instance these were based on coal gasification under pressure, and shortly thereafter on the newer naphtha reforming processes.

At the same time that high-pressure gas production processes were first introduced, the scheme to import liquefied natural gas from

NATURAL GAS TRANSMISSION SYSTEM

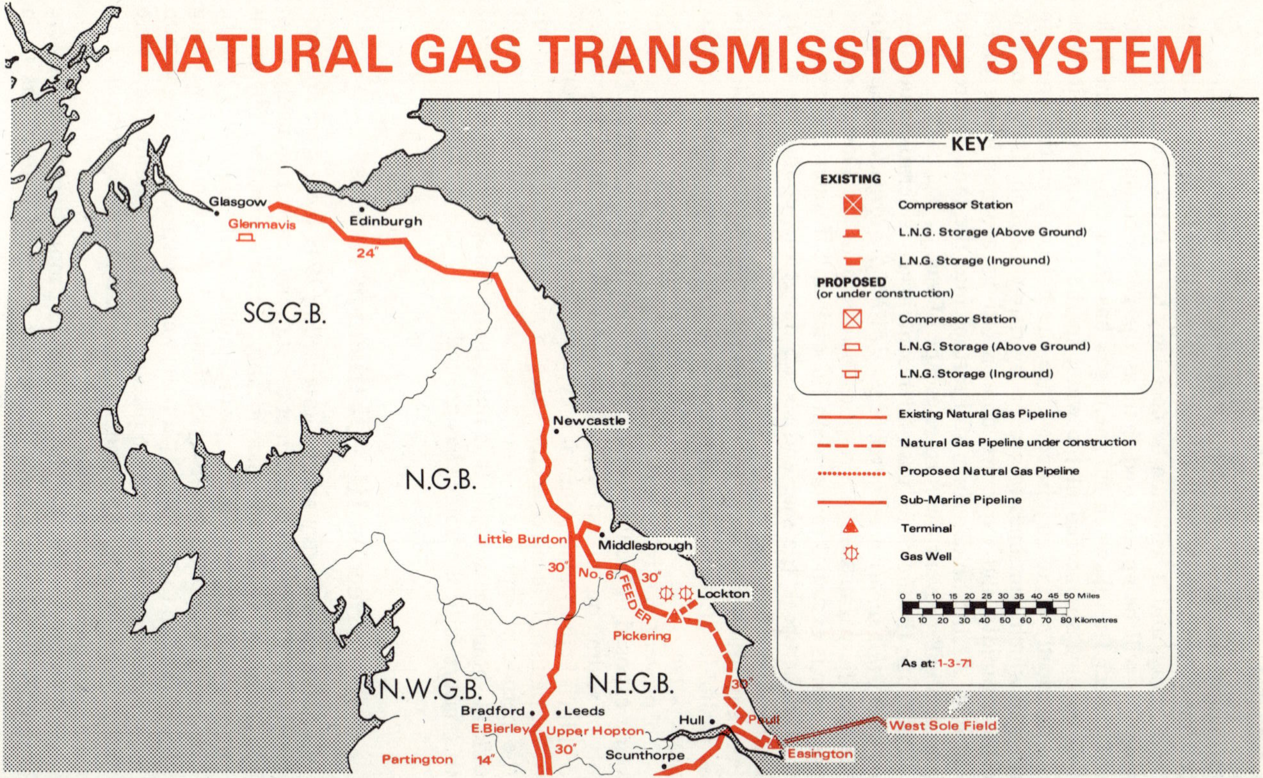

KEY

EXISTING

⊠	Compressor Station
◆	L.N.G. Storage (Above Ground)
▮	L.N.G. Storage (Inground)

PROPOSED (or under construction)

⊠	Compressor Station
▯	L.N.G. Storage (Above Ground)
▯	L.N.G. Storage (Inground)

——	Existing Natural Gas Pipeline
– – –	Natural Gas Pipeline under construction
··········	Proposed Natural Gas Pipeline
——	Sub-Marine Pipeline
▲	Terminal
☼	Gas Well

0 5 10 15 20 25 30 35 40 45 50 Miles
0 10 20 30 40 50 60 70 80 Kilometres

As at: 1-3-71

Glasgow

Glenmavis

Edinburgh

24"

SG.G.B.

N.G.B.

Newcastle

Middlesbrough

Lockton

No. 6' FEEDER 30'

Pickering

N.E.G.B.

Little Burdon

30'

Hull

Paull

30'

Easington

West Sole Field

Leeds

Bradford

E.Bierley

Upper Hopton

Scunthorpe

N.W.G.B.

30'

14"

Pertington

94

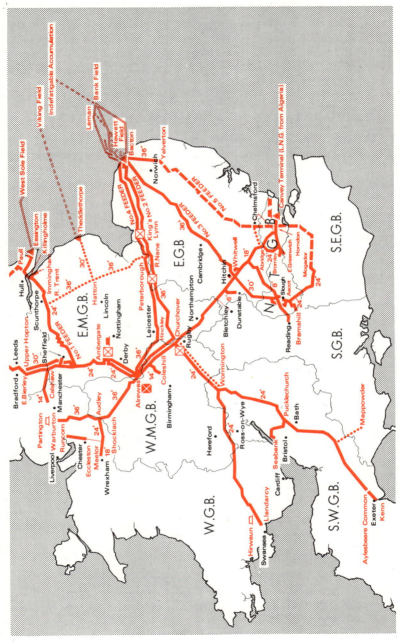

Fig. 2–13. The Gas Council's national natural gas transmission system (supergrid).

Algeria was also developed; this led to the construction of the first national pipe-line scheme designed for operation at 1,000 lbf/in² (69 bars). The advent of large supplies in the North Sea again changed the industry and led finally to the planning of the supergrid national transmission system.

1. NATIONAL GAS TRANSMISSION SYSTEM

The supergrid is designed to link all the Area Gas Boards and Fig. 2-13 shows the development of the system at the present time (1971). The main feeders run generally from east to west as the three supply terminals are situated on the East Coast at Canvey, Easington and Bacton (Plates 40/42).

Canvey only handles liquefied natural gas (LNG) which is imported by sea from Algeria and is stored in above- or in-ground storage units, virtually at atmospheric pressure but at a temperature of −165°C. The LNG is pumped to vaporisers where the liquid is changed to gas and passed into the transmission system.

Both Easington and Bacton handle North Sea gas which is brought in by pipeline. Large feeder mains of between 24 and 36 in. (610–914 mm) diameter then connect with the supergrid. Interspersed along these mains are a few compressor stations although the 'natural pressure' is used to a great extent to drive the bulk of the gas through the system. The compressors operate at a delivery pressure of 980 lbf/in² (68 bars) and are driven by gas turbine engines which may be of the aircraft or industrial engine type. The stations may or may not be manned.

Throughout the whole of the natural gas distribution system will be found regulator or governor stations. The purpose of these regulators is to reduce the pressure of the gas as it passes from one part of the system to another. This may be where it passes from the national grid into the Area Board's grid system.

2. AREA BOARD'S TRANSMISSION SYSTEM

In each Gas Board's area the gas is received from the supergrid at high pressure and is then passed from:

(a) the supergrid into lower-pressure grid;

(b) lower-pressure grid into district feeder mains;

(c) district feeder mains into local low-pressure district mains through district governors or into gasholder stations through volumetric governors.

Jet boosters are installed at many gasholder stations to utilise the pressure available in the local feeder main system to draw gas from the conventional gasholder and to raise its pressure to that required for the distribution of natural gas through the local low-pressure mains, thereby eliminating or reducing the use of mechanical boosters. In this way, the energy contained in the North Sea gas is harnessed to supply most of the customers in the Area Board's system.

Valves are installed on each side of all branches from the grid and the branches themselves are also valved. Many of these valves are under computer control in the Area Board's Central Control Room.

The regulator installations vary in size from the small type found on the consumer's meter to the large installations on the grid system. Those installations found on both the national and area transmission grids will vary as to type of construction; they may be above ground in the open with no protection; above ground in buildings; partly in the ground or with a surrounding bund of earth; or they may be completely enclosed underground.

3. FINAL DISTRIBUTION

The gas supplied from gasholders is transmitted at a low pressure, which may be as little as 12 in. (305 mm) water gauge (approximately $\frac{1}{2}$ lbf/in^2 (0·034 bar)). Gas supplied direct to the consumer may be at a much higher pressure and this has therefore to be reduced by governors before being passed to the consumer. Low pressure mains are chiefly made of cast iron, but mains used for high pressure gas transmission are of steel.

Local distribution mains are fitted at intervals with valves to enable any particular section to be shut down, but as it is generally the custom to interconnect the mains in order to avoid dead ends, the valves at both ends of the section must be closed in order to isolate it completely.

4. SAFETY PRECAUTIONS

Recommendations on transmission and distribution practice are contained in a 'Pipeline Code' (IGE/TD/1) issued by the Institution of Gas Engineers. The Code which has many unique features, has been based on a study of the design and operating experience in a large number of other countries.

While most of the Code lays down criteria by which the risks of failure can be reduced, the Code also recognises that there are finite possibilities of failure. The chances of a severe failure in a large pipeline are remote, but if one should occur the consequences would not be acceptable without some proximity requirement. In general, the Code limits the consequences by ensuring that the routes of high pressure large diameter pipelines avoid heavily populated areas, and by other alternative precautions.

(a) Types of failure

Normally two types of failure occur in pipelines; leaks or breaks (or ruptures as they are often called). There are many causes of these two failures, but the consequences can be classified into four categories: blast, debris scatter, fire and seepage.

A leak is an escape of gas from a hole in the pipeline. The hole size is usually considerably smaller than the pipe diameter, and it does not enlarge during the incident. Following a leak there can be a jet of burning gas or it can produce a cloud of combustible gas. The gas can seep underground for some distance and give rise to a hazard in installations connected to underground ducts or on the surface at places some distance away from the pipeline.

Following a rupture in a large diameter pipeline, the consequences depend on pressure. Above 350 lbf/in^2 (24 bars) the amount of combustible gas which can be released is so large that the possible accident would be intolerable in urban areas. Also, the probability of the escaping gas igniting increases with pressure. Burst tests which have been carried out on buried pipelines resulted in large quantities of earth, rocks and pieces of pipe being hurled up to 280 ft (85 m) from the pipeline. This damage radius is roughly constant in the pressure range 350–1,000 lbf/in^2 (24 to 69 bars); at 100 lbf/in^2 (7 bars) the distance is very much reduced.

(b) Flames

Experimental work shows two distinct types of flame: the flame jet and a trench type. The flame jet is seen when the gas momentum is not destroyed by impact, and a long, relatively non-luminous jet of burning gas is obtained. The trench fire is very luminous (Plate 43) with a wide base. The gas loses its momentum by impact and does not entrain sufficient air to give complete combustion, hence giving a yellow, smoky flame.

(c) Leaks

The consequences of gas leaks within buildings are well known and Gas Boards have established measures to prevent these. Leaks from high pressure pipelines, however, may travel considerable distances underground before coming to the surface. Another feature is that an external source of ignition is required to produce a fire.

(d) Siting of pipelines

In the United Kingdom pipelines are normally buried and are intended for subsequent operation *without inspection for an indefinite period*. It is not possible at this stage to design a pipe to be safe for an indefinite period unless inspection and testing at regular intervals is undertaken. The Code, therefore, attempts to limit the consequences of accidents by classifying pipelines according to the gas pressure and siting them in areas where the minimum number of people will be exposed to risk.

Pipelines which on failure could produce the more severe types of fire are accordingly limited to rural areas where pressures in excess of 350 lbf/in^2 (24 bars) may be used. There have been so few very large incidents up to the time of writing that when the probability of such an incident occurring at any particular spot is considered along with the low population density and proximity, then the risk to any particular building is very low indeed. Operating pressures below 350 lbf/in^2 (24 bars) may give rise to fire which although intense, is localised. There should be time to evacuate those people in the immediate vicinity of the pipeline before the fire spreads to surrounding buildings. In town central areas which are often crowded and contain many multi-storey buildings, the Code limits the maximum operating pressure to 100 lbf/in^2 (7 bars) in order to reduce the probability and scale of a serious fire. Experience has demonstrated the feasibility of controlling escapes of gas at this pressure by immediate temporary localised repair without loss of supply to other consumers.

(e) Proximities

Between 350 and 1,000 lbf/in^2 (24 and 69 bars) it is accepted as impossible to eliminate fire damage to people and property. Damage due to blast and debris scatter should not be a problem at the recommended proximities. Below 350 lbf/in^2 (24 bars) fire is still the major hazard and proximities are such that there is adequate access for fire-fighting and repair crews. People should have time to evacuate before secondary fires trap them within buildings, etc. Where conditions are excessively crowded, further reduction in flame size is demanded by reducing pressure to 100 lbf/in^2 (7 bars), recognising that proximities must be reduced in order to supply gas at all. In addition to the flame considerations, operating experience of distances required to reduce seepage into houses, etc., has been used to produce code proximity values.

(f) Special precautions

Pipeline design and siting are based on the fact that they must operate safely without routine inspection and testing after commissioning, so the Code is concerned with limiting the consequences of an incident. Three basic approaches are recommended:

(i) Enclosing the pipeline in a sleeve. The principle of sleeving is to duct gas from the failure site and release it in a safe area, and to eliminate debris damage at the pipeline failure. Short sleeves (up to half a mile (804 m) in length) are effective safety measures with certain corrosion preventative measures. Longer sleeves require high design standards.

(ii) Preventing damage from outside agencies. Barriers of mass concrete may be used as a protection from pneumatic drills or large automatic digging equipment.

(iii) Preventing deterioration of a pipeline during its life. This will involve some means of monitoring the pipe's condition, possibly in association with pressure testing.

4. FIRES INVOLVING PIPELINES AND GAS MAINS

A fire resulting from a leak or fracture of a high pressure pipeline should not be extinguished by fire brigade personnel except on the definite instructions of a responsible official of the Gas Board, because the large volume of gas released would create a far greater explosion hazard. A message should be sent via Brigade Control notifying the Gas Board of the incident, so that the appropriate isolating valves may be shut to control the flow of gas. At the same time branches should be laid out to cover all surrounding risks to life and property.

Similarly, fires in low pressure mains should be allowed to burn under control until extinction is authorised by a Gas Board official, except in extremely isolated instances in open country where there is no possibility of unburnt gas collecting to form dangerous pockets and it may be desirable to extinguish the flame.

Gas from a fractured main may be found to have escaped into adjacent buildings, and in such circumstances the officer in charge should ensure that the buildings affected are thrown open for ventilation as soon as possible and that the occupants are requested to leave the buildings until all traces of gas have been removed. All naked lights in the buildings (not forgetting pilot lights) and in the vicinity should be extinguished and smoking should be prohibited.

5. FIRES IN PREMISES USING GAS

Town or natural gas when properly used presents no greater hazard than many other commodities in general service. It is widely employed in commercial and industrial premises for heating, drying ovens, furnaces, etc., and in domestic property for cooking, heating and refrigeration. A gas fire presents very similar hazards to a coal or to an electric fire insofar as any flammable material such as clothes which are being aired will be set on fire if they are accidentally brought into contact with it.

(a) Domestic premises

After it leaves the meter, gas is piped to the points where it is to be consumed, generally in steel or copper pipes, although in older premises 'compo' pipes may still be in use. To facilitate fitting, the meter is often connected into the line by lead pipe. A meter may be located in a wide variety of places: in a room; under the stairs; outside a door on the landing; or in a specially designed built-in compartment—the diversity being often due to the conversion of a house into tenements, flatlets, etc., in which each occupier has a separate meter. Should a fire occur close to a meter, the lead pipes generally melt and the escaping gas ignites, thus feeding the fire and possibly (where the meter is located below stairs, on a landing, etc.), cutting off the retreat of the occupants. The use of lead pipe for connecting a meter into the system has now been abandoned by Gas Boards; instead either copper or iron piping is now used.

The first precautions which a fireman should take when entering a room in which a leakage of gas is suspected is to arrange for thorough ventilation. An escape of gas sufficient to build up an explosive concentration may then be avoided.

(b) Industrial premises

Very much the same remarks apply in the case of industrial premises as were made in the case of domestic premises, but the installation will, in general, be better cared for and operated by the occupiers. Gas-fired boilers may present some slight explosion or flashback if they are not lighted correctly.

(c) Dealing with fires involving gas

Gas which is issuing from a pipe and is on fire should not be extinguished except by cutting off the flow. Once this has been done the fire may be dealt with in the same way as any other fire and appropriate methods can be used. Gas may, depending on the circumstances, be cut off by one of the following methods:

(i) Turning off the tap on the appliance.

(ii) Turning off the control cock which will be found on the supply side of the gas meter.

(iii) Turning off the gas (generally in large premises only) by means of the valve fitted outside the premises.

(iv) In the case of malleable pipes, by flattening them with blows from a hammer or the back of an axe.

(v) Plugging the pipe with wet clay, soap, chewing gum, etc. Sand or earth should not be used because they may run into the pipe and enter the system.

Once the gas has been cut off and the fire extinguished, all windows and doors in the premises should be opened in order to ventilate thoroughly. Firemen should be detailed to work through the building verifying that all taps to gas-burning appliances, including those controlling any pilot lights, have been closed.

Electric wiring is often run in close proximity to gas pipes below the floor. If a fault develops in the wiring, the heat caused by the short circuit may melt lead gas pipe or ignite any gas which may escape from a faulty joint in the pipe. Such a fire will continue to burn while the flow of gas continues and will rapidly ignite the woodwork of the floor. In the early stages of such a fire, however, the only symptom may well be hot woodwork and the firemen may wish to verify that this does in fact indicate the seat of the fire before he undertakes cutting away operations. In such a case, men should be detailed to work rapidly through the premises shutting off all gas taps at the appliances but leaving the control cock open. It will then be possible, by the movement of the dials on the meter, to verify whether gas is escaping from the piping system, and the heat will confirm the location of the fire.

Part 6B Chapter 3

Electricity and the Fire Service

Section I—Introduction

THE presence of an electrical installation at, or close to, a fire presents an added risk to the fireman although, if the electricity can be isolated, the extra hazard is completely removed and extinguishment of the fire can proceed, the extinguishing medium to be used depending on the material which is burning. It is no longer considered that electrical fires constitute a 'fire class' in themselves (*see* British Standard 4547), since any fire involving, or started by, electrical equipment must in fact be a fire of Class A, B or D (*see* Part 6A of the *Manual*, Chapter 1, 'Practical Fire fighting', Section III). It is only when the current cannot be cut off that special extinguishing agents which are non-conductors of electricity will be required.

Electricity is a highly technical subject and it is not proposed in this chapter to deal with the theory of electricity and its allied subject magnetism. Any fireman wishing to pursue a study of these subjects is referred to one of the many textbooks available, but a short explanation is given below of the units to be encountered in electricity. A glossary of electrical terms is included at the end of this chapter.

1. ELECTRICAL UNITS

Electricity when flowing along a wire (known as the conductor) is called a current, and this is a measure of the number of electrons passing a particular point in the conductor. This rate of flow is measured in units called amperes (symbol A). Energy must be provided to cause the electrons to flow and this energy, which may be derived from a number of sources, is termed the applied voltage or electromotive force (emf). This is measured in volts (symbol V); the greater the applied voltage, the greater the current flowing.

An analogy can be drawn between electricity flowing in a circuit and water flowing through a pipe. In hydraulics, the pipe offers a resistance to the passage of water and this resistance is proportional to the diameter of the pipe. Similarly in electricity, the conductor offers a resistance to the passage of the electrons; the greater the size (diameter) of the conductor, the lower the resistance. The resistance of a conductor is measured in ohms.

There is a direct relationship between voltage, current and resistance. For example, if a circuit has a resistance (R) of 1 ohm and a voltage (V) of 1 volt is applied at its end, a current (A) of 1 ampere will flow. This fundamental principle is known as *Ohm's Law* which states: 'the value of a current passing through a conductor is directly proportional to the potential difference between the ends of the conductor, and inversely proportional to the resistance of the conductor.' This can be expressed mathematically as $R = V/A$.

2. THE RESISTANCE OF A CIRCUIT

The resistance of a circuit depends on a number of factors, namely:

   (i) The length of the conductor. An increase in length results in an increase in resistance.

  (ii) The cross-sectional area of the conductor. The greater the cross-sectional area, the lower the resistance.

 (iii) The material of which the conductor is made. Some materials are better conductors than others (*e.g.* silver is a better conductor than copper). Some materials offer such a high resistance (*e.g.* dry air) that virtually no current will flow.

 (iv) Temperature. For most materials, the hotter the material, the greater its resistance, although carbon is an exception, and actually decreases in resistance when the temperature is raised.

It can be seen from Ohm's Law that the potential difference (V) becomes greater as the value of the resistance (R) increases in order to maintain the same current (A) flowing. For example, a conductor having a resistance of 10 ohms may have a potential difference of 50 volts recorded across it. If the length of the conductor is doubled and the current flowing is retained at the same value, the potential difference will be 100 volts. It is because of this basic principle that the transmission of electricity is by extra high voltage, so that the size of the conductors can be kept to a minimum.

3. CONDUCTORS AND INSULATORS

Electricity is always endeavouring to find a path to earth, that is, to escape from its conductor and reach the ground or a conducting path which is connected to the ground. Some materials offer such a high resistance to the flow of electricity that the current cannot force its way along them; they are then said to act as insulators. Others which offer little resistance are said to be good conductors; copper and aluminium are two examples of good conductors and so are extensively used for electric cables. Water is also a good conductor, so a fireman with wet clothing or holding a wet hose who touches a live conductor will form an electrical path to earth and will receive a shock which could be fatal.

Conductors must be insulated in order that they may carry the current to the point where it is to be utilised and to prevent the current flowing to earth. Although air is a good insulator under certain conditions and is the cheapest, some other form of insulation must generally be used except for overhead lines in the open country and for switchboard connections. Where bare conductors are used, they

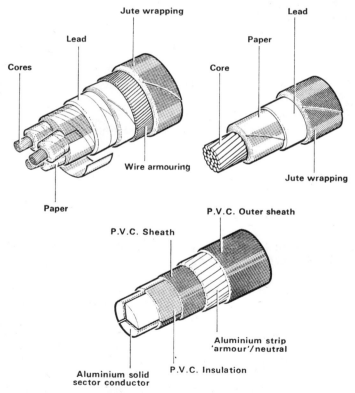

Fig. 3–1. Examples of the type of insulation to be found on distribution cables.

must be supported and at the points of support, arrangements must be made to prevent adjacent conductors from touching. Insulators of porcelain or glass, but sometimes of other insulating material, are employed.

In most positions, however, the use of bare wire is impossible and the conductor must be continuously insulated. For many years vulcanised rubber and oil-impregnated paper were the materials used for insulating cables, often with lead sheathing and wire-armouring for protection and to prevent the ingress of moisture (Fig. 3-1). However, most medium and low voltage cables and all flexible conductors nowadays are insulated by pvc (polyvinyl chloride) or other plastics such as pcp (polychloroprene) or csp (chloro-sulphonated polyethylene). These plastics are extremely durable and whilst not strictly non-flammable, will only burn whilst a source of heat such as a naked flame is continuously applied.

A mineral powder (generally magnesium oxide) within a copper sheathing is also used as an insulating medium for cables which are laid in hot places, such as near furnaces or boilers. These cables are known as MICS (mineral-insulated copper-sheathed) or alternatively MICC (mineral-insulated copper-clad) cables and are also being used increasingly in general situations where extra protection is required.

Section II—Generation and distribution

1. GENERATION

Electricity is generated as alternating current and distributed either as direct current or alternating current. Direct current flows from the positive to the negative terminal of the conductor, but with alternating current there is a rapid change (or alternation) in the direction of flow which occurs many times a second. The number of changes per second is called the frequency and is expressed as so many hertz (Hz) (cycles per second); this is standardised at 50 Hz in this country.

A generator is a machine which produces a difference in voltage between its terminals, the voltage difference being dependent on the design and speed of the generator; when the terminals of the generator are connected to an external circuit, an electric current flows through the circuit. Alternating current is generally used for transmission and distribution as the voltage can be increased or decreased according to requirements by means of apparatus called a *transformer*, and alternating current is particularly suitable for transmission over long distances for which very high voltages are required.

This is because if the voltage is increased, the current is reduced and hence the equivalent resistance for any given length of conductor passing the same amount of power is less, so enabling smaller conductors to be used. Electricity distributed by supply undertakings is now almost entirely in the form of alternating current which can, if necessary, be converted (or rectified) into direct current for any specialised use.

(a) Alternators

Alternating current generators are called alternators, which in this country are generally driven by steam turbines, although gas turbine diesel engine or water turbines (in hydro-electric schemes) may be used for driving alternators, particularly in privately owned stations. The public generating stations are linked together and to the main centres of consumption by a network of high voltage overhead conductors generally known as the 'grid'.

(b) Power stations

Power station alternators vary in size between 10,000 and 500,000 kilowatts (kW). The large modern power stations therefore comprise a boiler room (Plate 45) where the steam is raised (in the atomic power station (Plates 47 and 48), the steam is heated by atomic reactors), a turbine room in which are located the turbo alternators (Plate 46), the switchroom and the control room. To reduce the fire hazard, each of these rooms is generally separated from the others by fire-resisting doors.

The type and construction of the building varies enormously, but modern power stations are generally fire-resisting and consist of a steel frame with brick or reinforced concrete panel walls, although some are of semi-outdoor construction where the boiler house is not enclosed. Some old power stations may have a certain amount of timber in the roof, but in the modern stations flammable materials are limited in the structure of the building. However, considerable quantities of insulating oil and other insulating materials used in the electrical equipment will be found, together with lubricating oil used on the turbines and generators. Most present day stations use hydrogen in a closed circuit for cooling the alternators. Some factories and commercial buildings, etc., may have small gas turbine or diesel-driven alternators in places of varying suitability.

2. TRANSMISSION AND DISTRIBUTION LINES

(a) Systems

All power stations in the United Kingdom feed into the national grid system and the majority of power transmission is by overhead

line. Until after the Second World War, these lines were supplied at
a maximum of 132,000 volts (132 kV) alternating current (Plate 49),
but since then the systems have been increased through 275,000 volts
to 400,000 volts (275 to 400 kV), and even higher voltages are under
development. Generally these systems are under the control of the
Central Electricity Generating Board (CEGB) in England and Wales
and Scottish Generating Authorities in Scotland.

Although high voltages are used to transmit the large quantities of
power from one part of the country to another, it is necessary to
convert to lower voltages before the power can be used by consumers.
This is done in several stages by means of transformers. Higher
voltages are usually reduced to 132 kV, and from 132 kV a reduction
is generally made to 33 kV, thence to 415/240 volts, usually through
an intermediate stage of 11 kV. Current which is supplied at 415 V
used to be known as 'medium voltage' and that at 240 V as 'low
voltage' but with the entry into Europe voltages are being re-
classified in bands. Band I = 0–50 V (which was known as extra
low voltage—ELV) and Band II = 50–1000 V. Further bands are
to be made for voltages over 1000. Firemen should therefore appreciate that if 'low voltage' current is mentioned, the voltage is still

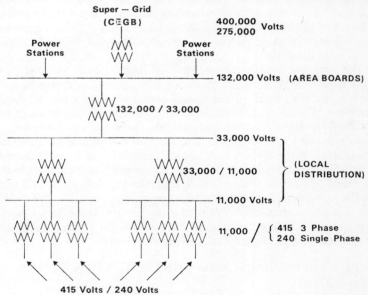

*Fig. 3–2. Diagram showing the transmission and distribution systems
emanating from the national grid down to domestic consumer supplies.*

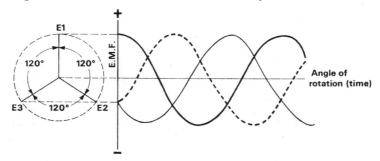

Fig. 3–3. The generation of high voltage alternating current in the 'three-phase' system, shown in diagrammatic form.

high enough to cause severe shock or even death if live conductors are touched. These local distribution systems are under the control of Area Electricity Boards.

Fig. 3-2 shows the transmission and distribution network in diagrammatic form. It should however be emphasised that transmission lines may be designed for one particular voltage and yet be operating at a lower one. The majority of extra high voltage (EHV) lines are double circuit, *i.e.*, one transmission line (3-wire) is carried on each side of the tower or pylon (Plate 51) and may be energised from separate sources at different voltages. A simple rule of thumb to ascertain the voltage is to count the number of insulators in a string, *i.e.*, those supporting a conductor, and multiply by 11 kV.

Control of CEGB transmission is becoming increasingly centralised and is now operated from about six control centres. Similarly, area

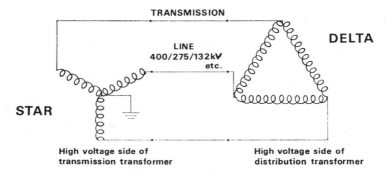

Fig. 3–4. In high voltage transmission there are three conductors, but no neutral.

109

distribution system control is being centralised, but to a lesser extent, and some lines will continue under local control.

(b) Three-phase system

Alternating current is normally generated by what is known as the *three-phase* system, that is, a system in which the current flowing is in three interdependent circuits, which are mutually displaced in phase by 120 electrical degrees (Fig. 3-3). For high voltage transmission (11 kV upwards), there are three conductors or lines between the generator and the voltage reducing transformer (Fig. 3-4), but when the current is finally reduced below 11 kV to medium voltage, a common return conductor (neutral) is introduced (Fig. 3-5). The voltage between the three-phase lines A, B and C is 415 volts, but the voltage between each phase line and the neutral is $\sqrt{3}$ of the phase voltage, *i.e.*, 415/1·73=240 volts.

These voltages are now the national standard declared voltages for normal consumer use (except for special higher voltage equipment).

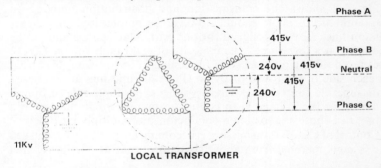

Fig. 3–5. The reduction of high voltage current to medium/low (415/240) voltages in the three-phase system shown in diagrammatic form.

(c) Safety procedures

The operation of overhead lines is subject to detailed safety regulations. These regulations precisely define who is a 'competent' person who is permitted to work on overhead lines and this authorisation may only relate to a specific part of the system, outside of which that person may not be considered 'competent'.

The basic principle of operation is that all current-carrying parts of the system are treated as 'live' until they are isolated from the rest of the system, proved to be 'dead' by approved instruments and efficiently earthed either at the points of isolation or at either side of the point of work. No work is allowed until a 'permit to work' has

110

been issued and this permit clearly delineates the precautions which must be taken and the area within which work is permitted. These precautions are of the utmost importance when it is appreciated that:

(i) many lines are automatically controlled and can be switched on under computer control;

(ii) many lines have automatic reclosers so that they are re-energised automatically after a fault;

(iii) an isolated line parallel to a live line may, if not efficiently earthed, carry induced lethal voltages;

(iv) even single circuit isolated lines may be charged due to atmospheric effects and carry lethal voltages.

Authorised persons climbing live towers are subject to strict control rules, which prohibit working on the lower part of towers within specified distances of conductors. This distance, for example, is 15 ft (4·5 m) for voltages above 132 kV and below 275 kV. Work is also limited to within the body of the upper portions of towers. The tools which may be carried under these restrictions are limited to 12 in. (305 mm) in length, and also any man working on a tower must be continuously watched by another person on the ground.

(d) System control

Irrespective of the voltage involved, every part of the system is under control. Within the control network, access to other control points is usually direct and rapid via telephone or radio. Thus CEGB transmission and main Area Board distribution networks are always under immediate control of 'competent' persons, but local lines at lower voltages may be under the control of local staff on telephone standby in the homes or offices.

It is important that fire brigade personnel should have quick access to the control system, and certain ex-directory telephone numbers are available at brigade controls for this purpose. These are, of course, only for use in a serious emergency, and the normal publicised numbers should be used for routine matters.

3. SUBSTATIONS

(a) Types

The point where electricity is transformed from one voltage to another is known as a substation, and these can vary greatly in size and type. A rural outdoor substation, for example may only occupy a space of about 6 ft by 6 ft (1·8 × 1·8 m) whereas a 400 kV switching and transforming substation will cover several acres (hectares) and may be indoor or outdoor.

(i) *Pole-mounted substations.* A pole-mounted rural distribution substation (Fig. 3-6) does not usually exceed 11 kV, and has a transformer with open high voltage terminals and open or enclosed

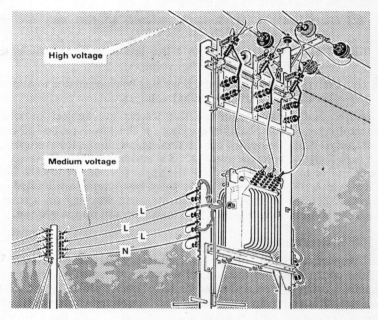

Fig. 3–6. A pole-mounted rural distribution substation.

medium voltage terminals. The high voltage current may be fed to the transformer from overhead or underground cables, and the medium voltage local distribution may also be overhead or underground.

(ii) *Outdoor distribution substation.* The high voltage side again does not usually exceed 11 kV, but may be up to 33 kV. This type of sub-station (Fig. 3-7) generally consists of a transformer with no accessible live parts, extra high voltage (EHV) switchgear with no accessible live parts, and a locked MV distribution board.

(iii) *Indoor distribution substation.* This usually takes the form of a separate building or a room in a building at or below ground level. It will contain one or two transformers, EHV switchgear and MV distribution boards, generally with accessible live busbars. Voltages do not normally exceed 33 kV.

(iv) *Outdoor 'grid' substations*. These substations (Plates 50 and 52) vary from single transformer units fed by a single overhead transmission line to a multi-transformer unit with several transmission lines radiating from it. The larger sites may include a control building housing MV and sometimes EHV switchgear. Voltages may be up to 400 kV.

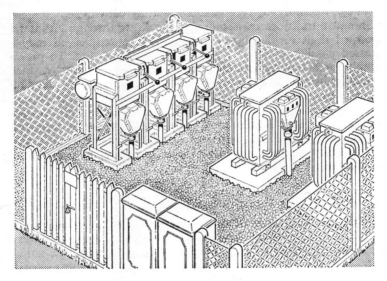

Fig. 3–7. An outdoor distribution substation.

(v) *Indoor 'grid' substations*. These are comparatively rare except in London and large developed areas where space is difficult to find. They are in effect more compact versions of the outdoor 'grid' substation (as (iv) above).

(b) Transformers

The more usual type of transformer consists of insulated copper conductors wound round iron cores, which may be immersed in oil in a tank. In the larger types (Plate 56), *e.g.* those used for voltages down to 33 kV, there are separate radiators for cooling the large quantities of oil. When the warm oil has risen to the top of the tank, it flows down the radiator, and the cool oil is then returned to the

113

bottom of the tank. Pumps are sometimes used to assist oil circulation and forced ventilation through the radiators may also be found; in these cases the pumps for oil and air circulation are automatically operated when the temperature of the winding reaches a predetermined level.

Smaller transformers (*e.g.* 11 kV and below) have cooling tubes on the outside of the tank instead of radiators and rely on natural air circulation for cooling. The quantity of oil depends on the size of the transformer and may be as much as 10,000 gallons (45 500 litres) in a large transformer, such as those used by the CEGB.

Should a transformer sustain damage either through an internal electrical fault or through some external cause, the oil may be released possibly at high temperature or even on fire. To prevent escaping oil flowing around other transformers nearby, many modern substations are so constructed that each unit is bunded in a separate compound which is filled with shingle to a sufficient depth to take the full quantity of oil which could be released. Provision may also be made for draining away the oil from the compound through a flame trap. Many transformers are provided with a water spray, carbon dioxide or vaporising liquid extinguishing system which is automatically operated in case of fire.

(c) Switchgear and circuit breakers

(i) *High voltage.* When a switch is opened there is a tendency for the current to arc across the gap, and at high voltages the distance the current will jump is considerable. Consequently high voltage switches used for transformers and feeders (see below) are usually filled with oil to quench the arc when the switch is opened (Plate 55). Some switches are automatic in operation; others are manual and are operated when it is necessary to open or close a circuit.

A circuit breaker is a special type of switch which is normally designed to operate automatically to protect a circuit against overloads or faults (Plates 53 and 54). Those on high voltage circuits have their contacts immersed in a tank of oil and operate when the current reaches a predetermined level. A very high pressure is set up in the oil when the circuit breaker opens, and so the tank is robustly constructed. A gas vent is also provided to release the gas which is generated when the breaker operates.

(ii) *Medium voltage.* The distribution side of a transformer which supplies medium voltage current to consumers is connected to a distribution board. This is a fuse board containing four busbars, one for each of the three phases and one for the neutral. The board is normally contained in a locked metal case if outdoors, but is open if inside a substation building.

The switching arrangement for isolating transformers from the distribution board is normally through isolating link switches, but sometimes a circuit breaker is connected between the transformer and the busbars. Cartridge type fuses are generally inserted between the busbars and the distribution cables and used to isolate them.

(iii) *Feeder cable switchgear.* The high voltage cables used to connect one substation to another are known as HV feeders, and three types of switch may be employed, namely, the automatic oil circuit breaker, an oil immersed isolator (which is a manually-operated oil-immersed switch) or an air break isolator (which is a switch normally mounted outdoors on a pole or gantry and operated from ground level.

(d) Ventilation of substations

When substations are situated in buildings, ventilation is necessary as a considerable amount of heat is dissipated by transformers, particularly when working at full load. Where ventilation is provided, means also exist for shutting off the ventilation in the event of fire although with modern switchgear and protection, the risk is not great, but as oil is used for cooling, there is the possibility that this may become ignited.

4. METHODS OF DISTRIBUTION

From the substation electric current is distributed to the consumer either by overhead lines or by underground cables; sometimes the two methods are combined, some cables running overhead and some underground.

(a) Underground systems

The cables which run from the distribution boards in the sub-station are called distributors, and until recently each cable generally carries four cores—one for each of the three phases and one for the neutral, although sometimes there is a fifth core to provide a separate control wire for public street lighting. Underground cables are continuously insulated and armoured.

(b) Overhead cables

Overhead cables are normally uninsulated, unless there is a possibility of contact being made with them, and they are used mostly in rural areas. The cables run from the distribution board in the sub-station to poles at the start of the distribution system. The phase cores and the neutral cables are connected to the overhead conductors at the top of the pole and consumers' services are tapped at the nearest pole to the premises concerned.

(c) Junction or link boxes

At intervals on underground cables link boxes (or feeder pillars) may be constructed to interconnect feeders and distributors to smaller cables, to enable cables to be tested and to facilitate the making up or isolating of connections.

These boxes are set in a brick pit below the ground with a cover at pavement level for access. There may be several cables entering the box, and they will be connected to one side of a link for each phase. The other side is connected to a busbar, in the same way as a distribution board. The box is filled with a bituminous compound, with only the contacts exposed. If a fault or overload occurs, the com-pound may become overheated, and being enclosed a considerable pressure can build up. The gas being flammable, an explosion can occur if sufficient heat is generated to ignite the mixture; as a rule, however, explosions are confined to EHV boxes.

In country districts and housing estates, kiosks take the form of steel or fibre glass feeder pillars instead of underground boxes, with a danger notice on the door. These kiosks are used as disconnection, feeder or distribution boxes. Only 'competent' persons on the staff of the electricity undertaking are permitted to have access to them.

(d) Service cables

From the street distributors, service cables are taken to supply each individual consumer and terminate at a main fuse or cut-out in the consumer's premises. Apart from the main fuse and meter, the installation is generally the property of the consumer and there-fore varies considerably in type and layout. Details of the wiring of consumers' premises are discussed in Section III.

5. SHORT CIRCUITS

Whilst air and most other gases are good insulators, electric current can, if the insulation becomes faulty, leak between two conductors or between one conductor and earth, the amount of the leak depending, among other things, on the voltage, the condition of the insulating material and the distance between the conductors. If, therefore, a breakdown occurs in the insulation separating adjacent conductors or a conductor from the earth, what is known as a *short circuit* takes place; that is, the current instead of following its normal path finds a quicker return path. The electrical resistance in such a case may be negligible, whereupon a heavy current will flow and will cause intense local heating combined with overloading of the cables, which may become dangerously overheated unless the circuit is broken.

Such a breakdown in the insulation may take place in many ways. Insulating material will deteriorate with age or from other causes, and a condition may be reached where their insulating properties are insufficient to prevent a short circuit. The perishing of rubber is a good example of this, and is one of the main reasons why pvc has superseded rubber as an insulating medium. Cables or wiring may be subjected to mechanical stress through vibration caused by external influences, whilst damp is a frequent cause of the breakdown in insulating properties. Alternatively, excessive heat through external causes, such as steam pipes, industrial processes for which the system has not been designed, will also lead to rapid deterioration. Further, insulation is not infrequently destroyed by nails driven into walls and penetrating the wiring; workmen's picks or pneumatic drills striking cable ducts; abrasion and (although rarely) rodents.

As has been stated, if a breakdown of insulation occurs, excessive current will probably flow through the fault, and if the fuse or circuit breaker fails to operate, overheating will result. For a fire to occur in such circumstances, it is only necessary that there should be combustible material in close proximity to the heated wire or to the hot spark. Fire can readily be started through a short circuit whether or not a cable is insulated. Likely places which are susceptible to damage by leaks and short circuits are below manhole or inspection covers containing cable boxes, in the base of street lighting standards and in pillars which contain electrical equipment, although effective steps taken to prevent the entry of moisture will reduce or eliminate the risk.

6. PROTECTIVE DEVICES

When an electric current passes along a conductor it generates heat, the amount of which depends on the square of the amount of current flowing and on the resistance of the conductor. When a cable is installed, the size is calculated according to the probable maximum current it will be called on to carry. If this maximum is exceeded, either because of excessive load placed on the circuit, or because of a short circuit, overheating will occur and the wire may reach a temperature sufficient to ignite the combustible insulation with which it is surrounded. To prevent this, an electric circuit is fitted with a fuse, or in the case of a circuit carrying a heavy current, with a mechanical device, to break the circuit in the event of an overload.

The operation of a fuse in an electrical circuit is based on the principle that heat is generated when current flows through a conductor. The fuse is a short length of wire having a low melting point and forms part of the circuit, the size of the fuse wire being calculated for the normal expected load. If this is greatly exceeded, the passage of the current causes the temperature to rise and the fuse wire to melt, thus breaking the circuit. The current for which the fuse is set to melt is very much less than that which would allow a dangerous temperature rise in the rest of the circuit. The fuse thus acts as the weak link in a chain. This explains the danger of replacing fuse wire with incorrect substitutes or with fuses of a heavier capacity than those for which the circuit is designed.

In installations of greater power, the use of fuses is impracticable for technical reasons, and automatic circuit breakers, which operate when the current rises to a dangerous level, are installed. Such circuit breakers are designed to open automatically if a fault occurs, or they can be opened manually if necessary, for example to test the mechanism. They can often be closed manually or automatically if they open due to a fault, to ascertain whether the overload was of a momentary nature only. It should never be assumed, therefore, that a circuit, especially a high voltage one, is dead when a circuit breaker has operated, if handling apparatus, particularly overhead lines. If a line has been brought down because of an accident and is lying on the ground, it may not be making sufficient contact with the ground to operate the contact breaker. Furthermore, the contact breaker may be closed automatically several times after a period of time, to test whether the fault has cleared (*see* pages 145/6).

Section III—Internal distribution

1. SINGLE-PHASE TWO-WIRE AND EARTH SYSTEMS

(a) The service point

Small consumers, such as domestic householders, are supplied by the Area Board with a single-phase two-wire and earth system. In overhead supplies, the service lines terminate at insulators attached to the building; from these terminals short lengths of insulated cable are run to the Board's cut-out inside the building. Underground service lines with insulated cables terminate in a sealing box chamber.

At the service point a cut-out is then provided. This consists of a fuse or perhaps a circuit breaker which protects the Area Board's supply cables if severe overloading occurs. In domestic premises they are rated at 60 to 100 amps. In modern practice the neutral conductor is not fused, and a solid bar link or other solid connection is installed. This is because the neutral conductor, which is common to all three phases, is connected to the star point of the transformer at the substation and is earthed there. Thus the neutral conductor is always near zero potential. It is now general practice for Boards to supply also an earth terminal which is connected to the cable sheath and to the consumer's metal work; in some cases neutral and earth are combined.

Finally the service cable is connected to the Board's meter, which records the units of electricity consumed. The service cable may be connected to more than one meter if different tariffs operate in a particular consumer's premises.

(b) Internal distribution after the meter

A typical older small-consumer type of installation would consist of distribution and fuse boards and would comprise:

(i) *A main switch fuse.* This is a single-phase double-pole switch with main fuses, or phase fuse and neutral link. Alternatively, a main switch might comprise a single-phase double-pole switch without fuses or links.

(ii) *Intermediate fuse boards.* These will be installed as necessary according to the requirements of the consumer.

(iii) *Final distribution fuse boards.* One or several of these may be installed as necessary. From these fuse boards pairs of wires (live and neutral) and usually an earth wire are led off as separate ways to form the individual sub-circuits. In modern installations, these components would be united in one 'consumer unit' wired to the Board's meters, and only the live conductors of the final sub-circuits are fused. Occasionally, old installations may be found with fused neutrals and similarly in older installations, it may be found that each socket outlet is fed independently with its own live and neutral wire from the final distribution fuse board.

In typical modern installations, the socket outlets are fed by ring circuits where each live conductor forms a loop, both ends of which are connected to the same fuse-way at the distribution board. Each socket may be fed from either side according to the load on the other branches.

2. THREE-PHASE FOUR-WIRE AND EARTH SYSTEM

If the load is not very great, as for example in a block of flats or in small commercial or industrial premises not using heavy or large power machinery, the supply may be tapped off a normal low voltage service cable which the Area Board would terminate in the building as a service point.

Connection of the service cable is made in the same way as for a two-wire system with fuses or cut-outs inserted in all three line conductors. After the meter, the supply is fed through a three-phase main switch fuse into a busbar chamber, where circuits may be taken off the busbars to the final distribution fuse boards. The final sub-circuits may be fed off separate way from the distribution fuse boards as already detailed. Arrangements of this kind do not require a separate intake room provided there is no ready access to the busbar chamber.

3. THREE-PHASE THREE-WIRE SYSTEM

(a) Intake equipment

This system would be for large users at premises where the power load is high. In a typical arrangement the Area Board would supply power at 11 kV and the transformation to medium/low voltage would take place in a substation installed by the Board on the premises. The equipment is usually maintained by the Area Board, who would require accommodation for the equipment and access for their employees. The equipment includes high-voltage oil-filled switchgear, a normal distribution transformer and the service point for a three-phase four-wire system. The meter would be inserted on the medium or high voltage side of the transformer.

(b) Internal distribution

The three-phase four-wire and earth system (the neutral is added at the transformer) is now available for distribution on the premises according to whether it is required for lighting or heating (single-phase two-wire circuits) or power for electric motors, which may be three-phase three-wire circuits for which no neutral is required.

A typical arrangement would consist of:

(i) *A main distribution board*. This is adjacent to the transformer and contains busbars of heavy section, the incoming cables to the busbars being usually protected by suitable three-phase main control-switch fuses or by circuit breakers. Connected to the busbars would be sub-mains protected by switch fuses or by circuit breakers. These sub-mains will terminate in sub-distribution boards.

(ii) *Sub distribution boards.* A sub-switch room may be provided, but in many consumer premises, depending on the load and complexity of distribution, wall-mounted panels may be used. The equipment is similar to that in a main distribution board, but of smaller size. Connected to the busbars are circuits terminating normally in the final distribution boards.

(iii) *Final distribution boards.* This last stage distributes supplies to the final sub-circuits of apparatus, lighting and heating, etc.

4. PROTECTION AGAINST EARTH LEAKAGE

As has already been explained, electricity can only be safely used if the conductors or windings of apparatus which convey it are insulated, not only against contact with other conductors, but also against contact with any metal in which they are encased. Insulation may fail as a result of ageing, the ingress of moisture, mechanical damage, heat or corrosion, and precautions have to be taken to protect personnel and installations against the consequent dangers. These may be severe or fatal shock, or equipment overheating to a sufficient degree to constitute a fire risk.

(a) Earthing

Earthing is the safeguard normally applied against the consequences of contact between any current-carrying conductor and the casing containing it. The effect of earthing the casing of apparatus is to provide a return path to the earth point of the supply transformer. The total resistance of this return path should be low enough to pass sufficient current to blow the fuse or operate the circuit breaker in the event of a contact between conductors and metal casing, thus isolating the circuit.

(b) Earth-continuity conductor

The earth-continuity conductor consists of a special conductor (sometimes laid in with the insulated cores of the cable) connecting the earth terminals of all metal-cased appliances and of all socket outlets (and hence of any properly wired appliances plugged into the sockets) to the consumer's earthing terminal.

In installations using metal conduit, ducts or trunking, or metal-sheathed and/or armoured cables, the earth-continuity conductor is sometimes formed wholly or partly by the metal cladding of such systems. It is then vital that all joints should be mechanically sound, electrically continuous and protected where necessary against corrosion.

(c) The earth-fault loop

The earth-fault loop (line to earth loop) starting and ending at the point of fault, comprises the following sections:

   (i) the earth-continuity conductor from the point of fault onwards;

   (ii) the consumer's earthing terminal;

   (iii) the metallic return parth (*i.e.*, cable sheath and/or armouring of the supply cable, or the continuous earth-wire of an overhead line) where available, or through the ground as an alternative return path where no metallic return path is available;

   (iv) the path through the earth neutral point of the transformer and the transformer winding;

   (v) the line conductor back to the point of fault.

For the earthing to be effective, the total earth-loop impedance of an installation must be matched to the minimum fusing impedances of the protective gear in use to prevent a dangerous rise of voltage on the casings of electrical apparatus.

(d) Connections to earth

Fig. 3-8 shows six methods of providing an earthing connection for electrical circuits, as follows:

(i) *Water pipe earthing.* This method has become unreliable because of the extensive use of plastic piping, and is now forbidden as the sole means of earthing in the Institute of Electrical Engineers' Wiring Regulations (14th edition).

(ii) *Local-mass earthing* (other than water mains pipe). Plates, rods, steel frames of buildings are sometimes used, but in practice these rarely provide a low enough value of earth-loop impedance and may be subject to variation due to site and weather conditions, *e.g.* dampness or dryness of the soil, etc.

(iii) *Cable sheath and/or armouring.* This is the most reliable system available and should be used whenever possible, unless the system of supply is as provided in (iv) below.

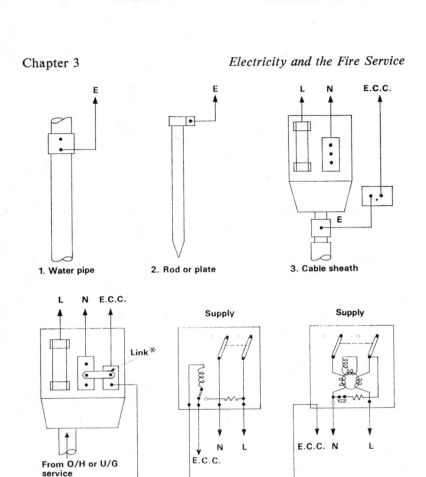

1. Water pipe   2. Rod or plate   3. Cable sheath

4. Protective multiple earthing (P.M.E.)

5. Voltage operated earth-leakage circuit-breaker (E.L.C.B.)

6. Differential-current operated earth-leakage circuit-breaker (E.L.C.B.)

To Type 1 or 2 Earth Electrode

L-	Line Conductor	
N-	Neutral Conductor	
E-	Earthing Lead	
E.C.C.	Earth Continuity Conductor	

*May only be installed by the Electricity Board

Note:
All earthing lead connections at the earth electrode must be fitted with a permanent label indelibly marked with the words
SAFETY, ELECTRICAL EARTH -
DO NOT REMOVE

Fig. 3–8. Six methods of providing an earthing lead connection for electrical circuits.

123

(iv) *Protective multiple earthing.* In this system the earth-continuity conductor connecting all exposed metal work of the electrical installation is itself connected to the local supply neutral whether the supply system is overhead or underground. This system is extremely reliable and is being increasingly used throughout the country.

(v) *Voltage-operated earth-leakage circuit breaker.* This system is often found not to have been installed properly in the first instance and/or to have been rendered ineffective in various ways afterwards. It is not easy to make it selective, and it may be subject to nuisance tripping through transient dampness; metallic shunts or parallel earth paths are the most frequent cause of ineffective operation. Its use is not advised except in very special circumstances.

(vi) *Differential current earth-leakage circuit breaker.* This type of earth-leakage circuit breaker provides shock protection at least as good as by direct earthing methods; it is selective in operation and provides a greater protection in respect of fire risk. The high-sensitivity type, operating at about 25 milliamp out-of-balance current, makes a fatal shock to earth almost impossible. Nuisance tripping should not be bad, and experience has shown that the so-called nuisance tripping is always fault tripping. The type operated on differential currents of 0·5 to 1 amp for up to 100 amp rating does not protect against shock; it can be used where the earth-loop impedance may be as high as 80 ohms for the 0·5 amp and 40 ohms for the 1 amp.

(e) Fires caused by earth faults

Fires can result from earth faults giving rise to local overheating, tracking or arcing, each of which can ignite insulating or combustible material in the vicinity. The following are some examples of circumstances where there is a high impedance which prevents the protective gear from operating:

(i) Failure of insulation allowing an undesirable leakage to take place between a phase conductor and an earthing conductor or earthed metal work, *e.g.* persistent arcing between a conductor and conduit.

(ii) Local overheating at a point of high resistance in the earth fault path itself, *e.g.* at loose or corroded joints in the earth-continuity conductor.

(iii) Earth fault current, unable to dissipate due to high impedance in the earth fault loop, finding alternative paths to earth by tracking or arcing to adjacent metal work, *e.g.* arcing between an earthed conductor (conduit) and a composite gas pipe.

This could puncture the gas pipe and cause the escape and ignition of gas.

5. WIRING SYSTEMS FOR CONSUMER INSTALLATIONS

All wiring systems consist of conductors which are either bare or insulated and which are usually provided with some means of mechanical protection and fixing in the route the conductors take. The difference is mainly in the materials used.

(a) Cables used for wiring

Cables used for wiring can be single or multi-cored. Single cables are now pvc insulated for general use, but vulcanised rubber insulation with tape and braid reinforcement may still be found in old premises. They are very tough and are used by the supply authority and for conduit wiring. Multi-cored cables have each core insulated separately and the whole encased in a pvc outer sheath. Tough rubber sheathed cables may still be encountered; these resist most corrosive fumes but deteriorate under sunlight and the rubber is, of course, combustible. PVC-sheathed cables are almost non-flammable and are unaffected by most chemicals, petrol, oils and moisture. They are not quite as pliable or resistant to high temperature and pressure as vulcanised rubber, but other plastics are used in these circumstances.

Lead-alloy sheathed cables are sometimes to be found, but are no longer used for new work. These are weatherproof and resist some acids, but are attacked by alkaline fumes and corrode in contact with oak under damp conditions.

Mineral-insulated copper-sheathed cables (MICS) are being increasingly used for general work although originally designed for use in extremely hot situations, and where intrinsic fire safety is essential. They consist of a number of conductors (1 to 7) embedded in highly compressed magnesium oxide insulation enclosing a continuous, solid drawn copper (or aluminium) sheath, and are resistant to damp, fire and mechanical damage.

Under the IEE Regulations both power and lighting circuits require a separate earth-continuity conductor and this often takes the form of a bare wire inserted between the other two insulated conductors within the cable. In MICS the sheathing forms the earth-continuity conductor.

(b) Wiring systems and methods

The choice of a wiring system must take into account the conditions in which the circuits are to be installed, the appliance or apparatus they are designed to serve, and whether it is to be a surface or buried system. Most cables can be laid directly and permanently under plaster, but heavier installations employ metal conduit through which insulated single-core cables can be threaded (Fig. 3-9). The cables can then be withdrawn and replaced if required or when re-wiring becomes necessary. The conduit can be laid in the walls and floor when the building is constructed.

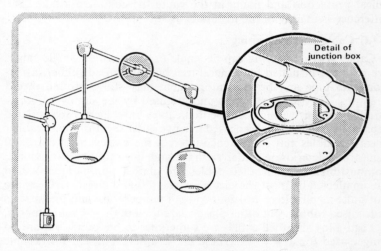

Fig. 3–9. Steel conduits forming an electrically continuous path carrying twin cables. Inset: one of the special junction boxes employed. Note: the conduit is shown exposed, but it could be buried in the plaster.

Clip or saddle-fixed wiring is now used for many installations. The pvc-sheathed cable or MICS can be laid on the surface of walls or can be buried in the plaster, as the building is constructed.

Conduit-carried wiring is often found surface-fixed, especially if the wiring is done after the building has been constructed. Strong, durable, non-corroding, non-rusting plastic or fibre conduit may be used, in which case an earth-continuity conductor is needed. Surface-fixed conduit may be made of steel or aluminium and is supplied in heavy or light gauge. This conduit can be made water-tight, but steel tends to corrode from condensation. Aluminium conduit is resistant to corrosion, is light and does not need painting. The whole installation must be electrically and mechanically continuous and properly earthed. Screwed conduit is best and grip socket satisfactory, but tubes slipped together and not properly locked are not electrically satisfactory.

Another system employs cable trunking, in which large section metal or plastic trunking is used instead of conduit to accommodate large numbers of cables of all types. This is usually a surface system so as to give easy access to cabling for rearrangement.

In many factories and workshops the plant layout is often subject to modification. It is essential therefore to have complete flexibility of the electrical installation and this is often met efficiently and economically by cable or busbar trunking systems. These are heavy section conductors in a steel trunking generally mounted overhead and tapped to serve a machine or other apparatus; a lead is taken from the fuse box (or tapping box) to each machine. The lines may be separate leads from the distribution point or arranged in rings fed from both ends.

(c) Rising mains

In large blocks of flats and commercial buildings, the Area Board or landlord sometimes install rising mains consisting of bare or lightly insulated conductors. These are carried vertically through all floors up to roof level either totally enclosed in earthed metal casing or in a specially provided chase, channel, trunking or shaft fixed to insulators. They comprise three line and neutral busbars, which are tapped at each floor as required. An earth-continuity conductor is also provided. The opening in the floors through which the busbars pass should be efficiently sealed with non-combustible material for the full thickness of the floor, particularly as a precaution against fire.

(d) Points of good practice

(i) *Switches.* Single-pole switches must always be inserted in the live conductor. If they are installed in the neutral (Fig. 3-10) they will successfully interrupt the flow, but will leave the major part of the circuit live to earth, with consequent hazard of electric shock.

(ii) *Joints.* All joints should be in proper joint boxes (*see* Fig. 3-9) or soldered, or made in such a way that they offer minimal resistance.

(iii) *Temporary wiring.* This (as, of course, should all wiring) should conform to the Institution of Electrical Engineers' Regulations (Section H, Regulations H1–3).

(iv) *Openings for cable passage.* The holes made for all wiring passing through floors and walls should be properly bushed with non-combustible materials.

127

(e) Flexible wiring

Electric circuits in premises normally terminate in a fixed electricity consuming device, such as a lamp, motor, heater, etc., or in a socket outlet or other device to which a flexible lead may be attached, the other end of which is connected to the current-consuming apparatus. They may be of various types of construction, depending on the use to which they are put.

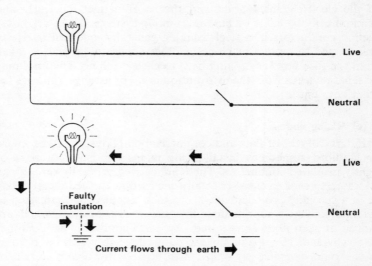

Fig. 3–10. Diagram showing how wiring in which the switch has been inserted in the neutral or earthed conductor can remain live even though the switch is open.

The most common type of flex consists of two or three separate conductors, each with one or two layers of coloured rubber or pvc insulation, finished off with silk or cotton braided together, or with a pvc sheath. Modern twin-wire flexes often consist of two bare wires laid parallel and fused into a plastic sheath.

For many years the colour coding for electric flex in this country has been red for the live conductor, black for the neutral and green for the earth. As from November 1970, however, all three-core flexes attached to domestic electrical appliances for wholesale must be coded in the following colours: *brown* for the live conductor, *blue* for the neutral and *green and yellow* for the earth (Statutory Instrument 1969, No. 310).

Where not subject to handling or heat, flexible leads will give reasonably good service, the length of which will depend largely on atmospheric conditions. Owing to the close proximity of the two conductors, deterioration of the insulation will lead to short circuits, and many fires have been caused in the past due to old or worn flexes being retained in use.

6. ELECTRIC LIGHTING

There are three main types of electric lighting in use, namely:

(a) incandescent lamps;

(b) vapour lamps;

(c) luminous discharge tubes.

Another type of lighting, namely (d) arc lamps, may still be encountered, but these are rapidly being replaced by modern types of lamp.

(a) Incandescent lamps

The incandescent lamp is the most generally used form of electric lighting. The current passes through a fine high-resistance wire filament, raising it to white heat. The filament is enclosed in a glass bulb which is generally filled with an inert gas—the gas filled lamp. Operating voltages are standardised at 240 v., but some areas may be found where the voltage differs from this.

(b) Vapour lamps

Another type of lamp is without a filament. Instead, a small quantity of mercury or sodium is contained in a gas-filled quartz tube enclosed in an evacuated glass bulb. When the current is turned on, the mercury is heated and vaporises and the current passing through the vapour causes it to glow. The colour of the light depends on the materials used; mercury gives a bluish-green light and sodium an orange-yellow light. Normal voltages can be employed for these lamps, but each must be fitted with a choke and a capacitor to limit the current passing. The choke and capacitor are usually integral with or close to the lampholder.

A modified form of mercury vapour lamp is the fluorescent tube, which has come into wide use for lighting purposes. In it, ultra-violet light emitted by the mercury vapour strikes a thin layer of fluorescent material deposited on the inside of the tube and causes it to emit visible light.

(c) Luminous discharge tubes

When a high voltage current is passed through a tube containing certain gases at very low pressures, the gas becomes luminous and emits a colour which depends on the gas in use. For example, neon gives a red light, carbon dioxide white and hydrogen green. Because the tubes can be bent into a variety of shapes, they are widely used for advertising purposes on the fronts of buildings and in shop windows. These tubes (Fig. 3-11) work at 3,000 volts or more,

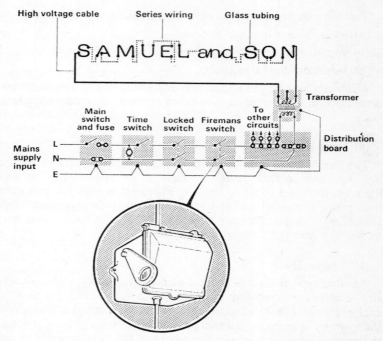

Fig. 3–11. Diagram showing the layout of a small luminous discharge tube advertising sign.

depending on the length of the tube, transformers being employed to step up the voltage to the required figure. The wiring therefore constitutes a serious hazard to firemen, since it may run in many directions over the face of a building against which it may be necessary to pitch a ladder. The transformers, which are usually about 12 to 15 in. (305–380 mm) square, are mounted close to the discharge tubes and may be in considerable numbers, depending on the length of tubing to be lighted. Thus, the average sign for a theatre or cinema may require twenty or more such transformers.

According to the Electricity Supply Regulations, 1937, para. 31(*a*), all such installations must be provided with a 'fireman's switch', which is mounted on the fascia of the building out of reach of the public but accessible to the fire brigade (Fig. 3-11). This switch isolates the current from the transformers and renders the whole of the installation dead. Before pitching an escape or ladder against a building on which luminous discharge signs are fitted, this switch should be opened with a ceiling hook by pushing it upwards.

(d) Arc lamps

Although arc lamps are not used very much nowadays, some may still be found. The arc lamp consists of two rods of high resistance carbon and the controlling mechanism. When a current is passed, the ends of the carbon are separated automatically and an arc is maintained, the glowing particles of which emit a brilliant light. If the supply is alternating current, a choke and a transformer are used to reduce the current.

Section IV—Electrical hazards and safeguards

With few exceptions, fires of electrical origin occur due to lack of reasonable care in the maintenance or use of electrical installations and apparatus. The power that provides heat and light and drives electric motors is also capable of igniting insulation or other combustible material if the power is misused, or if the equipment is not adequate to carry the load, or is not properly installed and maintained. The most common causes of fires in electrical installations are:

(i) short circuits, due to the failure of the insulation;

(ii) overheating of cables and equipment, due to overloading, lack of ventilation or the presence of local resistance;

(iii) the ignition of flammable gases and vapours by sparks or heat occurring in the operation of electrical equipment;

(iv) the ignition of combustible substances by electro-static discharges.

1. FAILURE OF INSULATION

The danger of fire arising from faulty insulation has already been dealt with in Section II, par. 5 (pages 116/7). It has been found that leakage or fault current in the earth-continuity path results in a higher fire risk than that which is caused by short circuits between line and neutral. To ensure adequate safeguards against fire through faulty insulation, the insulation resistance and the earth-continuity system should be regularly tested, and circuit breakers or fuses, together with the earthing system which is complementary to them, should be correctly designed and maintained. Fuses should not be rated higher than the capacity of the smallest conductor in the circuit they are protecting.

2. OVERHEATING OF CABLES AND EQUIPMENT

(a) Overloading of circuits

Electrical equipment and circuits are normally rated to carry a certain safe current which will keep the temperature rise in the smallest conductor in the circuit or appliance within permissible limits. Where, for any reason, the actual flow of current is higher for any length of time than rated, this temperature rise will be greater until, under normal circumstances, the fuse or circuit breaker will operate to prevent dangerous overheating. If, however, the fuse is over-rated or the circuit breaker is faulty or wrongly set, protection will not be achieved and damage will follow.

The normal cause of overloading of circuits is that the equipment and cables are too small for their purpose. Bayonet cap adaptors and socket outlet adaptors, possibly with bad or corroded contacts, are typical examples, and the only safeguard is to make sure that the size of all cables and apparatus is correct for the current they are to carry.

Another cause of overloading is due to mechanical breakdown of electric motors and the machinery they drive. The same basic safeguard applies. Motors and control gear should be of dimensions appropriate to the loads they have to carry. Together with the machinery they drive, they should be maintained in good condition. It should be noted that fuses do not provide close protection against the overloading of motors, and in some cases severe heating may occur without blowing the fuses. Electric motors which are not under direct supervision sometimes have an inbuilt thermal overload trip incorporated as this is much better than a fuse to give protection against sustained overheating.

(b) Inadequate ventilation

Ventilation is necessary to maintain safe temperatures in most electrical equipment, and overheating is liable to occur if ventilation is obstructed. Refrigerators, for example, require an adequate space to be left around them to allow the heat generated to be dissipated and to prevent the motor becoming overheated. All electric equipment of this nature should be kept clear of obstructions that restrict a free supply of air to the frame or case of the apparatus and to the ventilation apertures.

(c) Overheating in circuits through local resistances

Heat can be generated locally due to high resistance at that point. Such a high resistance could be caused by badly made or corroded joints or connections, or at connections where only a few strands of the core are joined. Dirty or pitted switch contacts and loose fitting plug or socket connections will also cause local overheating. Fuses will not give protection against this form of overheating as the current consumed by the circuit is less than normal.

Correct installation is the answer to such local heating. All joints or connections should be soldered or mechanically clamped and made to anchor all strands of the conductor securely. Regular inspections of installations carried out in accordance with the Regulations for the Electrical Equipment of Buildings (issued by the Institution of Electrical Engineers) will safeguard against local overheating. (Reference is made in the Regulations that joints in cables, except buried cables, should be accessible for inspection.)

3. IGNITION OF FLAMMABLE GASES AND VAPOURS

Most electrical equipment either sparks in normal operation, or is liable to spark under fault condition. Some electrical appliances, such as electric fires, are specifically designed to produce high temperatures. These circumstances create fire and explosion hazards which demand very careful assessment in locations where processes capable of producing flammable concentrations of gas or vapour are carried on, or where flammable liquids are stored.

Mechanical and structural precautionary arrangements dealing with these dangerous materials have been codified in British Standard Code of Practice: CP 1003, which deals with electrical apparatus and associated equipment for use in explosive atmospheres of gas or vapour, other than mining application. Part 1 of the Code deals with the choice, installation and maintenance of flameproof and intrinsically safe equipment, and Part 2 deals with the methods of meeting the explosion hazard other than by the use of flameproof and intrinsically safe equipment. The principles and recommendations laid down in CP 1003 are the basis for all installations of this kind, and their implications for the fire service should be fully understood and acted upon when dealing with fires and explosion risks from flammable liquids, gases or vapours.

(a) Classification of danger areas

CP 1003, Part 1, lays down three sets of conditions, each defining a type of danger area, viz. Div. 0, Div. 1 and Div. 2.

In Div. 0, flammable or explosive substances are present in concentrations within the lower or upper limits of flammability, and the conditions require the total exclusion or segregation of any electrical equipment. If, under special circumstances, this is impracticable, recourse must be made to special measures, such as pressurisation or the use of intrinsically safe equipment.

Div. 1 covers areas where flammable substances are processed, handled or stored where during normal operations an explosive or ignitable concentration is likely to occur in sufficient quantity to produce a hazard. A risk of this nature would be met by the use of segregation, flameproof equipment, intrinsically safe equipment, pressurised systems or ventilation.

Div. 2 is an area within which any flammable or explosive substance is so well under control that the production (or release) of an explosive or ignitable concentration in sufficient quantity to constitute a hazard is only likely under abnormal conditions. In these areas the risk of an explosive concentration forming arises only under freak conditions, and the chance of electrical equipment failing at that very instant is very slight. Vapour-tight apparatus or totally-enclosed equipment, such as squirrel cage induction motors which have no sparking contacts, may therefore be approved by the appropriate approval authority as satisfactory safeguards.

(b) Safeguards

To deal with the conditions defined under (a) above, CP 1003 recommends the following five ways of prevention of risk which are considered satisfactory safeguards each on its own or, if necessary, in combination of two or more.

   (i) Flameproof equipment.

  (ii) Intrinsically safe equipment.

 (iii) Segregation (or isolation).

 (iv) Ventilation.

  (v) Pressurised system.

(i) and (ii) are dealt with in Part 1, and (iii), (iv) and (v) are described in Part 2.

There are no definite pre-set rules for the application of the safeguards to each individual danger area and its hazards, and each hazard is considered according to its character. In the following paragraphs, therefore, an appreciation of the features of each of the five safeguards is given.

(c) Flameproof equipment

Flameproof equipment is tested and certified by the British Approval Services for Electrical Equipment in Flammable Atmospheres (BASEEFA), except for mines, as safe for use in areas related to four groups of explosive gases and vapours, namely:

Group I   Methane (fire damp).

Group II   This covers the majority of gases or vapours encountered in industry.

Group III Town gas, coke oven gas, ether, ethylene and ethylene oxide.

Group IV   Hydrogen, acetylene, carbon disulphide, ethyl nitrate and blue water gas.

Group IV gases are known as 'excluded' gases and very little flameproof equipment has been approved in this section.

The difference in the flameproof equipment as authorised for the various groups is mainly in the maximum permissible dimensions for any gaps which may exist between joint surfaces and for any other openings in the structure, such as gland shafts.

(i) *Definition of flameproof enclosure.* British Standard 4683: Part 2: 1971 defines flameproof enclosure as:

'An enclosure for electrical apparatus that will withstand an internal explosion of the flammable gas or vapour which may enter it, without suffering damage and without communicating the internal flammation to the external flammable gas or vapour for which it is designed, through any joints or structural openings in the enclosure.'

The British Standard goes on to specify the minimum gaps or clearances in the joints. Threaded joints must have a minimum of five full threads engaged.

(ii) *Cables.* Flameproof apparatus must be connected by cables appropriate for the purpose, although they may not be officially certified. Examples are lead covered wire-armoured cables, cables in solid drawn steel conduit with certified inspection boxes, and MICS cables with flameproof jointing fittings.

(iii) *Fuses and circuit breakers* have to be rated strictly for the current values of the apparatus and operated well within their short-circuit rating in order to avoid disruptive effects in the event of a serious fault occurring.

(iv) *Earthing.* To enable protective gear to operate satisfactorily, the metal enclosures of flameproof apparatus and conductors have to be efficiently earthed.

(d) Intrinsically-safe equipment

For certain special purposes, such as control circuits, telephones and small inspection lamps where flameproof equipment would be unsuitable, intrinsically-safe equipment and circuits find a useful application. The principle of intrinsic safety is that the available electrical energy is limited so that any spark which occurs is insufficient to ignite gas or vapour for which the equipment is certified. The testing authority is BASEEFA, and at present certificates are issued in respect of the following two classes of flammable substances:

(i) butane, pentane, hexane, carbon monoxide, acetone, cyclohexane, cyclohexene, benzene and iso-octane;

(ii) hydrogen, towns gas, coke oven gas and blue water gas.

The classification of gases for intrinsically-safe equipment is given in B.S. 1259 and is different from the grouping of gases adopted for flameproof apparatus as described in B.S. 4683: Part 2. This is due to the fact that the physical processes in the ignition of gas are different for intrinsic safety from those which apply to flameproofing. In order to emphasise the distinction the word 'class' is used for intrinsically-safe apparatus.

The minimum igniting current is not a constant for any gas or vapour, but varies with the circuit characteristics, such as the inductance and voltage of the circuit. It is necessary to restrict the current to a safe value having regard to such factors, and the essential technical features of the components are specified in the certificate when it is issued.

(e) Approved apparatus

Some electrical apparatus may be certified as 'approved' without necessarily being intrinsically safe; for example, the filament of an incandescent lamp may be a source of ignition if the bulb is broken. It is necessary, therefore, to protect the lamp by a tough window or well-glass which itself is protected by a robust metal cage or guard. The internal space around the lamp bulb is also restricted in order to limit to the minimum practicable volume the amount of gas which can enter the apparatus and surround the lamp bulb.

A miner's cap lamp, fed from a secondary battery strapped on the user's chest and protected by means of a fuse and resistor and other features of construction, is another example of apparatus which may be certified without it necessarily being intrinsically safe. In such circumstances, it would fall into the category of 'approved' apparatus.

A further example of apparatus embodying certain equipment which is not of recognised flameproof type is provided by the battery truck in which the switch and control gear and connections are certified flameproof while the battery is of special construction. The construction of the battery, rate of hydrogen evolution and type of container must comply with the requirements of BASEEFA. Charging connections should be made by means of a flameproof socket and plug interlocked with the isolating switch to prevent the withdrawal of the plug with the switch in the 'on' position, and to prevent the switch being moved to this position with the plug withdrawn.

(f) Segregation

In some instances the electrical equipment may be kept out of rooms in which vapours of gases may be present. This method has only limited application because electrical equipment, especially lighting, may be needed within the places concerned. Motors and control gear may be placed outside the room containing the risk, and these could drive machines via shafts passing through glands in the walls. Segregation is always adopted where the risk is from hydrogen or blue water gas since, at the time of writing, no flameproof apparatus is certified for these gases.

An intrinsically safe circuit is usually installed within the area of risk and control outside. It is important that the part of the circuit outside the area of risk should be specially safeguarded from becoming accidentally energised from a power circuit by reason of a fault—the part of the circuit within the area of risk would then become highly dangerous. An example might be an intrinsically-safe circuit to (outside the area of risk) an auxiliary contact on a power circuit breaker. In such circumstances, the intrinsically-safe circuit at the auxiliary contact must be so segregated and enclosed as to prevent, under fault conditions which may occur in practice, an electrical fault developing between the power circuit and the intrinsically-safe circuit. This may involve the provision of barriers and liberal clearances and insulation creepage distances between the power circuit and the intrinsically-safe control circuit such as amply to safeguard the installation from the danger mentioned above.

(g) Pressurisation

Where pressurisation is adopted, a small positive pressure provided by air or an inert gas from an uncontaminated source is maintained in an enclosed part of electric equipment, which is being monitored by pressure relays protected by an intrinsically-safe circuit, and arranged to isolate the equipment in the event of failure of pressure. Arrangements for purging the system must also be provided. Where the air used for pressurising also forms the means of cooling a pipe-ventilated motor, it must be supplied from an independent or auxiliary fan, and the fan motor, if situated within the danger area, must be of flameproof construction.

Another application of pressurisation to the risks arising from the excluded gases lies in the use of the air-turbo hand lamp, in which a small self-contained turbo-generator, operated by compressed air, provides current for the lamp; the whole of the apparatus being surrounded by air under pressure. Failure of this pressure causes the generator to stop.

(h) Ventilation

Either natural or mechanical ventilation may be used to ensure dilution, by means of added air, of the flammable gases or vapours. 10,000 ft³ (283 m³) of air to each gallon (4·55 litres) of solvent evaporated is considered satisfactory for the majority of industrial solvents. Care has to be exercised in designing ventilation to ensure proper control of containing the mixtures, otherwise flammable gases could be evolved and could ignite.

(j) Ignition of dusts

Certain finely divided organic dusts constitute an explosion risk of high degree. The appropriate safeguard is provided by the use of totally-enclosed dust-excluding electrical apparatus.

4. STATIC ELECTRICITY

Static electricity is probably best known when it discharges in the form of lightning, and this causes a number of fires each year. Although detailed statistics are lacking, it is probable that many fires are also due to static electricity in other forms. It is impossible to prevent the formation of static electricity, but it presents no problem if it is conducted to earth before it has time to build up a charge sufficient to cause sparking. Precautions taken against static electricity are normally based on this principle. In explosives factories, rigorous precautions are taken to prevent the build-up of static charges and, for example, all metal work, even to the hinges on doors, is carefully earthed.

Friction between two non-conducting surfaces is a ready cause of static electricity; thus if fur or silk is rapidly brushed considerable charges accumulate, and unless conducted to earth, will spark. It is for this reason extremely dangerous to clean such articles in petrol or any similar flammable liquid. Even if the most stringent precautions are taken to exclude lights, sparks may occur which will ignite the flammable vapour present.

The method of formation of static electricity can be found in any textbook on electricity and magnetism. For practical fire-fighting purposes, it is usually associated with substances which, whilst non-conductors, are also flammable. Thus if petrol (a non-conducting liquid) is allowed to emerge as a jet from a nozzle, the latter rapidly becomes charged with static electricity and, unless a path is provided to conduct the charge to earth, a point is reached where the insulating property of the surrounding air breaks down and a spark occurs. Since petrol vapour is flammable, this spark may easily ignite it and possibly cause a serious fire.

To dissipate the charge which would be built up when petrol is discharged from a road tanker, for instance, arrangements are always made to provide a conductor to earth. Conductive rubber tyres are normally fitted and special earthing arrangements are made when a tanker is being loaded.

Non-flammable liquids and vapours will also build up charges of static electricity under suitable conditions. For instance, escaping steam from a fractured line on oil refining processes could build up a charge on the plant itself, and special precautions are always taken to prevent this charge accumulating. Under appropriate conditions a static charge can be built up on rubber-tyred vehicles, and Plate 51 in Part 6C of the *Manual* shows an earthing connection on a solvent dispenser used in a rubber factory. Such vehicles are fitted with a trailing chain or other device which will conduct the charge to earth. Conducting rubber, which is rubber treated to give it sufficient conductivity to dissipate static electricity, is being increasingly used in places where there is danger of the building up of static charges. A typical application is its use for the type of trolley used in hospital operating theatres, which are almost invariably fitted with rubber tyres and tend to build up static charges because of their movement. In an operating theatre the dissipation of static charges by sparking is dangerous on account of the ether or other flammable vapours so often present, and many operating theatre fires have been traced to this cause. If conducting rubber tyres are not used a trailing chain is always employed.

In industry the passage of belting over pulleys is a frequent cause of static electricity. The belt, usually made of some non-conducting material, builds up a charge, sometimes of considerable strength, as it passes over the pulley. Where there is no possibility of fire risk such charges may be allowed to dissipate by sparking out, but in the presence of flammable vapour or dust means must be taken to eliminate this risk. A series of rollers running on the belt or copper brushes are often employed for the purpose. They require care and supervision at all times to ensure that they are fulfilling their role. Conducting rubber belts can be used to dissipate the charge as it is built up if the machinery on which they run is correctly earthed.

Certain industrial processes are more prone than others to result in the generation of static electricity, and notes to this effect where appropriate are included in Part 6C of the *Manual*, 'Special and Unusual Risks'.

5. ELECTRIC SHOCK

If a fireman comes in contact with a live circuit he may receive an electric shock; this can have fatal results, although a feature of electrical accidents is the large percentage in which injury is due to burns alone. It cannot be too strongly emphasised that, although in some cases severe electric shock directly affects the functioning of the heart, the effect in most cases is on the nerve centre in the brain which governs the functioning of the respiratory muscles. For this reason artificial respiration should *always* be applied, and will often be successful. The effect of electricity on the human body is still not fully understood, but it is certain that it varies greatly in different persons. Experiments show that alternating current (a.c.) potentials at a frequency of 50 hertz (Hz) and greater than about 30 volts may produce a severe shock for most people if good 'contact' is made, and that in practice good contact with even lower voltages may produce shocks liable to cause an accident. The effect of the frequency of the applied current is not altogether established, but most authorities agree that frequencies of 20 to 70 Hz and currents in excess of 22 milliamps are most dangerous, whilst direct currents (d.c.) and currents of very high frequency have a much less severe effect.

The immediate effect of an alternating current is to cause the muscles to contract involuntarily; accordingly, if an a.c. conductor is inadvertently grasped it is impossible to let go. There is also the possibility of indirect effects; for example, a shock received by a person when climbing a ladder may cause him to fall and sustain injury. It should be emphasised that it is not necessary to touch one of the conductors of a circuit to receive a shock; any conducting material which is electrified through contact with a circuit will suffice.

The principal dangers to the fireman lie, first, in unwittingly, in the dark or smoke, touching a conductor which has been displaced by the fire or which has electrified other conducting material and, second, in directing a jet of water or foam on to live electrical equipment (*see* par. 6 below). When a fireman is standing in water, as he must so often do in the course of his work, the danger from touching an electric circuit is greatly increased as, even when a fireman is wearing a non-conducting helmet, damp and perspiration beneath the helmet, combined with its wet exterior, tends to provide a path for the current through the body. Few deaths of firemen through electrocution have occurred, however, and of these the majority have been due to the cause first mentioned. Risk of injury due to touching live wiring or electrified material may be greatly reduced by the observance of certain simple precautions.

In buildings seriously damaged by fire, electric wiring will often be exposed and dislodged, and it is therefore unwise to attempt to touch any wires, except with the necessary safeguards, until it is certain that the circuit has been rendered dead.

All switches in a building which has been affected to any considerable extent by fire should be treated with caution. It is always wise to push them on or off with the sleeve (if it is dry), or with the fireman's axe, provided that the handle is dry or is of the insulated type.

If it is necessary to touch a conductor in a building, the *back* of the hand should be employed. If it is live, the shock will then jerk the hand clear and will not cause it to contract on to the wire as would happen if the palm of the hand were employed.

6. MINIMUM DISTANCES FOR SAFE APPROACH

There has been a number of experiments carried out in this country and abroad on the hazards associated with the use of water jets and sprays on electrical equipment. The Joint Fire Research Organisation of the Department of the Environment and Fire Offices' Committee have published a Fire Research Technical Paper* in which the results of their experimental work are summarised. The electrical conductivity of the most commonly used extinguishing agents is discussed, together with the factors which determine the severity of shock, and criteria for the safe operation of fire-fighting equipment. Most of the work done on the subject has been concerned with water as the extinguishing agent, and the hazards associated with the use of hand extinguishers are also considered.

The JFRO have issued a Research Digest giving the minimum safe approach distances for water sprays and jets, and these are shown in Table I, from which it will be seen that sprays are safer than jets under comparable conditions; also that the distances for jets increase with nozzle diameter and the voltage of equipment.

There is little practical information on the conductivity of foam jets and sprays. In the absence of specific data, foam should be

TABLE I

A Summary of Electrical Conductivity Tests

Line of voltage of equipment (volts)	Minimum safe distance of approach (feet)					
	Jets					Sprays
	Nozzle diameter in inches					
	$\frac{1}{4}$	$\frac{1}{2}$	$\frac{3}{4}$	1	$1\frac{1}{2}$	
Transmission						
275,000	19	35	55	71	89	17
Primary Distribution						
132,000	14	29	47	64	83	9
66,000	14	23	38	54	74	7
33,000	11	18	30	44	63	5
22,000	10	15	25	38	57	4
11,000	9	14	22	32	45	4
6,600	8	12	19	27	38	4
3,300	6	10	16	23	31	4
Secondary Distribution						
420	4	5	7	10	14	4

* Fire Research Technical Paper No. 13: 'The shock hazard associated with the extinction of fires involving electrical equipment', by M. J. O'Dogherty, B.Sc.(Min.), B.Sc., Dip.A.M., Department of the Environment and Fire Offices' Committee Joint Fire Research Organisation: (Her Majesty's Stationery Office).

TABLE I(a)

Line of voltage of equipment (volts)	Minimum safe distances of approach (metres)					
	Jets					Sprays
	Nozzle diameter in millimetres					
	6	13	19	25	38	
Transmission						
275,000	5·8	10·7	16·8	21·6	27·1	5·2
Primary Distribution						
132,000	4·3	8·8	14·3	19·5	25·3	2·7
66,000	4·3	7·0	11·6	16·5	22·6	2·1
33,000	3·4	5·5	9·1	13·4	19·2	1·5
22,000	3·0	4·6	7·6	11·6	17·4	1·2
11,000	2·7	4·3	6·7	9·8	13·7	1·2
6,600	2·4	3·7	5·8	8·2	11·6	1·2
3,300	1·8	3·0	4·9	7·0	9·4	1·2
Secondary Distribution						
420	1·2	1·5	2·1	3·0	4·3	1·2

applied as a spray, using the appropriate distances shown in the Table. Owing to the short range at which water and foam from hand extinguishers are used, combined with the high conductivity of certain types, it is necessary to avoid their use altogether on fires involving live electrical equipment.

In the vicinity of high voltage electrical equipment, there can be a risk of flashover from the equipment to the operator or his apparatus. It is always desirable to maintain the maximum practicable distance at all times, to avoid inadvertent movement inside the minimum safe distance.

7. USE OF RUBBER GLOVES

Rubber gloves or gauntlets (*see* Part 1 of the *Manual*, Chapter 13) are carried on many fire brigade appliances for use when it is necessary to work on, or voluntarily to come in contact with, electrical apparatus or circuits. It cannot be too strongly emphasised, however, that the rubber gloves issued are only *tested* to 15,000 volts, and British Standard 697 which covers their manufacture only recommends their use on voltages up to 3,300. (Electricity Boards only allow their use on MV.) *They are no safeguard where equipment working at higher voltages is concerned, the only safe course being to wait until the current is cut off and the circuit earthed before it is touched.*

Rubber gloves are generally stowed, liberally treated with French chalk, in waterproof metal containers, and should be kept out of sun and heat. Damp or water will reduce the insulation effect of the gloves and, when they are in use, every effort should be made to keep them dry. Rubber gloves have their greatest use in dealing with voltages normally encountered in business, industrial and private premises; for removing persons in contact with electric wiring, for working on electric wiring which may prove a danger to operations, and other work of a similar nature. On some appliances a rubber mat and rubber boots are provided in addition to the rubber gloves, for obtaining increased insulation when dealing with electrical apparatus.

8. REMOVING PERSONS FROM ELECTRIC. WIRING

(a) General

It has already been stated that the human body acts as a conductor of electricity, a condition which is greatly intensified if the skin is wet, as is usually the case at fires. If, therefore, a person is in contact with live electric wiring, his body will form part of the circuit, and any effort to touch him is equivalent to touching the circuit. The same precautions must be taken as if it were necessary to touch the wiring. Where high voltages are involved, the only solution lies in isolating the current. At lower voltages (3,300 V and below) rubber gloves, a dry hooked stick, a ceiling hook or a length of dry hose may be used to pull the victim clear of the wiring. A steel-shafted umbrella should *not* be used for the purpose. On normal household lighting and power circuits, it will suffice if several thicknesses of a dry non-conducting material, such as sheets of dry newspaper, a coat, rug, gloves, etc. are employed.

At equal voltages a.c. has more powerful physiological effects than d.c. When a person is pulled clear of a heavily loaded d.c. circuit, however, severe burns may result from arcing. It is for this reason preferable to switch off the current whenever practicable, and if it can be done speedily. Immediately a person has been removed from an electric current, even though signs of life may be absent, artificial respiration with or without the use of resuscitation apparatus, should be resorted to and only discontinued when the patient revives or a

Plate 45. An example of a coal-fired boiler at a power station.

Plate 46. The turbine hall at High Marnham power station, Nottinghamshire showing the five 200 MW turbo-generator sets. This station has an output of 1,000 MW.

Plate 47. The interior of the CEGB's 500 MW nuclear power station at Dungeness. The biological shield above the reactor is a concrete slab which is pierced for the reactor vessel standpipes. A secondary floor of removable concrete slabs forms the principal working area in the charge hall.

Plate 48. The nuclear power station at Dungeness in process of being charged. The reactor core is pierced by 3,932 channels in each of which are stacked seven fuel elements of solid natural uranium rod encased in special cans.

Plate 49. A typical 132 kV double circuit transmission line.

Plate 50. An aerial view of an outdoor 132/275 kV substation.

Plate 51. A 400 kV tension tower, part of the CEGB's 400 kV Sizewell to Sundon transmission line.

Plate 52. Part of an outdoor 275/400 kV substation showing how the connecting conductors are kept well above ground level.

Plate 53. The air-blast circuit breakers of an outdoor 132 kV substation. The high voltage conductors are carried on to the tower on the right. Note the exterior fence and the interior enclosures.

Plate 54. The type of 7,500 MVA air-blast circuit breakers used at a 275 kV substation.

Plate 55. Switchgear, oil circuit breakers and isolators in a 275 kV substation.

Plate 56. A 275 kV transformer at an outdoor substation. Here again all high voltage line conductors are well above ground level.

Plate 57. *Part of the main control room at Ferrybridge power station. All the boiler/turbine units together with auxiliary plant and gas turbines are controlled from this central control room. The 2,000 MW output is fed into the national grid by three double circuit 275 kV overhead lines.*

Plate 58. *The 25 kV overhead traction installation on the Eastern Region of British Railways.*

Plate 59. The retractable pantograph on the roof of the motor unit which collects the current for the train from the contact wire of the overhead system shown in Plate 58.

Plate 60. An example of an untidy domestic electricity installation which leads to a high fire risk. Arcing has occurred on the side of the larger fuse box and elsewhere.

doctor pronounces life extinct (*see* Part 1 of the *Manual*, Chapter 12, 'Resuscitation').

(b) Overhead transmission lines

It is of course obvious that it is extremely dangerous to climb a standard tower carrying high voltage transmission lines, and even more so on towers on which additional equipment, such as transformers, switchgear or boosters, is mounted. As a general rule no tower should be climbed without authorisation and a clear indication from a Board official of the dangers and of the distance necessary for safety. In particular, no rescue of persons on live high voltage conductors should be attempted until full clearance has been obtained. Any manoeuvring, or use of metal or metal-reinforced, ladders in the vicinity of towers or under transmission lines, should be specifically prohibited unless under conditions closely controlled by a 'competent' Board official.

Occasions will doubtless arise where circumstances demand action by firemen without technical supervision, and it is impossible to prescribe in detail the precautions necessary to ensure electrical safety in all instances. Initial action should *always* be to contact the appropriate control centre at least to obtain verbal advice. Identification of the tower concerned is of the utmost importance, and any identification markings on the tower should be given. Immediate rescue action is not always necessary, and a pause is often advisable to consider the implications of delaying removal of the person to allow competent Board staff to attend.

A particular rescue problem arises where overhead transmission lines have fallen on to vehicles, or a vehicle is in contact with them. Ground clearances of lines are sometimes as low as 20 ft (6 m) at mid-span and this may be further reduced by ice or snow loading conductors; clearances may also be reduced by earthworks or tipping without the knowledge of the Board. Any vehicle in contact with power lines should be treated as 'live' even though the lines may appear to be dead. Generally a person within a vehicle is quite safe from electrocution and the hazard is from fire, often due to arcing through tyres. Electrocution frequently takes place in the panic of the person inside of the vehicle leaving after contact with the overhead line; if the person is able to jump clear of the vehicle, this is the obvious course to be taken, but the danger of touching any part of the vehicle and the ground at the same time is obvious. If the person is unable to jump, or is trapped in the vehicle, he should be left there until the vehicle can either be pulled safely clear of the line, the line confirmed to be dead, or earthed competently.

145

Power lines found lying on the ground, even those apparently intended for low voltage, should in no circumstances be moved. In some instances transmission lines can continue to operate with one conductor on the ground, and full voltage would automatically be restored immediately it is lifted from the ground. In other cases, it is possible for a line to be re-energised whilst the conductors are being moved.

It should be remembered that transmission lines may often not be isolated to permit access without appreciable delay while alternative supplies are established or important installations notified. The sudden interruption of supplies may itself endanger life: hospitals, lifts, cranes are typical examples, and the interruption of an important connection between the system and a power station, for instance, may affect whole areas of the country. Requests for isolation should therefore only be made in extreme cases.

Section V—Fire-fighting procedure

In the case of a fire involving electrical apparatus, the first essential is to try to render the circuit dead; this will be carried out in large installations by the employees of the premises or undertaking involved and, in small premises, by switching off at the main or at an appropriate point in the system. Where it is not possible to switch off the current, the fire must be attacked in a way which will not cause danger to the fireman, *i.e.*, by the use of non-conducting extinguishing media. Carbon dioxide, vaporising liquid, dry power, dry sand, ashes, etc. are the substances normally used, and extinguishers or supplies of these materials will usually be found in larger premises where electricity is generated or consumed. Foam can be used for fires involving oil, provided that there is no danger of the stream reaching apparatus which is still live.

Carbon dioxide or vaporising liquids are non-damaging to electrical equipment, an extremely important factor in view of the delicacy and complexity of apparatus such as is used on switchboards in generating stations, substations, telephone exchanges or other electronic equipment such as computers. Sand should only be used where it will do little damage, as on cables, and never on machinery. When extinguishing a fire known to have been started through an electrical fault, the current must in any event be switched off; otherwise, there is a serious risk of a renewed outbreak, as the continuance of the current will probably result in re-ignition. After extinguishing such a fire, therefore, careful watch should be kept for renewed outbreaks until the fault has been rectified or the current turned off.

The fire brigade will normally be called to fires which may involve two main classes of electrical equipment:

(a) Fires in generating stations, switchgear and transformer stations, and distribution mains administered by the electricity supply authority;

(b) fires in premises where electricity is utilised or is generated in limited quantities incidental to the main user.

1. FIRES IN GENERATING STATIONS

In nearly all cases generating stations are staffed day and night (although peaking gas turbines are remote-controlled), and consequently a fire is likely to be discovered in its initial stages and possibly dealt with by the station staff with the fire equipment which they would have available. The presence of the staff would be of major assistance if a fire assumed sufficient proportions to result in the fire brigade being called. Such fires are usually caused either by an electrical fault or by oil coming into contact with a superheated steam pipe by way of a fault in the lagging.

Generating stations usually contain large quantities of oil required for lubricating plant and equipment including turbines, and for operating the governor mechanism, in addition to that contained in switchgear and transformers. It is essential, therefore, that no time should be lost in attacking any outbreak, and the fire brigade officer should co-operate closely with the station staff in order that the area of the fire may be restricted to the smallest possible limits, thus enabling the station to continue generating electricity in those parts which are not immediately affected. It will be appreciated that electricity supply authorities use every endeavour to maintain supplies and it is essential for fire brigade personnel to assist in that direction.

In addition to the large quantities of oil, there is a considerable amount of other flammable material such as paint on steelwork and insulation on cables. Burning insulation and, in particular, the bitumen used for sealing joints gives off dense clouds of smoke, and it is often physically impossible for men to work without the use of breathing apparatus. The outer covering of bitumenised jute used to protect cables against corrosion is often removed from those sections under cover in a power station.

Although it would be safe to use any fire extinguishing medium in many parts of a generating station, the use of water should be avoided if possible. However, before commencing any attack, the Station Engineer in charge at the time should be consulted in order to ensure that no danger is likely to be incurred from electric shock. Cable racks, tunnels, etc., will often be found at generating stations and may present a difficult problem should fire break out in them.

2. FIRES IN TRANSFORMERS

Many oil-cooled transformers have external bushings or multiple shed porcelain insulators on the top of them (Plate 56). These are liable to be fractured by heat and, if this happens, a certain amount of oil will be released which, if it ignites and is left to burn, will heat the transformer tank causing more oil to overflow and feed the fire. Unless the fire is extinguished in its early stages, a major conflagration will probably result and, in the absence of barriers, ignited oil will spread to other flammable material in the vicinity. Where each transformer is not separately bunded, burning oil can flow around others in the group, or 'bank' as it is generally termed, and will rapidly involve them also. Such a fire may be disastrous and cause the temporary shut-down of power over a considerable area.

In the same manner, high voltage switchgear, which if not of the air blast type, is also oil-filled (though oil is present in smaller quantities), is in many cases also compartmented to a limited degree. Such compartments are often protected by fixed automatically-operated installations (*see* Part 4 of the *Manual*). Cables pass from cubicle to cubicle and fire may, therefore, spread along such cables in the ducting system although, in correctly constructed modern installations, suitable seals are provided wherever the cables pass through a fire-resisting partition. Care is also taken that ducts in which the cables lie are not so constructed as to trap the burning oil and allow it to come in contact with the cable. Once it is certain that the current is off, fires involving oil can be extinguished by the use of foam or, where applicable and absolutely unavoidable, by water spray.

There is however one most important point with which all firemen should be conversant. Cutting off the current to a high voltage installation, such as a cable, transformer or switchgear, does not necessarily render it safe. Owing to what is known as 'capacity', a residual charge of what is really static electricity may be present in the apparatus, and this charge is frequently sufficiently powerful to cause electrocution. For this reason electrical equipment must always be 'earthed' before it is touched. This is usually effected by means of a long pole with an insulated handle having at one end a metal contact connected to a conductor, which should be effectively earthed before contact is made with the equipment which it is suspected may be charged.

Where cubicles containing transformers, switchgear, etc., are protected by fixed carbon dioxide or vaporising liquid installations and the installations have operated, only men wearing breathing apparatus should be allowed to enter the premises in order to verify whether or not the outbreak has been extinguished by the installation, and if not, what further steps are necessary. Although scrupulous cleanliness should be the rule in such installations, there is always the possibility that odd scraps of cotton waste, etc., may be lying around, and the fire brigade should not leave the premises until a thorough check has been made to see that every vestige of fire has been dealt with, and that no smouldering material remains which could cause re-ignition.

Apart from transformers and switchgear, or apparatus containing oil, there is little fire risk involved where transmission is carried out by means of overhead lines, although where the lines are carried on wood pole supports, and the route lies across scrub or bush-covered country, there is some slight risk of scrub fires setting the wood pole supports alight and bringing the cables down.

3. FIRES IN SUBSTATIONS

(a) Grid substations

On the grid system, substations are of the outdoor type (Plate 50), but they may also, occasionally, be indoor. Because the voltages employed range from 6,600 to 400,000 volts, it is essential that firemen should not enter the substation or attack any fires which might occur in them until they have received notification from an Electricity Board official that entry and fire attack can be safely made. In this connection, the appropriate fire brigade officer in every locality should make himself fully acquainted with the grid substations in his area, and should arrange a definite procedure with the Board's officials so that no time will be lost in attacking any outbreak of fire.

Certain of the grid substations are permanently attended, but others are not. Close co-operation with the responsible officials in the locality will ensure fire brigade officers know which substations are, and which are not, constantly attended, and the procedure which should be adopted in each case.

It has been stated above that no grid substation should be entered until an assurance has been received that this can be safely done. There are two exceptions when entry can be made: if a fire is on the ground or a man is lying on the ground inside the substation and apparently injured. The reason for this is that live open high voltage bushings are never located less than 8 ft (2·5 m) above exposed ground level, or where this is not possible, protective screens are provided round the equipment to ensure safety. Once inside, however, the fireman must on no account climb on equipment or use ladders, nor must he employ any fire appliances with the jet directed above ground level, or beyond the safety screens, if these are fitted. Should a man be seen lying on the top of a transformer or switch, he must not be touched until word is received from a Board official that rescue work can be carried out.

Many substations in rural areas are situated at a considerable distance from water mains and, not infrequently, from any static supplies. When planning predetermined attendances for such a risk, therefore, it may be wise for a water tender to be included as part of the first attendance.

(b) Other substations

Substations, other than grid substations, are of various types, and those which the fireman is most likely to meet are located on commercial or industrial premises, where they may be outdoors or inside the buildings. The voltages at these substations vary considerably, but they should all be treated with circumspection until information has been received from a responsible official of the Electricity Board that the supply has been cut off. Similar precautions must be taken on industrial premises containing substations operated by the factory occupier.

Under the Electricity Regulations, the door to any compartment in which high voltage equipment is installed must carry a suitable warning notice. No standard is laid down but the notices are generally in such form as 'DANGER 33,000 VOLTS'. The plate often carries the address and telephone number of the electricity undertaking and, where this is not the case, the fire brigade officer may well make the suggestion that this information should be included.

4. FIRES IN CABLE BOXES

Where the transmission or distribution of electricity is carried out by underground cables, the chances of fire occurring are remote except at a cable or link box or feeder pillar, where the main cables may divide into a number of circuits. A fire may be caused by an explosion which may blow off the cover of the box. This can occur through a fault in the cable with the consequent formation of an arc which ignites the gas generated during the development of the fault.

Should a fire occur in an underground cable and should the street box cover have been lifted, the box should not be filled with sand unless the fire is actually visible, in which case a small quantity of sand may be used to extinguish it; to fill the box with sand is a mistake, for the fumes require a vent. Burning cable insulation gives off dense fumes which fill the ducts. If a street box is filled with sand, the duct becomes sealed, with the result that the expansion of the heated gases will either blow out the sand or, which is more likely, will cause the fumes and fire to travel along the duct to other boxes. The best policy is to cover any exposed property and await the arrival of representatives of the electricity undertaking, who should have been notified at the earliest moment. Underground cable or link boxes and feeder pillars are generally located sufficiently far from a building for any risk of fire spread to be almost, if not quite, negligible.

5. FIRES IN INDUSTRIAL PREMISES

Most industrial premises use considerable amounts of electricity. Where the demand is heavy the supply is often brought in at high voltage and transformed down as necessary on the premises (unless the firm has its own generator). Substations on industrial premises, therefore, often contain transformers and switchgear. The supply is invariably alternating current, and so, if the supply for technical reasons is required by the factory or industrial user as direct current, the substation will also contain coverting plant, which will be of the rotating or rectifier type. In both cases, it should be taken for granted that the incoming supply is at high voltage and it is most important that the current should be isolated before attacking the fire.

From the substation or switch-room the current, which is then usually at 240/415 volts, although some equipment such as motors may operate on current up to 3 kV, generally passes through a local switch and fuse board before it is conveyed to the individual apparatus by cables similar to those already described. In the case of a small fire, it may only be necessary to isolate circuits near the fire, and this will avoid shutting down large numbers of machines.

6. FIRES IN PRIVATE DWELLINGS

The majority of fires of electrical origin which occur in private houses are caused by faulty electrical appliances or circuits, or by carelessness. Where a faulty circuit causes a fuse to 'blow', the householder, instead of having the circuit properly tested and repaired, sometimes replaces the fuse with heavier fuse wire, and it has even been known for copper wire, nails, etc. to be used. The protective value of the fuse (which is in effect a safety valve) is nullified by these devices, and will result in the circuit carrying a load considerably in excess of that for which it was designed, with the result that overheating in the circuit will occur, and possibly a fire.

Worn or damaged flex is frequently a cause of fire. Where it is subjected to considerable movement, wear and tear, its life is short, and owing to the abrasion or overheating of the insulation, the wires may easily become bare. When used on table lamps, portable electric fires, electric blankets, etc., dangerous conditions can readily be set up. Flex is rarely replaced in the average household until the insulation has broken down and it has caused a short circuit, thus blowing the fuse. Flex is often allowed to trail over carpets, wooden floors and so on, and if the fuse fails to operate, or has been tampered with, a short circuit may well start a fire. For this reason the switch on portable apparatus should not be used for isolating the circuit, but should be incorporated in the wall socket, so that when the appliance is switched off, the flexible lead (if the wiring is correctly installed) is dead also. For perfect safety, it is far better to remove the plug from the wall socket.

Portable electric fires switched on and forgotten may also be responsible for starting a fire, as they may be knocked over by animals or children (if children are in the household, all fires must be properly guarded), when the fire will immediately ignite carpets or furnishings. Electric irons without a pilot light may be inadvertently left switched on (an oversight which is easy because there is no visible indication) and, if not thermostatically controlled, a steady rise in temperature will take place until they ignite the table or board on which they are standing. Tests have shown that this can occur within ten minutes (*see* also Part 6A of the *Manual*, Chapter 3, Section II, 'The Investigation of Fires'). Faults in television sets may lead to overheating which may result in the cabinet in which the set is contained igniting and spreading the fire to the room. There are innumerable ways in which faulty circuits, or safe circuits incorrectly used or fused, may be responsible for an outbreak of fire. Electric blankets are another source of danger if incorrectly used or if not regularly serviced, and many deaths have been caused by people not switching electric underblankets off before getting into bed, or by folding them or placing other objects on them whilst switched on.

Voltages in private houses rarely exceed 240 v., so that the danger of serious shock is limited to touching exposed wiring or coming into contact with electrified materials. The subject of cutting off the electric supply is dealt with in Part 6A of the *Manual*, Chapter 1, 'Practical Fire Fighting'.

Some care should be taken when dealing with a fire involving the meter and fuse installation of a private house because it is generally mounted on a wooden board which falls away from the wall when it burns through; the ends of the service cable may then be exposed. The correct action at a fire of this type is to extinguish the flames and as soon as possible thereafter to switch off the current. At any fire involving electric cables and installation, the electricity undertaking should, of course, be notified, and the occupier should be advised not to approach or use the installation until it has been rendered safe. An example of an untidy domestic electricity installation which led to an outbreak of fire is shown in Plate 60.

7. FIRES INVOLVING STORAGE BATTERIES

Storage batteries are usually of the lead-acid or nickel-iron type and will be found in many premises, of which the following are the more important:

telephone exchanges and telephone repeater stations;

power stations;

Admiralty depots;

some electrical engineering works and research laboratories;

railway signalling installations;

racecourse totalisers;

hospitals and cinemas (for emergency lighting);

garages, particularly those of firms with fleets of electric delivery vehicles, such as milk floats.

When correctly installed and maintained, storage batteries present little fire risk, but the unsuitable conditions under which they are often re-charged not infrequently leads to a fire. If a fire has been caused by a short circuit, the circuit should be broken if possible by opening the switch or disconnecting the leads; otherwise, the conditions which caused the fire will persist until the battery is fully discharged. The fire should preferably be tackled with a spray branch—not because of the risk of shock, but because needless damage may be caused if a high-pressure jet is allowed to strike the cells. Water should be kept away from cells which are not involved in the fire, because it will adversely affect the electrolyte. Any electrolyte which has been released by the failure of a cell should be diluted with a stream of water.

Salt water should never be used on fires in which lead-acid type batteries are involved, since under certain conditions free chlorine may be generated. If fresh water is not available, firemen should work in breathing apparatus, those not so protected keeping well to windward. Chlorine (*see* also Part 6C of the *Manual*, Chapter 16, 'Dangerous Chemicals') is, however, readily detectable by smell, so it will immediately be evident if there is any serious danger. Nickel-iron batteries which use an alkaline electrolyte are free from this danger.

8. FIRES INVOLVING ELECTRIC RAILWAYS

(a) Systems

Electricity is used to a limited extent for the propulsion of passenger-carrying vehicles on the roads, but increasingly for the haulage of passenger and freight trains on the railways.

The current is fed to the vehicle by means of a special conductor, the return side of the circuit being either another conductor or the axles, wheels and running rails carrying the vehicle. The conductor or conductors may be overhead, as with trolley buses, tramways and the high voltage railway systems, or at rail level (third or third and fourth rail) with most direct current systems, including London Underground railways.

(b) Operating voltages

Operating voltages range from 600/750 or 1,500 for direct current systems to as high as 25,000 volt (25 kV) in the latest alternating current systems.

In overhead systems, the higher the working voltage, the greater becomes the clearance necessary between conductors and rolling stock, bridges and tunnels, to prevent arcing. Because of such limitations, parts of the earlier electrification of existing railways used 6,250 volts a.c., a comparatively low voltage for alternating current systems. The passage of trains between 6,250 V sections and 25,000 V sections required automatic switching of transformer connections in the locomotive or multiple unit train. Parts of the Eastern and Scottish Regions of British Railways operate on this dual-voltage system.

As a result of experience gained from existing 25 kV railway systems, it is more than probable that all future main-line electrification by British Railways, excluding certain extensions of existing third-rail routes, will be at 25 kV, 50 Hz a.c.

(c) Overhead supply

All railways in England and Scotland having overhead systems operate at 6,250 or 25,000 V, a.c., except the Manchester–Sheffield–Wath line, where the supply is 1,500 V, d.c.; this line may eventually be converted to 25 kV a.c.

Electricity is supplied to railway feeder stations by the Central Electricity Generating Board or other electricity boards. From the railway feeder stations or sub-feeder stations, 6,250 or 25,000 volts is fed to the overhead line equipment. The latter consists of a *contact wire* suspended by a *catenary wire*, which is, in turn, supported by a complex system of suspension cables, arms and tensioning devices (Plate 58). The greater part of the suspension system is electrically 'live' and is carried on insulators.

The height of the contact wire on existing a.c. electrifications is normally 16 ft 10 in. (5·13 m) but for future electrifications this will be reduced to 15 ft 6 in. (4·72 m). At low bridges it is reduced as necessary down to a minimum of 13 ft 9 in. (4·19 m) for 25 kV and 13 ft 5 in. (4·09 m) for 6·25 kV. At public road level crossings this height is increased to 18 ft 6 in. (5·64 m). The current for the train is collected from the contact wire by a retractable pantograph on the roof of the locomotive or motor-unit (Plate 59). Wherever possible overhead line equipment over each running line is kept electrically separate from that over other lines, and is also divided into sections by means of switching gear at feeder stations, sub-feeder stations and track-sectioning cabins, all of which are unattended, closed and locked. The switchgear they contain is remotely controlled by supervisory control in the Electrical Control Room. Each section is further divided by means of switches mounted on the overhead line equipment, and operated manually from ground level, or in some cases by remote control.

(d) Third rail systems

Third rail systems operate on voltages between 600 and 750 d.c., the current being picked up by shoes from a rail or conductor outside and two to three inches (50–76 mm) above either running rail. A fourth rail between the running rails is found in some systems, *e.g.* London Underground Railways; this rail is part of the return circuit and may carry current at voltages up to 250.

The main electricity generating and distribution system is very similar to that for overhead systems, except that alternating current is converted to direct current at substations for supply to the conductors, the overall control of circuits being supervised from a control room. Local isolation of sections may also be carried out by manual operation of track-side switches.

(e) Control and communication

On British Railways main lines all electric circuits for traction purposes are controlled from the Electrical Control Room, which is continuously staffed by one or more Electrical Control Operators. In addition to the normal control and communications system, special *electrification telephones* are provided at the track side and certain other locations. They communicate directly with the Electrical Control Room and are used only for the operation and maintenance of the electricity supply system and for reporting any derailment, mishap, fire or emergency which may necessitate the electricity supply being switched off and the electric system rendered safe.

The location of electrification telephones is indicated by a red telephone on a white background together with the word '*Electrification*', or on the Eastern Region by black and white diagonal stripes with red horizontal bar underneath.

It is important to remember that cutting off the current does not mean that possession of the line has been obtained and diesel trains may still pass.

(f) London Underground Railway control

A safety device found in the tunnels of the London Underground Railways consists of two bare copper wires, about 6 in. (150 mm) apart, which are carried the length of the tunnels on a series of insulators. If these two wires are brought into contact with each other, a circuit breaker operates, cutting off the traction current to the conductor rails and a relay switches on emergency lighting in the tunnels.

A portable telephone handset (low impedance) carried in the driver's cab can be connected by clips to the tunnel wires and this will enable the driver to establish communication with the substation that controls the current to the affected section. If the wires have not already been brought together, the action of connecting the telephone handset will operate the circuit breaker.

Whenever a driver has so operated the circuit breaker, he is required to inform the substation attendant of the reason for cutting off the current, otherwise the supply may be restored in the belief that a defect had caused the tunnel line apparatus to function. If the substation attendant fails to answer within three minutes, the driver should then remove the telephone handset and in its place connect by a cable and clips a special telephone (high impedance) which is fitted in the driver's cab. He can then establish direct communication with the Traffic Controller. The action of connecting the special telephone to the tunnel wires does not operate the circuit breaker controlling the traction current.

Sited at the tunnel entrance of each Underground station is a telephone in circuit with the tunnel wires. On lifting the receiver and pushing a button (where fitted), the current to the conductor rails will be cut off. It is necessary to replace the receiver as soon as possible, otherwise the special cab telephone in the train cannot function.

On overground sections communication can only be made by telephone at stations or signal cabins.

(g) Electrical hazard

Great care must be taken not to come into contact with any conductor rail. It should be assumed (unless the contrary is known) that the presence of overhead conductors on the permanent way of a railway indicates the existence of alternating current at 25,000 volts.

It is highly dangerous to approach closely, either directly or by any article which may be carried, the *contact* wire, the *catenary* wire or any other part of the suspension system which is carried on insulators. Current passing through running rails on any system is not dangerous to life, but on third and fourth rail systems it is advisable to avoid stepping on *any* rail because of the risk of confusing conductor rails and running rails.

(h) Procedure

All railway employees and other persons who may need to go on to any overhead-electrified railway are warned not to approach within 9 ft (2·74 m) of any overhead electrical equipment without special authority. Any maintenance work or other need to approach more closely is strictly controlled and in most cases requires the electrical isolation of the overhead line equipment, and rendering safe by earthing.

Following a request for isolation, whether as a result of an emergency or otherwise, no approach must be made to any overhead line equipment until confirmation has been received from the Electrical Control Operator that it is safe to do so. On third rail systems, short-circuiting bars carried on the trains, may be placed across the conductor rails to initiate cutting off the current and to prevent the restoration of the supply.

(j) Fire protection

(i) *A.c. electrified lines.* Electric locomotives carry one 12 lb

(5·44 kg) BCF extinguisher in each driver's cab. The extinguishers are marked with a yellow band to indicate that they may be used on electrical equipment if necessary before the current is switched off. About half the locomotives have a fixed CO_2 installation (15 lb—6·8 kg) to protect the inner transformer compartment. This is operated manually from the exterior of the locomotive, the control being accessible from ground level. The remainder of the locomotives are now (1972) being progressively fitted with fire detectors and a fixed BCF installation (40 lb—18·14 kg) which is similarly operated manually from the exterior.

Multiple-unit trains carry one 3 lb (1·36 kg) BCF extinguisher in each driver's cab and also in each guard's compartment. These are additional to the standard provision of water (gas pressure) extinguishers in coaching stock as given below.

(ii) *D.c. electrified lines (excluding London Underground Railways)*. Electric locomotives carry one 12 lb (5·44 kg) BCF extinguisher in each driver's cab. The Southern Region of British Railways operates also some electro-diesel locomotives which have a dual function: to work as normal electric locomotives on electrified lines and as diesel-electric on non-electrified lines or when electric power is not available. These carry the same portable extinguishers as the electric locomotives, but also have a fixed CO_2 installation to protect the diesel engine compartment. Multiple unit trains have the same provision of extinguishers as the a.c. multiple-unit trains (see (i) above).

On coaching stock generally, 2-gallon (9·1 litres) water (gas pressure) extinguishers are provided in guard's compartments, brake compartments and the corridors or vestibule ends of passenger coaches, dining cars and sleeping cars. A 2½-lb (1·13 kg) CO_2 gas extinguisher is provided in the kitchens of restaurant and buffet cars.

Railway staff are warned not to use any water-type extinguisher on a fire involving electrical equipment until the current is switched off. All substations and switching stations are provided with CO_2 extinguishers.

(k) Causes of fire

Fires may arise from faults in the electric traction motors or ancillary equipment in trains, in feeder circuits and cables of distribution systems. Fires may also occur from causes not associated with electrical equipment, as a result of derailment or other accidents, and may involve either passenger or freight trains. In the latter case further difficulties may be encountered if highly flammable liquids in bulk, *e.g.* in tank wagons, become involved.

If a train driver becomes aware of any serious defect or overheating of the electrical equipment of the locomotive or electrical heating of the train, he is required to bring the train to a standstill (in the case of overhead systems, first lowering the pantograph), and endeavour to isolate the defective equipment.

(l) Fire fighting

If a fire breaks out in a locomotive or motor unit, the driver is required to lower the pantograph immediately so as to cut off the electricity, and also stop all fans and blowers to reduce draughts. Before fighting any fire on an electric locomotive, the 'external emergency battery isolating switch should also be operated.

When the fire brigade is called to deal with a fire or other incident on any railway property (whether or not the railway is electrified), immediate contact should be established with the appropriate Traffic Control and/or Electrical Control Room, to which requests should be made for the stopping of trains, switching off of electricity supplies and any other relevant or emergency measures.

If the nature of the incident necessitates firemen going on to the tracks, the officer in charge should post look-outs on each side of the incident to warn of approaching trains until the railway authorities can arrange for the stopping of trains or other proper safeguards. Warning horns (blown by the mouth) for this purpose are carried on a number of fire brigade appliances.

On railways having an overhead electrification system, the danger of approaching nearer than 9 ft (2·74 m) to any live overhead line equipment applies also to the use of water for fire fighting and to any fire brigade equipment. In all cases, immediate isolation of electrical power to the affected sections is necessary. Pre-planning and liaison between the fire service and the railway authorities will ensure the effectiveness of measures required in an amergency.

(m) Rescue of injured persons

(i) *Overhead line equipment*. No attempt must be made to touch or rescue a person injured by electric shock or otherwise where any part of the injured person or of the rescuer is, or is likely to be, closer than 2 ft (610 mm) from any overhead line equipment, until the electricity supply is cut off and the equipment rendered safe.

Where an injured person is more than 2 ft (610 mm) away from and below any overhead line equipment, it is advisable, if possible, to have the electricity supply cut off before attempting rescue. There would, however, be no danger in touching the injured person, as there would be no harmful electric charge retained in the body.

(ii) *Conductor rail systems* (*not exceeding 750 V.*). If an injured person is touching a conductor rail, the electricity supply should, if possible, be cut off before any attempt is made to remove him. If the electricity cannot be cut off without delay, it may be possible to pull or push the person clear of the live rail using a dry rope or wooden pole. For methods of rescue from live electrical equipment, *see* par. 3 (a) on page 149.

9. FIRES IN MOTOR CARS, ETC.

Fires of electrical origin in motor vehicles are by no means uncommon. They normally result from short circuits caused by damage to, or deterioration of, the electric wiring system, which in the modern motor vehicle may be of some complexity. They may also be caused by overloading parts of the circuit by the attachment of additional equipment, such as cigarette lighters, radio sets, etc. As the wiring is normally permanently connected to the battery without a master switch, such fires may occur at any time and not only when the vehicle is in use. Owing to the low voltage of the battery there is no electrical danger in tackling such a fire, the first step in which should be to disconnect one of the main leads from the battery to prevent the fault continuing. The fire can then be dealt with by any appropriate extinguishing medium (*see* Part 6C of the *Manual*, Chapter 5, 'Fires in fuels').

Glossary of common electrical terms

Alternating current (a.c.). An electric current which alternately reverses its direction in a circuit in a periodic manner, the frequency with which the alternations occur being independent of the nature of the circuit. The frequency in this country is standardised at 50 cycles per second = 50 Hertz, (written 50 Hz). A cycle contains two reversals, viz. from one direction to the opposite and then back to the original direction.

Ammeter. An instrument used for measuring current and provided with a scale graduated in amperes or multiples or sub-multiples thereof.

Ampere (amp.). The practical measure of electric current. Named after the famous French physicist (1775–1836). As an indication of the order of magnitude of the ampere, a 2 kW electric radiator on a 240 V circuit takes a current of $\frac{2000}{240}$ = 8·3 amps.

Battery. Two or more primary cells or accumulators electrically connected and employed as a single unit. There are two main types of cell used for the production of electric current, primary cells and secondary cells or accumulators. A primary cell is a voltaic cell for the direct conversion of chemical energy into electrical energy, and consists generally of two dissimilar materials immersed in an electrolyte. It is characterised by the consumption of one of the two materials forming the cell. For all practical purposes, a primary cell is irreversible. A secondary cell or accumulator is a voltaic cell which is reversible and which, after discharge, can be brought back approximately to its initial (charged) chemical condition by passing a current through it in the direction opposite to that of the discharge.

Busbar. A relatively short conductor forming a common junction between a number of circuits which are separately connected to it.

Capacitor. A piece of apparatus capable of storing electrical energy as electric stress in insulating material and generally consisting of conducting surfaces (known as the plates or electrodes) at a small distance apart and separated by an insulating material. When a voltage is applied between the plates, the capacitor is said to be charged, and the quantity of electricity on the positive plate is known as the charge of the capacitor. When the plates are brought to the same potential the capacitor is said to be discharged. Formerly known as a condenser.

Choke or choking coil. A piece of apparatus used to limit the amount of current which can be consumed by certain types of electrical appliance such, for instance, as a luminous discharge tube.

Circuit. A number of conductors connected together for the purpose of carrying a current. When they form a continuous uninterrupted path through which a current can circulate, the circuit is said to be closed; when the path is not continuous, the circuit is said to be open.

Dead. A term applied to a conductor or circuit when it is not live (*q.v.*).

Delta connection. A method of connection used for the three windings of a piece of three-phase electrical equipment; the windings are connected in series, the three-phase supply being taken from or supplied to the junctions. The vector diagram of the current or voltage in the windings is in the form of a triangle and the symbol Δ *connection* is therefore often used. (*See* Fig. 3-4.)

Direct current (d.c.) or continuous current. An electric current flowing in one direction only and substantially free from pulsation.

Distributing main. An electric line from which electric energy can be supplied to the service lines of consumers.

Distribution pillar. *See* 'feeder pillar'.

Earth. (a) The conducting mass of the earth or of any conductor in direct electrical connection therewith. (b) A connection whether accidental or intentional between a conductor and the earth. (c) (*As a verb.*) To connect any conductor with the general mass of the earth.

Electrode. A conductor by means of which a current passes into or out of a liquid or gas (*e.g.* the electrodes of an electrolytic cell, of an electric furnace or of a discharge tube). The term is also applied to conducting elements separated by an insulating material as in a capacitor.

Electrolyte. A conducting medium or solution in which the electric current flows by virtue of chemical changes or decomposition. The term electrolyte is frequently used to denote a substance which, when dissolved in a specified solvent, produces a conducting medium.

Electro-magnetic induction. If an alternating current or a direct current of varying strength is passing through a conductor, then any other conductor in the vicinity lying approximately parallel to it will have an electromotive force (*i.e.*, a force which tends to cause a movement of electricity in a circuit) induced in it. If the ends of the second conductor are joined so as to form a closed circuit, then an electric current will flow. In practice, the respective conductors usually take the form of coils or insulated wire. Electric generators, static transformers and induction motors depend upon electro-magnetic induction for their operation. The principle was discovered by Michael Faraday over 100 years ago.

Feeder. A line which supplies a point on a distributing network without being tapped at any intermediate point.

Feeder pillar. A pillar containing switches, links, or fuses for connecting feeders with distributing mains.

Filament. A thread-like conductor usually of carbon or metal which may be rendered incandescent by the passage of an electric current.

Four-wire distribution. The usual system of distribution employed on three-phase a.c. systems; it consists of three phase wires and one neutral wire.

Frequency. *See* alternating current.

Generator. A machine which converts mechanical energy into electrical energy. One which generates direct current is usually called a dynamo while one which generates alternating current is usually called an alternator.

High voltage or High tension (HV or HT). A voltage up to 1000 V— see under 'Voltage'.

Joint or Junction box. A closed box usually placed underground, to which the ends of feeders and distributing mains are brought with the object of connecting them to each other and protecting them from mechanical damage.

Kilowatt (kW). A measure of power equal to 1,000 watts. A kilowatt is equal to 1·34 horsepower.

Kilowatt hour (kWh). The energy expended in one hour when the power is 1,000 watts.

Live (alive). A term applied to a conductor or circuit when a potential difference exists between it and the earth.

Low voltage or Low tension (LV or LT). A voltage normally not exceeding 250 V.

Main. A conductor or an assemblage of conductors used for the transmission and/or distribution of electrical energy.

Medium voltage. This term was used to indicate a voltage normally exceeding 250 V but not exceeding 650 V—see under 'Voltage'.

Meter. Literally any measuring instrument. In the absence of a prefix such as 'am' or 'volt', the use of the term is usually restricted to an integrating meter. The ordinary meter used to measure a public supply of electricity is a kWh meter and indicates on a series of dials the number of units consumed.

Milliamp. Equals a thousandth of an ampere (*q.v.*).

Mineral-insulated copper sheathed cable (MICS). Special cable consisting of a seamless copper sheath filled with compacted magnesium oxide as an insulating medium through which run copper conducting wires (up to seven in number). Also known as mineral-insulated copper-clad cable (MICC).

Negative. In practice applies to direct current only. The negative terminal is usually either painted black or marked with the symbol (−).

Network. An aggregation of conductors intended for the distribution of electrical energy.

Neutral conductor (neutral wire). One of the conductors of a three-wire or four-wire system. The neutral is usually earthed, and under conditions of balanced load carries no current. In a three-wire d.c. system it is at an intermediate pressure between the positive and the negative conductors, and so was called the neutral.

163

Ohm. The unit of electrical resistance. A resistance of one ohm will pass a current of one ampere when a potential difference of one volt d.c. is applied at its ends. This fundamental relationship between current and voltage is known as Ohm's Law.

Open circuit. *See* circuit.

Parallel. (a) Two or more conductors are said to be in parallel with one another when the current flowing in the circuit is divided between the two conductors. (b) Machines, transformers, cells or the like are said to be in parallel when terminals of the same polarity are electrically connected together.

Polarity. (a) *Magnetic.* That quality of a body by virtue of which certain characteristic properties are manifested over certain regions of its surface. These regions are known as poles. (b) *Electric.* A term applied to electrical machinery or apparatus when it is desired to indicate which terminal is positive and which is negative.

Polyvinylchloride (PVC). Used as an insulating and protective medium for electric cables.

Positive. In practice applies to d.c. only. The positive terminal is usually painted red or marked with the symbol $(+)$.

Potential difference. A difference between the electrical states existing at two points tending to cause a movement of electricity from one point to the other.

Rectifier. A device without moving parts used for converting alternating current to direct current.

Ring main. A main closed upon itself or by bringing the ends to a common busbar, and in which the direction of flow of energy at some point depends on the distribution of load.

Series. Two or more conductors are said to be in series when they are so connected that they are traversed by the same current.

Service line. A line connecting a consumer's installation to a distributing main.

Single-phase. Alternating current (*q.v.*) flowing through a single circuit. With single-phase current two conductors are normally employed as for d.c.

Star connection. A method of connecting the several phases of a three-phase supply; the terminal voltage is $\sqrt{3}$ times the phase voltage. (*See* Fig. 3-5.)

Substation. An assemblage of equipment at one place, including any necessary housing, for the conversion, transformation or control of electric power.

Switching station. A substation for controlling the distribution of electrical energy by means of switchgear, without transformation or conversion.

Three-phase. An a.c. system employing either three or four conductors in which the changes in direction of the current in the conductors do not occur at the same time but in a regular sequence. Such a system has certain economic and technical advantages for transmission, distribution, transformation and power purposes.

Unit (of electrical energy). One kilowatt-hour; it is approximately equivalent to 3,415 British thermal units, or $2 \cdot 6552 \times 10^6$ foot-pounds.

V.I.R. cable. Cable having conductors insulated with vulcanised rubber.

Volt. The practical unit of electromotive force and potential difference named after the Italian scientist Volta (1745–1827). It is that electromotive force or potential difference which, applied steadily to a conductor the resistance of which is one ohm, produces a current of one ampere.

Voltage. With the entry into Europe, voltages are being re-classified into bands. Band I = 0–50 V and Band II = 50–1000 V. Further bands are to be made for voltages over 1000.

Voltmeter. An instrument for measuring voltage and provided with a scale graduated in volts or multiples or sub-multiples thereof.

Watt. The practical unit of power named after the engineer James Watt (1736–1819). It is the amount of energy expended per second by an unvarying current of one ampere under a voltage of one volt.

Part 6B   Chapter 4

Fires in Aircraft

THE problems of the fire service attending an aircraft accident are unique, differing from other major civil disasters by the combination of high life and fire risk, varying in magnitude with the size of aircraft and the location of the accident. The very infrequency of serious aircraft accidents adds to the operational difficulties because it is almost impossible for one officer to accumulate experience which he can later employ to advantage.

Aircraft accidents fall into two main areas of operation—firstly, on the aerodrome where there are adequate resources available to deal with the situation, and secondly, off the aerodrome where there are vastly different conditions which may apply, particularly if the accident occurs in urban or rural environments. There is also the problem of military aircraft with their special hazards associated with armaments, different emergency escape features and ejection seats.

Aircraft have to be very strongly constructed to withstand the forces sustained in flight and in landing, so that forcible entry for rescue purposes can be very difficult to achieve. This strength will, however, be insufficient to preserve the integrity of the structure when it collides with the ground or other substantial obstructions in the process of landing or take-off. It is in these accidents, with rapid deceleration, that the most severe loss of life occurs, and as the fuel is released in fuel-mist and liquid forms the risk of fire is great. There are many potential sources of ignition in aircraft and some of these can promote ignition some time after the initial accident. In any accident there are always persons at risk, possibly trapped in the wreckage, which may be contaminated with released fuel together with much of the surrounding area.

If an aircraft is considered as a potential fire situation, professional firemen would probably reject the whole structure as unsuitable for use by persons, as it has, very broadly, the characteristics of an aluminium house situated between two fuel storage installations, both of which contain mechanical equipment designed amongst other things to generate heat and electric current in very large quantities. The situation is even worse than this simple description indicates as

166

the fuel containment is interconnected and led through the occupied portions of the aircraft. In some aircraft fuel is also stored in the wing centre-section within the fuselage, whilst in others the fuel is led to the rear of the fuselage to supply rear-mounted engines.

This chapter deals firstly with the construction of civil fixed-wing aircraft, then with such constructional details of military fixed-wing aircraft as are different from civil aircraft. Then follow details of rotary-wing aircraft (helicopters). Aerodrome facilities and equipment are next considered and, finally, rescue from and fire fighting in aircraft, both on and off aerodromes. It is, however, impossible in a single chapter to do more than cover the essential details of aircraft types, construction, fire and rescue procedures, because aircraft design is continually under review.

Section I—Civil aircraft

Before the subject is examined in more detail, it may be of assistance to introduce some information on modern aircraft with particular reference to those aspects which may be significant when dealing with an aircraft accident.

Aircraft come in a variety of sizes, from small models seating from two to ten persons, used for training, pleasure, agricultural and business purposes, to the very large types, seating almost 400 persons including the crew. Aircraft could quite easily become larger because one military aircraft, the Lockheed C-5A 'Galaxy' has been expressed in civil aviation form as the L-500, with a passenger capacity of 900. The speed of aircraft has already exceeded that of sound and the Concorde (Plate 61) can fly at Mach 2. Fuel loads already at the 40,000 gallon (over 180 000 litres) level with the Boeing 747 (the 'Jumbojet'—Plate 62) could reach 45,000 gallons (204 000 litres) with the L-500 and might easily exceed this figure with the larger aircraft of the future.

1. FIXED-WING AIRCRAFT

(a) Fuselage construction

There are two main types of construction: (i) stressed skin and (ii) braced girder, although this latter type is rapidly becoming obsolete.

(i) *Stressed skin construction.* Most large modern aircraft are of stressed skin construction and although the size and shape of aircraft vary considerably, the basic design of the structure is similar. The tapering shape of the fuselage is formed by a series of vertical metal frames placed transversely from nose to tail (Fig. 4-1). The cross-sectional shape of the fuselage varies so much that any two frames are rarely identical in size and shape. Metal stringers running horizontally along the length of the fuselage are spaced around the circumference of the frames. Stringers, which are continuous along most of the length of the fuselage and are of thicker gauge metal, serve as attachment points for other assemblies, *e.g.* cabin flooring; these are called longerons.

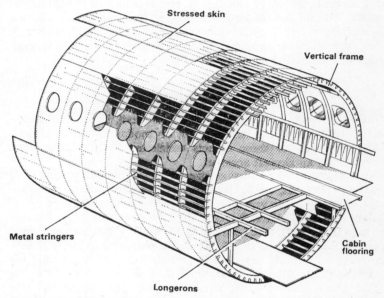

Fig. 4–1. Sketch showing the basic design of stressed skin construction of the fuselage of an aircraft.

The skin is not merely a sheet metal covering. As the name implies, it is 'stressed' skin which contributes to the rigidity of the airframe and the thickness of the skin varies according to the stress it must take. The skin panels may be riveted or bonded to the frames and stringers. Often several panels are bonded to a number of stringers to form a separate assembly, which is then riveted to the frames and longerons. Where the skin is bonded on, there is no external indication of the underlying framework.

(ii) *Braced girder construction.* Although the stressed skin construction is used almost exclusively, there are a few old types of very light aircraft, such as Auster, Tiger Moth and Anson, with fuselages of braced girder construction. This consists of a lattice of welded steel tubing, three or four lengths of which are longerons which run fore and aft, and these are braced by a pattern of struts. This frame takes the stress, strain and load of the aircraft. For weather protection and streamlining, a fabric covering is fitted over a framework of formers (plywood shaping members) and stringers (light spruce members) running parallel with the longerons.

(b) Mainplane and wings

Spars run from the centre section to the wingtip, or from wingtip to wingtip, *i.e.*, through the fuselage. Their vertical height is the same as the thickness of the mainplane, so they vary in size according to their position in the wing profile, and they are tapered towards the wingtip. Some aircraft have only two spars, but many have several spars varying in length according to the wing plan form (swept wing, crescent wing, delta wing, etc.). The ribs form the aerofoil profile of the mainplane. They are closely spaced at right angles to the spars. Again the skin is a structural member, not a covering; the upper and under surface skin panels are riveted or bonded to the spars and ribs.

(c) Centre section

The centre section of the aircraft (*i.e.*, the junction of the mainplane and the fuselage) may be constructed as a separate assembly; the front and rear fuselage and the outer wings are then built around it.

(d) Metals used in aircraft construction

It is important for the firemen to have some knowledge of the metals forming the major structure of an aircraft, and the manner in which they are incorporated, since their resistance to fire, impact and cutting will have a pronounced effect upon fire fighting and rescue operations. Fig. 4-2 shows how large a part light alloys play in aircraft construction as compared with steel.

(i) *Light alloys*. The metal most used in aircraft construction is aluminium alloy. The composition of the alloy varies from one aircraft to another, but the following broad descriptions are typical:

A. *Duralumin* is an alloy of aluminium with about 4 per cent of copper and about 1 per cent each of magnesium, manganese and silicon.

B. *Alclad* is duralumin with a surface finish of pure aluminium.

C. *Magnalium* is a lighter alloy of aluminium with about 2 per cent of copper and 2 to 10 per cent of magnesium.

Fig. 4-2. Diagram of an aircraft showing the use of light alloy and steel.

These alloys are used for skin surfaces and as pressed sectional members, or as channels for framework, spars and stiffeners. Their sheets are readily pierced and severed; heavy sections can be cut with an axe, hacksaw or power-operated cutting tool.

(ii) *Magnesium* (*and its alloys*). Magnesium alloy castings or sheets are used to minimise weight where bulkiness is no object. Usually such components are sub-assemblies rather than parts of the framework. Examples are control consoles, engine mounting brackets, crankcase sections, cover plates and many other engine parts. Magnesium is rarely used at positions where forcible entry will be necessary.

(iii) *Stainless steel and titanium alloys*. Although light alloys are adequate for most of the airframe structure, it is necessary to use stainless steel or titanium where greater strength or resistance to heat is required. They are used for engine parts and reinforcement areas to skin surfaces on leading edges of mainplanes on certain high-speed aircraft, for tubing for structural members and for airscrews.

2. AIRCRAFT ENGINES

Aircraft engines are designed to accelerate a mass of air rearward, and the reaction from this is the thrust which propels the aircraft. The mass of air may be accelerated by an external propeller (piston and turbo-prop engines) or by an internal compressor and turbine assembly (turbojet and turbofan engines).

(a) Piston engines

These engines may be either of the radial or inline cylinder type. Large engines are usually radial and present a greater fire hazard; the cylinders are installed in a circle radiating outwards from the crankcase. The crankshaft extends forward to drive the airscrew assembly and a sufficient distance to the rear to drive auxiliary equipment, such as the generator, oil pumps, etc. The number of cylinders varies with the size of the engine and in some of the larger engines there are two or three separate rows of cylinders, which are referred to as 'banks'. The fire hazard in the cylinder section is not so great as in other parts and (unless the cylinders fracture releasing fuel, or the crankcase is holed releasing oil) is confined almost exclusively to electrical wiring or oil lubricant pipe-lines.

Immediately to the rear of the cylinders, there is an accessory section, which contains important engine equipment and is of special interest to firemen because it contains the carburettor and built-in super-charger, the main fuel lines and pumps which furnish the engine fuel supply, oil lines and pumps and, in many cases, the oil tanks. The generator, magneto electrical connections and in some instances the storage batteries and other necessary engine equipment are also located in this section.

The accessory section has little unoccupied space and contains various equipment some of which involves moving parts. Access to this section is gained by removing the rear cowling, which is normally fastened with toggle or 'dzus' fasteners; these are readily unfastened. However, many instances may occur where the intensity of a fire will prevent removal of the cowling and it would then be necessary to gain access elsewhere. The cowling is constructed of metal somewhat thicker than the aircraft skin, but it can be readily pierced with an axe. Effectiveness of the carbon dioxide extinguishing agent can be increased by keeping the cowling in position and using penetrating nozzles as are fitted to wheeled CO_2 appliances at the majority of airports. A special skin piercer is also used by airport fire services and fire access panels or points are often provided on each side of the cowling through which CO_2 or BCF applicators or wing piercing equipment can be inserted.

There may be a so-called 'fire-wall' or bulkhead separating the forward section of the engine containing the cylinders and the accessory section; this is generally known as a 'shoulder cowl'. There is a main fire-wall or bulkhead between the accessory section and the adjoining parts of the aircraft. The term 'fire-wall' is sometimes a misnomer as a continued fire can burn through the cowling, over the top of the bulkhead and so penetrate into the nacelle and wing spaces.

Bulkheads are of asbestos sandwiched between two layers of light gauge steel, but in some aircraft stainless steel or titanium is used. Bulkheads are pierced with openings for cables, control linkages, fuel pipe-lines, etc. Bulkheads are intended to localise a fire which may occur in the engine sections, giving the pilot sufficient time to carry out his 'cockpit fire drill'.

(b) Piston engine hazards

The most common points of fire hazard in piston engines are the fuel lines, oil lines, the induction systems which are under pressure from super-chargers, the amount of fuel carried and the heated exhaust ducting. Piston engine starting fires, which are most due to over-rich mixture, are fairly frequent, but immediate action by the pilot minimises the danger and damage. The pilot will normally shut off the fuel supply and switch off the ignition. Carbon dioxide or vaporising liquid is generally the most effective extinguishing media in the confined space of an engine nacelle and results in clean and non-damaging extinction. Foam is only used in extreme cases as the engine would need to be completely dismantled after foam had been used.

(c) Turbine engines

Large transport aircraft are mainly powered by turbine engines (familiarly known as 'jets'). In these, a compressor draws air into the engine and forces it through combustion chambers where it is heated and accelerated to drive a turbine which is on a common shaft with the compressor. Engine-driven accessories are also installed, usually well forward of the combustion chambers, and include such items as hydraulic and oil pumps, generators, etc. Airflow cools the engine, entering at the forward part and being ducted round the engine.

Air enters through a duct in the air intake casing, passes through compressors (multi-stage and operating on an axial flow basis), and is distributed at high pressure through 'elbows' into the combustion chambers. Here the highly compressed air is sprayed with fuel (a special aviation grade of kerosene—*see* par. 3) and burned. The exhaust gases then pass through the turbine section and thence through the exhaust cone at the rear of the engine, the hot gases giving a forward thrust to the aircraft.

The use which is made of the turbine differs between:

(i) *Turbojets*, in which the turbine accelerates the mixture of combustion gases and hot air out of the engine through a tail-pipe which may be fitted with variable exhaust cones or nozzles.

(ii) *Turbo-props*, in which the common shaft between the turbine and compressor is extended forward through a reduction gear to turn a propeller.

(iii) *Turbofans*, in which there are two compressor assemblies on a co-axial shaft from the turbine, and the forward compressor acts as an internal airscrew as well as supplying air for the other compressor and turbine to function as a turbojet.

If a turbine engine fails to start when it is turned over, the surplus fuel which has been delivered to the combustion chambers may cause 'torching' (excessive flaming at the tail-pipe) when the next attempt to start is made. Normally the pilot can deal with this by keeping the engine running with the fuel cock turned off. Alternatively some of this fuel may drain out of the engine to the ground and be ignited later by exhaust gases. Incidents of this kind, however, have become infrequent through the introduction of combustion fuel drains which pass surplus fuel back into the system (instead of to the ground) and through improved precautions in start-up procedures.

The rotary components of a turbine engine attain a high momentum, and this is resisted by little more than their own weight. They continue to revolve at high speed after the engine is shut down, and the run-down period is considerable.

3. FUEL SYSTEMS

Fuels used in aircraft are broadly divided into two categories: (a) petrol or gasoline, which is used in piston engines, and (b) kerosene, which is used in turbine engines.

(a) Gasoline fuels

There is one standard gasoline fuel, whose flash point may be −40°C or slightly higher. This is supplied in several grades with a different knock rating to suit the compression ratio of different engines (NOTE: a higher octane rating of a fuel does not increase the degree of fire hazard—see page 265). Each grade is identified by figures representing its knock rating, and by its colouring:

> AVGAS 115/145   contains purple dye
> AVGAS 100/130   contains green dye
> AVGAS 73   contains no dye.

(b) Kerosene fuels

There are three kerosene fuels used for turbine engines:

(i) AVTUR (also known as JP 1 and ATK), which has a flash point above 37·8°C. There are two grades: AVTUR/40 and AVTUR/50, neither of which contains a dye.

(ii) AVTAG (also known as JP 4 and ATG). This is a gasoline (known as a 'wide-cut' gasoline) which has some of the properties of kerosene, with a flash point of −20°C. There is only one grade and it contains no dye.

(iii) AVCAT (also known as JP 5 and ATC); this has a flash point above 65°C and is specially distilled for use in naval carrier-borne aircraft.

(c) Physical properties

It will be seen that AVGAS and AVTAG fuels at normal temperature and pressure conditions will give off vapours that are capable of forming ignitable mixtures with air near the surface of the liquid or within the vessel in which they are stored. The kerosene grades of fuel will not form ignitable mixtures at normal temperatures and pressures, but it should be remembered that kerosene fuel in the form of a spray or when heated is much more readily ignited than when in bulk, and in a crash it may be sprayed on to hot engine parts or exhaust ducts; it will then ignite very quickly. Once ignited, kerosene will burn as readily and will produce as much heat as a similar-sized petrol fire.

Although there is very little difference in the heat of combustion of the three normal types of aviation fuel, there is a difference in the rate of flame spread. Although difficult to measure, it has been found in controlled experiments that AVGAS and AVTAG have a flame spread rate of between 700 to 800 feet per minute (213–244 m/min) whereas the rate of flame spread for AVTUR under the same conditions is substantially lower; it is less than 100 ft/min (30·5 m/min). This slower rate of flame spread does not hold where the fuel is released in 'mist' form. Although AVTUR offers a certain safety advantage over other types of fuel, it does not appreciably reduce the severity of fire situations in aircraft accidents to permit any lessening of appropriate standards of fire protection.

(d) Fuel tanks

Fuel is carried in a number of tanks (Fig. 4-3), structurally separate but interconnected, in the wings and, in many instances, in the fuselage. The principal types of tank are:

(i) *Rigid tanks.* These are usually made of aluminium or duralumin sheet with internal baffles which reduce liquid swirl and also brace the tank. They may be installed in wing sections or fuselage depending on the type of aircraft. The tank is often covered with fabric and is provided with a vent pipe, an overflow, a base sump (from which any water due to condensation can be drained) and a fuelling orifice. Pressure fuelling valves are fitted on some aircraft and all types are provided with a bonding point to guard against the formation of static electricity sparks which could cause ignition of the fuel vapour and air mixture. Rigid tanks are usually set in cradles and secured by metal straps.

(ii) *Integral tanks.* These are compartments formed by the airframe structure itself, which are sprayed internally with a synthetic rubber composition to seal their joints and make them fuel-tight. Generally they are either box sections formed by the spars, ribs and skin of wings, or quarter section, saddle section or cylindrical compartments formed by bulkheads or frames and skin in the fuselage.

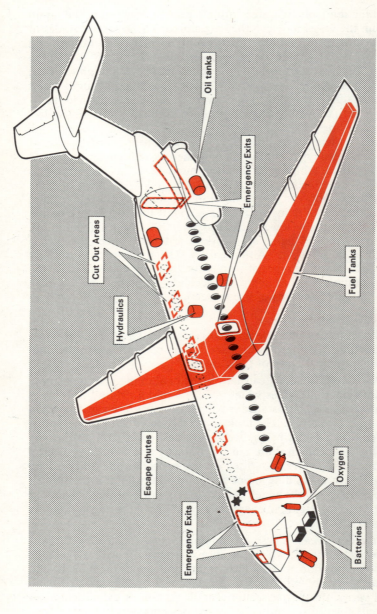

Oil tanks

Emergency Exits

Cut Out Areas

Hydraulics

Fuel Tanks

Escape chutes

Emergency Exits

Oxygen

Batteries

Fig. 4–3. A typical fuel-tank layout of an aircraft. Some tanks run through the fuselage as well as through the wings. Tanks are interconnected and have cross feed valves; tank vents are normally situated at the trailing edge of the wings.

Plate 61. The prototype 002 Concorde taking off from Heathrow Airport, London.

Plate 62. The Boeing 747 (Jumbo jet)

Plate 63. A comparison of relative sizes of modern civil aircraft. At the top are two VC10s, in the centre the Boeing 747 and below is a DC8.

Plate 64. A BEA Trident Two.

Plate 65. The nose loader and stairway required to enable passengers to enter the Boeing 747.

Plate 66. The passenger walkways (also known as fingers) and nose loaders at one of the aircraft aprons at Heathrow Airport.

Plate 67. The Control Tower at Heathrow. The Air Traffic Control was re-designed in 1971 and is the most modern control complex in Europe.

Plate 68. Part of the Air Traffic Control situated at the top of the control tower shown in Plate 67.

*Plate 69. A demonstration show-
ing the effect of water on burning
magnesium.*

Plate 70. One of British Airport Authority's fire-fighting appliances, the Nubian Major, with the foam monitor mounted on the roof.

Plate 71. The Cardox appliance of BAA which can discharge CO_2 from the specially-designed boom applicator whilst the vehicle is in motion.

Plate 72. A typical civil airport rescue tender. This appliance carries the necessary equipment for effecting a quick rescue at aircraft accidents.

Plate 73. Another type of foam tender to be found at an aerodrome fire station.

Plate 74. The Nubian Major appliance producing foam. The monitor is controlled and directed by a member of the crew from the position behind the cab.

Plate 75. An accident involving an Ambassador aircraft at Heathrow in July 1968. The aircraft crashed along one of the aircraft aprons and damaged three Tridents.

Mainplane distortion due to an accident could cause splitting of the joints with consequent fuel spillage to add to the fire hazard.

(ii) *Flexible tanks.* These are flexible plastic bags fitted into compartments in the wings or fuselage and secured by a pattern of press-studs. For others fuel-resisting conductive rubber is used in conjunction with canvas or nylon, and, quite often, a covering of fibreglass.

The advantages of flexible tanks include a greater ability to stand the shock of heavy landings and, being flexible, they may adopt the new shape of a mainplane damaged in an accident. They may still, however, split in a severe crash or be ruptured by a jagged metal component, and the plastics used in their construction can burn fiercely emitting toxic vapours.

(iv) *Auxiliary fuel tanks.* Most types of aircraft are able to carry additional fuel tanks when required. These are carried externally under the wings, at the wingtips or under the fuselage (slipper or ventral tanks). These external tanks are aerodynamically shaped and their construction depends largely on their size; small tanks of about 30 gallons (136 litres) fixed to wingtips are likely to be moulded fibreglass; large tanks of 100 to 1,700 gallons (455 to 7 728 litres) are likely to be metal stressed skin on a framework similar to that of the fuselage. In some cases these tanks can be jettisoned in an emergency. The additional hazard is obvious.

4. POWERED AND PRESSURISED SYSTEMS

The internal spaces in an airframe are packed with system components and their connecting pipework, cables and ducts. These represent many potential sources of fire distributed throughout the aircraft, a means of spreading and intensifying fire especially by the bursting of pressurised containers, and a degree of congestion which resists the penetration of some fire extinguishing agents into the airframe.

(a) Hydraulic systems

Hydraulic power is used for the operation of undercarriage, flaps, brakes and, in special cases, power-assisted control systems. The fluids used are special mineral oils (coloured red), a mixture of castor oil and alcohol (coloured blue) or synthetic (coloured yellow or purple) which are contained in reservoirs varying from one to thirty gallons (4·5–136 litres) capacity. Operating pressures are often over 1,000 lbf/in² (69 bars) so care should be taken if pipelines have to be

177

cut. Carbon dioxide is the most effective inerting medium when alcohol is present.

(b) Electrical systems

An aircraft electrical system supplies current for lights, radio, intercom system, booster pumps, hydraulic pumps, airscrew pitch gearing, heaters and numerous other electrical devices. As an example, the RAF Hunter has over 400 electric or electrically-operated components, and any aircraft is fitted with several miles of electric wiring distributed throughout the whole of the airframe.

The electrical system differs from that which is fitted to the normal motor car in that it is more extensive and the batteries (both lead acid and alkaline may be found) are not generally used as a source of current for the engine ignition systems. On aircraft direct current, with a generator as the primary source of power, is employed, and conventional wet-cell batteries for storage. Most aircraft now have engine-driven alternators with rectifiers to convert part of the output to direct current. Batteries, either 12 or 24 volt, constitute a reserve to supply extra power for momentary peak loads and for starting operations when an external source of power, such as a ground power unit, is not available.

When an aircraft accident occurs it is probable that a large number of electric wires will be severed or otherwise damaged, and any subsequent movement of the aircraft may produce an electric spark of sufficient intensity to ignite fuel vapour. For this reason, aircraft debris should only be disturbed when necessary for rescue operations or when the fire is of such proportions that the effect from a short circuit is immaterial.

(i) *Batteries*. The location of the batteries varies with the type of aircraft. They may be in the fuselage, wings or engine nacelles. In multi-engined aircraft, each engine may be provided with its own battery (generally located in the engine nacelle or in the undercarriage housing), or there may be a central battery position serving the whole system. Special equipment, such as radar, is provided with a large number of separate batteries, which are usually installed apart from the main batteries.

(ii) *Ignition system*. An aircraft ignition system is of importance to the fireman mainly because of the terminology used in connection with it. The term 'ignition switch' in relation to a motor car means a battery switch, but this is not usually the case with aircraft. The reason for this difference is that the ignition system of a car is supplied from the battery whereas in piston-engined aircraft the ignition system is operated by magnetos. Practically all piston engines are equipped with dual magnetos.

The magneto switches are found at the pilot's and/or flight engineer's position. They are usually of the toggle type and are off when they are in the 'down' position. The master switch (sometimes called the main switch) is the principal electric switch and through it all electrically-operated services are connected to the power supply. It can be used to cut off simultaneously electric energy from all cables and equipment. When the master switch is off, the circuit between the batteries and the switch is still closed and in consequence it is advisable to disconnect the battery terminals where an aircraft accident has occurred without fire. The master switch is also to be found near the pilot's and/or flight engineer's position.

(iii) *Auxiliary power unit*. Many modern aircraft are equipped with an auxiliary generator powered by a small engine (generally a turbine). This is used to take the load off the batteries when starting the engines and it can be operated after take-off to restore the batteries to normal. The units are located in various parts of the fuselage, sometimes in the waist section or under the flight deck, but more generally in the tail cone area.

(c) De-icing system

The system is designed to prevent the formation of ice on leading edges, propellers and windscreens. The fluid used has a large alcohol content and is contained in tanks varying from three to fifty gallons (14–227 litres) capacity. Carbon dioxide is the most effective extinguising medium for fires when alcohol is present.

(d) Pressurisation and air conditioning

The fuselage of a pressurised aircraft is specially strengthened and each exit door is pneumatically sealed. A pressurised system consists of engine-driven air compressors which maintain the requisite air pressure within the fuselage. The air is filtered, refrigerated and then brought to normal atmospheric pressure and temperature, after which it circulates through the fuselage (flight deck, passenger and luggage compartments). It is discharged to atmosphere through a controlled restriction designed so as to maintain the pre-determined pressure within the cabin; these controlled restrictions are known as 'spill valves'. The system is controlled electrically and regulated by the aircraft captain from a panel situated in the cockpit.

When an aircraft is to fly at a height above, say, 8,000 ft (2 438 m), the pressurisation system is brought into operation as soon as the engines start, whereupon the compressors commence working and in consequence no difference in air pressure is felt inside the aircraft during the climb. On descending below 8,000 ft (2 438 m), the spill valves are so operated as to gradually reduce the pressure inside the aircraft to normal atmospheric pressure.

(e) Compressed gases

Compressed air is used in an emergency if the hydraulic system fails. Nitrogen is sometimes used for pressurising fuel tanks to assist fuel feed and for inhibiting empty tanks. Oxygen is used for breathing purposes and the system is supplied from a number of oxygen cylinders containing gaseous oxygen at 1,800 lbf/in^2 (124 bars). The capacity of the cylinders varies from between 400 to 2 250 litres, and as many as twelve cylinders may be carried. The oxygen is usually piped to a pressure reducing valve which reduces the pressure to about 400 lbf/in^2 (28 bars) and then to a demand regulator from which it is generally supplied to a mask.

5. SEATING IN CIVIL AIRCRAFT

Civil aircraft seats and their attendant safety straps are of particular importance for the fireman faced with a rescue operation. Passenger seats usually embody a simple method of adjustment for passenger comfort and pilots' seats always have a certain measure of adjustment to 'fit' the pilot to his controls. Whenever the opportunity occurs, firemen should study the adjustments which can be made to the various types of aircraft seat, because a few inches (mm) of movement of the seat by means of the normal adjustment may free the occupant and enable a rescue to be made expeditiously.

The seat-mounting rails permit the installation of seat units in a host of configurations in any aircraft (Fig. 4-4). The pitch interval (*i.e.*, the distance measured horizontally between corresponding points of adjacent seats), can vary between 29 and 42 in. (737 and 1 067 mm). Much depends on the class (first, tourist, coach), the airline and the duration of flight. Short-haul inclusive tour flights or domestic routes are likely to have seating more closely related than would be the case on an inter-Continental flight. Additionally, the width of individual seats in seat units varies as between first class and tourist class, so that four abreast seating may be found in the first class cabin whilst there may be six abreast seating in the same aircraft for tourist passengers.

A third variable is aisle width; it is possible to provide a few more inches (mm) between seat units where fewer seats occupy a given

TYPICAL INTERIOR VIEW (B.A.C. VC.10)

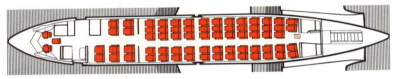

MIXED-CLASS SEATING PLAN (B.A.C.1-11 400 SERIES)

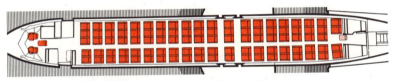

HIGH DENSITY SEATING PLAN (B.A.C. 1-11 500 SERIES)

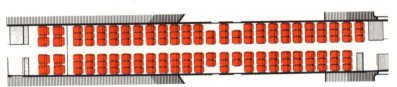

TYPICAL SEATING PLAN (B.A.C. VC. 10)

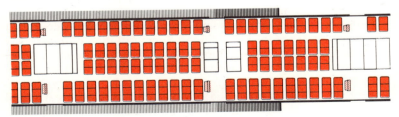

TYPICAL SEATING PLAN PORTION (BOEING 747, JUMBO JET)

Fig. 4–4. Examples of various seat configurations in civil aircraft.

cabin width. In the wide-bodied aircraft, *e.g.* the Boeing 747, seating in the tourist cabin can be nine abreast with two longitudinal aisles, and lateral aisles between blocks of seats.

All seats are provided with lap-straps which passengers are required to fasten on take-off and landing. The fastening is simple in operation; all lapstraps are undone by a single positive action irrespective of type design, normally by lifting a clasp and pulling the straps apart. Members of the crew on the flight deck have a full harness consisting of leg and shoulder straps, whilst cabin staff have conventional lapstraps.

Passenger lapstraps are designed for instant release in an emergency and are simple because they are used in many cases by inexperienced people. A few seconds' examination will indicate to the fireman how to to release the strap. Only in exceptional circumstances is the release or buckle likely to be damaged sufficiently to render necessary the use of a knife and lapstraps are always easier to undo in the normal manner than to cut.

6. AIRCRAFT ACCESS AND EXITS

(a) Doors

The normal means of entrance into an aircraft is through the door. Aircraft having closed cabins are provided with at least one normal exit in the form of a main door, and most public passenger aircraft have a number of exits to facilitate the rapid escape of all occupants in the event of an emergency landing. The main door is generally on the port side midway down the fuselage or nearer the tail, but in large aircraft there will be other doors as well, the number and size being related to seating capacity. Where cabins are divided into two or more compartments, there will be an exit door in each compartment, unless the passageways connecting the compartments are such that they would not become blocked or retard passenger movement in the event of a minor crash.

Doors often open outwards and hinge on the forward side so that the slipstream tends to shut the door. Some variation of design may be found, such as sliding doors, and sometimes doors may be hinged at the top or bottom for special purposes. Normal door exits open from the inside and the outside using one handle only. Operation of the handle is rapid and obvious, and handles are arranged and marked so that they are readily located and operated, even in darkness. Handles are very often recessed or flush positioned with the door skin when locked, and can be released by press button.

(b) Windows

These are usually completely fixed, very often double glazed and are made of transparent plastic. In modern pressurised aircraft, they are kept as small as possible and are extremely strong, as are the frames in which they are mounted. Windows, other than those specially constructed as emergency exits are, therefore, an unpromising means of access to the inside of pressurised aircraft. On some types, however, they may afford easy access if large enough.

(c) Emergency exits

(i) *Emergency doors.* All aircraft have a number of emergency doors as exits according to the size and type of the aircraft. Passenger emergency exits are of a size and number related to the carrying capacity of the aircraft, and easy access is provided to enable passengers to reach the exits even in darkness. The means of opening are rapid and obvious, handles are not removable and exits can be opened from both inside and outside.

Emergency exits and their means of access and opening are plainly marked both for the occupants and on the outside of the aircraft for the guidance of rescue personnel. The actual markings vary from one type of aircraft to another and all are necessarily brief, but the method of opening and direction in which a handle has to be turned is always clear. Fig. 4-5 shows the method of emergency access to two typical passenger aircraft.

(ii) *Emergency hatches.* In many aircraft selected window panels are so constructed that they can be removed for emergency access (Fig. 4-19). There may be similar emergency hatches on top of the fuselage, to allow for escape when an aircraft is ditched, or beneath it, although this generally only applies in small or military aircraft. Whatever type of emergency hatch is installed, the method of removal will be clearly marked.

(iii) *Break-in points.* These are areas marked on the fuselage (Fig. 4-6) where it is possible to cut through the airframe to force an entry if necessary. These are not weak points in the airframe structure, but they are marked between frames so that it is necessary to cut through skin and stringers only, and they are located where there is no internal obstruction once the structure has been cut away, *i.e.*, where there is no equipment, furnishing or pipework on the inside of the cabin wall. As their locations are decided according to the arrangement of interior fittings, they are often awkwardly placed for rescue purposes, well above ground level on the outside or well above floor

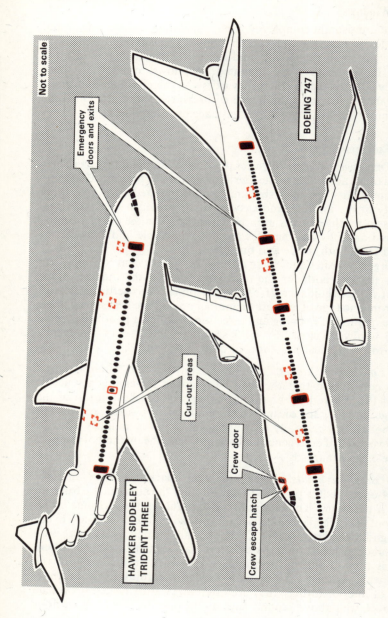

Not to scale

BOEING 747

Emergency doors and exits

HAWKER SIDDELEY TRIDENT THREE

Cut-out areas

Crew door

Crew escape hatch

Fig. 4–5. Method of emergency access to two typical passenger aircraft.

level on the inside. Whenever possible, other emergency access points should be investigated before any cutting away is attempted.

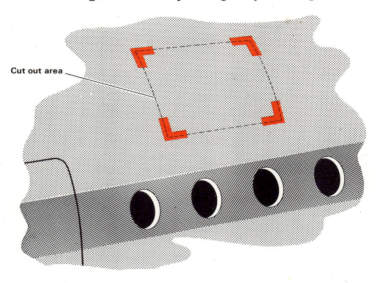

Fig. 4–6. Typical 'break-in' marking on the fuselage to denote where it is possible to cut through the airframe for an emergency entrance.

7. FIRE PROTECTION SYSTEMS AND FLIGHT RECORDERS

Most aircraft have fire detection and fire extinguishing systems. These are independent of each other; the fire detection system operates automatically, but the fire extinguishing system operates only when the pilot switches it on (or when a crash switch is operated—*see* below). Some small aircraft have only a fire extinguishing system with no detection system.

These systems are installed in the engine bays, and in some aircraft also in fuel tank compartments.

(a) Fire detection systems

Fire detection systems are electrically operated with circuits so designed to distinguish between different compartments or zones. The detector unit is a heat-sensing element. The most common type consists of a length of stainless steel tubing containing a co-axial central conductor wire and a filling material to insulate the wire from the tubing. The resistance of this filling material decreases as the temperature increases until sufficient current flows between the wire and the tubing to operate an alarm relay. The alarm is registered simultaneously by illumination of one of the groups of fire warning lights and by the sounding of an alarm bell in the cockpit indicating which zone is affected.

(b) Fire extinguishing systems

The fire extinguishing agent is a vaporising liquid (either BCF or BTM) and is contained in cylinders under pressure. The agent is released when a miniature cartridge in the cylinder outlet is detonated electrically by the pilot pressing a button switch in the cockpit. The duration of the discharge is very brief—between one and five seconds—but often a pair of cylinders are so connected that the pilot can choose between discharging them simultaneously or consecutively.

(c) Crash switches

On older types of aircraft there is also provision for the fire extinguishing system to be discharged automatically by special switches which are actuated by conditions which occur during a crash landing. The 'crash switches' do not operate if a fire occurs in a stationary aircraft on the ground. In this situation, the cockpit switches must be used and electrical power must be available.

In addition to the actuation of the fire extinguishing system, the function of 'crash switches' may include other fire prevention measures, such as closing the low pressure fuel cocks, cutting out the electric generators, isolating the batteries from non-essential circuits and switching on cabin emergency lighting.

(d) Accident conditions

Despite the installation of crash switches, it cannot be assumed that the installed fire extinguishing equipment would have any real effect during an aircraft accident. If the aircraft is subjected to forces greater than those required to operate the switches, disruption of the electrical circuits or the spray ring piping will make the system useless. The small cylinders of fire extinguishant are only intended to cope with a wholly enclosed fire in a particular compartment, so they have no effect outside their own enclosures. Fires originating from escaping fuel, or in other compartments or outside the airframe would not be affected by the discharge of the fire extinguishing system, and would rapidly overwhelm whatever localised control the system might have achieved.

In other words, the fire extinguishing system could be effective in an aircraft accident only if the forces involved are low enough for the system to remain serviceable, for the airframe compartments to remain intact and for any escape of fuel to be localised. Because of the small size of the fire extinguishing cylinders, they will be affected by heat far more rapidly than other larger cylinders. If these cylinders are not discharged during an accident and fire occurs, they may burst at a comparatively early stage.

(e) Flight recorders

Flight recorders are carried on most civil aircraft used for passenger transport and may also be found on aircraft used for freight, private or business purposes. Normally installed in the rear fuselage section and often referred to as *black boxes* in non-technical literature, these recorders may also be finished in fluorescent red paint and could be spherical in shape; their function is to record details of aircraft performance throughout all stages of operations, and this recorded data may be of importance when an accident has occurred.

Special care should be taken by fire brigade personnel to ensure that no additional damage is sustained by these devices, and the following advice on how to achieve this is given by the Accident Investigation Branch of the Department of Trade and Industry:

   (i) After an accident additional damage may be caused to a flight recorder by involvement in fire or by incorrent handling in attempts at recovery.

  (ii) No attempt should be made to recover a recorder unless there is a risk that it may be irretrievably lost, for example, in swampy ground or due to tidal action on the seashore or river bank.

 (iii) Everything possible short of removal should, however, be done to protect flight recorders from additional fire damage.

 (iv) In conjunction with the police, the officer in charge should take steps to safeguard the recorder in situ pending the arrival of properly authorised officers of the Accident Investigation Branch of the Department of Trade and Industry.

Section II—Military aircraft

The primary object of fire fighting in military as in civil aircraft is to save life. The conduct of fire fighting, however, whilst remaining basically the same for both types has, in the case of military aircraft, to take into account the peculiar hazards likely to be encountered at the scene of an accident. The great majority of crash landings will occur at or in the immediate vicinity of airfields where trained rescue personnel will be available, but on other occasions military aircraft may crash land away from any such base and the initial rescue operations may have to be attempted by local authority firemen.

The types of roles of military aircraft and the complementary weapon systems, plus the many and varied designs of modern ejector seats, makes it impossible to describe these items in detail in this section, so the importance of a close liaison between officers of the Royal Air Force and local authority fire brigades cannot be over-stressed.

1. CONSTRUCTION OF FIXED-WING MILITARY AIRCRAFT

The constructional details of civil aircraft given in the previous section are applicable in whole or in part to military aircraft, and several types of civil aircraft, such as the VC10 and Britannia, are used by the RAF in a passenger role or for air trooping. Items peculiar to military aircraft which have not been dealt with in Section I are summarised below, but it must be emphasised that the subject can only be covered briefly in each case and only items of a direct fire service interest have been included. Fire brigade personnel are urged to take every opportunity of visiting military aerodromes in their fire area to learn at first hand the special constructional and other details.

(a) Auxiliary fuel tanks

Some military aircraft, such as bomber or strategic reconnaissance aircraft which are required to fly long-range sorties, are fitted with one or more metal, saddle section or cylindrical tanks. These are installed in the bomb bay, which may also contain a limited load of weapons or pyrotechnic stores.

(b) Auxiliary power plant

An auxiliary power plant is installed in several large aircraft (*e.g.* Argosy, Belfast, Victor, Vulcan). This is an additional small turbine engine which is used not to propel the aircraft, but as a supplementary source of power or pressure for the aircraft's systems. The following are examples of the uses of this unit:

(i) to drive an electric alternator in addition to those driven by the main engines;

(ii) to supply pressurised air to pneumatic turbo-starters on the main engines;

(iii) to supply pressurised air to a nuclear installation.

This unit is contained in an enclosed compartment with titanium or stainless steel bulkheads, usually close to the main engines (in the Belfast it is in the port undercarriage blister). It is provided with a separate air intake scoop and exhaust ducts, and a cylinder of oxygen is mounted in its air intake. It uses normal aviation turbine fuel which is supplied either from a separate tank connected to the aircraft's main fuel system or directly from the main fuel system.

(c) Fuel systems

In addition to the aircraft fuels which are listed in Section I (page 174), some military aircraft use AVPIN (isopropyl nitrate) in liquid fuel engine starter systems. This is an unusual fuel in that it is a mixture of hydrocarbon and nitrate compounds, and is capable of continuing to burn without any air supply (this is known as a 'monofuel'), once it has been ignited because its molecules contain oxygen.

The principal physical properties of AVPIN are:

(i) it is very volatile (flash point 10°C);

(ii) its vapour is 3·5 times heavier than air;

(iii) it is lighter than and is not miscible with water (specific gravity 0·79);

(iv) it has wide limits of flammability (2 to 53 per cent by volume in air);

(v) it gives off toxic fumes when burning.

(d) Compressed gases

Military aircraft often have liquid oxygen (LOX) systems. These are supplied from one or more LOX converters, which are spherical or cylindrical insulated containers with evaporating coils and valves to regulate the rate of evaporation of the liquid according to demand. One litre of LOX produces 845 litres of gaseous oxygen.

Oxygen cylinders or LOX converters and their associated equipment are usually located near the cockpit, but some transport aircraft have additional storage cylinders at the sides or rear of the passenger cabin.

Other cylinders of compressed gases may be found in military air-craft, and these can be identified by their colour and by the lettering on them, which gives the name of the gas (along the body of the cylinder) and the chemical formula (around the neck). The principal compressed gases to be found are air (light grey), carbon dioxide (white), nitrogen (light grey with black neck) and oxygen (black).

(e) Identifying symbols

The symbols which are used for the identification of system pipe-lines and components in military aircraft are shown in Fig. 4-7. The pipework of the systems is marked for identification of purpose

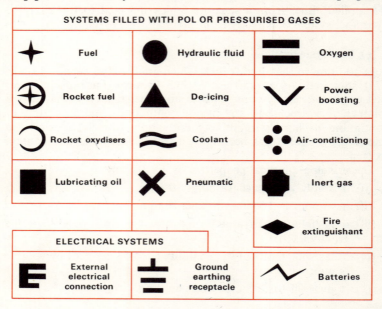

Fig. 4–7. Some of the symbols used in military aircraft to identify system pipelines and components. (Note: POL = petrol, oil, lubricants.)

at each side of every union, cock or other connection. The markings are printed slips bearing the identifying symbol and the general title of the system (*e.g.* fuel, hydraulic, pneumatic, etc.).

2. COCKPIT CANOPIES

Cockpit canopies (Fig. 4-8) are only found in military aircraft, such as fighters and bombers. They are slightly domed, hinged or sliding hoods over the seat positions (behind a windscreen of laminated safety glass or perspex panel, which is separate and fixed). Where the cockpit has tandem seating, there may be two separate hoods (*e.g.* Javelin and Phantom) or one longer hood (Gnat). On bomber aircraft only, the canopy may be jettisoned by the use of explosive bolts or other means, fired electrically by the pilot.

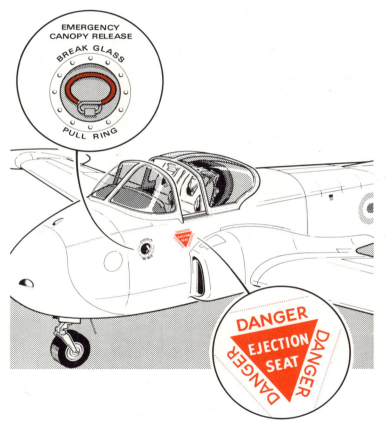

Fig. 4–8. Sketch showing a typical cockpit canopy.

When closed, the canopy is secured to the airframe by two locks, one at each side of the cockpit. Sliding canopies are permanently fitted into a guide rail on each side, and the guide rails are secured by the canopy locks. With hinged canopies, the hinge at the rear does not secure the canopy to the airframe: it is an opening hinge which allows the canopy to be detached when it is raised beyond a certain angle. If the canopy is opened normally by an electro-hydraulic or electro-pneumatic jack, there is an arrangement for disengaging the jack.

Canopy locks are linked to the aircraft's canopy jettison and seat ejection (*see* par. 3 below) systems, and they are opened automatically when either firing handle is pulled.

3. SEATING IN MILITARY AIRCRAFT

(a) Transport aircraft

Passenger seats in military transport fixed-wing aircraft (except light aircraft) are rearward-facing and grouped in pairs or threes on either side of a central aisle (*see* Fig. 4-4). This central aisle is narrow; in most types of aircraft its width is between 13½ and 17 in. (343–432 mm). Seating may be removed from transport aircraft in order to carry freight in the cabin. When a mixed load of passengers and freight is carried, the freight is stowed at the front of the cabin; seating then occupies the remaining space to the rear.

When paratroops are carried, individual seating is not provided. Folding 'benches' of webbing on tubular frames are fitted along the cabin walls, and additional rows may be erected along the centre; alternatively the paratroopers' heavy equipment may be lashed in the central area. The maximum number of paratroops which an aircraft may carry is greater than the maximum number of seated passengers.

(b) Pilot ejection seats

Most types of high speed fighter and bomber aircraft are fitted with ejection seats which are designed to enable the pilot and crew to leave the aircraft in an emergency. When travelling at speeds bordering on the speed of sound and higher, the slipstream would normally make this impossible; the ejection seat, however, is a means of 'firing' the occupant, together with the seat, into the air, so that he clears the slipstream and tail unit by main force. Subsequently, the pilot leaves the seat, and by opening his parachute, reaches the ground safely.

The type of seat at present in use by the RAF uses an explosive charge and is ejected upwards; that used by the United States Air Force (who have some forces stationed in this country), while differing in many details from that of the RAF, particularly as regards its actuation controls, does the same. It cannot be too strongly emphasised, however, that there is much development in the design of ejection seats, and that frequent variations in type and design are to be found. Consequently the information given in this chapter is of a general character, and as has already been said, firemen should take every opportunity of familiarising themselves with the types used in aircraft in their locality. Means exist for the distribution of the latest information on the subject and this, together with close liaison between the fire service and military authorities, must be used to keep up to date on all aspects of ejector seat design.

(i) *Martin-Baker ejection seats.* Most British and Commonwealth high-speed military aircraft are fitted with one or other of the various types (known as 'marks') of Martin-Baker seat (Fig. 4-9). The seat has also been adopted as a standard fitment by NATO and may therefore be found in some aircraft of European and American manufacture.

The main components of the apparatus are: the pilot's seat, propellable vertically upwards by means of an explosive cartridge; a locking catch, termed a 'sear', with which the firing pin for the cartridge is connected; a blind for the protection of the pilot's face, provided with a handle; and a gun for the firing of a steel bolt attached to a 'drogue', or small parachute.

When he requires to 'bale out', the pilot pulls the face blind handle forwards and downwards over his face. This action also has the effect of withdrawing the sear from the firing assembly, firing the cartridge and ejecting the seat. Alternatively, the seat may be fired by means of a second handle between the pilot's thighs. At the same time, the drogue gun is fired automatically and the steel bolt pulls out the drogue. The latter steadies the seat and pilot after ejection. On certain types of aircraft, an explosive canopy jettison mechanism is fitted. The entire escape action is still carried out by the one action of pulling either firing handle, but the first firing blows the canopy clear and the second firing ejects the seat.

(ii) *Folland lightweight ejection seats.* This seat was originally developed for its 'lightweight' properties for installation in the prototype 'Midge' aircraft and is currently a standard fitment in the Folland Gnat trainer. It may also occasionally be fitted in certain aircraft under development.

The seat structure is made almost entirely from light alloy and the main frame consists of two vertical side tubes joined at the top and bottom by two side beams. The seat itself, consisting of a shaped back and pan is designed for a normal back-pan type parachute with a survival pack including dinghy, forming a seat cushion. The operation of this type of ejector seat is similar to that of the Martin-

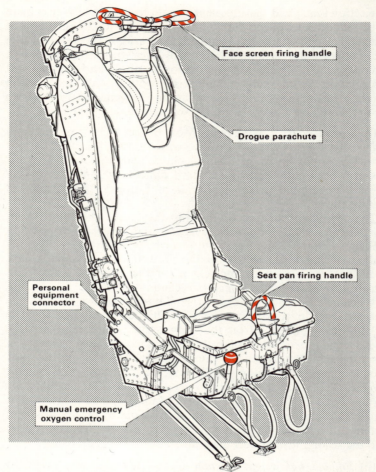

Fig. 4–9. A typical Martin-Baker ejection seat. (Note: the firing handles are generally coloured yellow and black.)

Baker, except that no drogue gun is fitted. The firing mechanism is operated by the pilot pulling the face blind forward and downward over his face, which releases the firing pin; this strikes the explosive charge and ejects the seat.

(iii) *American ejection seats.* The manufacture of the ejection seats fitted to American military aircraft is not confined to any one design, consequently the seats differ in detail, but achieve the same purpose as the British counterpart, and Fig. 4-10 shows the type of ejection seat as fitted to Phantom aircraft. It can be seen that there is a great similarity with the Martin-Baker ejection seat as incorporated in British military aircraft, although the firing controls are different; they are, however, coloured yellow and black as in British aircraft.

The seat is made safe by the insertion of a safety pin in the seat catapult firing mechanism located at the extreme top of the ejection seat. The ejection seat cannot be fired if the canopy has not been jettisoned, and the canopy cannot be jettisoned when in the fully open position. Nevertheless, even if the canopy is found, or can be,

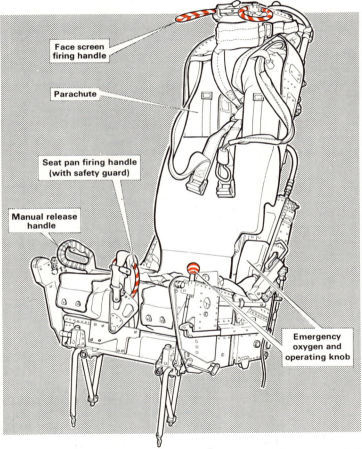

Face screen
firing handle

Parachute

Seat pan firing handle
(with safety guard)

Manual release
handle

Emergency
oxygen and
operating knob

Fig. 4–10. An ejection seat as fitted to USAF Phantom military aircraft. The firing handles are also coloured yellow and black.

195

opened fully, extreme caution should be taken when working in the cockpit and rescuers should stay clear of the ejection seat handles.

Section III—Rotary wing aircraft

Rotary wing aircraft, or helicopters as they are more popularly known, can be divided broadly into two categories:

(i) Small helicopters with two to five seats and a maximum fuel load of up to about 200 gallons (900 litres). These have a single engine driving a main rotor and a coupled tail rotor. The Scout, Sioux and Wasp are examples.

(ii) Larger helicopters which carry 10 to 30 persons and have a maximum fuel load between 200 and 700 gallons (900–3,200 litres). Usually these have two engines geared to drive a single main rotor and a coupled tail rotor. The Wessex, Whirlwind, and Sea King are examples (Fig. 4-11), although the Whirlwind and some types of Wessex have a single engine. Other helicopters of similar capacity which have two engines each driving a separate rotor (fore and aft) have been produced in the United States, but to date there are no British examples since the Belvedere.

1. CONSTRUCTION

The construction of the airframe of a helicopter is similar to the fuselage framework of fixed wing aircraft, but generally it is lighter. There are several reasons for this: it is not stressed to carry a main-plane; the cabin is not pressurised for high altitude flight; the under-carriage assemblies are comparatively small. The structure of a helicopter is more likely to include structural members of smaller cross-section, sheet metal of thinner gauges and very light alloys such as magnesium or elektron (a magnesium alloy with three to twelve per cent aluminium and about one per cent each of man-ganese and zinc).

Helicopters operating over water are often fitted with wheel flotation equipment which can impede rescue operations if the crash has occurred on land. This equipment is in the form of an inflatable bag fitted in a metal container on each wheel. A water-actuated device blows off the metal cover and at the same time inflates the bag to approximately 5 ft (1·52 m) in diameter. Whilst the device is protected against normal rainfall, a branch in close proximity may easily operate it. Care should be taken not to stand directly at the side of the wheels in case the disc does blow off, as this could cause

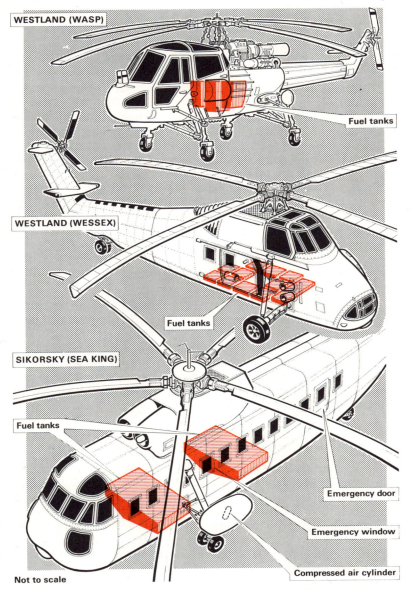

WESTLAND (WASP)

Fuel tanks

WESTLAND (WESSEX)

Fuel tanks

SIKORSKY (SEA KING)

Fuel tanks

Emergency door

Emergency window

Compressed air cylinder

Not to scale

Fig. 4–11. Three examples of typical rotary-wing aircraft (helicopters) showing the position of the fuel tanks.

serious injury to nearby personnel. In the event of accidental infla-
tion, the bag can be deflated by cutting it.

2. ENGINES

Most types of rotary wing aircraft have turbo-shaft engines, which
are essentially the same as turbo-prop engines, but are geared to
drive a rotor head instead of a propeller. The positions of the engines vary, but generally helicopters have an engine or coupled
engines in the nose (Wessex and Whirlwind), twin engines above the
cabin (SA 330 and Sea King) or an engine behind the cabin (Scout,
Sioux, Wasp and SA 341).

On larger helicopters, the engines are enclosed under a cowling
with inset fire access panels, but on some smaller types the engine is not
covered. The engine bay is separated from the airframe by fire-
resisting bulkheads and, usually, where there are twin engines, they
are separated from each other by a fire-resisting bulkhead.

3. ROTORS

Single engine helicopters have one main rotor overhead and a
small stabilising rotor at the tail. Two-engined craft have two main
rotors and no stabilising rotor. The tail stabilising rotor is perhaps
the greater hazard in that it is always at body height; it is coupled to
the main rotor and will continue to revolve for the same period after
the engines have been stopped. Some helicopters have a metal cage
around the tail rotor as a safeguard; on others the blades are
coloured to show a visible disc when they are in motion.

Section IV—Aerodrome equipment and facilities

This section deals with aerodrome organisational aspects which may
not seem immediately relevant to the local authority fire services.
Even where an aerodrome has its own fire services, it is essential that an
emergency plan should exist between the aerodrome authority and
the local fire authority to provide for aircraft accident or emergency
situations. When an accident occurs the local authority fire service
will be operating with the aerodrome rescue and fire-fighting services,
supporting their appliances and using the fire protection facilities of
the aerodrome.

In view of these factors an outline of aerodrome organisation and
equipment is given below.

1. CIVIL AERODROMES

Civil aerodromes in Great Britain are licensed by the Civil Aviation Authority, and it is a requirement of the licence that an efficient emergency organisation must be maintained, of which the fire and rescue service forms a part. A number of aerodromes are operated by the Civil Aviation Authority themselves; a British Airports Authority has been created with responsibility for London (Heathrow), Edinburgh, Gatwick, Prestwick and Stansted airports, and some other aerodromes (*e.g.* Birmingham, Liverpool, Manchester, Glasgow and Teesside are controlled by an Airport Committee of the local authority. Local authority firemen man the Liverpool aerodrome fire appliances, but at others, airport firemen are employed by the British Airports Authority, the Civil Aviation Authority or the fire authority. The size of the aerodrome and the type and frequency of aircraft using the airport determines the number of fire appliances, personnel and special equipment carried.

2. AIR TRAFFIC CONTROL

All movement of civil aircraft to and from this country as well as across the country is regulated by Air Traffic Control (ATC). A branch of the Royal Air Force performs a similar function in respect of Service aircraft, but the movement of all aircraft, both civil and military in the Control Zones or areas of Air Traffic Control, must be regulated by the ATC (Plates 67 and 68).

The ATC officer on duty is responsible for alerting the emergency services in the event of an accident on aerodromes, this is normally by means of a direct telephone link between the ATC and the aerodrome fire service watchroom. The call will be passed on to the local authority fire brigade by the aerodrome fire service dutyman or by other agencies which can ensure the prompt transmission of the call.

3. MARSHALLING ARRANGEMENTS

A further condition of the licence of civil aerodromes is that Emergency Orders must be prepared for any aerodrome so that adequate preparations are made for the efficient operation of all emergency services when an accident or fire occurs. It may not be possible or practicable for the vehicles and appliances of the fire, police and ambulance services to go direct to the scene of the accident, and at the larger aerodromes it is usual to have one or more 'rendezvous points' to which incoming appliances will report.

At these points there may be an internal telephone linked either to the aerodrome fire station watchroom or to the Air Traffic Control (ATC) through which the officers in charge can receive instructions. If the appliances and vehicles have to proceed into a movement area, a guide vehicle equipped with R/T communication with ATC can lead a group of vehicles so that there is no risk of interference with aircraft. At smaller aerodromes, a less complex arrangement is often adopted, having regard to the size of the aerodrome and the aircraft movement rate, but in all cases it is desirable to post a person at the aerodrome main gate to direct incoming appliances to the scene of the accident.

4. TYPES OF EMERGENCY

The responsibility for initiating emergency action by the aerodrome fire service rests with Air Traffic Control who classify emergencies under one of three headings: (a) local standby, (b) full emergency and (c) aircraft accidents.

(a) Local stand-by

When an aircraft approaching the airport is known or is suspected to have developed some defect but the trouble is not such as would normally involve any serious difficulty in effecting a safe landing, the aerodrome fire service will be called to stand-by.

A full attendance will be turned out and stationed, as instructed by ATC, at the pre-determined stand-by points for the runway in use. Any subsequent action is the responsibility of the officer in charge of the aerodrome fire service, who will order the appliances to return when he is satisfied that they are no longer required.

When weather has deteriorated to such an extent as to render the landing of aircraft more difficult or more difficult to observe, a local stand-by may be called even though no in-flight emergency has been indicated by the pilot of the landing aircraft.

(b) Full emergency

When it is known that an aircraft approaching the airport is in such trouble that there is danger of an accident on landing, a full emergency may be called by ATC. The aerodrome fire service will turn out a full attendance to the pre-determined stand-by points for the runway in use, as for a local stand-by, but in addition, the local authority fire brigade will also be called and will make a predetermined attendance. Ambulances, the civil aviation constabulary, if employed, or the local police are also informed. Not all aerodromes have a resident police organisation, but most have a security unit which may act in a similar fashion. A constable will direct incoming appliances and ambulances to the rendezvous point.

(c) Aircraft accidents

Calls to aircraft accidents will normally be received from the ATC, but if a call is received from other sources, or if an accident is observed, the aerodrome fire service will, if the location is on the airport, turn out a full attendance to the accident, and will pass the call to the local authority fire brigade. Amongst others, the ambulance service and civil airport constabulary will also be notified. If the accident is off the aerodrome, the attendance of the aerodrome fire service will be made in consultation with the ATC. The size of 'off aerodrome' attendance will, of course, have regard to the distance of the accident from the aerodrome boundary, the degree of support likely to be available from the local authority fire brigade and the anticipated traffic pattern at the aerodrome. It is usual to have an agreed attendance area outside the aerodrome boundary, but it is always possible to obtain a specialised appliance, *e.g.* one with a particular powered tool, or the assistance of officers who are familiar with aircraft, outside the attendance area.

(d) Domestic fires

The aerodrome fire service attends all domestic fires on the airport, and notifies the local authority fire brigade accordingly, who may provide an additional attendance.

(e) Additional facilities

Where an aerodrome is near the sea or any large area of water, the Emergency Orders generally provide for the summoning of assistance from the RNLI, Coastguard or other marine craft users, as well as the initiation of air-sea rescue procedures where this is appropriate. In mountainous, swampy or heavily-wooded country, the support of Service helicopter units may be requested.

(f) Attendances

The predetermined attendance to domestic fires and for full emergencies and aircraft accidents on the aerodrome is agreed beforehand with the local authority fire brigade. The domestic attendance will vary according to particular risks; for example, in some instances the aerodrome fire service alone may constitute the first attendance, although, of course, all calls are reported to the local authority fire brigade control. For other incidents the local authority fire brigade appliances augment the first attendance.

Where the senior member of the aerodrome fire service is in command at any fire or other incident he is responsible for initiating any necessary assistance messages, and for using the standard fire service message phraseology for this purpose. If a senior local authority officer attends he will take command of the incident, but if a senior member of the aerodrome fire service remains throughout in command, he will decide when to return local authority fire brigade appliances to their stations.

5. SPECIALISED APPLIANCES

The characteristics of the typical fire appliances used at civil and military aerodromes, as compared with conventional fire appliances, are as follows:

  (i) Their ability to travel across open country. This involves four-wheel drive, independent suspension and high ground clearance.

  (ii) Large capacity tanks. They must carry a sufficient amount of fire extinguishing agent to suppress large flame masses without reliance on other sources of supply.

  (iii) High output rates. An aircraft fire must be suppressed in the minimum time to make survival possible and rescue feasible. The delivery systems are designed for very high output rates.

  (iv) Pre-arranged delivery equipment. At most survivable accidents, the appliance is positioned close to the aircraft and complete delivery lines are stowed ready for one basic operation generally through a single delivery length.

(a) Foam tenders

Various types of foam tender/pump are to be found; two types are shown in Plates 70 and 73. Generally there are foam deliveries on each side of the appliance and often a foam monitor mounted on the roof. Foam compound and water are carried in separate tanks with varying capacities. 100 gallons (455 litres) of foam compound and 800 gallons (3 637 litres) of water would be average capacities of the tanks. Foam-making branchpipes and monitor can be operated separately or together (Plate 74).

Modern appliances would have an automatic foam proportioner device (*e.g.* the 'Vactrol 2' is one type used) and this governs automatically the amount of foam compound and water supplied to the branches as the throttle is operated.

(b) Carbon dioxide tenders

Carbon dioxide cylinders are mounted in banks and these are connected via manifolds to delivery hose reels. The operation of the discharge lever generally actuates the whole bank of cylinders but provision is also made for some cylinders to be operated individually. The delivery hose reels terminate in a discharge horn. A Cardox appliance of BAA is shown in Plate 71.

(c) Rescue tenders

Rescue tenders (Plate 72) carry specialised equipment specifically for dealing with initial rescue, and include such items as:

Searchlights and floodlights
Stretcher-ladders
Electric or pneumatic cutting tools
Breathing and resuscitation apparatus
Grab and ceiling hooks
Cable cutters

A dry powder installation is also often included on rescue tenders, to enable a quick knockdown of fire to be made. The dry powder cylinder has a CO_2 container mounted on it to expel the powder which is directed through delivery hoses to two pistol-grip type of nozzles. When both nozzles are in use, the overall discharge time with a 200 lb (90·7 kg) dry powder cylinder is about 60 seconds. An effective throw of about 20 ft (6·10 m) is obtained.

(d) Protective clothing

Various types of clothing designed for protection against radiant heat and flame lick may be found on aircraft tenders, but none is designed to allow deliberate entry into a flame mass. The clothing is not gastight and the wearer inhales the surrounding air so he must keep clear of super-heated gases. The clothing includes a suit, boots, a helmet with visor, and gloves. Aluminised asbestos is often used for protective clothing.

It is recommended that supporting local authority firemen should *not* wear such protective clothing without previous training or experience in its use.

6. WATER SUPPLIES AT AERODROMES

The system of water supply usually provided at aerodromes for fire-fighting purposes is classified under two headings: (a) primary, (b) secondary.

(a) Primary water supplies

The primary supply consists of a below ground water mains system which is usually fed from street mains of the local water undertaking. The size of the airport main is therefore generally determined by the size of the water company's supply, usually mains of 6 in. (152 mm) or larger. The supply is often fed into a ring main system which forms a complete circuit, which has the advantage of reducing friction loss, water will flow in either direction and a section may be isolated by sluice valves without interfering with the supply of other parts.

(b) Secondary supplies

Additional water for emergency purposes is in the form of tanks (either below or above ground) of varying capacities, or storm water catchments may be found at some airports. Natural supplementary supplies consist of ponds, rivers, streams or the sea.

(c) By-pass valves

The water supply to aerodromes is usually metered and in an emergency it is necessary for a valve to be operated to by-pass the meter. All members of aerodrome fire services will be familiar with the location and method of operation of by-pass valves.

(d) Fire hydrants

Fire hydrants are placed at strategic points around airports at positions governed by the fire hazard, and are indicated by hydrant plates. Generally hydrant outlets are below ground level and stand-pipes have to be shipped to get to work. Some airports, however, are provided with above ground (pillar) hydrants. (See Chapter 5, Fig. 5–19, page 296).

(e) High level water storage tanks

High level water storage tanks are provided on many aerodromes and are usually 30 to 45 ft (9·14 to 10·67 m) high although some may be as high as 80 ft (24·38 m). Tanks may hold up to 100,000 gallons (454 610 litres).

(f) Ground level reservoirs

The purpose of ground level reservoirs at aerodromes is to provide an increase in the pressure in the fire mains by drawing water by booster pump from a large reservoir, usually containing 100,000 to 200,000 gallons (454 610 to 909 220 litres) of water. The pumps are usually in pairs (one petrol and the other electric). The running, care and maintenance of booster pumps is undertaken by the Aerodrome Works Department, but aerodrome fire personnel will be acquainted with the location and method of operation of the pumps.

(g) Catchment facilities

At some airports catchment facilities are provided whereby surface water drainage is stored and can be boosted as required to pressures as high as 125 lbf/in^2 (8·6 bars). Such a system is commonly referred to as 'dirty water' supply and is generally made available to hydrants sited adjacent to runways, taxiways and near to large airport buildings.

7. MILITARY AERODROMES

The Ministry of Defence (Air Force Department) maintains crash rescue services at all flying stations. At non-airfield stations, fire stations are maintained to provide immediate response to a fire, but are not self-sufficient and rely mainly on the resources of local authority fire brigades. In aircraft crash fire fighting and rescue work, the time factor is critical and the Air Force Department has an establishment of firemen and special appliances at flying stations held specifically for aircraft rescue and fire fighting. This establishment is primarily geared to enable rescue to be effected from the type of aircraft normally using the airfield. The firemen may be either civilians employed by the Air Force Department Fire Service or RAF Regiment firemen, but the fire section will not consist of a mixture of both.

When a fire occurs at an RAF station, an officer appointed by the CO, usually a civilian station fire officer or a suitably trained RAF Regiment officer, will take charge, but if the local authority fire brigade is called, control of fire-fighting operations is handed over to the senior officer of the local authority brigade, and RAF or AFDFS personnel give their support, as required. Where the RAF station is equipped with special appliances and fully-trained crews (as at the major civil airports), arrangements are generally made for the senior member of the RAF fire crew to direct operations or to advise the senior local authority fire brigade officer on the conduct of operations.

Whenever flying is in progress or aircraft are being moved or serviced on the ground, the station fire service rescue and fire-fighting appliances are kept manned and in a state of immediate readiness. The appliances used at RAF stations are similar to those already described for civil airports.

Section V—Fire fighting and rescue

The primary object in aircraft accident operations is to save life and fire fighting should be conducted so as to create conditions in which survival is possible and in which rescue attempts may proceed. Control of the fire situation is the first objective and total extinguishment of the fire may not save the aircraft.

Although fires do not always occur at the moment of impact, the damaged aircraft contains sources of potential ignition which can initiate a fire some time after the accident has occurred. Once a fire is started, it may spread rapidly to involve all of the exposed fuel and reach lethal proportions in which survival is impossible.

At aerodromes the initial attack is likely to be made with the specialised appliances maintained at the airport as their communication link with Air Traffic Control enables them to enter restricted areas under control and surveillance. If a full emergency has been initiated by ATC the appliances will have taken up their predetermined stand-by positions on the runway to be used. The aerodrome emergency plan will ensure that any local authority fire brigade attendance already available or which may arrive subsequently can be directed to the scene of the incident without delay. Where a pilot is unable to land at an airfield, he will try to select flat terrain, such as playing fields or open pastureland, but in many cases the pilot has no alternative and has to make a 'crash' landing in a remote and sometimes inaccessible part of the country which may or may not be inhabited. An aircraft, however, may crash in a built-up area, in which case the incident may well attain 'major disaster' proportions.

1. FEATURES OF AIRCRAFT FIRES

An aircraft fire usually breaks out suddenly and reaches maximum intensity in a very short period of time. A considerable proportion of the space in an aircraft is occupied by highly flammable systems (Fig. 4-3). Of these the ignition of escaping fuel creates the dominant feature of aircraft fires. This can result in a very rapid development of fire from ignition to peak intensity with the generation of intense heat. Escaping fuel will flow outward over a large surface area and will present widespread flame frontages with flames of considerable length and large volumes of dense smoke. The situation may be worsened by distortion of the airframe structure and melting of pipework by heat resulting in a release of more fuel and other changes in the fire situation. The magnesium content of an aircraft can also aggravate the intensity of the fire.

2. FIRE FIGHTING ON AERODROMES

Once a pilot has knowledge that a serious defect has developed or is likely to develop, he will naturally do his utmost to ensure the safety of his aircraft, crew, passengers and cargo, and a predetermined 'drill' is carried out by all members of the crew. When in possession of the facts, the ATC authorities will give the aircraft its instructions and immediate priority to use any air lane that is free of traffic with a view to landing at the nearest airfield. Other aircraft may be directed to alter course to keep the area in the vicinity of the distressed aircraft clear, and in some circumstances an aircraft may circle an airfield for a considerable time to exhaust excess fuel.

(a) Positioning of appliances

The positions adopted by the first aerodrome fire appliances will have regard to a number of tactical considerations. Wherever possible, due to the nature of the extinguishing agents to be used and the exposure of the fuselage to fire, advantage should be taken of the wind direction, the attack being mounted downwind if at all possible. Modern foam-producing appliances have the ability to produce foam whilst in motion and this gives them greater tactical advantages than were possible with older machines which had to stop before foam production could start. With either type of appliance, it is essential to avoid placing the vehicle in jeopardy by parking it in areas of exposed fuel or leaving it where it may be in hazard as fuel flows down slopes to where it is positioned.

Positioning of appliances must be swift and decisive, with due regard to terrain and the existing fire situation. In certain instances, it may be necessary to keep appliances on paved or consolidated surfaces and to use extended hose lines to reach the aircraft which is located on soft or impassable ground. Although this inevitably adds to the time taken to mount the attack, it is preferable to the immobilisation of appliances. At all times the officer in charge must recognise the need to withdraw men and appliances should there be a massive release of fuel which places his force in unacceptable danger.

(b) Methods of attack

The main objective in fire fighting is to isolate the fuselage from the effects of fire and radiated heat, to preserve exit routes in use by occupants and to facilitate access to the aircraft for rescue purposes. If fire is in the engine nacelles or wings only, a stop should be attempted at the wing roots. If, as is likely, fuel is leaking from tanks and spreading on the ground, the object should be to keep this whole area of fire down long enough for rescues to be effected. With a wind blowing, it may be possible to keep one side of the aircraft relatively free of smoke and heat, and fire-fighting efforts should be concentrated on this. All parts of the fuselage exposed to fire should be protected if possible as aircraft skin material is very rapidly penetrated. Additionally, the effect of an external fire is to decompose sealant and trim material within the passenger cabin causing smoke and fumes to be evolved in quantity.

A mass application of foam should be the main attack on the fire in an endeavour to achieve maximum cooling and a rapid suppression of the fire. Since, however, foam like other extinguishing agents has limitations, a suitable backing-up agent must be available to deal with those pockets of fire which are inaccessible to direct foam application. Carbon dioxide, dry powders or vaporising liquid (halogen) agents are the most suitable for this purpose. The use of these backing-up agents should be confined to running liquid fuel fires, the inhibition of enclosed spaces such as wing voids, or to deal with special fires such as in engine nacelles or undercarriage assemblies.

Foam branches should be positioned as closely as possible to the fuselage, the initial discharge being directed along the line of the fuselage so that the foam drives the fire outwards. When selecting the ideal position for the branchpipe, it should be remembered that the wind has considerable influence upon the rate of fire and heat travel. The position should be chosen with this in mind, thus utilising the wind whenever possible to assist in foam application. Great caution should be used when applying foam to the fuselage as there is a risk of flushing fuel under the fuselage where it can present a serious hazard. Similar care should be taken to avoid the possibility of a jet disturbing the foam blanket already laid on a liquid fuel surface.

The basic methods of applying foam are discussed in detail in Chapter 5, 'Fires in Oil Refineries' and the same methods can be used on aircraft. One is to use a long striking branchpipe or monitor and allow the foam to fall on to the area, or alternatively a diffused jet can be used at close range. Foam can often be applied by deflecting from another surface, such as the contour of the fuselage or mainplane.

The officer in charge will have to decide quickly which particular pattern of equipment positioning is best suited to his available resources. At an aircraft fire there is little time for individual briefing of crew members and the initial layout may well have to be adjusted to cope with existing circumstances, but it is necessary that crews should know exactly what is their first action immediately on arrival, and this calls for specific training of airport fire service firemen well in advance. There should be a standard layout of equipment even when fire has not broken out; at least one jet should be manned and in readiness to go into immediate action should a fire start.

(c) Combined agent technique

Fig. 4-12 shows three examples of the positioning of appliances using two foam tenders and a dry powder, carbon dioxide or halogen (vaporising liquid) unit. The object is to attack with the wind as feasible and to knock down bulk flame with the supporting dry powder, carbon dioxide or vaporising liquid unit. The foam tender crews protect the fuselage to prepare a rescue path even if against the wind and to cut off the fire at the wing roots. Arrangements should be put in hand for reinforcing water and foam supplies.

(d) Technique using one foam tender

The basic principles of fire fighting at smaller airports where only one foam tender is immediately available are shown in Fig. 4-13. In this case the technique is to attack from an upwind position, aiming to blanket the area of fire or spilled fuel adjacent to the fuselage. If a water tender or pump is available it keeps the foam tender supplied with water. Once a rescue path is available, every effort should be made to keep it open. Screened areas which cannot be reached with foam should be inhibited with dry powder, carbon dioxide or vaporising liquid as available.

(e) Ground incidents

Fires sometimes occur in aircraft on the ground from a variety of causes, generally as a result of engine starting or closing down operations, from an accidental spillage of fuel during filling operations or as a result of collision with another aircraft, vehicle or structure whilst taxying.

When attending such an incident, drivers of appliances should avoid passing through smoke at speed in the vicinity of the fire as ground crews and possibly passengers may be on the far side of the smoke zone. Warning horns, sirens or bells should be sounded continually up to the moment of positioning. Fire appliance indicating flashing or revolving lights should be kept in operation until arrival.

(f) Low speed accidents

Typical of this type of accident are those that occur when an aircraft is landing, taking off, overshooting or undershooting on a runway. The term low-speed is a relative one as speeds on landing and

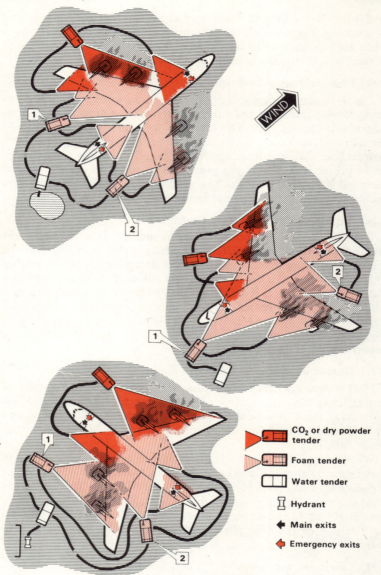

Fig. 4–12. *Three examples of the positioning of appliances when using two foam tenders supported by a dry powder, carbon dioxide or vaporising liquid unit.*

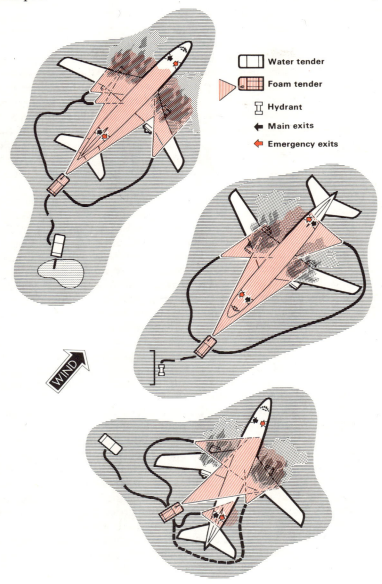

Fig. 4–13. Three examples of the positioning of one foam tender with a back-up supply of water.

211

take off can exceed 100 mph (160 km/hr). Because of the lower speed, the chances of occupant survival are high and conditions for rescue are therefore sometimes favourable.

Probably the commonest example of the low speed accident is the belly landing, which can result from a failure of the undercarriage retracting gear or the hydraulic supply itself, or from the necessity of landing the aircraft at very short notice before the undercarriage has had time to reach the correct landing position (Plates 80 and 81). Fuel lines and even tanks may be ruptured by the scraping of the lower part of the aircraft on the ground, and tremendous heat and sparks may be produced at the same time. This result is more likely on the concrete or tarmac of an airfield than on the soft ground beyond it.

After a belly landing, a large aircraft is likely to be substantially intact and there is some prospect of cabin doors or at least escape hatches being openable from the inside, and of the majority of the occupants being able to make their own way out. If fire breaks out, an immediate attack should be made to keep it clear of the fuselage and especially at the escape points while the crew organise the evacuation of occupants. There is little to be gained in such circumstances by entry into the aircraft of fire-fighting personnel, since this may obstruct exit gangways and may not be necessary unless the crew are incapacitated. Later, however, when walking occupants are out of the way or when fire conditions may be making evacuation difficult, rescue operations as such are more appropriate and should be undertaken with speed. Everything depends on the immediate subduing of fire, if it has broken out, or the prevention of an outbreak by blanketing with foam.

Fire does not always break out, but can do so at any time following the accident. Where an accident without immediate fire has occurred, equipment should be laid out and a constant readiness maintained. Free fuel should be covered with a blanket of foam. If fuel is leaking from ruptured tanks or supply lines, an endeavour should be made to seal off the flow. Airport firemen with their more expert knowledge may be able to isolate master and magneto switches and to disconnect, where possible, batteries (the ground lead should be disconnected first). A check should be made to ensure that all passengers and crew have been evacuated. No smoking and no naked light should be permitted, and no one, except recognised authorities, should be allowed to touch or to enter the aircraft.

(g) Effect of metals on fire fighting

Aluminium will ignite when heated to 800°C, but the major

airframe alloys, duralumin, alclad, etc., are not ignited in aircraft fires. A possible reason for this is that the melting point of aluminium is 200°C below its ignition temperature, so that it fuses and drips to the ground some time before it can be ignited. In doing so, it will often escape into an area where temperatures are significantly lower, and in this molten form it is easily covered and effectively sealed by the mass discharge of foam.

With magnesium the fire hazard is, of course, very great. Large sections are not easily ignited but when this does happen, the metal burns violently and almost explosively (Plate 69). Magnesium fires are not likely to be extinguished by the mass discharge of foam normally approved for aircraft fires, whilst on the other hand the application of water intensifies the already brilliant glare and there may be sporadic and spectacular flashes showering glowing particles around the area. This activity resembles a firework display, but the quantity of water which magnesium is capable of breaking down is only three-quarters of its own weight, and as the magnesium and water are in contact only at their surfaces, the proportion of a continuous stream of water which is broken down is relatively small. If a stream of water is maintained, most of it is able to cool the magnesium until it solidifies and the fire will be extinguished. Magnesium alloys burn only when molten and their melting points are about 600°C, the actual figure depending on the composition of the alloy.

It is wiser, therefore, to use a hand-controlled branch, commencing with a spray and converting it slowly to a jet. When a jet is used, care should be taken to keep it low and to protect the face. Once the first explosion danger has passed, the metal should be attacked with a concentrated jet to achieve swamping, working progressively over the burning surface.

Both titanium and stainless steel would have to be subjected to temperatures above 2,000°C for some time to ignite, and this is not likely at an accident where the fire services are in attendance. If titanium is ignited, however, it should be remembered that it is the only metal used in aircraft construction which releases its product of combustion (titanium dioxide) into the air. This is non-toxic but is an extremely dense vapour which would make visibility difficult.

(h) Brake and wheel assemblies

Excessive braking is liable to produce a rapid build-up of heat in brake and wheel assemblies. It has been found, especially with large aircraft, that this may result in brake or wheel fires or delayed tyre failure due to the transmission of heat from the brakes (Plate 78). Tyre failure of this sort can occur some time after the aircraft has come to rest if very high temperatures have been reached in the brake and wheel assemblies. For this reason, an aircraft with an overheated wheel should be isolated until natural or assisted cooling lowers the temperature to an acceptable level.

Cooling of the wheel assembly is beneficial, but unless it is carried out very carefully it might cause damage which would not necessarily be apparent and might only subsequently be revealed. Aerodrome firemen, when called to an aircraft with overheated brakes, generally refrain from applying cooling water unless they are satisfied that a fire is developing which is likely to involve the wheel assembly, tyres or associated components.

If water has to be used, it should be applied in as fine a spray as possible and should be directed so as to cover the whole wheel assembly. Spot cooling must be avoided. The affected wheel should be approached from the front or rear and men or appliances should not be positioned alongside the wheel because of the risk of injury or damage should rim failure occur. Because of the risk of collapse of landing gear struts, the number of persons working beneath any part of the aircraft should be kept to a minimum consistent with operational requirements; all other persons should be kept clear.

(j) Foaming of runways

It is considered in some quarters that in certain circumstances (*e.g.* in an emergency belly-landing with wheels up or when an aircraft has defective nose gear) it may be advantageous to provide a foam blanket on a runway before the aircraft makes the emergency landing, although the concept has not gained universal acceptance. The suggested advantages of such a foam blanket are the reduction of the extent of damage, the reduction of friction and thereby the decrease (by permitting slippage) of the deceleration forces imposed on the aircraft and the reduction of friction sparks which might ignite fuel spilled as the result of the impact. On the other hand, there must be sufficient time available for accomplishing the production and distribution of the foam blanket before the aircraft alights, and there must be adequate facilities at the airport to divert traffic on to other runways.

In this country, the practice of foaming runways is not carried out at civil airports, but at two military aerodromes which are geographically sited strategically at RAF Manston and RAF Leeming, special equipment and appliances are available for foaming runways. The method adopted is that special trucks equipped to dispense foam through ground sweep nozzles or special boom nozzles are used to deliver foam from devices to the rear of the sides of the appliance.

The length, width and depth of the foam pattern will vary with the type of emergency, the type of aircraft, the quantities of foam available and the time factor. To be effective, a continuous layer of foam in the proposed slide path is essential as any interruptions, holes or breaks might result in the generation of sparks. The foam should be evenly distributed at least 2 in. (50 mm) in depth.

Following the foam-laying operation, the aerodrome fire crew would take up stand-by positions which recognise the risk of the aircraft leaving the runway on landing, more particularly where the undercarriage is not symmetrically arranged. After the aircraft touches down, the fire-fighting and rescue vehicles should follow the aircraft and be ready to get to work.

3. FIRE FIGHTING OUTSIDE AERODROMES

When an aircraft in flight develops an emergency condition the pilot will make every effort to land at an aerodrome, his ability to do so depending on the nature of the emergency and the time this provides for selecting a suitable aerodrome. It is possible, however, that conditions may cause the aircraft to fail to reach the aerodrome and although the pilot may seek a relatively level and open area for his emergency landing this may not be sufficient to prevent an accident. Additionally, a sudden structural failure in an aircraft may lead to its uncontrolled descent despite the skills of the aircrew. Aircraft accidents may therefore occur wherever aircraft fly and it is is in these landings, on unprepared surfaces and critical conditions, that the most serious damage and loss of life is likely.

(a) Locating the incident

One of the fire officer's main objectives in approaching the scene of a reported aircraft accident is to locate the aircraft or wreckage at the earliest possible moment and to reach it by the quickest route. If the aircraft was in touch with ATC up to the time of the accident and the call originates from that control, there may be a clear indication of the aircraft's whereabouts and some details of the type of plane, number of passengers, etc. Failing any exact location in advance, a good knowledge of local topography will play a vital part and for this reason personnel in rural areas particularly on aircraft routes, should be familiar with the local names of farms, hotels, etc.

A circling aircraft may be an indication of the whereabouts of a reported accident, or at night, the glow of a fire may identify it. It is important to know the condition to be expected on the roads in the locality, especially in winter, and the best avenues of approach for heavy vehicles.

Once the first attendance has found the scene of the crash, any assistance message should include exact details of the location and it is useful to post a guide if necessary to direct subsequent appliances; a bystander if available may be pressed into service for this task.

(b) Cross-country travel

It is always better to keep appliances on hard surfaces, even though the route may be a little longer than to risk their becoming bogged down and immobilised. When driving on hard rough ground, a low gear should be engaged and the vehicle should be driven as slowly as necessary to retain control of the steering, avoiding drops or bumps which might exceed the ground clearance of the vehicle. All appliances driven through fields should follow the same track, where possible, to enable any following vehicles to find the way easily. A vehicle should never be left blocking a path or roadway, as this may be the only traversable route to the incident; if a vehicle has to be left unattended, it should be properly parked, or, if merely unable to proceed, it should be backed into a convenient field or opening.

(c) Approach of appliances

In the final stages of the approach to the accident, it is essential to keep a careful watch for survivors who may have been thrown from the aircraft or have made their escape. If the approach route corresponds to the slide path of the aircraft there may also be debris to be avoided. Near the aircraft the ground may be contaminated by released fuel and this will present a hazard. Appliances should not manoeuvre or position in such locations and ideally a position up-wind and up-contour should be adopted to avoid fuel vapours or liquid fuel travel.

The siting of appliances should in general be the same as for an accident on an airfield (*see* page 207), but of course hard standing may not be available, and the terrain may be very rough. Similarly, any vehicle not in use should be parked clear of the aircraft accident and in a position of safety.

(d) Fire fighting

If the crash occurs in the country, only one appliance may attend initially, without any special equipment or foam, and Fig. 4-14 shows a plan of attack using equipment generally available in municipal or rural areas. The basic principles are, of course, to attack with the wind as feasible, and to approach along the fuselage with spray nozzles to cool it and to drive any free fuel away from the occupied portion. Where rescues have to be made, a rescue path must be protected. Fire extinguishment may not be possible, but preservation of fuselage integrity and the reduction of temperature is essential. As more assistance becomes available, additional branches can be got to work from the pump as the water supplies allow.

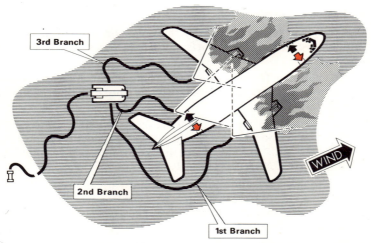

Fig. 4–14. A suggested plan of attack using one appliance. The number of branches which can be got to work will depend on the reinforcing help available.

If no fire is present on arrival, any spilled fuel adjacent to the aircraft should be blanketed with such foam as it may be possible for the initial appliance to produce. This will limit the burn-back risk if the spillage is ignited during rescue operations.

(e) Survivors

A sharp lookout will have been made for survivors when approaching the scene of the accident. It should be remembered that some may have been thrown clear and may have crawled a considerable distance in their efforts to summon help. It will be necessary to find out the number of persons aboard the aircraft, which, in the case of a large passenger aircraft, may be several hundreds. It is a police responsibility to do this, but in the absence of the police, a message should be sent to brigade control asking that this information be provided. The nearest ATC centre will be able to obtain this information, and it will speed the answer if the ATC centre can be given the aircraft registration letters or numbers, the aircraft type or the airline or service operating the flight. All, or any part of this intelligence will assist in identifying the flight and, in time, will produce the details of passengers.

(f) Post-accident discipline

This duty will be taken over by the police on arrival, but in the meantime, fire brigade personnel may have to assume some of the following tasks:

(i) No smoking. This must be strictly enforced. Neither survivors, onlookers nor rescuers must be allowed to smoke in the vicinity of the crash.

(ii) Onlookers must be kept back as far as possible in an uphill and upwind direction to minimise the risk from a possible explosion. If radiation hazards are suspected, smoke from the fire should be avoided (*see* par. 7, 'Special Hazards').

(iii) Souvenirs. Under no circumstances must any person be allowed to remove any part of a crashed aircraft; apart from the fact that this would be theft, it may also be harmful. The part taken may be the one required by the accident prevention officers to help them determine why the aircraft crashed.

(iv) If the aircraft has crashed in the vicinity of buildings, their occupants should be advised to leave the buildings by the farther side and remain in a safe area until further notice. Meanwhile, all doors and windows facing the aircraft should be closed, gas or electricity turned off at the mains and any oil lamps or stoves or other domestic fires should be extinguished.

(v) Personnel should be instructed to recover any aircraft documents which may have survived as these can contribute to the accident investigation.

(vi) Nobody should be allowed to touch any control lever or switch except as far as it is necessary to do so for rescue purposes. Any alteration in control setting or switch position which is made must be reported to the accident investigation team.

(vii) The location of any bodies recovered should be recorded as accurately as possible, particularly those from the flight deck.

(viii) Flight recorder. The location of the flight recorder should be identified if possible and it should be protected from further damage by fire. No attempt should be made to recover it unless it is likely to be lost, *e.g.* if it may sink into marshy ground or fall over a cliff. In certain circumstances unskilled removal of a flight recorder may damage the recorded information (*see* also page 187).

(g) Crashes on to buildings

This type of accident can have such disastrous results and present so many problems and complications that the fire brigade crews attending may be required to use their skill and knowledge of fire fighting, rescue, special services and salvage at one and the same time. It is evident, therefore, that each incident must be tackled according to the circumstances found at the time, commencing with the officer in charge making a rapid but accurate assessment of the situation.

The aircraft will normally have broken up on impact and the wreckage will have caused widespread damage to surrounding property, hence the need for an inspection of the area as soon as practicable. Fires can be widely separated and spread with great speed due to scattered fuel, fractured gas and electrical services, domestic fires and other causes. Roofs and upper storeys of buildings may suffer considerable damage and the collapse of floors and walls can well aggravate the rescue problems. Serious or superficial injuries may be caused to people within and outside the buildings already threatened by fire or other dangers, as well as to the occupants of the aircraft. In general, such an incident may well be classified as a 'major disaster' (*see* Part 6A of the *Manual*, Chapter 1, Section IV).

A search of properties should be undertaken by a responsible person or persons with a view to casualties being removed from further danger. Buildings adjacent to the incident should be evacuated, fires in neighbouring homes extinguished, gas and electric mains turned off, smoking prohibited and all other steps taken to avoid the risk of any gas/air mixture which may be present. It is almost certain that fuel tanks will be severely damaged and the contents distributed over a wide area. Partly empty tanks or damaged engines may explode causing further damage and casualties. Immediate steps should be taken to prevent fuel running down the gutters and so out of the immediate danger area, as the risk of a 'flash back' is obvious. A generous assessment of assistance required should be made and appropriate local authority department and public undertakings should be advised via brigade control. If fuel enters sewers or drains, it should be washed down with as much water as possible, and the Borough Engineer of Surveyor should be informed of the action being taken.

If no fire has occurred, all fuel and engines should be covered with a blanket of foam and the same precautions taken as described in preceding paragraphs.

(h) Nose dives and cartwheel accidents

On soft ground a nose dive high speed crash usually results in a large crater within which is contained the wreckage of the fuselage and engines, a quantity of fuel and possibly the bodies of the occupants. Under such conditions, there is little hope of rescue being carried out. Engines may penetrate as much as 20 ft (6 m) into the ground and throw up a large mass of earth. In some cases, an explosion may ensue and scatter parts of the wreckage. Those parts of the aircraft in the crater will burn fiercely often with small underground explosions.

Where possible a foam seal should be applied, otherwise it may be necessary or advantageous to flood the hole and apply a foam blanket on the water, or to apply high expansion foam to completely cover the wreckage. No salvage work should be undertaken until the debris is thoroughly cold.

An aircraft striking the ground violently with its wing tip may turn over before finally coming to rest. Here again, wreckage and fuel will be spread over a wide area, the aircraft may break its back and throw the occupants clear. Fittings within the aircraft are likely to be torn free and rescue operations will be difficult. A search for injured persons should be carried out over the accident area, and when rescue operations are completed, the remaining fires should be suitably tackled with foam or water if water supplies permit. Fires which do not involve property and cannot easily be reached may be allowed to burn themselves out.

(j) Crashes into water

Where airports are situated adjacent to large areas of water, there is a risk that an aircraft accident may result in the aircraft crashing into the water, so the aerodrome fire-fighting equipment generally includes some type of inshore rescue craft. In such an accident the possibility of fire is appreciably reduced due to the suppression of ignition sources, but the surface of the water will probably be covered with fuel, whether burning or not.

As soon as possible, pockets of fuel should be broken up or moved with large velocity jets, or neutralised by covering with foam or a high concentration of chemical agents. Calm surfaces will usually present a greater problem than choppy or rough surfaces. If wreckage is on the bank, foam equipment should be laid out in readiness to check any fire which may threaten it. If the aircraft is half in and half out of the water and has not taken fire, rescue operations should be carried out with great care, since fuel rising to the surface may come into contact with heated parts of the engines, or with the exhaust of boats used to reach the aircraft.

Where occupied sections of aircraft are found floating, care should be taken not to disturb their watertight integrity. Removal of occupants should be accomplished as smoothly and quickly as possible, as any shift in weight or lapse of time may result in the section sinking. Rescuers should beware that they themselves do not become trapped and drowned. Where occupied sections are found submerged, there remains the possibility that there may be enough air inside to maintain life. Divers, if available, may be the only way to reach trapped occupants.

4. RESCUE FROM CIVIL AIRCRAFT

The rescue of persons involved in an aircraft accident should be undertaken with the utmost speed. Whilst care is necessary in the evacuation of injured occupants so as not to aggravate their injuries, removal from the fire-threatened area is the primary consideration.

Although the principal objective is to save life, it is always possible that a fire may occur during rescue operations, if it has not already happened, and so rescue operations must go hand in hand with the fire-fighting measures already described in preceding paragraphs. Details are given below of the methods of access and exit as applicable to civil aircraft, but because of the great differences between various types of aircraft and between aircraft of the same type used by different operators, firemen liable to attend aircraft accident fires are recommended to keep their knowledge up to date by frequent visits to aerodromes in their locality.

(a) Approach to aircraft with engines running

In certain circumstances it may be necessary to approach an aircraft which has declared an emergency and which has one or more of its engines running. This will hamper rescue operations to some extent, particularly at night when vision is limited.

Firemen should not approach nearer than 25 ft (7·5 m) from the intake of an operating jet engine to avoid being ingested and not nearer than 150 ft (45 m) from the rear to avoid being burned by the blast. Fig. 4-15 shows the best method of approach to a jet engined aircraft if the engines are still running.

It is a basic practice never to walk through the propeller disc (the swept area of a rotating propeller) at any time, and the propellers should never be touched, even when at rest. Most propellers have blade markings in paint which indicate the disc when the blades are rotating, but it is not easy to see these at night. The use of lighting equipment is essential when moving around aircraft under power at night.

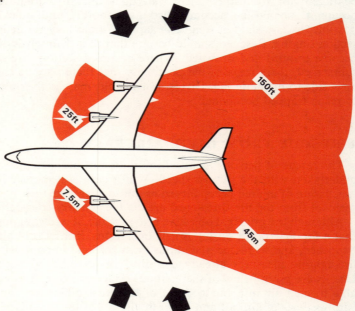

Fig. 4–15. *Diagram showing recommended lanes of approach to turbine-engined aircraft and safe distances to avoid jet streams.*

(b) Main passenger doors

The first approach should be made by way of the passenger doors. It is always easier to carry a person through a door than to manipulate him through a window. Large modern aircraft often have several doors: two on the port side as passenger entrances and two opposite these on the starboard side for cabin and galley servicing, would be fairly typical. There are instances, however, where the main passenger entrance is up through the underside of the fuselage (*e.g.* Caravelle and BAC-111).

Doors can be opened from outside the aircraft. The operating handles are normally recessed and flush fitted to the skin of the fuselage. Fig. 4-16 shows some of the normal emergency methods of

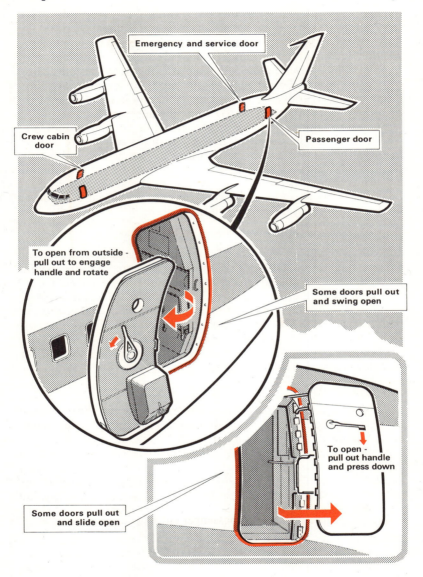

Fig. 4–16. *Two methods of opening doors in an emergency. Note that there is a contrasting band of colour around the perimeter of the door.*

223

opening doors and although these vary from one aircraft to another, the operating instructions are always clearly indicated.

A recent innovation which will eventually become standard requires the definition of doors (and window exits) by a contrasting band of colour around their perimeter which is clearly visible against the airline livery. This eliminates the need for looking for joints, although this is probably not necessary in any case because of the operating instructions associated with all emergency exits.

Failure to appreciate the correct method of opening a door may lead to difficulty in rescue operations, as doors can jam if handled inefficiently. Should a door be found to be jammed, it will usually be quicker to force it by applying leverage at the right spot than to achieve entry and rescue through another opening. Firemen who are on duty at airports should take every opportunity to learn the correct methods of forcing the various types of door.

(c) Emergency stairs

Modern giant aircraft make it impossible for passengers to descend from normal doors without the use of stairs or steps, and some aircraft have built-in airstairs (as in the case of the DC-9 and BAC-111) where the manual opening of the port side doors in aircraft accident conditions will merely reveal folded airstairs which block the exit path. Airstairs are lowered by engine-powered hydraulics in normal circumstances, but may have to hand-pumped from within if there is a failure of hydraulic power. They can, however, be lowered from outside (Fig. 4-17) in an emergency.

(d) Escape slides

Large civil aircraft usually carry one or more escape slides to assist in the evacuation of passengers in emergencies, owing to the height of the cabin floor above ground level. The slides (Fig. 4-18) are generally made of heavy quality nylon and are stored inside the main fuselage near the door that they are meant to serve, or occasionally between a pair of doors, one either side of the fuselage so that one slide may serve either door. The Boeing 747 has escape slides at all passenger doors.

The slides are rigged when necessary by the cabin crew and are sufficiently long to reach the ground even if the nose wheel gear is collapsed and the tail up in the air. Hand ropes are often provided to hold the slide when extended. The type of slide and the method of rigging may vary, both in aircraft types and with different operators. In the most modern aircraft the design permits automatic deployment of slides when the door is opened from the inside in an emergency

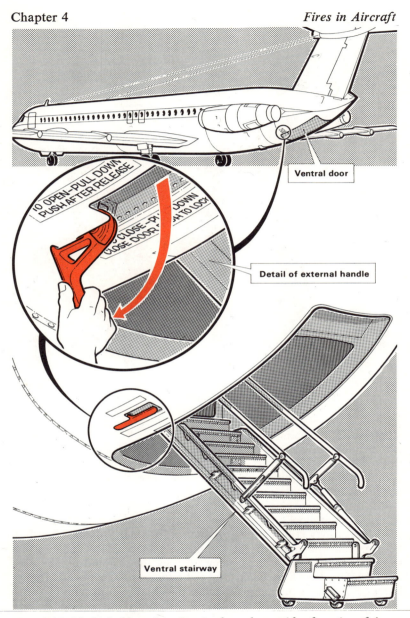

Ventral door

Detail of external handle

Ventral stairway

Fig. 4–17. Method of lowering airstairs from the outside of an aircraft in an emergency.

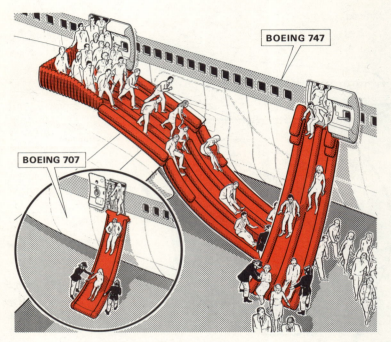

BOEING 747

BOEING 707

Fig. 4–18. Diagram showing the use of escape slides of a Boeing 707 and a Boeing 747 (Jumbojet).

situation. The system can be disarmed so that it is not activated by normal door operation, and it is automatically disarmed when the door is opened from the outside. A 'cold gas' generator may be used to inflate the slide, although pressure vessels containing compressed air or carbon dioxide are more common.

If it is found that the escape slide has been inflated while still in the cabin so that it blocks the door, an attempt should be made to remove it so that it may still serve its original purpose. If it cannot forcibly be removed and deployed, it should be punctured to deflate it. If slides are in use when rescue crews arrive, they should not be disturbed unless they have been damaged by use or fire exposure. In the latter case, ladders or emergency stairs if available (for example on an airfield) should be placed in position for immediate service. Where slides are in use, rescue crews should stand by at the foot to aid passengers to their feet and so keep the slide area clear for other evacuees. Passengers using overwing exits for evacuation will normally slide off the rear edge of the wing or down the wing flaps (if extended), and they should be given assistance to prevent leg injuries.

(e) Emergency methods of escape

Emergency methods of escape (*see* Section I, par. 6) are fitted on all civil aircraft. Certain windows (Fig. 4-19) are arranged to fall inwards or outwards (on unpressurised aircraft only) on the operation of release mechanism, normally from inside the aircraft. In view of the design requirements for pressurisation, almost all large pressurised civil aircraft have certain inward opening windows which are normally located over the wings and are intended primarily as the escape routes in a ditching accident. With very few exceptions, these window exits are openable from inside and outside the aircraft.

When it is impossible to gain access via passenger doors, the emergency exits should be tried. A number of these exits are arranged to give access to the wings; these are very often the most accessible to the rescuer. It must be borne in mind that the windows are heavy and must be firmly handled when being removed.

The location of emergency exits can be recognised by outline of the joint between the hatch and fuselage and by the marking of the release devices (*see* also par. (b) above). The use of overwing exits presents some hazard if the aircraft is in the normal position with gear extended, so these exits in most of the larger aircraft are fitted with an escape line. This consists of an escape rope made fast above the exit. Rescue crews should immediately assist passengers who may be descending by means of ropes.

Emergency exits for the crew are provided in some aircraft as movable portions of the flight deck glazing, or roof hatches in cockpits. There is a connecting door between the flight deck and the passenger cabin and passengers can in some cases (but not in mixed configuration aircraft, *i.e.*, passengers and freight at the same level) be led out via the flight deck. This does not apply to the Boeing 747.

(f) Breaking in

As previously explained, entry by breaking in to any aircraft should be a last resort, but may have to be undertaken. Many modern aircraft have pressurised cabins to provide suitable conditions for passengers when flying at high altitudes, and this means that a large part of the fuselage consists of a double skin with a suitable insulating material interposed, and all openings are heavily sealed. Non-pressurised aircraft are also fitted with internal linings. There is

Escape rope

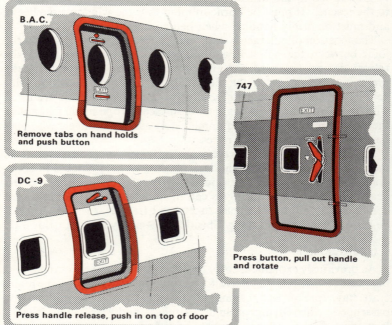

B.A.C.

Remove tabs on hand holds
and push button

DC -9

Press handle release, push in on top of door

747

Press button, pull out handle
and rotate

*Fig. 4–19. Some methods of opening emergency windows. These also have
a contrasting colour around the periphery.*

also a considerable amount of electric wiring, and in some of the larger aircraft, oxygen lines run through the aircraft.

Modern processes of metal bonding have replaced riveted joints in many cases, thus rendering the position of the heavy internal members less obvious. In such cases cutting-in should be confined to those areas specially indicated as suitable for forcible entry (*see* Fig. 4-6). Where the position of the heavy internal members is revealed externally by double or treble rows of rivets, no attempt should be made to cut through at these points.

The underside of a fuselage is unsuitable as a break-in point because it would normally give access to baggage compartments and/or cavities beneath the fuselage floor (Fig. 4-20). For this reason the position of the floor of the passenger cabin is sometimes marked externally by a red dotted line. The sides of the fuselage will normally be obstructed by passenger seats and are specially reinforced in the vicinity of the wing roots.

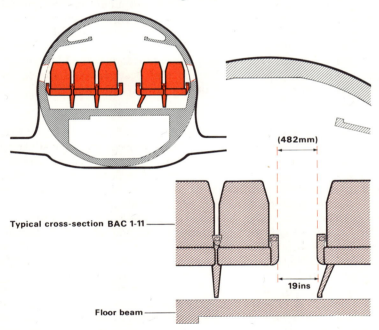

Fig. 4–20. *A typical cross-section through the passenger cabin to emphasise the limited aisle space available for movement within the cabin, and the impracticability of breaking in below the floor, or above and below the cabin windows.*

229

Although externally areas immediately above window frames appear very desirable for break-in points, they should be avoided. Within the aircraft these areas are occupied by luggage racks and/or air conditioning trunking which would prevent forcible entry. Breaking into pressurised aircraft is, therefore, not likely to be successful unless power tools are available, and care should be taken in their use to ensure that further injuries are not caused to trapped occupants. Care should also be taken when using powered tools which may provide a source of ignition in a fuel-soaked environment. Abrasive discs are particularly hazardous in this connection. When entry has been made, all jagged edges of metal or perspex should be suitably covered so as to avoid injury to both rescuers and rescued.

(g) Safety straps

Although there are many different types of lapstraps (as there are in motor cars) to be found in civil aircraft, they all incorporate a quick-release mechanism and are easier to undo in the natural manner than to cut. If, however, difficulty is experienced, the straps should be cut at their narrowest part. Extreme care should be taken in order that injuries are not caused or that injuries already suffered are not aggravated. When using a knife, the blade should be inserted between the outer garments of the seat occupant and the safety strap, and a decisive cut made in an outward direction.

(h) Rescue procedures

Having effected an entry into the fuselage or flight deck, the fire-man will invariably be confronted with tangled wreckage. Bearing in mind the number of passengers who may be involved and the fact that passengers and crew may be incapacitated, the rescue must be well organised. It is of little value to commence rescue operations until a clear 'working space' has been provided. When a 'clear way' has been achieved, it may be necessary to make the aircraft safe, but if any switch or control mechanism is operated, the fact should be remembered so that the information can be given to officers of the Accident Investigation Branch at a later date. However, extreme caution should be exercised by any individual who is not wholly familiar with aircraft systems. The guiding principle should be to leave matters as they are unless the rescuer is absolutely certain that his remedy in making an aircraft 'safe' is operationally essential and technically sound.

A quick 'sizing-up' of the situation should be made to determine the priority in relation to rescue, and as operating space may be limited (Fig. 4-4), the number of rescuers entering the fuselage should be kept to a minimum. As has already been stated, the distance between seats will depend on the configuration according to the class or type of aircraft, but in any case it is very limited and the situation can be worse if seating has been torn from its fixings. Rescue procedure should progress on the 'chain' principle, all walking casualties being evacuated first. All civil airline personnel, male and female, are drilled in rescue procedure, and their guidance will be invaluable and should be followed.

Cases of haemorrhage should be treated without delay, although it may not be possible to effect an immediate removal of a passenger trapped in a precarious position. Nevertheless consideration should be given as to whether or not first-aid must be given while a reasonable clearance of broken wreckage is being made. Unless the emergency is extreme or the physical condition of such persons dictates otherwise, medical advice should be sought during extrication. Ambulance attendants have an extremely high standard of first-aid knowledge and their help, if available, should be sought. Common sense and careful work will accomplish much more than excited and unco-ordinated effort will ever achieve.

Because of lack of space the use of stretchers may be denied, or at best the stretcher may have to be carried above head level or turned on its side between the rows of seats.

If in the course of operations outside the aircraft it is decided to ventilate to assist rescue work, all exits opened or allowed to remain open for this purpose should be on the downwind side of the fuselage. Ventilation, other than for rescue, should not be started until directed by the officer in charge.

Finally, a thorough detailed search should be made for survivors, irrespective of whether all are accounted for or not; there is always the possibility of the involvement of persons on the ground at the accident site.

(j) Treatment after removal

Casualties should be carried to an upwind (and if possible uphill) position at least 50 yards (metres) from the aircraft, unless ambulances are already in attendance. They should be kept warm and not laid on damp grass and should be covered (both under and over the casualty) with whatever material can be improvised. Cigarettes should not be offered—there is a danger that internal injuries may be aggravated in addition to the risk that fuel may still be present in the clothing of survivors.

Clothing should be examined to ensure that it is not smouldering and that it is not contaminated or saturated with fuel; if the latter is the case, anyone who might handle the casualty should be warned. First-aid treatment should be limited to stopping the flow of blood and treating for shock, but as much detail as possible about injuries should be given to ambulance attendants before the casualty is taken to hospital. Gloves should be worn by personnel carrying out rescue work to avoid the danger of infection from broken pieces of bone, etc. Should personnel be scratched immediate disinfecting treatment should be given to obviate blood poisoning.

5. RESCUE FROM MILITARY AIRCRAFT

The means of entry into military aircraft differ with the purpose for which the aircraft is designed. Single- or double-engined machines, such as fighters and trainers, have only the cockpit canopy as an entrance. On larger aircraft with more than two occupants (such as bombers and transports) a main entrance door is provided for normal access. In addition, there may be emergency exit doors or panels and ditching hatches in the sides, top and bottom of the fuselage. This offers rescuers a choice of entrances into large aircraft. It is recommended that the sequence set out in the following paragraphs should be used when possible at the scene of a crash.

(a) Main entrance door

As with civil aircraft, entrance by the main door should be tried first. The door is indicated by the word 'ENTRANCE' and has stencilled instructions on the use of the external release mechanism. This entrance is on the left (port) side of most aircraft—an exception being the Vulcan bomber, in which the main entrance is in the underside of the fuselage nose behind the air bomber's blister, and another being the Canberra where it is on the right (starboard) side.

Door handles on modern military aircraft are normally housed within the door and flush with the fuselage skin. The handle flies out to thumb pressure on a small button situated in the tail of the handle, which is then turned or lifted as instructed.

(b) Emergency exits

Should the main entrance door fail to open, due perhaps to distortion, and cannot be forced open by leverage, the emergency exit should be tried next. Instructions on how to release the panel are stencilled on the side of the fuselage. Emergency exit and parachute escape panels are designed to fall free of the aircraft when released and are not hinged. The panel should be held firmly until it is on the ground in order to avoid injury. Both doors and exit panels are often marked as areas for breaking-in in case they are jammed. The normal method of opening should always be tried first.

(c) Parachute and ditching escape panels

These panels are normally opened by the aircrew from inside the aircraft before leaving in an emergency. The panels are marked externally with interrupted lines showing where access can be gained by cutting if necessary.

(d) Canopies

Canopies are opened in different ways on different aircraft and operating instructions are printed on the fuselage by the canopy release handle; the normal method of gaining access to the cockpit of an aircraft on the ground is to *open* the canopy, whilst the emergency method is to *remove* it. The normal method of opening a canopy is usually less suitable for rescue purposes for one or more of the following reasons:

    (i) Insufficient space is gained.

    (ii) Several normal canopy opening systems are dependent on electric and hydraulic or pneumatic power.

    (iii) The switch for normal canopy opening is not always positioned where it can be reached, *e.g.* the external canopy opening switch on the Hunter (mark T) is inside the nose-wheel bay.

It is important, therefore, not to confuse the normal and emergency canopy releases. It is advisable to use the emergency facility whenever haste is necessary (and it is reasonable to assume that there is a degree of urgency in any situation when rescue work is necessary, since the risk of fire is high, even if it has not occurred already), so that the maximum space for rescuing the crew can be obtained. The procedures for removing the canopy when outside the aircraft vary considerably but on all aircraft there will be instructions near the cockpit for emergency canopy release (*see* Fig. 4-8).

(i) *Sliding canopies.* There is an external canopy release handle which, by means of a cable, opens the canopy locks and deflates the canopy seal. The canopy must then be lifted off by hand complete with its guide rails.

(ii) *Hinged canopies.* These canopies generally have a jettison mechanism, which is operated by means of an external canopy jettison release, the position of which is marked on the fuselage with operating instructions. When the handle is pulled a cable withdraws the sear from the canopy firing unit, the cartridge fires, mechanical linkages open the canopy locks and the canopy is thrust upwards by the rams, pivoting on a rear hinge until it is released.

It is impossible to predict how a canopy jettisoned by this means will behave when there is no slipstream to carry it away. It should not be assumed that it would behave as a high velocity missile travelling towards the rear of the aircraft, partly because of its shape and partly because the canopy jettison cartridge is less powerful than the multiple seat ejection cartridges. In some instances, a canopy jettisoned on the ground has merely reared upright and then rolled away, as the wind and the contours of the airframe happened to take it, to a position in front of the mainplane leading edge. In any event, firemen who are aware that a canopy is being jettisoned should be able to watch its flight and avoid its fall, but as it could land up to 30 ft (9 m) away from the fuselage, vehicles and personnel should be kept clear. If the canopy is not blown clear, but only lifted slightly by explosive bolts, it will have to be lifted clear.

(iii) *USAF canopies*. With American type fighter aircraft, the method of canopy release again varies with type, but the release will normally be found on the port side behind a small panel operated by thumb studs.

If a handle attached to a length of wire is found, particular care should be taken as this may operate an explosive charge designed to jettison the canopy when in flight. If actuated, the canopy may be ejected 40 to 50 ft (12 to 15 m) over the tail of the aircraft. Levers or switches should never be operated by putting an arm through a broken canopy because if the canopy is jettisoned accidentally, serious injury may result.

(e) Breaking through perspex

Should entry by the main or emergency exits fail, it may be necessary, depending on the type of canopy fitted, to either smash the canopy at the rear or gain entry into the cockpit by other means. When breaking perspex the following points should be remembered:

(i) The perspex should not be broken above or near any member of the crew, because of the risk of injury.

(ii) Breakage should also be avoided directly above an ejection seat (*see* (f) below) as there is a danger of actuating the seat with possibly disastrous results. The sear is always exposed and requires only $\frac{1}{2}$ in. (12 mm) to travel to explode the cartridge.

(iii) The break should be made just above the metal sill (Fig. 4-21), using the flat of an axe in preference to the cutting edge and using the sill as a 'stopper' to prevent the axe head going through into the cockpit.

(iv) Perspex should not be struck with excessive force. This could result in the rescuer's wrists being lacerated on the broken and jagged edges of the window material.

(v) If necessary, the entire perspex panel should be cut from the metal frame.

(vi) In modern aircraft laminated perspex may be encountered. This is virtually unbreakable, and although it can be broken through layer by layer, it is better not to waste further time if the windows do not respond to a hard blow with an axe head.

Fig. 4–21. Method of breaking in through the perspex canopy using a large axe.

(f) Ejection seats

Ejection seats have already been described in Section II, par. 3 (b), and from a perusal of this section it will be seen that the inadvertent operation of the ejection mechanism while the aircraft is on the ground is dangerous to the occupant and to any person in the vicinity of the cockpit. Extreme care must, therefore, be taken to ensure that the firing mechanism is rendered safe before attempting to extricate the seat occupant. Although the various types of ejector seat differ to some extent, all have incorporated some means of making this possible.

(i) *Martin-Baker ejection seats.* One or more safety pins (Fig. 4-22) attached to a large metal label (usually coloured red or black)

235

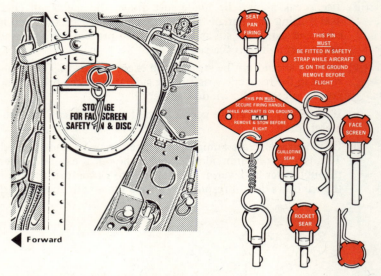

Fig. 4–22. Right: Typical safety pins for inserting in the sear to render an ejection seat safe. Left: Method of stowing the safety pin on the side of the seat.

are stowed in pockets or brackets on the seat itself, or in the cockpit according to the type of seat. Before any attempt at rescue is made, a safety pin should be removed from its place of storage and placed in a hole in the sear. Where an automatic canopy jettison mechanism is fitted, the canopy gun is situated at the top of the ejection seat and employs a sear of similar design to the ejection seat sear. This mechanism should be made safe in exactly the same way as the ejection seat by inserting a safety pin in the sear at the rear of the top of the seat (Fig. 4-23).

On some aircraft the canopy is connected to the seat by means of a restrictor wire (Fig. 4-24) and if the pilot has attempted to eject, the removal of the canopy will fire the seat. This will be indicated by the face blind (Fig. 4-25) being out, or the seat pan handle being loose. If this proves to be the case, the canopy *must not* be removed until the restrictor wire has been made safe. Under these conditions it will be necessary, depending upon the type of canopy fitted, either to smash the canopy at the rear or to gain entry into the cockpit by other means. Once access is gained to the cockpit, a check can be made to see if there is a cable connecting the canopy to the top of

236

the ejection seat. If there is, this cable will have to be disconnected from the canopy by removing the quick-release pin connecting the cable to the canopy or, if available, pliers or wirecutters may be used to sever the cable. A conscious effort must be made at all times to ensure that the cable is not pulled taut and the restrictor removed.

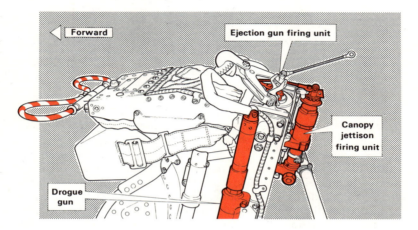

Fig. 4–23. A typical arrangement of sears and firing cables on a fighter aircraft.

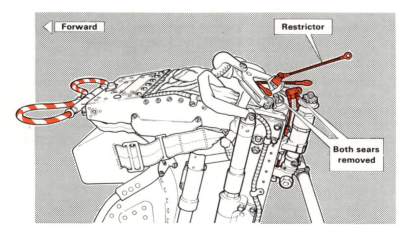

Fig. 4–24. A typical arrangement of the restrictor wire on a fighter aircraft.

237

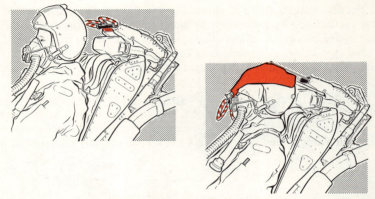

Fig. 4–25. Left: The face screen firing handle in the stowed position. Right: The face screen firing handle operated.

(ii) *Folland ejection seats.* As the firing machanism is enclosed, an external handle is provided so that the seat can be made safe. This safety lock handle is on the underside of the headrest box. During flight, the handle points towards the starboard side of the aircraft, and is held in position by an internal spring-loaded pin which engages in a recess in the pivot of the handle.

To render the seat safe to carry out rescue operations, the hand should be slid over the head rest, carefully avoiding the firing handle, and to the right of the pilot's shoulders will be found a small handle with a large red knob. Pulling this knob gently outwards, turning the handle towards the front of the seat until it can be turned no further and releasing the knob renders the seat completely safe.

(g) Release of aircrew

Aircrew are provided with harness, clothing and seating to ensure safe flying at high altitudes and to provide rapid and safe exit in an emergency. The present trend is to reduce harness release actions to a minimum; however, equipment is still in use which necessitates releasing seven items before a pilot can be removed from his seat. In earlier types of aircraft, the harness release actions are:

(i) Remove the oxygen mask from the pilot's face.

(ii) Disconnect the main and emergency oxygen tubes.

(iii) Disconnect the telemic (wireless telephone) lead.

(iv) Disconnect the parachute safety straps.

(v) Disconnect the dinghy straps (three).

(vi) Disconnect the 'anti-g' suit tubes, if fitted. (In some aircraft corrugated rubber tubes are incorporated in the pilot's clothing for the passage of air under pressure.)

(vii) Disconnect the seat safety straps.

There are several different types of connection here, but they are all easy to release.

The personal equipment connector (PEC) has been brought into service on several types of aircraft to reduce the number of items to be disconnected when releasing aircrew by grouping some of them in a box with a single release (Fig. 4-26). The PEC is easily recognised; it

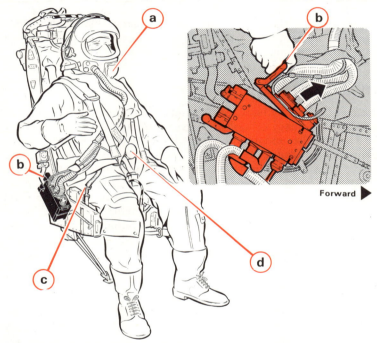

Fig. 4–26. The personal equipment connector (PEC). Left: location of the PEC. Right: removing the upper portion of the PEC.

is on the right-hand side of the seat pan. Where a PEC is fitted, the following actions are necessary to release the occupant:

(i) Remove the oxygen mask (a).

(ii) Press the thumb release and raise the handle (b) of the PEC. The top plate comes away when this is done.

(iii) Disconnect or cut the dinghy release straps (c).

(iv) Turn and press the release mechanism of the combined seat and parachute harness connection box (d).

Certain types of ejection seat used by the RN and the RAF have a manual over-ride control which will release the pilot's harness completely. The manual over-ride lever is positioned either on the left-hand or right-hand side of the ejection seat, depending on the type of seating arrangement. Raising the manual over-ride lever will release the pilot's harness. If the mechanism fails to work, it will be necessary to cut the straps.

The release of aircrew should be performed as carefully as circumstances permit. If the wearer is unconscious, he should be held firmly so that he will not slump forward; if the aircraft is on its side or upside down, he must be supported to prevent a fall.

6. HELICOPTER ACCIDENTS

Being of relatively light construction, these aircraft will not stand up well to the heavy or violent forces encountered on impact (Plate 88). Usually the undercarriage, rotors and tail units disintegrate, leaving the wreckage of the cabin or fuselage as the main debris. This part of the wreckage normally carries the engine and fuel tank, and it should be approached with due caution. If the aircraft's rotor becomes damaged in the air and is put out of commission, the effect of a nose dive crash is likely to ensue. Normally, the possibility of serious fire is less in a helicopter accident than with fixed-wing aircraft because of the smaller fuel capacity, but the hazards associated with fuel fires and fuel tanks remain the same as for other types of aircraft.

(a) Approach

Should a helicopter crash-land with the engine still running and the rotors turning, the greatest care should be taken if it is necessary to approach the aircraft to effect a rescue. If the engine is cut off, the main rotor will continue to turn for some time with the tips of the rotor blades sagging lower and lower as they lose speed. It must be assumed that these will sag below normal head level and could cause a serious accident or death to the would-be rescuer. It is advisable, therefore, to watch the rotor blades and, if necessary, to approach the aircraft in a crouching position or on hands and knees.

A good approach would be from the rear because the main rotors are canted to rise above the tail, keeping to the other side of the tail

Plate 76. The burnt out shell of a military aircraft which has been completely destroyed by fire.

Plate 77. A Boeing 727 which crashed at Gatwick Airport in January 1969. Forty-five people were killed, but 12 survived. The picture shows how wreckage can be strewn over a large area.

Plate 79. The Boeing 707 accident at Heathrow in April 1968 (Whisky Echo) when four people died but 122 survived. Carbon dioxide is being applied at the front and foam to the rear and centre sections.

Plate 78. A fairly frequent form of ground accident. Burst tyres evolve heat and smoke and sometimes fire.

Plate 80. A military aircraft landing on its nose, as a result of which fuel tanks have ruptured and burst into flames.

Plate 81. An aircraft crash with the undercarriage still up, but no fire. The pilot escaped without serious injury.

Plate 82. An example of an aircraft crashing on to a built-up area. The potential dangers and complications of this type of accident are obvious.   Photo: Associated Newspapers.

Plate 83. The crash of a BEA Trident just off the Staines By-pass road on the 18th June 1972, just after taking off from Heathrow Airport.

Plate 84. In this Trident crash the aircraft broke in two with the fuselage and tailplane finishing 100 yards (91.4 metres) apart.

Plate 85. *The search being made for possible survivors at the Trident accident, but all 118 passengers and crew were killed, mostly on impact.*

Plate 86. *Heavy lifting gear being used to facilitate the recovery of bodies. Because the crash occurred on a Sunday, the roads for miles around were jammed with the vehicles of sightseers.*

Plate 87. Foam was used to extinguish the fire in this crashed helicopter. The vulnerability of the pilot and passengers can be seen.

Plate 88. Because of its light construction a helicopter is easily damaged when a crash occurs.

from that on which the stabilising rotor is mounted, and remaining close to the fuselage where the main rotor is always above body height. Any approach from the front or sides means passing through the circle swept by the main rotor where it is at its lowest. (This applies only in crash conditions: normally anyone approaching a helicopter under power should keep in view of the pilot and obey his instructions.)

(b) Rescues and fire fighting

The absence of wings makes a helicopter more likely to roll on to one side in a forced landing or crash. Rescuers should be prepared for this situation because it usually necessitates climbing up on to the side of the helicopter to gain access to the cabin. The doors and windows are located in the sides: there is certainly no access through the belly, and the top is likely to be obstructed by distorted rotor blades.

Smaller types of helicopter have access doors with opening instructions marked on the outside. Larger types have additional cabin doors with opening instructions also marked on the outside. The side windows of the cockpits of medium and large helicopters are sometimes utilised as emergency exits. Some helicopters have extensive frontal areas of perspex which can be broken or cut through if other means of access cannot be used. The rescuer, however, should first ensure that such entry will avoid further obstacles; for example, a control panel or similar equipment may be positioned where it would prevent the rescuer from getting in after removal of the perspex.

Cutting tools may be necessary to extricate trapped occupants, particularly from sections where girder work has collapsed. Small outbreaks of fire involving magnesium alloys can be tackled with water spray (but *see* page 213 regarding the effect of using water on magnesium). Very small sections are more easily dealt with by cutting them away and dispersing the fragments. When this is being done, care should be taken to ensure that such action does not lead to re-ignition of any spilled fuel.

(c) Military helicopters

Certain military helicopters may be armed with machine guns or missiles. Magnesium flares may also be carried outboard in special launchers. The same care should be taken on approaching military helicopters, in the positioning of appliances and in the selection of rescue routes as for fixed-wing aircraft.

7. SPECIAL HAZARDS

Apart from the normal risks attached to fire-fighting operations following an aircraft accident, certain special hazards may arise, and guidance is given on the most important of these in the following paragraphs.

(a) Bombs

High explosive or training bombs do not normally explode on impact of a crashed aircraft since the fuses are not likely to have been set, but it must be emphasised that there is always some risk attached to them as their behaviour is totally unpredictable. Risk to personnel and appliances must be accepted where there is a possibility of saving life and where the fire situation could endanger lives—in nearby buildings, for example. Apart from these situations there is no justification for the exposure of personnel to risk.

Crashed military aircraft involved in fire and believed to be carrying bombs should be treated with great respect. HE bombs are carried to a limited extent only on training flights, and if the aircraft crashes and takes fire the bombs may explode in the resulting heat. There are, however, many instances of HE bombs failing to explode even after the aircraft has completely burnt out. Following a crash, the risk of explosion of bombs carried by the aircraft is always present, and it is therefore vital that no attempt whatsoever should be made by anyone other than qualified bomb disposal personnel to move or in any way interfere with bombs, whether the bombs have been subjected to heat or not.

The RAF uses practice bombs of various types and weights, some of which are filled with smoke-producing compounds whilst others are filled with a flash composition, sometimes in conjunction with a smoke-producing compound. All are initiated by some type of detonator and/or HE burster charge. Whilst the danger from an explosion of one of these bombs filled with smoke composition only is not unduly great, other than when the explosion takes place in close proximity to persons or property, the explosion of a bomb filled with flash composition can be lethal. It should be noted that the flash produced by some types of flash bomb is of such an intensity (millions of candle power), as to constitute a danger to the eyesight. Precautions should therefore be taken to protect the sight even at a distance from the bomb.

If during rescue operations, bombs are seen in such a position that they may become heated, they should be cooled with a spray branch.

Should a Service officer be present, his advice concerning the danger of explosion of bombs or ammunition should be taken.

(b) Small arms ammunition

The risk of small arms ammunition being initiated in an aircraft crash is remote unless fire occurs. If a fire does occur and the ammunition is involved, it may be burnt by excessive heat, and fragments of cartridge cases and projectiles may be propelled up to a distance of 50 to 75 yd (45 to 68 m). There is no risk of mass explosion, but small or added explosions will take place with increasing frequency as the fire takes hold.

Wounds resulting from the initiation of small arms ammunition are possible under such circumstances; particularly where heavy calibre ammunition is involved. There is also the possibility that the powder charge or incendiary or tracer cores may contribute to the spread of fire. Nevertheless experience has indicated that small arms ammunition stowed in aircraft involved in a crash is more spectacular and frightening than an actual obstacle to fire fighting and rescue operations.

The best protection in all cases of necessary exposure is to keep low, to avoid passing in front of the muzzles of guns and in front of rockets, and to have all belts of ammunition or racks of bombs or cases of flares, etc., kept cool by spray branches.

(c) Mechanisms operated by explosives

Small detonators are used to operate emergency mechanisms, *e.g.* canopy jettison, undercarriage lowering, etc., on many aircraft, and these may be actuated by the heat of a crash fire, but they would have only a minor effect.

(d) Rocket projectiles

If an aircraft carrying air-to-air missiles is involved in a crash fire, the missile warheads may be exploded by heat similarly to an HE bomb. It is less likely that the rocket propellant would be ignited, and it is impossible to predict the result if the propellant were ignited because the missile might still be attached to its pylon, or the pylon might be distorted, but it cannot be regarded as likely that the missile would be fired from the aircraft.

Air-to-air missiles are carried externally on pylons, and these are likely to break free from the aircraft during a crash landing. If so, they are less likely to be involved in any subsequent fire but the unpredictable character of explosives makes it necessary to find any such weapons and to keep all personnel well away from them until bomb disposal technicians can deal with them.

(e) Pressurised containers

Although these are not weapons or explosives, it is appropriate to mentioned pressurised containers of liquids and gases because these may be burst violently by heat expansion during a crash fire. Virtually all military aircraft are fitted with pressurised containers with distribution systems for aircraft services. These containers may not be burst by heat, however, since it commonly happens that the distribution piping is ruptured or melted, and allows the pressure to be released before the contents of the container reach a critical temperature.

(f) Radioactive materials in transit

Some civil aircraft carry consignments of radioactive isotopes or other radioactive materials for industrial or medical use. Usually the consignments are fairly weak sources and are carried in special sealed and marked containers, but moderately strong sources may also be carried, in which case shielding containers are used which have been designed to prevent damage in the event of fire or other accident.

The properties and hazards of radioactive materials are dealt with in Part 6C of the *Manual*, Chapter 11, and the control procedure necessary when dealing with a fire involving substantial radioactive sources is detailed in Part 6A of the *Manual*, Chapter 3, 'Control at a fire'.

(g) Nuclear weapons

Medium and heavy bombers and large military transport aircraft occasionally carry nuclear weapons on special operational manoeuvres which involve moving aircraft from one airfield to another. The storage and movement of nuclear weapons are governed by precautionary regulations. Nevertheless, it is impossible to ensure that an accident cannot occur, although a full yield nuclear explosion could not result, as an important factor in limiting the consequence of an accident is that a nuclear weapon consists of a number of assemblies or components which can be stored and transported separately, and this is the normal practice. Even when a weapon is fully assembled, however, the arming and firing sequence demands such an extremely close synchronisation of events that an accidental detonation would never reproduce the whole sequence.

In appearance the weapon is similar to a conventional HE bomb. In bomber aircraft, it is carried in the bomb-bay in the fuselage of the aircraft and in transport type aircraft it is carried as components in metal containers in the main cabin.

All nuclear weapons contain high explosive (HE) when they are fully assembled and a conventional explosion may occur when a nuclear weapon is involved in an accident. In addition fire or explosion of the HE may lead to the spread over a limited area of radioactive dust which can be harmful if inhaled or ingested, or if it gets into a cut or abrasion. If an aircraft is known or suspected to be carrying a nuclear weapon it should be dealt with in the same way as for an aircraft carrying HE bombs.

(i) *Special Safety Organisation.* The RAF have a Special Safety Organisation (SSO) to deal with the problems arising in the event of such an accident and the RAF fire crew attending a fire in an aircraft involving a nuclear weapon or component would be part of a Special Safety Team (SST), who are specially trained and equipped to deal with the situation.

(ii) *Fire-fighting procedure.* The Air Force authorities will, through the police, notify all appropriate fire brigade headquarter controls of any aircraft carrying nuclear weapons which they know to be in distress or to have crashed. The officer in charge of a fire appliance called to an aircraft crash may therefore receive from his brigade headquarters early notification if the aircraft is carrying a nuclear weapon, but this information may not reach him until after he has arrived and has got to work.

In the absence of any such information, the officer in charge at the scene of a crash of a medium or heavy bomber or large transport aircraft of the RAF or USAF should observe the precautions appropriate to an aircraft known to be carrying a nuclear weapon.

No one should approach closer than 300 yd (274 m) except to save life or to fight fires until it is confirmed that a nuclear weapon is not involved and there is no further danger of an HE explosion. At this distance in open country, personnel will be relatively safe from the direct blast effects of an HE explosion but cover should be used for protection against flying debris. In broken country, or in a built-up area where buildings provide good protection, the extent of evacuation will have to be decided by the officer in charge at the time. No one should stay close to the aircraft longer than is necessary.

If an approach is necessary, it should be made from upwind, and the smoke from fires should be avoided. If it is necessary to enter smoke to effect rescues, breathing apparatus or a respirator should be worn.

The greatest care should be taken not to endanger the lives of firemen unnecessarily. While the decision whether and when to withdraw firemen must remain one for the officer in charge on the spot, risk to personnel and appliances may have to be accepted where there is a possibility of saving life and where the fire situation could endanger lives—in nearby buildings, for instance; where no such conditions apply, firemen should be withdrawn as soon as possible to a place of safety, particularly if the bomb or the metal containers are actually burning or are engulfed in flames. Men are reasonably safe from blast effects at a distance of 300 yd (274 m) in the open, though they should still lie down or take cover for protection against flying debris. Where good natural or artificial cover is available, a much smaller distance will suffice.

Foam should be used in the usual way to tackle the fire and to facilitate rescue operations, but should not be used for cooling the bomb or metal containers because, although the water drained from the foam will assist cooling to a small degree, it will not materially reduce the temperature. If the bomb or containers are visible and likely to become heated they should be cooled with water spray, if possible from branches supplied with water from standard 2¾-in. (70 mm) hose lines. These spray jets should be kept at work until the arrival of the RAF Special Safety Team (SST), who will then accept responsibility.

If the aircraft is on fire or if smoke is seen issuing from it, breathing apparatus or respirators should be worn in order to guard against the possible risk of inhalation.

Care should be taken not to handle or tread on debris of any kind since some of this can be dangerous and will require recovery by experts. Personnel should keep upwind as far as possible.

The RAF SST should reach any incident within a comparatively short space of time. The team will be equipped to monitor radiation and will be responsible for decontamination. When the SST arrives, the officer in charge of the team will accept responsibility for control of the incident, and the fire brigade officer should accept the advice of the SST officer regarding any necessary decontamination of uniforms and equipment, including respirators.

Any persons who have been within 300 yd (274 m) of the wreckage or who has passed through smoke plume from fires should remain in the vicinity until the arrival of the SST, so that their skin and clothing can be checked for the presence of radioactive substances which may have been released due to fire or explosion. They should be advised not to smoke, eat or drink until they have been checked by the SST; a check by the fire brigade's own radiac instruments cannot be considered sufficiently positive.

Glossary of aeronautical terms

Aerodyne. Any heavier-than-air type of aircraft.

Aileron. Primary control surfaces at each wing tip which operate differentially (*i.e.*, one goes up when the other goes down) to give lateral (rolling) control.

Anti-g suits. These are worn by pilots to counteract the effects of high 'g' loads by applying pressure to the lower abdomen and legs and preventing blood draining from the brain.

Autopilot. A mechanical or electric-mechanical device which will maintain an aircraft on a predetermined heading and altitude, controlling ailerons, elevators and rudder through a system of gyros.

Bicycle undercarriage. One in which the main landing wheels are one behind the other in line under the fuselage, usually with wing-tip outrigger wheels.

Bogie. A type of undercarriage with four or more wheels to each leg.

Braking propeller. A propeller the blades of which can be reversed in pitch so that they have a braking effect on the landing run.

Canard. An aeroplane of 'back-to-front' layout, with a horizontal tailplane (noseplane) ahead of the wing.

Canopy. The transparent fairing over a cockpit.

Cantilever. A structure supported only at one end; *i.e.*, a wing without bracing struts, or a single-leg undercarriage.

Co-axial propellers. Two independent propellers mounted on a common shaft and rotating in opposite directions.

Contrail. Short for condensation trail, which occurs when water vapour in the exhaust gases from aero-engines condenses in low temperatures at high altitudes.

Crescent wing. A swept-back wing of special type, in which the degree of sweep back is reduced from root to tip.

Delta. A wing or tailplane of triangular or near-triangular plan form, so called from the Greek letter Δ delta.

Dorsal fin. A small extension of the fin along the centre line of the fuselage.

Drag. The resistance of the air to an aircraft's forward motion.

Drogue. A type of parachute in the form of a conical canvas sleeve, open at both ends, like a bottomless bucket, which is used to check the way of the aircraft. Also, a funnel-shaped portion of in-flight refuelling gear trailed by a tanker aircraft.

Drone. A pilotless aircraft, radio controlled from the ground or from another aircraft, for use as a target.

Ejection seat. A crew seat which can be fired from the aircraft, complete with occupant, in an emergency; parachutes deploy automatically and the seat separates from the occupant.

Elevator. The moving portion of the horizontal tailplane which provides longitudinal (dive and climb) control.

Fatigue. Under repeated loads, such as experienced in flight, metal parts get 'tired' and lose strength. Fatigue failures may follow if the aircraft structure has not been properly designed.

Fin. The fixed portion of the vertical tail surface.

Flap. A surface on the trailing edge of the wing which can be lowered to increase the lift and/or drag for take-off and landing. Leading edge flaps are similar in operation and are used to improve lift and control at low speeds.

Flight refuelling. The system of transferring fuel from one aircraft to another while in flight. Two basic methods are used; the British probe and drogue and the U.S. flying boom.

Foreplane. A forward control surface on a canard layout; an alternative term for noseplane.

Fuselage. The main structural body of an aircraft, carrying the main planes, tail, etc., and providing the accommodation for the occupants and load.

GCA. Ground control approach, a radar landing aid in which a ground controller radios directions to an approaching aircraft which he watches on a radar screen.

Helicopter. A rotary-wing aircraft which, for the whole of its flight, derives the major part of its lift from a powered rotor system whose axis or axes are fixed and are substantially perpendicular to the longitudinal axis of the rotorcraft.

Hovercraft. Used loosely to describe any type of machine which rides over the terrain on a cushion of air but has no means of generating lift and therefore does not fly in the strict sense.

IAS. Indicated air speed—the reading on the air-speed indicator. Because of reduced static pressure as altitude increases, the IAS becomes a progressively smaller proportion of *true* air speed through the air as the aircraft climbs.

ILS. Instrument landing system. A radio equipment transmitting signals from the end of a runway to allow an aircraft to fly down a 'glide path' without seeing the ground below.

Integral tank. A fuel tank formed by the basic structure, usually of a wing, by making a fuel-tight seal of spars, ribs and skin.

Jet assisted take-off (JATO). A slightly inaccurate term for the rocket packs used to shorten the take-off run of heavily loaded aircraft.

Jet flap. A system of ejecting most or all of the exhaust from a jet engine through a slit in the wing trailing edge, so that the air flow produces the effect of a lift-increasing flap.

JP4. Designation of a 'wide-cut' gasoline aviation fuel for jet engines, with characteristics similar to petrol.

Kerosene. An aviation fuel, similar to paraffin, widely used in jet engines. The military designation is JP1.

Leading edge. The front edge of a wing or aerofoil surface.

Lift. The force in an upward direction which sustains an aircraft in flight. Lift must exceed weight, acting downwards, to achieve flight, while thrust forward must exceed drag to produce forward motion.

Mach number. A measurement of speed related to the speed of sound. A Mach number of 1 is the speed of sound, which varies from 760 mph (1 223 km/h) at sea level to a constant 660·6 mph (1 063·1 km/h) above 36,600 ft (11 156 m). Thus the term Mach= 0·5 means half the speed of sound, Mach=3·0 is three times the speed of sound and so on.

Monocoque. A common form of aircraft construction in which the outer skin, supported by light frames and stringers, is a primary load-carrying structure.

Nacelle. An enclosed structure containing the engine—or sometimes the crew—distinct from the fuselage.

Nose flap. A leading edge flap on a wing.

Noseplane. The forward lifting and control surface on a canard layout, taking the place of the tailplane.

Oleo. An undercarriage leg in which shock is absorbed by a piston moving up a cylinder containing hydraulic fluid or compressed air.

Overshoot. A misjudged landing approach in which the aircraft touches down too far down the runway to pull up safely. Also used to describe the procedure of 'going round again' to avoid touching down too far along the runway.

Payload. That part of an aircraft's total weight which can be used to carry passengers or freight (*i.e.*, for which revenue can be obtained).

Pod. A type of engine nacelle, separate from the main structure of the aircraft to which it is attached by a pylon.

Power control. A flying control, the movement of which is assisted or totally effected by a hydraulic, pneumatic or electric actuator, used in high speed aircraft in which the force of the airflow over control surfaces makes it impossible for the pilot to use conventional manual controls.

Pressure differential. The difference, measured in lbf/in^2 (or metric equivalent) between pressure inside an aircraft cabin and atmospheric pressure outside.

Pressure suit. Used by military aircrew at very high altitudes, where low atmospheric pressure makes normal breathing difficult or impossible.

Pressurisation. The process of making an aircraft cockpit or cabin airtight and maintaining a pressure inside it higher than that of the outside air pressure, which decreases linearly with increase of altitude to the point where survival would be impossible.

Probe. The receiving part of flight refuelling equipment which is inserted into the tanker's drogue to make a fuel-tight connection between the two aircraft.

Pylon. A streamlined fairing on a wing or fuselage to carry a fuel tank, weapon or engine pod.

Radome. Any dome-shaped or curved fairing over radar aerials on an aircraft.

RATOG. Initials of 'rocket assisted take-off gear', comprising small liquid or solid fuel rockets on an aircraft, used to shorten the take-off run.

Rotor. An external wing-like surface of narrow chord. A rotor system comprises from two to six rotor blades carried radially on a single vertical shaft to produce lift when rotated.

Rotorcraft. Any type of aerodyne (heavier-than-air craft) which is sustained in flight primarily by the lift from a rotor system. Also known as a 'rotary-wing aircraft'.

Rudder. A vertical control surface providing directional control.

Slab tail. A tailplane which operates as a single entity to give longitudinal control, instead of having separate elevators. Used on high-speed aircraft.

Slat. A small section of a wing leading edge which can be moved forward, to produce a slot between it and the wing. This improves the airflow at low speeds, giving better control.

Slipper tank. A type of external fuel tank, fitting flush to the fuselage or wing undersurface.

Slot. A gap through the leading edge of the wing, serving to control the airflow and so reduce stalling speed and improve control. Various types are fixed slot, valved slot, and controlled or retractable slot.

Sonic boom. The noise produced by the shock wave set up by an aircraft flying above the speed of sound.

Subsonic. Any speed below the speed of sound; less than Mach 1.

Sweep-back. The angle between the lateral axis of an aeroplane and its wings, usually measured at 25 per cent of the wing chord.

Tailplane. The horizontal stabilising surface at the rear of an aircraft, to which the elevators are usually attached.

Thrust. The force that moves an aircraft forward through the air, overcoming the drag. Also used in relation to the power produced by a jet engine.

Transonic. The range of speeds just below and just above Mach 1, at which an aircraft may experience buffeting, trim changes and other effects of shock waves.

Torsion-box. The main load-carrying portion of a multi-spar wing comprising front and rear spars, ribs and skin. Frequently contains integral fuel tanks.

VTOL. Initials of 'vertical take-off and landing', defined as the ability of an aircraft to reach altitude of 50 ft (15·24 m) within 50 ft (15·24 m) distance of the take-off point.

Part 6B   Chapter 5

Fires in Oil Refineries

OIL refining as a major industry in Great Britain is less than twenty years old. It is a development of the post-war era, mainly as a direct result of the economic situation in which Britain found herself after the Second World War, and of the enormously increased use of oil which the war itself and the years of reconstruction after it brought about. Up to that time, over three-quarters of the oil used in Britain was imported and stored in the form of finished products. In other words, it was refined elsewhere—mainly in the United States—and oil companies in Britain shipped in the products the market needed— the petrol, lubricating oils, diesel and aviation fuels, the fuel oil, and so on.

By the middle forties, however, shortage of dollars, shortage of refining capacity in the Western Hemisphere, and the fact that the main supplier, America, was herself becoming a net importer of oil, had made it necessary to change this pattern. One further factor was important; the great oilfields of the Middle East were then opening up. This was crude oil which could be obtained predominantly for sterling. The decision was therefore taken for Britain to have her own refineries, drawing their supplies of crude oil mainly from the Middle East. The refineries were built by the major oil companies operating in Britain at the time.

Oil has many uses: it is an illuminant—which is how it started to be used—a lubricant, or the raw material of thousands of chemicals, plastics, man-made fibres and detergents. Its greatest importance, however, is that it is a source of energy. In Britain we rely on coal, oil and atomic power for our basic energy needs, with a small percentage of hydro-electric power in addition. Neither gas (other than natural gas) nor electricity are 'basic' in the same sense that both are dependent on another source of energy for their manufacture. Britain is using at the present time about 300 million tons (304·8 million tonnes) of basic energy each year, expressed in terms of one ton of energy being equal to one ton of coal. Oil is providing each year about 40 per cent of the whole. When one considers that Britain's consumption of oil products may be half as great again ten years from now, then the need for, and the task that faces, the oil refineries becomes clear. In plain terms, the country used 78 million tons (79·25 million tonnes) of oil in 1967; by 1975 it may be using 120 million tons (122 million tonnes).

In the oil producing countries, crude oil is brought by pipeline from the oil wells to the coast and kept there in huge storage tanks. The oil is then pumped aboard oil tankers and brought to this country to be unloaded at the refinery. Powerful ships' pumps often unload it at a rate in excess of 12,000 tons (tonnes) per hour into storage tanks, some capable of holding up to 20 million gallons (90,000 cubic metres) or, in some cases, large tankers lying offshore may have to transfer into smaller tankers first. Now the oil is ready for the refineries to process.

Section I—Characteristics of mineral oils

Petroleum (crude oil) is generally found as an unstable, highly flammable, corrosive liquid. It has a dirty black colour and an objectionably nauseating odour. Although it is normally in a flowable form, the exception so far as viscosity is concerned is the crude oil from the bitumen lakes in Venezuela. Before turning to the refining processes, it is essential for the fireman to have a good knowledge of the characteristics of mineral oils, and to be able to recognise the conditions in which, given a source of ignition, hydrocarbon vapours will fire or explode.

1. GENERAL CHARACTERISTICS

(a) Vapour formation

Petroleum oils, at temperatures below their boiling point, vaporise only at the surface and in the presence of a vapour space. If the liquid is contained in a closed vessel, vaporisation will occur until the vapour space is saturated at that particular temperature, *i.e.*, until the space contains such a concentration of the vapour that condensation occurs at the same rate as vaporisation. When this condition obtains, the liquid and the vapour are said to be in equilibrium. The vapours produced tend to mix more or less readily with air or other gases in the vapour space, and if they are left alone, the space will eventually contain a homogeneous mixture of all the gases contained in it. This tendency of gases to mix is called diffusion.

The tendency of liquids to vaporise takes place more quickly with some liquids than with others. For instance, a small quantity of ether will vaporise almost immediately when exposed to air; petrol requires a longer time, whilst water will take longer still. This tendency of a liquid to vaporise is called its volatility.

(b) Flammable limits

It is the vapour which is given off from a flammable liquid that burns when combined with oxygen from the air, and oil which is not vaporising, or has no vapour space above it, cannot burn. Moreover, the air and vapour must be in certain proportions in order to burn. The concentration varies for different vapours; for instance the flammability range of petrol vapour in air is between 1·4—the lower limit—and 5·9—the upper limit, per cent of petrol vapour by volume; *i.e.*, petrol vapour requires a maximum of 98·6 per cent and a minimum of 94·1 per cent of air to support combustion. The flammable limits of some hydrocarbon compounds and petroleum liquids, *i.e.*, mixtures of hydrocarbon compounds are given in Table I. Hydrogen is included, as it is a regular by-product and is present in refineries

TABLE I
Flammable limits in air

	Explosive limit* (per cent in air)	
	Lower	Upper
Methane (gas)	5·0	15·0
Ethane (gas)	3·0	12·5
Propane (gas)	2·4	9·5
Butane (gas)	1·5	9·0
Pentane (liquid)	1·4	7·8
Hexane (liquid)	1·2	7·5
Heptane (liquid)	1·2	6·7
Petrol	1·4	5·9
Petroleum naphtha	1·1	4·8
Kerosene	0·7	5·0
Hydrogen (gas)	4·1	74·0
Methyl ethyl ketone (solvent) . .	1·8	11·5
Acetone (solvent)	2·5	13·0
Furfural (solvent)	2·1†	—
Ethylene	2·7	28·6
Acetylene (gas)	2·5	80·0

* Slight variations in these limits may be found according to the grade of the particular petrol, naphtha or kerosene.

† Decomposes rapidly above this limit.

254

and chemical plant in large quantities and is particularly hazardous, together with one or two other extremely dangerous substances.

It will be obvious that a gas (or vapour) with wide limits of flammability is potentially more dangerous than one which has a narrow flammable range, since the possibility of obtaining a mixture within the flammable range is greater. It is interesting to compare the flammable limits of the compounds in Table I with those of hydrogen, which are 4·1 to 74 per cent by volume.

(c) Flash point

The flash point of a liquid is the lowest temperature at which sufficient vapour is given off to flash *on the application of a flame* in the presence of air (*see* Part I of the *Manual*, Chapter 1, 'The Physics and Chemistry of Combustion'). The flame can be an arc, spark, naked flame or any other source of direct ignition. The flash point of some hydrocarbons is well below freezing point; petrol, for example, has a flash point of about −45°C. Flammable liquids with HIGH volatility generally have LOW flash points and are more hazardous than flammable liquids with LOW volatility, which usually have HIGH flash points, *i.e.*, lubricating oils, heavy fuel oils, diesel or gas oils. This characteristic gives low volatility oils a greater degree of safety with relation to fire.

(d) Self-ignition temperature

It should be noted, however, that heat alone can be a source for the ignition of hydrocarbon vapours without the application of a naked flame. For this to take place a source of heat must be provided. The temperature at which this will occur is called the self-ignition temperature (sometimes it is called the auto-ignition temperature); this is the lowest temperature to which a solid, liquid or gas requires to be raised to cause self-sustained combustion without initiation by a spark or flame.

If, for example, some petrol vapour is leaking and is diluted with air to within its flammable range, and then comes into contact with a source of heat such as hot brickwork or pipes which are above 246°C, then ignition will occur automatically. This is why if a non-cooling extinguishant, such as chemical dry powder, is used on a petrol fire, the flame may be quenched; but if there is an incandescent source of ignition or sufficient residual heat build-up, the vapour will almost immediately re-ignite if application of the extinguishant is discontinued before cooling by water spray or blanketing with foam is commenced.

The approximate self-ignition temperature of some hydrocarbon compounds is given in Table II. Hydrogen is again included for comparison.

TABLE II

Self-ignition temperatures

	Degrees centigrade
Methane, CH_4 .	538
Ethane, C_2H_6 .	514
Propane, C_3H_8	466
Butane, C_4H_{10} .	430
Pentane, C_5H_{12}	309
Hexane, C_6H_{14}.	234
Heptane, C_7H_{16}	223
Octane, C_8H_{18} .	232
Nonane, C_9H_{20}	206
Petrol	246
Kerosene	254
Lubricating oil	370/416
Fuel oil (Nos. 3 to 6)	260/407
Paraffin wax	245
Hydrogen	585

(e) Safe dilution point

Most petroleum vapours are heavier than air and will travel considerable distances following contours of the ground, depending on wind strength and direction. The farther the vapours travel from the point of escape, the more the vapours will be diluted with air until the volume of air will cause the mixture to become outside the flammable limit. The safe dilution point for petroleum vapour is generally accepted as 50 ft (15 m) from the source of emission, but in assessing the safety margin, the wind and prevailing conditions MUST be considered. Any heavy emission of vapour could, in favourable downwind circumstances, dilute at greater distances than this spreading over a wide area to a vapour to air ratio within the flammable range. If such a vapour cloud flashes over, the flame will propagate very rapidly over the whole of the vapour trail back towards the source of leak, and may cause a number of fires in its path.

(f) Toxicity

Apart from the flammability of petroleum oils, another important hazard is toxicity. The nature of the toxic hazards arising from hydrocarbons depends on the composition of the fraction, and the important fractions are hydrocarbon gases containing benzene and heavy aromatic oils.

Air containing only 0·1 per cent by volume of hydrocarbon vapour can cause irritation to the nose, ears and throat; heavier concentrations can cause dizziness and unconsciousness. A 0·5 per cent concentration could prove fatal.

Petroleum fractions containing benzene are those present in petrol. Benzene has a destructive effect on blood-forming organs, which occurs on repeated exposures to low concentration. Vapour inhalation should be prevented altogether. Heavy aromatic oils, which are encountered in the catalytic cracking plant, hydroformer and chemical plants, are dangerous, especially in contact with the skin. As a method of identification, lines and equipment containing aromatic products are sometimes marked with coloured bands.

Hydrogen sulphide (or sulphuretted hydrogen), which is to be found in fresh crude oil, sulphur plants and polymerisation processes, is extremely toxic and is highly corrosive in contact with metal. It can be easily recognised by its offensive smell of rotten eggs, and will tend to paralyse the olfactory nerves. It is important to realise that this gas can create a false sense of security through this effect of paralysing the sense of smell. Sulphur dioxide is another extremely toxic gas produced in the sulphur plants.

Chlorine (*see* Part 6C of the *Manual*, Chapter 16, 'Alphabetical List of Dangerous Chemicals') is another extremely poisonous gas which is to be found in oil refineries. It is used to produce chlorinated hydrocarbon solvents by the reaction of chlorine with light hydrocarbons, such as methane, ethylene and acetylene. Very stringent precautions are adopted to prevent escape of the chlorine gas.

2. CLASSIFICATION OF PETROLEUM OILS

Petroleum oils have been arbitrarily divided by the Institute of Petroleum into three classes to effect safeguards in handling and storage and the classes have been arranged according to the flash point of the oil. Flash points are a guide to the relative volatility of the oils and give an indication of their behaviour when heated. The classifications are:

Class 'A'

These are light fractions with a flash point below 73°F (22·8°C— but owing to our entry into Europe, this may be changed to 21°C). Included in this classification are the following petroleum spirits:

LNG (methane and ethane)
LPG (propane and butane)
Aviation spirit
Pentane
Benzene (benzole)
Coal tar naphtha
Crude petroleum
Heptane
Hexane
Octane
Petrol (motor spirit, benzine, gasoline)
Petroleum ether
Petroleum naphtha
Toluene
Xylene
Some jet aircraft fuels.

Liquefied natural gas (LNG) and liquefied petroleum gas (LPG)—which are not for technical reasons regarded as petroleum spirits—deserve special mention due to the fact that their flash characteristics are completely unrelated to other natural petroleum liquids. Special care should be taken with LNG and LPG as within their explosive limits in the presence of air, they will flash whenever there is any source of ignition present.

There are many other flammable liquids, especially solvents such as acetone, methyl ethyl ketone, etc., which should be included in any comprehensive Class 'A' list. Liquids in Class 'A' have very low but varying flash points and the greatest caution should be exercised when in the presence of air. Petroleum crude oil has no particular flash point, but is more hazardous than any of the liquids in Class 'A'.

Class 'B'

Medium oils which have a flash point between 73° and 150°F (22·8° and 65·6°C although this latter figure may become 55°C) comprise Class 'B'. These oils always present an element of danger, especially in hot weather. Jet fuels (kerosene), white spirit (turpentine substitute) and tractor vaporising oils are included in this class.

Class 'C'

Class 'C' petroleum liquids have a flash point above 150°F (65·6°C) and include gas oils, diesel oils, heavy fuel oils and the heavier lubricating oils. These oils will not give rise to a flammable vapour mixture unless they are heated and brought to a temperature above their flash point, which may in some cases be as high as 260°C. However, the difference between flash point and self-ignition is much less with the heavier oils than with the lighter oils. Under normal conditions, a dangerous vapour atmosphere will not exist inside a tank holding a Class 'C' liquid, and it is only when such tanks are subjected to heat from some external source, such as radiated heat from a nearby tank on fire, that they present a fire hazard.

Crude oils vary greatly in their characteristics, as the term 'crude' is used to define petroleum in its natural state as taken from the earth. They can range from an extremely light liquid to a very heavy product. Accordingly they are hard to classify precisely, but most crude oils contain sufficient light ends, or fractions, to bring them into the 'A' category since the flash point of an oil is governed largely by its most volatile constituents.

Section II—Refining processes

1. CRUDE OIL

Crude oil (correctly termed petroleum) is an intimate mixture of a large number of compounds which are formed mainly of only two elements—hydrogen and carbon. Some other elements are present but hydrogen and carbon represent approximately 12 and 85 per cent by weight respectively. Atoms of hydrogen and carbon can combine to form molecules of different sizes and different configurations. These compounds are called hydrocarbons and each will boil at a temperature which is characteristic of that molecule. In general, the greater the number of carbon atoms in the hydrocarbon molecule, the higher its boiling point.

(a) Classification of crude oils

Crude oils are classified according to the kind of hydrocarbon molecules which predominate. This classification is important since different types of crude oil yield a different quality of individual products. For example, there are *paraffinic-based* crudes which produce good quality base stocks for kerosene, diesel oil and lubricants; a fair proportion of raw petrol is produced by primary distillation, but it is of low quality. Other types of crude oil are *asphaltic-based*, producing good asphalt and fuel oil, and *naphthenic-based* crudes. There are also mixed-base crude oils in which no particular type of hydrocarbon predominates.

There are seven main fractions of crude oil, which are all groups of compounds boiling within certain temperature ranges. Two of these seven fractions are removed at the oil field itself; they are natural gases which are released from the petroleum when the liquid mineral suffers a reduction of pressure on reaching the earth's surface, but quite a substantial amount still remains dissolved in the crude oil and is released in the refinery when the petroleum is heated in the first stage of distillation, namely to evaporate the crude oil. These natural gases consist mainly of methane, with lesser amounts of ethane, butane and propane.

At least five fractions are normally produced in the refinery, namely:

(i) Liquefiable petroleum gas and refinery fuel gas, used for enriching town gas or as a fuel.

(ii) Naphtha, the base product of petrol.

(iii) Kerosene (or paraffin) and turbo jet fuels.

(iv) Gas oil, for diesel oil and for heating purposes.

(v) Fuel oils, which range from light fuel oil to heavy fuel oil and asphalt.

Additional base stocks for lubricating oils and asphalts are also produced in some refineries.

(b) Supplying the crude oil

The great oilfields of the world are in the Middle East and in America, although drilling is in progress in other parts of the world; strikes of natural gas and oil have now been made in the North Sea. At the time of writing, the crude oil has to be brought to this country by sea in tankers, and since the closure of the Suez Canal, reliance is placed on super tankers on the longer journey around the Cape; crude oil is also obtained from Libya and Nigeria. Most of the supplies of crude oil come from the Middle East, predominantly Kuwait, Iraq and Iran, and now Libya and Nigeria, but smaller shipments are made from Venezuela and elsewhere. (Venezuelan oil is used for making special lubricants and bitumen.)

Very large crude carriers (VLCCs), as the largest super tankers are called, berth alongside marine terminals and from their berths the crude oil is pumped through jointed metal booms or flexible hoses as far as two miles inland to the crude oil storage tanks. The next stage is the refining of the crude oil.

2. THE REFINER'S TASK

The petroleum refiner has two aims. He must make products which meet the high quality specifications of today's markets, and he must produce the right proportion of each product from the crude oil so that nothing is left over or wasted. To achieve these objectives the refiner uses four main types of process. He can use a separation process, such as '*distillation*' to split the crude oil into groups of compounds, or even to separate one particular compound from another. It may, however, be necessary to change one sort of compound into another in order to obtain the correct balance of production. This the refiner can do with conversion processes, breaking large molecules into smaller ones by '*cracking*', building small molecules into larger ones by '*polymerisation*', or converting low grade raw petrol into high quality motor spirit by '*reforming*'. Thirdly, the refiner may have to remove product impurities or render them harmless: examples of this type of process are '*hydrofining*' and chemical sweetening. Finally, there are many other processes, such as the blending of products, the manufacture of special products, such as bitumen, and the production of lubricating oils by solvent extraction. Fig. 5-1 shows in diagrammatic form the principal processes required to refine crude oil into a wide range of products.

3. THE REFINING PROCESSES

The refining processes described below are those to be found at one of the major refinery companies in this country, but the processes at all refineries are similar in principle, although they may vary in title and detail.

(a) Primary distillation

The initial processing of crude oil is by primary distillation (Fig. 5-2 and Plate 95), which separates it into fractions, each consisting of a group of compounds boiling within a predetermined temperature range.

The crude oil is heated in a furnace to a temperature of about 400°C, at which temperature about three-quarters of the oil has vaporised; the rest remains liquid. This mixture of liquid and vapour is then passed into a '*fractionating tower*', a column about 200 ft (61 m) high, divided horizontally by about thirty trays. Each tray in the tower contains 2–3 in. (51–76 mm) of liquid and there are devices in each tray which force oil vapours rising up the tower to bubble through this liquid. The tower is heated at the bottom by the

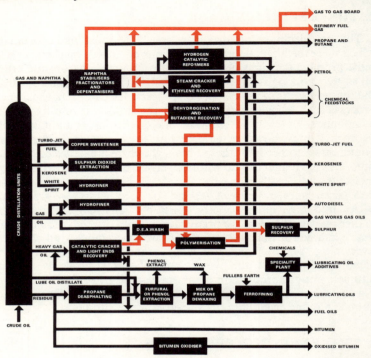

Fig. 5–1. Flow chart showing in diagrammatic form the principal refining processes.

hot oil vapour and liquid which enter. By removing some of the liquid from the top of the tower, cooling it and then re-introducing it, the upper part of the tower is cooled to about 93°C. In this way a temperature gradient is obtained, each tray in the tower being slightly cooler than the one below it.

The liquid portion of the feed falls to the bottom of the tower and is drawn off. This is the fuel oil fraction. The vapours rise up the tower, bubbling through successive trays, and when a particle of vapour reaches a tray which is at or below its boiling point, it condenses and joins the liquid on that tray. The lightest vapours do not condense in the tower but pass out at the top to be condensed and collected externally. These form the gas and naphtha fractions. The remaining fractions are withdrawn at intermediate points in the tower.

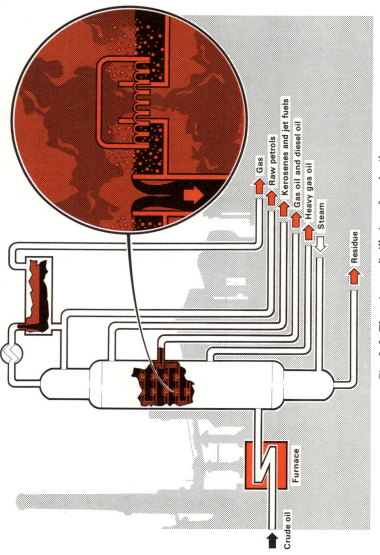

Fig. 5–2. The primary distillation of crude oil.

Gas

Raw petrols

Kerosenes and jet fuels

Gas oil and diesel oil

Heavy gas oil

Steam

Residue

Furnace

Crude oil

Distillation may also be carried out under reduced pressures. The boiling point of a liquid gets lower as the pressure on it is decreased and in this way heavy fuel oils can be split into fractions without making them so hot in order to vaporise them; this avoids the tendency of the big molecules to 'crack' or break up into smaller molecules of light oil.

(b) Fluid catalytic cracking

'*Cracking*' is a conversion process which breaks large oil molecules into smaller ones. One application is in 'cracking' a heavy gas oil to form high grade petrol and gas. One process used is known as 'fluid catalytic cracking' (Plate 96)—'catalytic' because a chemical substance called a catalyst is used (this helps the cracking reaction without being changed itself) and 'fluid' because the catalyst in powder form can be made to behave like a liquid when it is blown with air or hydrocarbon vapour.

Heavy gas oil feedstock is sprayed in to meet a stream of red-hot catalyst from the regenerator; the catalyst vaporises the oil and the vaporised oil fluidises the catalyst. Both flow into the reactor where cracking takes place. The cracked oil vapours pass to a fractionating column, in which the small molecules of petrol and gas formed by cracking are separated from the heavier and unconverted products as in the distillation process. Further fractionation separates the petrol from the light gases which are used for refinery fuel, or sent to Gas Boards (for making town gas—*see* Chapter 2), or fed to the polymerisation plant, or used to make chemical feedstocks.

During cracking, the catalyst becomes coated with carbon. It is transferred by a stream of air into a regenerator or kiln, where the carbon is burned off and the catalyst reheated—ready to begin its cycle again.

(c) Polymerisation

Polymerisation is the reverse of cracking; *i.e.*, building up small molecules into larger ones. Light gases, produced by the 'cat cracker' are combined to produce heavier materials, like butane and a further supply of high quality petrol. A polymerisation plant at an oil refinery could produce as much as 1,000 tons (1016 tonnes) a day.

(d) Reforming

This is a process by which the shape, rather than the size, of oil molecules is changed in order to improve product quality (Plate 97). The catalytic reformer processes naphtha with a low octane rating from primary distillation (*i.e.*, it has a low resistance to 'knocking' in a high compression engine), and reforms it into a high quality petrol with a high octane rating.*

The naphtha feedstock is first treated in a hydrofiner to remove any sulphur compounds, and is then passed through four furnaces and reactors which are in series. In the reactors, by using high pressures, an atmosphere of hydrogen and a platinum-based catalyst, the molecules of raw petrol are converted into aromatic configurations with high anti-knock properties. At a large refinery, the catalytic reformer could have a capacity of over 2,000 tons (2032 tonnes) a day, while a hydrofiner could process over 3,000 tons (3048 tonnes) of oil a day.

(e) Sulphur recovery

Sulphur is found as an impurity in most crude oils. Some sulphur compounds are corrosive and must be removed from products such as diesel oils and white spirit. In the hydrofining process, the oil is heated and mixed with hydrogen under pressure and passed into a reactor where, in the presence of a catalyst, the sulphur compounds are converted to free hydrogen sulphide (H_2S). This highly dangerous gas is easily separated from the oil. The oil is then scrubbed with steam and washed with a solution of caustic soda to remove any unconverted sulphur compounds.

The poisonous hydrogen sulphide from the hydrofiners is burned in a controlled reaction furnace with a limited amount of air to form sulphur. Some refineries produce as much as 75 tons (76 tonnes) of pure sulphur a day by catalytic refining of 5,000 tons (5080 tonnes) of oil.

(f) Sulphur dioxide extraction

Some products of primary distillation require 'cleaning up', *i.e.*, unwanted compounds must be removed from them. An example is found in raw paraffin. As it comes off the primary distillation tower, the paraffin contains a proportion of hydrocarbon molecules of aromatic form. These compounds make a lot of black smoke when burned in an open flame—although they burn very well in an internal combustion engine.

---

* It should be noted that the octane rating of petrols is merely an indication of the suitability of that fuel for use with certain types of high compression internal combustion engine, and depends partly on the chemical structure of the fuel and partly on the addition of compounds, such as 'alkyl lead', designed to reduce engine knock. The octane rating is primarily of interest to the motor engineer and does not have any significance in fire fighting, *i.e.*, it does not indicate the flammability of the fuel.

In a sulphur dioxide extraction plant—a typical plant at a modern refinery can process 3,000 tons (3048 tonnes) of kerosene a day—the aromatics are removed from the kerosene by washing them out with liquefied sulphur dioxide. The kerosene (paraffin) will then burn with far less tendency to smoke, and the aromatics extracted can be blended into other products.

(g) Copper sweetening

In some cases complete removal of sulphur compounds is unnecessary and it is sufficient to convert the malodorous compounds (mercaptans) into inoffensive ones (di-sulphides) by a treating process known as copper sweetening. Conversion of the mercaptans to di-sulphides actually occurs in the presence of air and a catalyst of copper chloride. A typical copper sweetening unit could have a capactiy of over 10,000 tons (101 60 tonnes) a day.

(h) Lubricating oil treating

Feedstocks for lubricating oil manufacture are prepared by vaccum distillation of the residue made during the primary distillation of crude oils. Each type of residue is split up by vacuum distillation into a number of fractions which provide a complete range of thick and thin oils, classified in terms of viscosity. Each feedstock contains aromatic compounds and other non-paraffinic compounds which adversely affect the viscosity temperature property of the oil. Viscosity Index (VI) is a measure of this property—the higher the VI, the less the viscosity alters with temperature change.

The phenol solvent extraction process removes the undesirable aromatic compounds and hence improves the VI quality of lubricating oils. This is a particularly important step in motor oil manufacture since high VI oils thin out less when heated to engine running temperatures and conversely thicken less under cold starting conditions. (At some refineries furfural is used as the solvent.) After phenol extraction, the oil is passed to the propane de-waxing plant where it is mixed with the solvent which has been liquefied by compression. (Other solvents used may be toluene/methyl ethyl ketone.) In the chiller-contactor, the propane is allowed to evaporate, so chilling the oil and causing the wax to crystallise. The wax is then removed by filtration.

The final steps in 'lube' oil refining are designed to improve the colour and stability of finished oils. Colour improvement is achieved by contacting the hot oils with activated clay in powder form. The dark colour bodies in the oil are absorbed on the clay particles which are then separated by filtration. A later process to achieve this is known as 'hydrofinishing' in which clay is used, but is a similar process to the hydrotreating of light oils. Another name for the process is 'phenolfining'.

4. CALCINED COKE

Calcined coke, commonly known as petroleum coke, was once a small by-product of petroleum refining, but because of present day demands and the product's versatility for use in the manufacturing of electrodes in the production of aluminium and steel, one major refinery in Britain has a large coking plant.

This coke must not be confused with coke produced as a by-product of coal. There are two types of calcined coke: 'regular' and 'premium'. The 'regular' coke is produced primarily for the manufacture of electrodes in the production of aluminium and the 'premium' for the manufacture of electrodes in the production of steel in electric arc furnaces. Two separate but similar units are used, the difference being in the initial liquid feedstock to the coke drums.

A liquid stream consisting primarily of 'thermal tar' is used for premium coke and a liquid stream of 'topped crude' is used for the regular grade. In both cases, the feed stream is fed through a bubble tower and heated by means of a furnace coil passing into the coke drums. A solid coke which is formed by polymerisation and condensation reaction, settles out and has to be removed from the drums by pumps using a conventional high water drilling rig at a pressure of approximately 3,000 lbf/in^2 (207 bars).

The coke lumps are then mechanically crushed and fed into a calciner kiln. These kilns are brick lined, sloping steel cylinders, 230 ft (70 m) long and 12 ft (3·7 m) in diameter, and rotate at three revolutions per minute. They are fired by fuel gas at the end opposite the coke feed-in. All volatiles contained within the coke are burned off as the product passes through the kiln. After the coke leaves the kiln it is water cooled and mechanically handled for loading into specially designed road or rail transportation to customers.

Fire hazards regarding the end product are negligible, but due to the very high temperatures involved during production, a potential fire hazard is always imminent. Water should only be used as a last resort, steam normally being utilised in all cases of fire. Steam lances (*see* page 303) are usually situated at strategic points on the plant.

5. MANUFACTURE OF CHEMICALS

The manufacture of chemicals is an important aspect of the oil business and is growing yearly. Already more than 70 per cent of all the organic chemicals made in this country have an oil base. Poly-thene, detergents, man-made fibres for house furnishings and cloth-ing, synthetic rubbers, building materials, tyres, paints, stockings, anti-freeze—these are some of the innumerable everyday products which emanate from petroleum chemicals. At most refineries are made chemical feedstocks, such as ethylene and butadiene, from which many of these end products are derived.

(a) Steam cracking

Steam cracking is a pyrolysis or high temperature thermal cracking process designed to produce olefins and diolefins as feedstocks for other chemical, plastics and rubber manufacturing processes. Heat is used to 'crack' a feed of raw petrol (naphtha); the feed is mixed with steam and heated to high temperatures in a large furnace. Under these conditions the molecules of naphtha are broken down or changed in shape to form light gases (such as ethylene, propylene, butylene and butadiene) and high quality petrol.

The cracked products are compressed and refrigerated, and then pass to a series of fractionating columns which separate a number of individual compounds (Plate 98). The most important of these is ethylene, which is the raw material for a tremendous range of plastics and chemicals. It is interesting to note that two olefin units at one refinery produce annually 475,000 and 100,000 tons (482 622 and 101 605 tonnes) of ethylene respectively.

(b) Butadiene production

Another chemical produced by a conversion process is butadiene, which is used for the manufacture of styrene—butadiene synthetic rubber. A feedstock of butene, which is produced in any cracking process, is subjected to a dehydrogenation process. By using a catalyst and high temperatures, two atoms of hydrogen are removed from each molecule of butene to produce butadiene.

(c) Butyl rubber production

Butyl rubber is a synthetic rubber made by co-polymerising iso-butylene and isoprene. It has very good resistance to atmospheric oxidation, particularly by ozone, which is the main cause of natural rubber deteriorating and cracking. It also has good resistance to heat, has a very low electrical conductivity, does not tear easily, is impervious to gases and liquids and has high shock-absorbing proper-ties. By altering the co-polymerisation conditions, a range of rubbers of different molecular weight or unsaturation can be made, which are mainly used for tyre inner tubes, electric cable covering, shock absorbers, gaskets, O-rings, extrusions, roofing, linings for agricultural silos and reservoirs.

6. PRINCIPAL PRODUCTS OF AN OIL REFINERY

Finally, here is a summary of the principal products of a modern oil refinery:

(i) *Gas*, which is converted by Gas Boards for use as town gas, or is used for fuel in the refinery's own furnaces.

(ii) *Propane* for heating, metal cutting and flame welding, lighting for caravans, etc.

(iii) *Butane*, a liquefied petroleum gas used as a fuel for heating and cooking, air-conditioning on farms, etc.

(iv) *Naphtha*, used in its raw state in the manufacture of town gas; also widely used as a petro-chemical feedstock and for reforming to petrol.

(v) *Petrol*, a fuel for motor cars and other spark-ignition internal combustion engines.

(vi) *Heptenes*, for use in the manufacture of plastics, such as PVC.

(vii) *Ethylene*, used in the manufacture of polyethylene, and an essential chemical for ethylene glycol, which is used in the manufacture of terylene and anti-freeze.

(viii) *Butadiene*, used in the manufacture of synthetic rubber.

(ix) *Butyl rubber*, for car inner tubes, shock absorbers and cable insulation.

(x) *Turbo-jet fuels* for civil and military jet aircraft.

(xi) *Kerosene* (paraffin), a fuel for portable domestic heaters.

(xii) *Tractor vaporising oil*, a kerosene fuel for all types of vaporising oil tractor.

(xiii) *White spirit*, a solvent used in the manufacture of paints, varnishes, enamels and polishes; also used for dry cleaning.

(xiv) *Autodiesel*, a fuel used in automotive diesel engines on roads and railways.

(xv) *Marine diesel*, a fuel for marine diesel engines.

(xvi) *Sulphur*, an essential chemical in the manufacture of sulphuric acid and fertilisers.

(xvii) *Lubricating oil*, for lubricating all kinds of machinery, motor cars, marine, aviation and industrial machines.

(xviii) *Lubricating oil additives*, for the improvement of engine performance and reduction of wear.

(xix) *Fuel oils*, for home heating, industrial furnaces, ship propulsion and electricity generation.

(xx) *Bitumens*, for road construction, roofing and waterproofing materials.

(xxi) *Calcined coke*, for the manufacture of electrodes for aluminium production and electrodes in electric arc steel-producing furnaces.

Section III—Storage tanks

Storage tanks are found in all shapes and sizes; the majority at oil refineries are vertical cylindrical tanks and giant ones now being built can hold as much as 20 million gallons (90 000 cubic metres) of oil, but horizontal cylindrical and spherical pressure vessels will also be seen. Some tanks may be refrigerated or heated. Crude oil tanks and those for volatile finished products, such as petrol, have roofs in the form of a pontoon which float on the surface of the liquid to obviate any ullage (or outage) space, and have seals round the periphery to prevent vapour escaping. The seals reduce the risk of fire, help to avoid loss of the valuable product, and minimise the not very pleasant smell of oil in its natural state.

The fireman may find the various terms indicating capacity, as used in the oil industry, a little confusing, but the change into metric equivalents should lead to some clarification. At the moment, the capacity of oil storage tanks is generally quoted in gallons or barrels (1 barrel=35 Imperial gallons=5·61 cubic feet), although the size of a tank may be stated in cubic feet. Under metrication, tank capacities will no doubt be reckoned in cubic metres, or small quantities may be given in litres (1 cubic metre=1,000 litres). On the other hand, because dues for shipping which are imposed by the Department of Trade and Industry (Marine Division), are rated on tonnage (under the regulations 1 ton = 100 cubic feet) oil tanker capacities are invariably quoted in tons. It is expected that under metrication tanker capacities will be given in metric tonnes, and these are in fact almost equal to Imperial tons (1 ton = 1·016 tonnes).

1. TYPES OF TANK

The types of cylindrical tank recommended for the storage of hydrocarbon oil having regard to volatility are shown in Table III.

TABLE III

Types of cylindrical tank recommended for petroleum oils

Class 'A' (flash point below 22·8°C)	(a) Floating roof. (b) 'Non-pressure' fixed roof with internal floating deck. (c) 'Pressure' fixed roof.
Class 'B' (flash point between 22·8 and 65·6°C)	(a) Floating roof. (b) 'Non-pressure, fixed roof with internal floating deck. (c) 'Non-pressure' fixed roof with atmospheric vents.
Class 'C' (flash point above 65·6°C)	'Non-pressure' fixed roof with atmospheric vents. (Tanks which contain heavy fuel oils or bitumens are insulated and heated.)

2. SIZES OF TANKS

Vertical cylindrical tanks can range in size up to 300 ft (90 m) in diameter, and more than 60 ft (18 m) in height. Horizontal tanks may be used for specific purposes, especially for underground tanks, and liquefied petroleum gas tanks up to 200 ft (60 m) in length are not uncommon.

Standard metric sizes are now recommended for vertical cylindrical tanks, and Table IV shows the capacity of some random sizes of metric tanks.

3. FIXED ROOF (CONE) TANKS

Oil storage tanks are generally constructed of a number of courses (or strakes) of mild steel plates, which are generally welded together, but may be riveted, if of older construction. Since the internal pressure on the tank is greater at the bottom, the side (or shell) plates increase in thickness from the top to the bottom. Strakes are usually 6 ft (1·8 m) in height, and this gives a method of easy calculation of the height of a tank.

(a) 'Non-pressure' roofs

Roofs of the non-pressure type of tank are conical or domed in shape and are self-supporting, *i.e.*, there are no internal columns to take the weight of the roof, but the steel plates rest on a supporting

271

TABLE IV

Nominal metric capacity of standard cylindrical tanks

Height Metres	Tank diameter in metres									
	10	15	20	25	30	42	48	60	72	84
	Nominal capacity in cubic metres									
5	392	883	1 570	2 454	3 534	6 927	9 074	14 137	20 357	27 708
6	471	1 060	1 884	2 945	4 241	8 312	10 857	16 964	24 428	33 250
7	549	1 237	2 199	3 436	4 948	9 698	12 666	19 792	28 500	38 792
8	628	1 413	2 513	3 926	5 654	11 083	14 476	22 619	32 571	44 334
9	706	1 590	2 827	4 417	6 361	12 468	16 285	25 446	36 693	49 875
10	785	1 767	3 141	4 908	7 068	13 851	18 095	28 274	40 714	55 417
15	1 178	2 650	4 712	7 363	10 602	20 781	27 143	42 411	61 072	83 126
20		3 534	6 283	9 617	14 137	27 708	36 191	56 548	81 429	110 835
25		4 417	7 853	12 271	17 671	34 636	45 238	70 685	101 787	138 544

Plate 89. *An aerial view of the Esso Refinery at Fawley, which occupies 1,250 acres (506 hectacres).*

Plate 90. *The Esso marine terminal at Fawley; this is 4,200 ft. (1,280 m) long and has five berths for ocean-going tankers. The berth at the top of the picture can accept partly laden vessels up to 300,000 tons (305 000 tonnes).*

Plate 91. *An aerial view of the jetties at the British Petroleum's Kent refinery with tankage and refinery unit in the background.*

Plate 92. *A typical example of the complicated mass of pipes and plant which is a feature of all oil refineries.*

Plate 93. An example of the BP integrated refinery at Vernon, near Paris. Particular attention has been paid to landscaping of the site.

Plate 94. A closer view of the process unit at Vernon. Note how compact this can be made in an integrated refinery.

Plate 95. A primary distillation unit. Fractional distillation is the first stage in the refining process, separating the crude oil into its basic groups of hydrocarbons by boiling them off.

Plate 96. A fluid catalytic cracking plant showing the preheat furnace on the left and the regenerator and reactor vessels at the rear on the right. Fluid catalytic cracking converts gas oils to high octane petrol and other distillate products.

Plate 97. A powerformer plant which produces petroleum blending components, liquefied petroleum gas and also a feedstock for an aromatics extraction plant producing benzene and toluene.

Plate 98. Chemicals are important products of an oil refinery. This is a general view of an ethylene recovery section of the chemical plant at Fawley. Much of this ethylene is supplied to the ICI plant at Severnside via a 78 miles (125 km) long pipeline.

Plate 99. Inside a floating roof tank. The access ladder automatically adjusts itself to compensate for changes in roof level.

Plate 100. Insulated storage tanks for LPG which is kept at a temperature of —45°C prior to being pumped into a pipeline connected to the North Thames Gas Board. The tanks are 100 ft. (30·5 m) high with a diameter of 86 ft. (26 m) and are insulated with a layer of polyurethane foam.

Plate 101. Spheres used for the storage of liquid butane gas under pressure. These have a capacity of about 1,000 tons (1 016 tonnes) each.

Plate 102. A cryogenic storage sphere for liquefied ethylene gas. The product is refrigerated to a temperature of —104°C enabling it to be stored at atmospheric pressure instead of under pressure as is normal practice.

Plate 103. A light portable trailer-mounted water monitor being demonstrated. This can deliver a stream of water or a wide curtain of diffused water at 500 gallons (2,273 litres) a minute.

Plate 104. Another type of insulated tank used for storing lubricating oil.

Plate 105. A cargo of crude oil being discharged at a marine jetty, showing the hard arm fully counterbalanced type of cargo handling equipment. Discharge rates in excess of 10,000 tons (10,160 tonnes) an hour can be achieved.

Plate 106. A road-tanker being loaded with white oils.

Plate 107. The damage which can be caused following a serious fire and explosion in process plant at an oil refinery.

Plate 108. This distillation plant releasing crude oil which was ignited gives a vivid picture of the proportions a refinery fire can attain.

Plate 109. Three foam branches being used at the fire shown in Plate 108. While these branches were at work at ground level, a serious fire situation was developing at higher levels.

Plate 110. A slop-over. The oil pours over the edge of the tank, but is not blown upwards as with a boil-over. The black smoke is typical of hydrocarbon fires.

Plate 111. A demonstration showing the effect of applying a water jet to burning propane.

steel framework (Fig. 5-3). The roof plates are fixed at the periphery to the top curb angle of the shell by a single fillet weld which is weaker than the shell seams or than the weld attachment of the shell to the base of the tank.

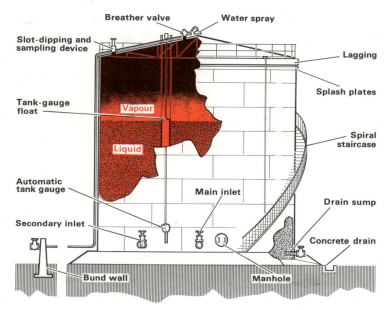

Fig. 5–3. A vertical cylindrical 'non-pressure' fixed roof tank.

This type of tank has only this weak roof-to-shell seam and no other form of emergency venting. Normal venting on a non-pressure fixed roof tank is by an open or free-flow atmospheric vent (Fig. 5-4) which allows the unimpeded flow of vapour in and out of the tank, but prevents the ingress of rain and air-borne dust.

(b) 'Pressure' roofs

Constructional details of 'pressure' roof tanks are similar to those of the 'non-pressure' type, but because of the higher internal pressure, they are limited to tanks up to 128 ft (39 m) in diameter. Pressure roof tanks, however, are provided with special breather vents (Fig. 5-5) which minimise the losses of vapour from volatile liquids that would result if the normal free-flow atmospheric vent was fitted. They also protect the tank from excessive pressure. The breather vent helps to

273

maintain an over-rich vapour in the ullage space of the tank and thereby prevents possible ignition.

Fig. 5–4. *A free-flow atmospheric vent as found on non-pressure fixed roof tanks.*

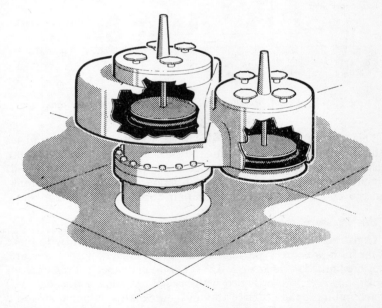

Fig. 5–5. *The breather vent as fitted to a pressure roof tank and which incorporates pressure and vacuum valves.*

Atmospheric and breather vents are sometimes fitted with flame arresters to prevent the propagation of flame into the tank. These take the form of perforated plates, non-corrodible wire gauzes, fine slots in a metal block, crimped metal or bunches of narrow metal tubes. It has been found, however, that flame arresters which have become clogged with paint, dust, scale or other waxy deposits may interfere with the normal working of the vents, and so regular maintenance is essential. This can be a problem in a refinery where there are hundreds of tanks. In addition, when the breather vents are closed, flame cannot pass through them and in the case of volatile oils, such as petrol, the vapour inside the tank would be too rich to ignite. Consequently some companies have dispensed with flame arresters.

4. FLOATING ROOF TANKS

Because the pressure fixed roof tank is limited in size, larger tanks require a different construction. The floating roof tank provides economical storage of volatile liquids with a high degree of safety and floating roof tanks of 300 ft (91 m) in diameter and 70 ft (22 m) high are becoming commonplace in refineries; these are capable of holding the full cargo of a VLCC. The steel roof floats on the oil (Fig. 5-6) and rises or falls as the liquid is pumped in and out of the tank. The essential feature of this type of roof is a vapour-tight seal between the periphery of the roof and the tank shell.

Fig. 5–6. The pontoon floating roof tank.

(a) Pontoon floating roof tanks

The early type of floating roof consists of a single deck with a vertical rim at the periphery and is known as a pan-type roof. A pan roof has one deck and is always in contact with the stored liquid. The sun's heat on the deck can cause severe boiling losses from volatile oils, and so the pan roof has been superseded by the pontoon floating roof which has an annular pontoon (Fig. 5-7) around the periphery, encircling a single centre deck. In addition to buoyancy,

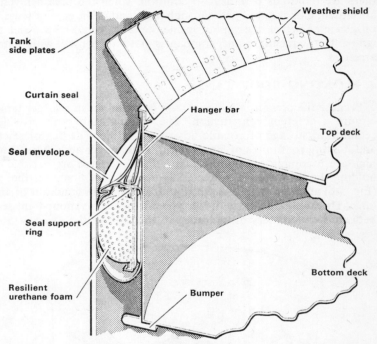

Fig. 5–7. The annular pontoon of a floating roof tank showing a resilient urethane foam fabric seal.

the pontoon provides air-space insulation from the sun's heat, and thus inhibits boiling of the oil in the annular area. The annular space between the floating roof and the shell may be rendered vapour-proof by means of a special fabric seal in tube form, the tube being filled with liquid, or by a resilient urethane foam fabric seal (Fig. 5-7). Either seal has the ability to conform to the tank shape so that there should be no vapour in the space between the roof and shell above the seal, but the liquid-filled seal has the disadvantage that it can be punctured by any sharp protrusion on the shell.

Another type of seal for floating roof tanks is the pantagraph hanger with steel shunts (Fig. 5-8). The stainless steel shunts are spaced about 10 ft (3·05 m) apart and provide a sure electrical bond

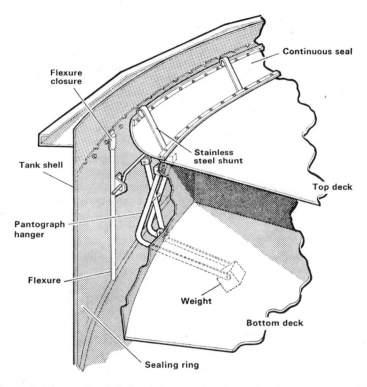

Fig. 5–8. The pantagraph hanger type of seal for floating roof tanks. The stainless steel shunts also provide an electrical contact across the seal.

between the floating roof and the sealing ring which is in contact with the tank shell. Insulated pantagraph hangers maintain the contact of the shunts with the tank shell.

Floating roofs are usually installed in open top tanks and therefore the top of the shell is generally strengthened by the addition of a wind girder (*see* Fig. 5-6) around the shell near the top as a protection against the shell 'blowing-in' during high winds. At some refineries, these wind girders have been provided with hand rails so that men can walk safely around the top of the shell for maintenance, inspection and fire fighting, especially of seal fires at the rim of the roof. Fire fighting can then take place from the wind girder on the outside of the tank, and men do not need to go down on to the pontoon roof.

Floating roof tanks are also provided with drains to remove rain water and discharge it outside the tank. Four types are normally to be found; open, siphon, pipe with swing joints or flexible hose. The first two types of drain discharge the water through the contents of the tank so that it collects at the bottom, where it can be drawn off through a connection at the base of the tank. The other two types convey the rain water to the outside of the tank without it coming into contact with the contents.

(b) Double-deck floating roof tanks

A further development of the floating roof to give better buoyancy and stability is the double-deck type of construction (Fig. 5-9). This provides an extension of the insulating air space between the two decks over almost the whole surface area of the liquid, and this has the advantage of shielding the oil from the effect of solar heat.

(c) Internal floating roof tanks

A further development in tank design is a tank which combines the fixed and floating roof type of construction (Fig. 5-10), generally

Fig. 5–9. Diagram showing the double-deck type of floating roof tank.

278

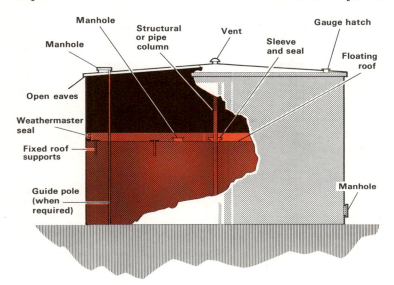

Fig. 5–10. An internal floating roof tank which incorporates an internal floating deck in a fixed roof tank.

known as the internal floating roof tank. A steel floating deck, similar to the pan-type floating roof, but without the elaborate draining system, is protected by a cone or domed roof with open eaves to allow ventilation of the small amount of vapour which may escape past the seals into the space above the floating deck. The roof may be column-supported, or the floating deck may be installed in a self-supporting fixed roof tank.

This type of tank is found in those areas where there may be bad weather conditions, especially where heavy snowfalls are prevalent.

5. PRESSURISED STORAGE TANKS

Standard tanks are not suitable for the storage of liquefied petroleum gases, such as protane or butane, owing to the high pressures required to maintain these gases in a liquid state; they are therefore stored in special pressure vessels. The ideal shape for a pressure vessel is spherical, as the internal pressure is the same at any point, but long, heavily-built small-diameter horizontal tanks with rounded ends are also used.

(a) Spheres

Spheres (Fig. 5-11 and Plates 101 and 102) are used at oil refineries for the storage of LPG in bulk, for ammonia or for ethylene under pressure. They are made of steel plates welded together in the same manner as for circular tanks, but they are supported on six or more steel legs, the number depending on the overall size of the vessel. The legs are enclosed in concrete except where they are welded to the sphere. Each vessel may have an individual fire wall or bund enclosure with a retention capacity of about 50 per cent of the contents of the tank, although, as a result of the Feyzin (France)

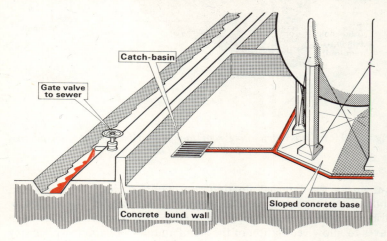

Fig. 5–11. A spherical pressurised storage tank, showing the catch basin or bunded enclosure, and the drain-away facilities.

fire, new installations are not bunded and do not hold leaking gas in the area, but arrangements are made to drain away leaking contents to a safer area.

The concrete floor of the area inside the bund (where they exist) is sloped towards a sealed catch basin (or pig trap as they are sometimes called) within the area, as remote as possible from the sphere, so that any spilled liquid, especially underneath the sphere, is directed into the catch basin. A gate valve (kept closed) is generally installed outside the fire walls in the sewer line from the catch basin to prevent any spilled liquid petroleum gas entering the refinery sewer system. Each enclosed area within the fire wall drains separately to the sewer system.

Safety valves are fitted at the top of LPG spheres as a precaution against possible over-pressurisation, and since the safety valves normally discharge vapour when they blow, it is the general practice for them to vent to the atmosphere. LPG spheres always have sufficient vapour space left in the vessel so that the liquid has room to expand as, if the vessel is overfilled, it can result in the safety valve blowing and discharging liquid. A small amount of vented liquid will vaporise into a very large volume of gas. Owing to location problems, it may be unwise to vent to atmosphere, and in these cases the vapour is routed into flare stack lines. Precautions are invariably incorporated to ensure that when a safety valve blows, liquid cannot be discharged directly into the flare stack, as this could lead to burning liquid LPG being vented from the flare stack.

Each sphere is protected externally by a water drencher system, and has a water draw-off and anti-freeze internal drain connection at the base to allow water in the tank to be drawn off and run into a catch basin. The water draw-off arrangements are safeguarded by two or more valves so that close down can be achieved despite possible ice formation.

(b) Horizontal pressure vessels

Horizontal pressure vessels for the storage of volatile oils or gases under pressure are easily recognisable by their rounded ends (*see* Plate 28 in Part 6C of the *Manual*). They are more stoutly constructed than normal vertical cylindrical tanks and, of course, incorporate suitable pressure-relieving devices. Fire walls (or bunds) may be provided, but in newer installations similar arrangements exist for collecting spilled liquid and directing it into safer areas. There is also water draw-off piping at the base of the tank similar to that on spheres.

6. REFRIGERATED TANKS

There is an economic advantage in refrigerated storage over pressure storage for very large quantities of liquid, and owing to the increase in the quantities of LPG which are being used in recent years, giant refrigerated tanks (Plate 100) of 100 ft (30 m) in height may now be found at oil refineries. At atmospheric pressure, propane boils at $-42°C$ and normal butane at $-0·6°$. By cooling to below boiling point and maintaining the liquids in a chilled state, it is possible to store them in tanks designed to operate at slightly above atmospheric pressure.

Cryogenic storage spheres (Plate 102) are also used for the storage of liquefied ethylene gas at a temperature of $-104°C$ enabling it to be stored at atmospheric pressure instead of under pressure as is normally necessary.

(a) Fully-refrigerated storage

Tanks are either of single- or double-wall construction. In single-wall construction, special low temperature steel is used and this is surrounded by an insulation layer of foam glass, polyurethane or similar material. With double-wall construction, the inner tank is enclosed by an outer tank constructed from low carbon steel and the annular space between the tanks is filled with an insulating material, *e.g.* perlite. As a safety measure, the annular space may contain an inert gas, such as nitrogen.

(b) Refrigerated pressure storage

Refrigerated pressure storage (sometimes called semi-refrigerated storage) combines partial refrigeration with low or medium pressure. These storage tanks are usually spherical in shape and can be 40 ft (12 m) or more in diameter.

7. TANK FITTINGS

(a) Access to the roof

Access to the roof of an oil tank is provided by means of a metal staircase which generally runs spirally from the ground to the top of the tank, or from a point some distance from the ground. On floating roof tanks, a second ladder leads down to the roof from the top of the spiral staircase (*see* Figs. 5-6 and 5-9 and Plate 99). The end of this ladder is free to move on rollers on a runway fixed to the roof as the roof moves up and down. Refinery companies discourage the practice of personnel climbing on to floating roofs because there is a risk of gassing if vapour is escaping from a seal. If the roof is low, vapour could collect above the roof, so refinery personnel are then only permitted to descend to the roof if they are wearing breathing apparatus and have a life-line attached to them, the free end of which must be held by another man on the staircase platform.

(b) Inspection manholes

At least one manhole will be found on the roof, whilst one or more are also fitted round the base. In some cases ladders run from the roof manholes down the insides of the tank, but generally the interior is reached through the base opening. Manholes are opened when necessary for ventilation purposes, or to give access for internal cleaning and maintenance for which large capacity tanks are fitted with a 4 ft (1·22 m) D-shaped hatchway, built and bolted into the bottom strake.

(c) Dip hatches

The level of oil in a cylindrical tank is ascertained via dip hatches which are fitted on the roof; on floating roof and non-pressure fixed roof tanks the dip hatch is a hole with a hinged lid, but on pressure-roof tanks, a special gastight fitting is installed which allows gauging and sampling to be carried out without loss of the internal pressure. Sampling of the contents of a tank is also done through the dip hatch by lowering a weighted corked can to the required depth, then jerking out the cork fastened to the lowering cord and allowing the can to fill

In modern oil refineries, remote-reading automatic gauging devices are used, but these often supplement rather than replace the older dip hatch.

(d) Vents

Atmospheric and breather vents (*see* Figs. 5-4 and 5-5) are fitted to permit air to escape when the tank is being filled and to enter when it is being emptied, otherwise the tank might be damaged by an excessive difference between the external and internal pressure.

(e) Pipeline connections

On vertical tanks one or more pipeline connections (*see* Fig. 5-3) are made through the bottom strake of the shell plates. Generally two such connections are used as it is then possible to use separate pipelines for filling and emptying. This reduces the risk of water contamination when the filling line is cleared with water. Two connections also permit blending to be carried out, and in this case on older refineries, one of the pipeline connections may sometimes be fitted with a 'swing-pipe' inside the tank (Fig. 5-12) with hoisting gear to enable the free end of the arm to be raised or lowered to any level. A swing-pipe was considered useful when blending, since it enabled the contents to be drawn off from the top and returned to the bottom, or vice versa, thus speeding the mixing process. However, except for floating swing arms, the installation of swing-pipes is not generally found.

Certain types of oil contain small quantities of water, sludge or other impurities and these tend to settle, so that the oil near the top is virtually free from such contamination, and an automatic water draining device is now generally incorporated instead of a manual drain valve. This prevents spillages of product in case a manual drain valve were to be left open.

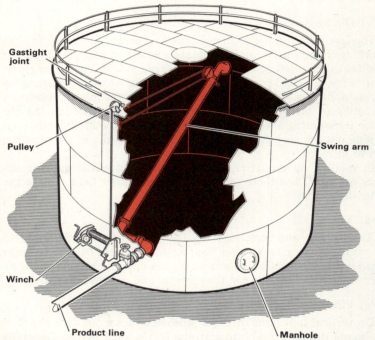

Fig. 5–12. *Cut-away view of an older type of storage tank with a swing arm and winch for raising and lowering the pipe.*

(f) Steam coils

Steam coils are fitted close to the bottom of tanks used to store bitumens and heavy oils in order to keep the contents fluid enough to be pumped. The coils consist of rows of steam pipes connected at alternate ends by hairpin bends. The steam supplied in this way is of no fire-fighting value and should be cut off in the event of fire as it merely serves to increase the temperature of the oil.

Section IV—Layout of oil refineries

A fireman entering a modern refinery is presented with a complex array of furnaces, fractionating towers, drums, heat exchangers, pumps and compressors, storage tanks, pipework, valves, buildings and, in many cases, huge cooling towers (Plates 95 to 98). All refineries have not only to convert the crude oil into a considerable number of saleable products, but also to be capable of receiving the crude oil and finally despatching the products to their destination. There must therefore be adequate tankage for the crude oil, inter-mediate products (*i.e.*, those which are not fully processed) and component products suitable for direct blending into finished product tanks for despatch.

Since practically all processes in a refinery are associated with heating and cooling and all products have to be pumped, provision has to be made for utilities in the shape of steam, electricity, fuel, cooling water or air, processing water and compressed air. Facilities have to be provided for the receipt of crude oil at jetties and for the despatch of products whether by road, rail, barge or sea.

The size of a refinery will vary with its capacity and diversification of processing and a modern refinery probably occupies some 30 to 40 acres (12 to 16 hectares) for each million tons (tonnes) annual capacity. The older refineries in Great Britain are generally dispersed affairs covering far more space than the modern integrated refineries, whereas in places like Rotterdam or Belfast, the whole processing plant is neatly contained in a small compact area, thus reducing the distance products and especially cooling water have to be pumped. One refinery in this country, for example, requires up to eight million gallons (36 million litres) of cooling water per hour.

Modern refineries present a much more compact appearance than the older ones, and a study of Plates 89/91 and 93/4 will show the difference between modern integrated refineries and the older more dispersed type, most of which were built in the early 1950s. In the older refinery design there tended to be a segregation of refinery activities into various areas, *e.g.* process, blending, despatch, and utilities, each area tending to be autonomous in its own operations. The unity of purpose required in the modern refinery has completely altered this concept and modern refinery design with its integrated operations from crude oil processing to despatch leads to a situation where the capabilities of each individual in the operating team can develop to the highest degree.

Whilst at the time of writing most of the refineries in the United Kingdom are dispersed ones, there are three in Wales, one at Teesside and one in Northern Ireland (Belfast) which are integrated and which only occupy a fraction of the area that the older ones cover. These integrated refineries have been constructed in the last decade, and there is no doubt that future refineries will be of the integrated type;

old refineries may also be modernised where practicable. Nevertheless the layout of most refineries can be broadly divided into five
sections: (i) the marine installations, (ii) the storage areas, (iii) the
processing plants, (iv) the maintenance areas and (v) the administrative section. There may also be a separate chemical plant.

1. THE MARINE TERMINAL

The marine terminal or jetties can be considered as the start of
operations where the tankers discharge their cargoes of crude oil.
At the large refineries, jetties are built well out into the sea or water-
way (Plate 90) so that they can accommodate deep-drafted loaded
tankers including, in some cases, the latest VLCCs. Besides loading
and unloading facilities, full provision has to be made for bunkering
tankers with fuel oil and for receiving their ballast water. Ballast
water is normally taken from the sea or river, and this accounts for
the muddy residue which accumulates in some storage tanks. The
water provided at the marine terminal is normally for refilling clean
water tanks. Tower-mounted fire-fighting monitors capable of discharging foam or water on to a tanker are often to be found on each
jetty.

(a) Conventional jetties

The conventional type of jetty is built alongside the shore, or is
connected to the shore by an approachway or trestle. Several tankers
can often be moored at the same time. Crude oil cargoes are discharged from the tankers by pumps on board in the pump rooms. In
most of the more modern ships which are designed with a free-flow
system between the tanks, oil is drawn to the pump room through a
cast-iron pipeline system in the bottom of the tanks, then discharged
up through the pump room into a deck pipeline system and then
ashore via flexible hoses connected from the jetty (Fig. 5-13 and
Plate 105). As the liquid is removed from the tanks, air enters the
ullage space through the vapour lines and dilutes the hydrocarbon
vapours present at the commencement of discharging.

Some tankers are fitted with an inerting system in which the boiler
flue gas is washed and cooled and is then pumped into the ship's
tanks to form a blanket of inert gas (with an oxygen content of about
5 per cent or less), over the liquid surface so that when the tank is
finally empty of oil, it is completely filled with the inert gas which
will not support combustion.

The atmosphere within a tank that has been discharged (but not
inerted) remains either explosive or over-rich until the tank has been

Fig. 5–13. The articulated metal cargo booms at the marine terminal for discharging crude oil from tanker to storage tanks ashore.

washed and ventilated, and stringent precautions are taken to prevent any possibility of sparking or static electricity igniting the vapour in empty tanks. (This subject is also dealt with in Part 7 of the *Manual*, Chapter 3, 'Fires in ships'). Ballasting consists of filling selected tanks with water after the cargo has been discharged so that the tanker is stable and in suitable trim for the next passage.

At each jetty there should be arrangements for stopping immediately the flow of oil in the event of failure of a manifold or hose, or their attachments, both on the tanker and jetty.

(b) Monobuoy mooring

A completely different type of marine terminal is the monobuoy mooring and floating buoy, usually known as the 'monobuoy'. With this type of floating buoy, VLCCs can remain in deep water and yet can discharge their cargo direct through a pipeline on the ocean bed to shore storage tanks.

The monobuoy (Fig. 5-14) is a single floating buoy about 30 ft (9 m) in diameter, which is moored to the seabed by chains and heavy anchors. Built into the centre of the buoy is a swivel that can rotate 360 degrees around a pipe assembly, which runs down to the sea bed and then to storage tanks ashore. Two flexible hose lines which will float on the surface of the sea are connected to the pipe assembly.

When a tanker is ready to discharge its cargo, it moors to the buoy, and this can be achieved in any direction according to wind, tide and weather conditions. The floating hoses are then picked up and connected to the manifold on the vessel. The ship's pumps are used to pump the oil through the pipeline to the tanks ashore.

Although at the time of writing there is only one monobuoy in use in this country, there is no doubt that as tankers increase in size and draught, this type of deepsea mooring will be more widely used.

2. STORAGE TANKS

(a) Crude oil storage

As the oil is pumped ashore from the tanker it is stored in crude oil tanks which are generally, but not always, conveniently grouped near the jetties. Due to the use of high tensile steel the tanks in the crude oil area are available in larger sizes and greater capacity is allowed in single bunds by the latest Institute of Petroleum Refinery Safety Code (1965) and by the model Codes of Principles of Construction* which were revised by the Home Office in 1968, and which relate to the siting and layout of storage tanks at major installations. The diameter of small tanks which may be sited in groups has been increased from 20 to 30 ft (6·1 to 9·4 m) and the total combined capacity of such groups has been increased from 3,000 to 8,000 water tons (3 048 to 8 128 tonnes) (Fig. 5-15).

A distinction is now made between large fixed roof tanks and large floating roof tanks. The recommended safety distances between tanks and between tanks and filling points are less for floating roof tanks than for fixed roof tanks because of the excellent accident record for large floating roof tanks. Before the present practice of bonding the roof pontoon electrically to the shell was adopted, a number of seal fires occurred in floating roof tanks, but these were

---

* Home Office 'Model Code of Principles of Construction and Licensing Conditions (Part II) for Distributing and Major Installations (1968)'. Published by HMSO.

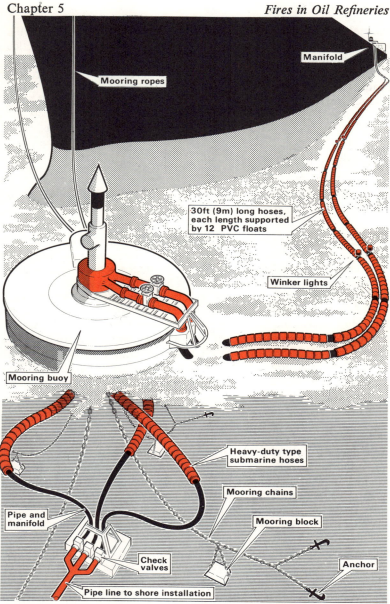

Mooring ropes

Manifold

30ft (9m) long hoses, each length supported by 12 PVC floats

Winker lights

Mooring buoy

Heavy-duty type submarine hoses

Mooring chains

Pipe and manifold

Mooring block

Check valves

Anchor

Pipe line to shore installation

Fig. 5–14. A very large crude carrier (VLCC) moored to a monobuoy and discharging its cargo of crude oil via a pipeline laid on the sea bed to storage tanks ashore.

invariably extinguished without difficulty by means of portable appliances. No seal fires have occurred (up to 1968) since the practice of bonding the roof to the shell was adopted. The only known case where the whole roof of a floating roof tank caught fire occurred in France in 1959; this was caused by a combination of bad maintenance, as a result of which a flammable mixture was allowed to

Fig. 5–15. Diagram showing the saving of space achieved by the use of larger tanks.

collect inside the pontoon space, and a direct lightning strike followed by an explosion which caused the roof to sink. For both types of tank, the recommended *minimum safety distance* between a tank and the outer boundary of the installation is 50 ft (15·24 m).

The total capacity of tanks in any one bunded enclosure was limited in the earlier Code to 40,000 water tons (40 642 tonnes). This figure has now been increased in the revised Code to 60,000 water tons (60 963 tonnes) in respect of fixed-roof tanks and to 120,000 water tons (121 926 tonnes) in respect of floating roof tanks. There is a further provision that the limit of 120,000 water tons (121 926 tonnes) in one main enclosure may be exceeded in suitable circumstances provided that the number of tanks in the group is not greater than three.

The earlier Code provided that the capacity of a main enclosure containing two or more tanks should be 100 per cent of the capacity of the largest tank, plus 10 per cent of the aggregate capacity of the remaining tanks. The revised Code provides that the net volume retained by the enclosure surrounded by a fire wall and/or a depression or impounding basin should generally be equivalent to the capacity of the largest tank in the group, but that a reduction of this capacity will provide reasonable protection in some instances and may be adopted where conditions are suitable. The recommendations of the earlier Code were based on the assumption that a bund should be designed to serve as an oil-retaining basin in the event of a major spillage. Experience has shown, however, that a bund will not fulfil this purpose since petroleum spirit will inevitably seep through the bund floor, even if the floor has been provided with a concrete base. The recommendations in the revised Code are therefore designed simply to ensure that any fire resulting from a spillage is retained within a small area, surrounded by a wall of sufficient height to enable firemen to approach close enough to fight the fire and to provide adequate protection from radiated heat.

(b) Intermediate, component and finished product storage

Storage tanks for intermediate, component and finished products may be found scattered over the older refinery, but the modern trend is to use fewer main blending and transfer open pump stations as opposed to the many old brick-built pump houses, with the tanks conveniently grouped round the pumps (Fig. 5-16). New refineries tend to have more tankage volume taken up with components and less with finished products.

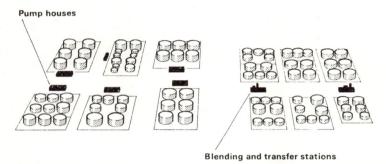

Pump houses

Blending and transfer stations

Fig. 5–16. Diagram showing a comparison between intermediate, component and finished product storage as is found in old refineries (left) and a modern integrated refinery (right).

3. PROCESS UNITS

It is in the numerous process units that there is the greatest diversification between the older and the modern refinery. Because all processes rely on vast quantities of cooling water (or air) which has to be circulated by pumps or fin fans, the less space there is between process units, the better use can be made of cooling water. After use cooling water is sometimes reclaimed and treated to remove contamination before being recycled for use, but where there is an abundance of water, new water is used continuously and the discharged water is passed through separators and returned to its source.

Fig. 5-17 shows a diagrammatic layout of the process units at old style and modern refineries from which the saving in space gives more economic operation.

Since about 1960, most refineries have been constructed as integrated processing complexes, but up to this time most units, in the older type of refinery, are operated independently, the product from each unit being fed into tankage. The next units in the processing line then draw their feed from this tankage as and when required.

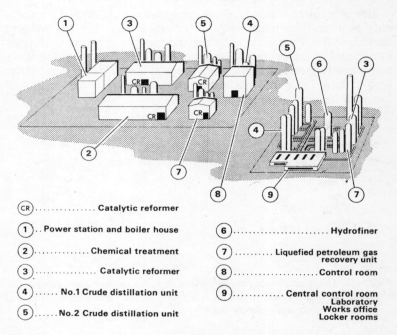

CR .... Catalytic reformer

1 .. Power station and boiler house   6 .... Hydrofiner

2 .... Chemical treatment   7 .... Liquefied petroleum gas
                                                              recovery unit
3 .... Catalytic reformer   8 .... Control room

4 ...... No.1 Crude distillation unit   9 .... Central control room
                                                              Laboratory
5 ...... No.2 Crude distillation unit   Works office
                                                              Locker rooms

Fig. 5-17. Diagrammatic representation of process units showing the economy of layout in an integrated refinery (right) as compared with an older refinery (left).

Many advances have been made since 1960 in the control of refinery process units. Control rooms may be centralised and automatic control of processes achieved by computers, but the older refineries may have a number of control rooms, one for each processing stage. However provision is invariably made to shut down a unit in an emergency by pressing a button on the control panel which will cut off feed to the unit, shut down fuel feed to the furnaces, cut out the firing and bring in emergency steam so that the shut down is carried out safely and as quickly as possible.

4. MAINTENANCE AND ADMINISTRATION

A team of engineers embodying all branches—civil, mechanical, electrical, electronic, chemical—as well as specialists in subjects such as welding and metallurgy—are required at any refinery. Maintenance work has to be carried out continuously but the workshops and service areas do not present any special problems for the firemen other than those which are inherent in workshops and stores.

Similarly the modern design of the administrative buildings is such that the minimum fire risk is involved.

5. DISTRIBUTION AREAS AND PIPELINES

The final function of the oil refinery is the distribution of the finished products to their destination. Bulk distribution is usually made by tanker, especially for overseas markets, where local refineries do not exist, but a large proportion of the products are distributed to installations direct by trunk pipelines or by rail. The remainder goes out by road tankers.

(a) Tankers and barges

Water transport is comparatively cheap and, where geographical conditions permit, is widely used for distribution purposes. Small tankers operate in coastal waters, supplying ports which are inaccessible to larger tankers. On inland waterways and estuarial waters, barges are also used being either self-propelled or 'dumb' barges.

Tankers and barges are loaded at the marine terminal or jetties and the same stringent precautions against spillage, etc. are taken as when unloading crude oil from large tankers.

(b) Road tankers and rail cars

Both road tankers and rail cars are used for taking bulk supplies of finished products from the refinery to installations and depots. Rail cars with a capacity of up to 100 tons (101 tonnes) are usually cylindrical tanks mounted on bogies, with transverse baffles to prevent surging of the contents when the rail car is in motion. The design of road tankers has altered in recent years and although cylindrical tankers are still used the more modern ones are more or less rectangular in cross-section (Plate 106). Their capacity is generally about 6,600 gallons (30 000 litres) or less.

Filling methods depend on the design of the vehicle compartment which may be fitted with a permanent perforated fill-pipe extending into a small well at the bottom of the tank, or filling may be through open-dome hatches. Filling via open-dome hatches has now almost completely superseded closed filling through fixed pipe connections owing to the need for higher loading rates.

Bottom filling may also be found but this method is rarely adopted as there are few loading racks which are suitable for this method.

Fig. 5-18 shows the method of top filling for road tankers and rail cars normally to be seen at refineries.

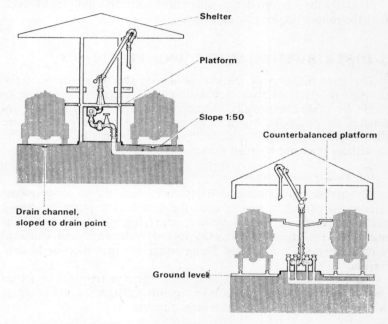

Fig. 5–18. *Diagram showing the method of filling tankers:* **Left:** *road tankers; right: rail cars.*

Although many thousands of tons (tonnes) of highly flammable petroleum products are transferred daily to road tankers and rail cars, few accidents occur, due to the prohibition or strict control over the use of naked lights and other sources of ignition. The design of the fill-pipe is such that when the end of the pipe is at the bottom of the tank, the liquid is directed smoothly along the tank bottom with the minimum of splashing. This helps to prevent the generation of static charges caused by splash filling. Bonding of the metal fill-pipe also prevents a static discharge between the pipe and tank hatch during filling or when withdrawing the fill-pipe after loading operations are complete. Earthing of the tank vehicle also ensures electrical continuity and has the same effect as bonding. Rail cars can be considered as adequately earthed via the rail lines, but isolation of the section of track on which the rail car rests is necessary if the system is electrified.

(c) Pipelines

Sometimes finished products are pumped direct into pipelines as this is now considered a more economical means of transporting certain petroleum products over particular routes. Pipelines eliminate handling operations and intermediate storage and result in a considerable reduction in road traffic.

The subject of the hazards associated with pipelines and the fire-fighting measures to be taken is dealt with on pages 330/3, as well as in Part 6C of the *Manual*, Chapter 5, 'Fires in Fuels'.

Section V—Fire protection and emergency planning

Because fire and explosion are the greatest potential hazards at an oil refinery, personal safety measures, fire protection and prevention are of top priority. Stringent precautions are always enforced to prevent fire starting: smoking is not allowed except in special designated safe areas, and only safety-type torches are used in flammable atmospheres. Plant operatives are required to take every precaution when working on plant or tanks to prevent accident or danger to life.

The emphasis on hazard from fire or explosion has shifted from the storage tank to processing plant where a fractured pipe could discharge highly flammable liquid on to heated surfaces or steam pipes. As a consequence there is a greater need for thousands of gallons (litres) of water a minute to be available for fire fighting so that pumps and monitors can be got to work immediately, than for installed equipment such as foam pourers on tanks which can become damaged or unusable as a result of fire or explosion.

1. WATER SUPPLIES

Water is still the most effective medium for controlling major fires in oil plant, and at a large refinery it will be needed in vast quantities if a fire occurs in processing plant. It is fortunate that refineries are frequently situated where there are unlimited supplies of water, either from the sea or large rivers, although direct access to this water is sometimes difficult. As a consequence, arrangements are made to make adequate supplies immediately available, generally by means of a grid or ring main running through the refinery, fed by fixed pumps of large capacity.

At one major refinery, for example, the ring main is fed by six fixed pumps (two electric, two steam and two gas turbine), feeding from tanks totalling over 8 million gallons (over 36 million litres) so that 10,000 gallons (45·5 kilolitres) of water per minute at a pressure of 120 lbf/in² (8·2 bars) is constantly available. Supplies are often interconnected and fed by either fresh or salt water, as convenient.

Hydrant outlets are provided at strategic points. Some refineries have pillar hydrants (Fig. 5-19) whilst others are below ground. Often 4-in. (102 mm) outlets are fitted in addition to the standard 2½-in. (64 mm) outlets.

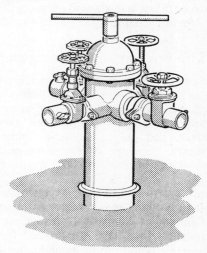

Fig. 5–19. Type of pillar hydrant to be found at some refineries with three 2½ in. (64 mm) and one 4 in. (102 mm) outlets.

In addition to ring mains, other water supplies are always provided, either in the form of static tanks with hardstanding for pumping appliances or open water such as the sea or river with access at jetties.

(a) Fixed water protection systems

Although there is a strong trend towards the use of mobile rather than fixed water fire protection systems, especially on storage tanks where such equipment extremely is vulnerable to explosion damage, some refineries have monitors permanently located in areas where large volumes of cooling water would be required for fire fighting. Fig. 5-20 shows a fixed monitor above ground level.

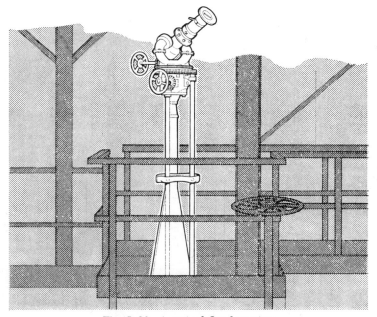

Fig. 5–20. A typical fixed monitor.

Monitors can be operated by one man, and should the area become untenable, the monitor can be set to the most advantageous angle and left unattended.

Fixed water drencher systems are also to be found covering storage tanks as a protection against damage due to radiated heat. Drencher systems have also contributed to the protection of steelwork on process plants, and are to be found on the supporting structures containing the process racks at many refineries. All liquefied petroleum gas spheres have water drencher systems.

(b) Mobile water monitors

Many refineries have water monitors which are mounted on trailers (Fig. 5-21 and Plate 103) or bipods. These can be quickly manhandled into position and fed through lines of standard hose. The monitors are often sited at strategic points throughout the refinery where they can be brought into use without delay. At some refineries, in order to ensure ready availability of an adequate number of monitors, some mobile monitors are kept stored upon a vehicle.

Fig. 5–21. A mobile trailer monitor.

2. FOAM

Oil storage tanks are being made in larger sizes than ever before, and this means that if a fire in a tank does occur, very large quantities of foam will be required to maintain a successful attack. Although chemical foam powder may be found in limited quantities in old refineries, the modern ones rely on mechanical protein foam; the compound can be stored in bulk quantities, it is easier to transport and it makes smaller demands on manpower than chemical foam.

Although serious fires in oil storage tanks are not frequent, marine tankers in excess of 150,000 tons (152 000 tonnes) capacity and storage tanks of 300 ft (90 m) diameter are to be found, so that fires when they do occur increase the demand for foam compound enormously. Very large foam monitors producing 5,000 gallons (22 730 litres) of foam per minute use 35/45 gallons (159/205 litres) or seven to nine 5-gallon (22·7-litre) drums of foam compound each minute. It is therefore obvious that the idea of using 5-gallon (22·7-litre) or even 40-gallon (182-litre) drums to supply these very large foam monitors is out of the question.

The major oil refineries, however, do not agree on the method of supplying foam compound in bulk. Some refineries use 2,000-gallon (9 092-litre) tankers which can be quickly hitched up to a mechanical horse and taken to the fire area, while others use 2,000-gallon (9 092 litre) self-propelled mobile bowsers or foam compound carriers. However, one major oil refinery believes that the answer to the bulk foam compound problem is to pump the compound either through fixed pipework or through temporary flexible hose lines as required. Consequently, two 2,000-gallon (9 092-litre) tanks containing foam compound are fitted with pumps which enable the compound to be pumped into specially laid foam lines. Outlets are supplied at strategic points, especially on the marine jetties, so that hose and foam-making branchpipes can be quickly coupled up. At a further oil refinery, bulk foam tankers can be driven to the jetties where the foam compound is then pumped into fixed 3-in. (76 mm) foam lines. Large foam monitors can be connected to down-fed pipes, and foam-making branchpipes used similarly by variable proportioning through foam inductors. Bulk storage of foam compound may also be found in elevated tanks, from which mobile foam bowsers ,may be quickly topped up.

Whatever the merits of one system as compared with the other, bulk foam supplies are always available, and the local authority fire brigade personnel who will attend a fire at an oil refinery on their ground should be well versed and exercised in the appropriate method to be used.

(a) Foam-making equipment

Most refineries have large foam monitors (Fig. 5-22) for dealing with major fires in oil storage tanks and other risks as well as a variety of smaller foam-making branches, generators, inductors, etc. for smaller oil fires and details of such foam-making equipment will be found in Part 1 of the *Manual*, Chapter 10. Large foam monitors are usually mounted on specially-designed trailers or bipods, so that they can be towed by appliances or other light commercial vehicles, or carried by firemen. Trailer-monitors can be quickly

Fig. 5–22. One type of large foam monitor which can deliver either a foam or a water jet.

detached from their towing vehicles and manhandled into position; during operations they are rigidly supported by adjustable drop legs.

Large foam monitors vary to some extent in their capacities, but generally require about 35/45 gallons (159/205 litres) of foam compound a minute to produce 5,000 gallons (22 732 litres) of foam per minute. This requires about 660 gallons (3 000 litres) per minute of water at an inlet pressure of about 170 lbf/in^2 (12 bars). The maximum capacity of a water monitor can be as much as 2,200 gallons (10 000 litres) per minute, but with a 2½-in. (64 mm) nozzle at 125 lbf/in^2 (8·6 bars) inlet pressure, about 1,600 gallons (7 274 litres) of water per minute would be delivered.

A large foam monitor at work requires three lines of hose supplying water at about 200 lbf/in^2 (14 bars) at the pump and when 'by-pass' induction is used, one line of foam compound/water at about 15 lbf/in^2 (1 bar) pressure at the outlet of the foam compound inductor on or near the pump.

Foam-producing appliances at refineries are being rapidly modern-ised with automatic variable flow control valves incorporated in the pump design to give a specified fluid flow of foam compound and water by means of orifice variation regardless of inlet pressure and flow. One type of control valve has a diaphragm as the only moving part; when flexed into the fixed orifice it compensates for increased pressures; another type uses a flexible synthetic rubber ring to achieve the same objective. A third type automatically proportions a pres-surised foam compound supply into a water stream at a predeter-mined ratio and maintains this ratio for a flow range of between 100 and 700 gallons (454–3 182 litres) per minute.

(b) Foam pourers and towers

Fixed pourers consist simply of a curved funnel which directs foam to the inside of a tank shell at the top of the tank so that the foam flows over the surface. The number of pourers installed will depend on the tank diameter but because fixed pourers are extremely vul-nerable to damage by explosion and fire, and due to high mainten-ance costs, fewer and fewer will be found as they gradually come into disuse.

Portable foam towers will be found at some refineries. These generally consist of aluminium or light-alloy telescopic tubes which are mechanically or hydraulically elevated. Sometimes the energy for elevation is provided by the foam pressure which raises the inner telescopic tube carrying the foam to its fullest extent. Foam may be supplied from a mechanical foam generator or foam-making branch-pipe.

Another system, which has been developed in Sweden, is shown in Fig. 5-23. The principal feature of this method is that after pressure has blown the cover from the foam container in the base of the tank, the hose is released and rises to the surface of the oil, where foam is discharged from the open end of the hose.

A further system is the National Foam System's sub-surface foaming which has been developed by a leading oil refinery company in this country. By this method high back-pressure foam generators are connected (when fire occurs) to valves welded on to the tank loading lines. Special fluoro-protein compound is required for this system.

3. DRY POWDER

Portable dry powder extinguishers which vary in size from 2 lb to 30 lb (1 to 14 kg) may be found at oil refineries to deal with spillage

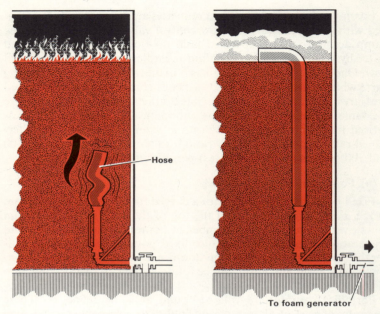

Fig. 5–23. Diagram showing the semi-surface system of applying foam to the surface of the burning oil.

oil fires, especially those involving liquefied petroleum gases. Dry powder is particularly effective in those circumstances where a quick knock down is required, but although it is a non-conductor of electricity, it has negligible cooling effect and does not form a blanket over the spilled liquid as does foam. Furthermore most dry powders are non-compatible with foam as they tend to break down the bubbles, although some types of dry powder extinguishers are foam-compatible.

Recently there have been developments in the use of mobile dry powder appliances to deal with more serious spill fires and larger wheeled units from 150 lb (68 kg) up to fully self-contained vehicles of three tons (3·05 tonnes) capacity may be found. These large vehicles are fitted with delivery monitors having a discharge rate of up to three tons of powder in 45 seconds.

4. STEAM LANCES AND SPEARS

Steam is a valuable agent when dealing with fires involving vapour or gas leaks from seals or flanges of pipework. It is also useful on fires involving hot vapour lines especially where the temperature at the emission point is above the flash point or auto ignition temperature of the vapour or gas. It has the effect of reducing the temperature at the point of vapour or gas leak without causing excessive contraction of the metal. It also reduces the concentration of oxygen in the free air surrounding the point of leakage.

Many of the process plants require the use of steam and so use can often be made of the availability of the medium in appropriate circumstances. Lengths of armoured hose to which a steam spear or lance is attached are accessible to all parts of the plant where gas or vapour leaks could occur. The steam is supplied from the plant steam lines for which valved connections are provided.

The steam lance (Fig. 5-24, *above*) is 6 ft (1·83 m) in length and is fitted with a hardwood handle, which is glued to the pipe and also recessed and secured with three jubilee clips. At the end is a hose connection to which special armoured steam hose is attached.

The steam spear (Fig. 5-24, *below*) comprises a hollow metal tube about 4 ft (1·2 m) in length by 1-in. (305 mm) in diameter. The discharge end is flattened into a fan-shaped nozzle to enable the steam

Fig. 5–24. Above: A steam lance. Below: A typical steam spear.

to be diffused as it is discharged. The spear is insulated with asbestos rope and two carrying handles are provided. Steam spears are really provided for operatives at the refinery for dealing with fractures of pipework which cause incipient fires. Care in the use of steam spears is essential to avoid touching exposed metal parts with the hands, otherwise severe burns may result.

5. REFINERY FIRE-FIGHTING TUGS

Many refineries maintain special fire-fighting tugs, and details of these are included in Part 7 of the *Manual*, Chapter 1, 'Fireboats and their Equipment'. They are provided specifically to deal with fires at marine jetties where the greatest risk is involved as tankers are discharging their cargoes of crude oil, or are loading finished products.

Large capacity fire pumps are a feature of these tugs with outputs in the region of 3,000 gallons (13 638 litres) per minute. Foam and water monitors are invariably a feature and foam or water jets of over 200 ft (60 m) are normal; the foam monitors can produce up to 5,000 gallons (22 730 litres) of foam a minute. The two fire-fighting tugs on the River Tees can each produce a total of over 10,000 gpm (45 460 l/min) of foam or 4,000 gpm (18 184 l/min) of water. Some tugs are equipped with hydraulic platforms which give additional height and manoeuvrability to the monitors, whilst others have their monitors located at the top of 60 ft (18 m) towers. Most refinery fire-fighting tugs carry a stock of foam compound of up to 6,000 gallons (27 276 litres).

6. EMERGENCY PLANNING

Because of the high risks at an oil refinery, it is essential that plans should be made in collaboration with the refinery management well in advance to deal with any foreseeable fire, explosion, toxic or other hazard which may occur. Details should be agreed of the initial and make-up attendances of local authority fire appliances to be sent in support of the refinery appliances, the special equipment, such as foam compound, which may have to be brought in, mobilising, control and communications arrangements, and such fire-fighting tactics as can be pre-planned to deal with known risks.

Incidents within the refinery will normally be reported to the works fire station and details of the call will be passed on to the local divisional or brigade control. In many cases, the refinery fire brigade may themselves deal with the occurrence and may only request an attendance from the outside brigade for more serious incidents.

However, it is imperative that the mobilising arrangements should be clearly framed so that there can be no possibility of misunderstanding so far as attendance is concerned. Any reduction in manning outside normal working hours should be taken into account when planning the initial attendance, which may vary to different sections of the plant according to risk, but there must also be a 'disaster plan' by which massive assistance can be summoned immediately if a serious situation has occurred or is imminent.

(a) Attendances

Maps should be prepared showing the various entrances to the refinery so that fire appliances responding will know their exact route and the entrance they should use. The maps should also show water supplies, communication points, rendezvous and assembly areas, and so on.

Appliances should in the first instance report to a specific rendezvous point (which will generally be the refinery fire station) and should then be directed on to an assembly area. Because of the congestion which can occur at a large refinery fire, the assembly points should be carefully sited so that appliances and equipment can be moved into the fire area without difficulty and loss of time.

(b) Control

Overall control at a fire is vested in the senior fire brigade officer present (some refinery fire officers hold a comparable local authority fire brigade rank), but there should always be complete liaison and accord between refinery and local authority fire officers. The extra technical knowledge of processes and plant of the refinery fire officer will invariably be invaluable to the local authority fire officer.

Specific arrangements should be made for incident control and allied responsibilities throughout the whole 24 hours and at weekends, including the recall by the refinery management of specialist personnel to incidents occurring outside normal working hours.

The main fire control point should be arranged with regard to communication throughout the whole refinery and to the local authority brigade control. In most cases, the refinery fire station will fit the bill, as it is generally well sited, constructed and equipped. An important point is that the main control should be usable in any situation which may arise, and where toxic gases may be released, it is essential that a respirable atmosphere should exist for a reasonable period within the main control point. A secondary control point should be considered in suitable circumstances.

305

Forward controls should be planned as appropriate so that they can report back without difficulty to the main control. These forward controls should preferably be completely mobile so that they can be quickly re-positioned as the situation requires. There should be a radio link to the main control, and a refinery fire officer's car, or a local authority fire officer's car (if on the appropriate wavelength) may be the logical choice as a forward control. At large fires where a control unit attends, it should be clearly laid down in the pre-planning whether this will be stationed at the main control, or will act as a forward control. Local requirements will dictate the most suitable policy in this respect.

(c) Foam compound requirements

At a major fire involving oil storage tanks, foam compound will be required in vast quantities (*see* Section VI, par. 3, 'Use of Foam'), and although all refineries maintain stocks of foam compound, a sustained attack with a number of super foam monitors may exhaust all available compound. It is essential therefore that the emergency pre-planning considers how and from where the additional stocks are to be collected.

The main problems are weight and time. A 5-gallon (22·7 litre) drum of foam compound weighs about 68 lb (30 kg); 33 drums weigh a ton (1 tonne) and contain 165 gallons (750 litres). A 10,000-gallon (45 460-litre) supply weighs 60 tons (61 tonnes) and involves 2,000 drums. All of these would have to be individually loaded on to lorries and transported from the store to the site. It is apparent, therefore, that even to collect smaller quantities involves men in arduous labour and it may take many hours to load up lorries and drive them to the fire. In many cases, a number of fire brigades have made mutual arrangements so that each brigade undertakes to collect and supply one or more lorry loads of compound. Also arrangements exist for the Army, Navy or RAF, or for compound manufacturers themselves, to supply foam compound in an emergency, and it is sometimes possible for this to be done in bulk by tankers. In some brigades arrangements exist for a control to be set up for the mobilisation of foam compound, and foam officers are appointed, both at brigade headquarters and on the fireground, to co-ordinate supplies.

Once the compound is delivered, it will still have to be decanted, generally into some form of bulk container, such as a mobile tanker, and here again it is a question of time and hard work, plus the difficulty of making space for the full and empty containers.

(d) Reliefs, feeding, etc.

The pre-planned emergency arrangements should also include the provision of relief crews and, where men are likely to be detained for lengthy periods, for the attendance of canteen vans, or some other form of emergency feeding. Other pre-planned emergency arrangements include such details as:

   (i) medical aid;

   (ii) the provision of dry clothing;

   (iii) safety officers to protect the safety of personnel;

   (iv) the provision of a safety launch when men are working on jetties;

   (v) arrangements for dealing with flooding and drainage;

   (vi) organisation for fire-fighting at sea (*see* Part 7 of the *Manual*, Chapter 3);

   (vii) liaison with police for signposting, clearance of sightseers, etc.;

   (viii) liaison with press and television;

   (ix) administrative matters for dealing with casualties and fatalities;

   (x) possible arrangements with the GPO to deal with extra work at exchanges.

Section VI—Fire fighting at refineries

1. PRECAUTIONARY MEASURES

Because of the attention which is paid to safe practices, losses due to fires are small, but the potential for severe fires exists and therefore fire fighting, if it is to be effective, should be planned and rehearsed in every detail. All refinery staff receive instruction in the use of the 'first-aid' appliances, such as extinguishers or steam lances. When flammable liquids or vapours escape from vessels or pipelines, the supply of fuel feeding the lines must be closed, and this action is often automatic at large refineries.

(a) Oil leaks

If a break or serious leak occurs in an oil line, the pumps should be shut down and any block valves closed by operatives. If the leak involves a tank or relatively large vessel, operatives should try to use available lines to pump out the oil. Trenches, dykes or diversion walls should be used to confine the oil. A traffic control should be established and vehicles should be excluded from the affected area.

Foam may be applied to cover oil spills in order to exclude air, but this is not normally necessary. Water spray applied at the point of emission of a leak may aid in the dispersal of vapours and prevent ignition.

(b) Gas leaks

In the event of a break in a gas or LPG line or vessel, all furnaces near the break should be shut down, as it is possible for vapour to be ignited if it comes into contact with hot metal or brickwork in furnace fire boxes for an appreciable period after the plant has been shut down. Every effort should be made to direct vapour away from hot surfaces by the use of water spray. The vapours from large LPG leaks may follow low contours of the ground and blanket large areas under certain weather conditions. It may be possible to disperse flammable mixtures by means of forced ventilation or by large quantities of steam or fine water spray. However, when using high pressure steam or water jets, one must remember that there is a possibility that static electric sparks could be generated which are capable of igniting the vapours.

2. USE OF WATER

Water is still the most effective medium for controlling large oil fires, but there are differences in the way it should be used as compared with, for example, Class 'A' fires (solid materials normally of an organic nature—*see* Part 6A of the *Manual*, Chapter 1, Section III, 'Classification of fires') and in the results it can accomplish.

(a) On 'high flash point' oils

When water is applied to wood or other similar combustible material, its principal effect is to cool the unburnt wood, stop the evolution of vapour from it, and thus starve the flames which result from the burning vapour. Ultimately it will quench the red hot embers to complete the extinguishment. Certain oils behave in a similar manner to wood, for example heavy fuel oil, lubricating oil or asphalt. At normal temperatures and pressure none of these produce any significant amount of vapour until heated to a high temperature. This is why they have a 'high flash point' (above 65°C). Once a fire is started in them, however, the supply of vapour is maintained, because the flame continues to supply heat to the oil surface to create more vapour.

If no preventive steps are taken the fire will continue until the fuel is consumed, but if water in the form of light spray is applied to the surface, the surface will be cooled down and the release of vapour will cease. The fire will then be extinguished.

So for some kinds of oil, water is well suited for the purpose of extinguishment, and accomplishes this in much the same way as it does with most Class 'A' fires. On non-volatile or 'high flash point' oils, cooling is the best means of extinguishment, but the water must be directed on the surface in the form of a fine spray. *Jets' must not be used.*

(b) Volatile oils

With volatile flammable liquids (for ease of reference those with a flash point of below 65°C), a different situation prevails. These oils give off sufficient vapour to burn at 'normal temperatures and pressure', and water reaching the oil surface will not be turned to steam; it will probably sink to the bottom without being greatly heated, so its cooling effect is negligible. The principal effect which it will have will occur within the flame itself, where any small droplets may be vaporised. This will remove some heat, but from the flame, not from the oil surface; in general, therefore, water is ineffective as an extinguishing agent on fires fed by gases or vapours from volatile oils, and in fact may spread the fire. There are, however, some important functions which water may perform.

(c) Cooling

Water can be used to cool or protect buildings, structures, tanks, etc. from heat or flame impingement. Steel structures are not likely to be damaged by radiant heat, but flame lick can heat them so that they soften and ultimately fail. Water properly applied in the form of fine spray or fog and in sufficient quantity can absorb the heat and so prevent damage. Experiment and practice have indicated that the rate should be about 0·2 gal/ft² (10 l/m²) per minute.

It is important to remember that most of the liquid petroleum products which will be encountered at an oil refinery have boiling points well below 100°C. Petrol, kerosene and stove oils all start to boil below 100°C, the boiling point of water. If a tank or vessel contains such an oil, the part of the shell which is *below liquid level* will be kept cool by the liquid inside. Even though the liquid contained in the tank is boiling, the steel which is in contact with it cannot get very hot. Water applied to the lower part of a tank which is wetted by the oil will run off, barely warmed and thus be largely wasted. Water only does its most effective job of cooling when it is converted into steam.

As far as tanks are concerned, it is generally safe to say that they will not need cooling below the liquid level unless flames are actually touching them. Radiant heat will not cause metallic equipment such as pipelines to fail if the liquid contents are kept moving, but a violent rupture would occur if the contents were not moving, with the result that hydrocarbons could be ejected and start further fires. The areas of equipment which are not visible because they are in the flame are the parts which need protection by cooling.

(d) Water application

Water applied to an oil fire may be used in two main forms—spray or a solid jet. Each has its advantages, disadvantages and scope of application.

In general the solid jet stream has the greatest range of driving force while the wide angle spray has short range but affords maximum protection for the firefighter. There are some in-between positions which combine the two, and in most cases, these will be the most suitable. A dense spray of water may be used as a barrier between flame and firefighter to protect against flame and heat, and to permit closer approach for an action such as to close a valve to stop the flow of fuel feeding a fire. The object is to use water in the right form, and at the place where it will have the greatest effect as a coolant or as an extinguishing agent.

(e) Other uses

Most of what has been said relates to the cooling effect of water, but there are other uses which may be just as important. The place where oil is burning may be very important. Oil floats on water, and flooding a fire may cause the burning oil to flow to an area where it could do a great deal more damage. But equally, it may be possible to use the flooding method to divert the burning oil into an area where it can continue to burn without doing any damage at all. This may be accomplished by the combined effect of floating, and by using the driving force of a jet of water.

If a container develops a leak at the base, adding water to the tank may float the oil above the level of the leak. This method has been used at a refinery to stop the flow of oil feeding an otherwise uncontrollable fire. Water for this purpose can be supplied at any level, but care must be taken *not to overflow* the tank. The rate of water input must match the rate of leakage once the bottom water level has been established.

If a stream of oil is issuing from an open end pipe or valve, fed at a lower pressure than the fire water nozzle pressure, it is possible to stop the escape of fuel by playing a hose stream into the opening. This has been successfully accomplished even though the leak had already taken fire.

3. USE OF FOAM

It is generally accepted that foam equipment should not be brought into operation until it is reasonably certain that sufficient equipment and foam compound is available or assured to extinguish the fire. A premature attack would not reduce the fire potential, and would only have the effect of wasting valuable and limited foam stocks. The object in the use of foam is to place a non-flammable layer between the surface of the liquid and the burning vapour above. The primary purpose of this layer is to cut off the radiant heat emitted by the zone of combustion which heats the surface of the liquid and causes the evolution of vapour—the only source of fuel for the flames. Secondary effects of the foam layer may also be the restriction of air supply and a limited cooling effect.

Although it is true to say that a foam attack should not be prematurely started, it does not mean that it should be delayed. For example, radiated heat from a fire in a tank which is situated in a refining area would soon affect nearby plant. As such tanks are usually not more than 40 ft (12 m) in diameter and bulk supplies of foam compound are virtually immediately available at major refineries, a quick attack with a super foam monitor as soon as sufficient pumps were available and adequate cooling jets covering the nearby plant were in operation, would no doubt prevent a spread of the fire and lessen the damage.

(a) Behaviour of foam

The application of foam is affected to a great extent by the fire conditions at the time. The updraught will vary with the fierceness of the fire, but in any case it will be obvious that a percentage of applied foam will never reach the oil surface at all, but will be blown up and away by the ascending vapour and flame. Whilst sometimes it is better to use a foam spray rather than a straight stream in order to build up a blanket of foam and to apply the foam as gently as possible, at a large oil tank fire, it may not be practicable to get close enough to apply foam gently, and large foam jets may have to be used from a distance. Under these conditions, the velocity of the falling foam will be reduced by convection from the fire.

Foam applied to the surface of heated oil breaks down continuously, the rate depending on the amount of surface exposed, the type and quality of the foam, and the temperature of the oil. To be successful, foam must be applied faster than it can be destroyed by the fire and by the radiation from the hot walls of the tank. It is therefore generally better to apply the foam from as many points as possible and with the largest possible foam generating equipment.

(b) Rate of application

In practice it has been found that the minimum rate of application of induced foam compound and water solution is about 1 gallon per minute per 10 square feet (4·5 litres per minute per square metre) of liquid area to be protected and this figure is not greatly affected by the foam expansion ratio. A reasonable estimate, therefore, is 1 gallon of *foam* per square foot (50 litres per square metre) of surface area per minute, assuming the normal 8/10 expansion ratio foam is being used.

The following formulae give very approximately the quantity of water and the number of No. 10 (or equivalent) foam-making branches required, when the diameter (D) of the tank is given in feet (metres).

	Imperial	*Metric*
Water required	$\dfrac{D^2}{10}$ gpm	$5D^2$ l/min.
No. 10 (or equivalent) branches	$\dfrac{D^2}{1,000}$	$\dfrac{D^2}{100}$

Table V shows the desirable minimum rates of foam compound, water and foam produced *per minute*.

It should not be inferred from the table that only one No. 10 foam-making branch would be adequate to deal with a fire in a tank 30 ft (9 m) in diameter. Two or more branches would no doubt be

TABLE V

Diameter (ft)	Area in sq. ft	Foam (gpm)	Foam compound (gpm)	Water (gpm)	No. 10 branches
30	707	700	3	100	1
45	1,590	1,600	6	200	2
60	2,828	3,000	12	400	4
90	6,362	6,400	24	800	8
112	9,852	10,400	39	1,300	13
150	17,670	17,600	66	2,200	22
200	31,416	32,000	120	4,000	40

TABLE V(a)

Diameter (metres)	Area in sq. metres	Foam (l/min)	Foam compound (l/min)	Water (l/min)	No. 10 branches
10	78	3 900	13·6	455	1
20	314	15 700	54	1 820	4
30	706	35 300	122	4 095	9
60	2 827	141 350	490	16 380	36

required bearing in mind the type of risk involved, the position of the tank in the bund, wind direction and velocity, length of pre-burn time, and whether the foam could be projected into the tank with maximum effect and minimum wastage.

From the table it will also be apparent that the increase in the size of modern oil storage tanks results in a large number of foam-making branches being required to deal with a tank fire. A tank 150 ft (45 m) in diameter requires the equivalent of 22 No. 10 foam-making branches, using 2,200 gallons (10 000 litres) of water and 66 gallons (300 litres) of foam compound every minute. As at least 30 minutes' supply should be on hand before foaming operations start, this will mean 66,000 gallons (300 000 litres) of water and about 2,000 gallons (10 000 litres) of foam compound. If large foam monitors were used, four would produce 20,000 gallons (100 000 litres) of foam a minute, but these would require $40 \times 4 \times 30 = 4,800$ gallons (22 000 litres) of foam and $660 \times 4 \times 30 = 79,200$ gallons (360 000 litres) of water for 30 minutes' application. The difference in the range of jets from large foam monitors and smaller branches should be allowed for when estimating the amount of foam which actually goes into the tank.

(c) Use of various types of foam branch

Because of the wide divergence of foam-making branches which may be in use at refineries, it may be helpful to tabulate the requirements of those which are likely to be found. Table VI shows the pump pressures and the amounts of foam compound and water needed to produce various quantities of foam.

(d) Methods of applying foam

Conditions at oil fires vary so widely that it is difficult to generalise on the methods of applying foam. As has been said, ample quantities should be available to enable the attack to be launched, and whilst stocks are being gathered and positioned, cooling branches should be laid out to cover surrounding risks.

313

TABLE VI

Foam-making equipment	Inlet pressure		Foam compound (approx.)		Water (approx.)		Foam (approx).	
	lbf/in²	bars	gpm	l/min	gpm	l/min	gpm	l/min
No. 10 FMB	100	7	4	18	100	450	800	3 640
No. 20 FMB	100	7	8	36	200	900	1,600	7 280
MFG 10	150	10·5	5	23	125	570	900	4 090
MFG 20	150	10·5	10	45	250	1 140	1,800	8 180
MFG 30	150	10·5	14	64	350	1 600	2,450	11 000
15 PFM	150	10·5	6	27	125	570	750	3 420
30 PFM	150	10·5	12	55	240	1 090	1,500	6 840
Jetmaster	150	10·5	20	90	350	1 600	2,500	11 400
Superjet	170	12	40	180	660	3 000	5,000	22 700
Merryweather 'Major'	150	10·5	36	164	680	3 090	5,000	22 700

As inlet pressures of about 150/170 lbf/in² (10/12 bars) are required for super foam monitors, pump pressures would have to be about 190/200 lbf/in² (13/14 bars), and pump outputs would therefore fall off considerably. Each monitor will require two high capacity pumps of 700/900 gallons (3 182/4 091 litres) per minute or three 350/500 gallons (1 591/2 273 litres) per minute pumps together with their attendant hose lines, if working from open water, but one pump will suffice if the mains pressure is 80/100 lbf/in² (5·5/7 bars). It is also important to remember that the hose must be of the best quality and in good condition to withstand these pressures. Inlet pressures for foam cannon designed on the 'branchpipe' principle (*e.g.* Minimax, 'L.24' and Pyrene 'slim-jet') may be operated at much lower pressures (*i.e.*, 90/100 lbf/in²—6/7 bars), but the foam jet ranges are then reduced and the foam quality is affected.

On a large diameter tank fire, four, five or even more foam monitors would be required, and this entails perhaps 10 to 15 pumps to supply them. When one considers the congested areas around tanks and process plant, the question of marshalling this number of pumps and foam monitors around a tank on roads not designed for such traffic poses quite a problem for the fire officer. The necessity for pre-planning and for exercises becomes apparent.

In addition to the equipment problem, there is the question of siting the monitors, and this can be critical. Fig. 5-25 shows a graph which gives the approximate heights of a foam jet at varying distances (in still air) which have been worked out by one fire brigade for the Merryweather 'Major' foam monitor; graphs for other types of monitor would be similar.

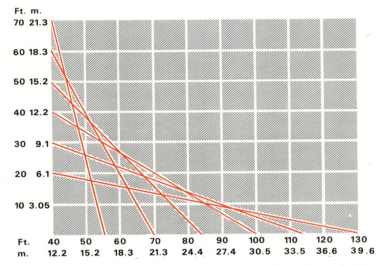

Fig. 5–25. Graph showing the approximate height which can be reached by a large foam monitor at varying distances.

From the graph it can be seen that to reach a 60 ft (18 m) high storage tank, the monitor must be positioned about 70 ft (21 m) away, but if the tank was only 30 ft (9 m) high, there is a great possibility that the foam would overshoot the tank if the monitor could not be placed 115 ft (35 m) away. This distance might be difficult to achieve if there were pipe bridges or other structures in the way. Lowering the inlet pressure to the monitor might be one solution as this would reduce the height of the foam jet, but it may in certain circumstances affect the quality of the foam. Air conditions and the intensity of the fire will, of course, influence these distances.

In tanks or bunds where there is sufficient ullage space to allow for the direction of the foam stream against the sides or back of the burning area the foam stream should be directed against the far side (if possible) of the tank or containing area above the surface of the burning oil, so that the velocity of the stream will be broken and the foam will fall gently over the surface. Direct application of high velocity streams will cause turbulence and possible submergence of the foam; if there is little ullage space some of the burning oil may be splashed out of the confining area.

Where it is impossible to reach the far side of the container, the stream should be directed against the side above the liquid. The foam will flow over the entire area and blanket the fire, except in the case of very large diameter tanks, where the foam burn back rate may exceed the rate of application of foam.

If approach cannot be made near enough to direct the stream against the side or back of the container, the fireman should aim the stream in front of the fire in such a manner as to bounce the foam on to the burning surface with the minimum of velocity. This, of course, only applies when the top of the container is very near the ground. As soon as possible approach should be made so that the foam can be directed into the container. On tall containers which cannot be reached from the ground, turntable ladders, hydraulic platforms or portable pourers may provide the necessary height to reach the fire.

Care should be taken to see that no break occurs in the foam delivery from an individual branch, as a result of which water could be applied through the branch. Not only is it dangerous for water to enter a container in this way, but it may break down the foam blanket already built up. For the same reason water and foam should not be used together on the same surface, or where the two can come into contact.

After the container has been completely blanketed, the surface should not be disturbed until it is certain that all hot metal has cooled sufficiently to prevent re-ignition. Branches should be kept in position so that any break in the foam blanket can be covered immediately.

4. EXTINGUISHING PETROLEUM FIRES

Fires at large refineries are often successfully dealt with by the refinery fire-fighting personnel, and the role of the local authority fire brigade is generally one of reinforcing refinery fire fighters when larger fires occur. The technical knowledge of refinery fire officers can be invaluable to a local authority fire officer if, by virtue of his rank, he will have to take command of a large fire at a refinery; good liaison is therefore essential.

Fire fighting to be effective involves both fire control and fire extinguishment. Prevention of fire spread often determines the success of extinguishing efforts. This involves the protection of tanks, other structures and pipelines that are affected by radiant heat or by direct flame impingement. Cooling streams of water should be directed so as to give adequate water coverage without waste. The maintenance of adequate drainage of a fire area will prevent floating blazing oil igniting unfired areas, and often provides a means of removing fuel with consequent salvage of product and plant. The construction of temporary drains, ditches and dykes is also a phase of fire control which is especially valuable if a boil-over (*see* par. (b)(ii)) becomes imminent. Blanketing unignited pools of oil with foam will also guard against fire spread.

Fires in storage tanks can be extremely hazardous, and as a general rule fire-fighting personnel should NOT be allowed to go on to the roof of a tank which is on fire, unless it is essential for rescue purposes. Refinery personnel with their technical knowledge will sometimes deal with small fires in tanks, particularly at the seal of floating roof tanks, at roof level; generally they will try to deal with the fire from the wind girder at the perimeter. Conditions on the top of a floating roof tank can be dangerous, especially when the pontoon is low, as vapour can collect above the pontoon if there has been a leak at the seal.

Successful fire extinguishment results from the systematic application of planned procedures. Those born of panic often add to the seriousness of the emergency, and at every stage, expert advice should be sought from operatives or refinery fire personnel who have a much greater and more intimate knowledge of the processes and risks involved. Refinery personnel will attend to such control procedures as elimination of fuel supplies by closing pipeline blocks or by re-routing flow elsewhere, depressurising systems, blowing down a complete unit or pumping out tanks. A water displacement procedure may be suggested whereby water could be introduced into equipment from which flammable liquid is leaking, although this can only be done if the temperature of the hydrocarbon is below the boiling point of water.

(a) Process unit fires

These are extinguished principally by fuel removal. This depends upon operatives being able to reduce pressure, introduce steam or nitrogen to the systems and to depressurise part or all of the unit involved.

The area and intensity of the fire will indicate the proper method of extinguishment. Small fires can be combated with dry powder or steam, and foam should be used where it can blanket the burning fuel. Water in the form of fine spray is most effective on large areas or intense fires that threaten damage to supporting structures and adjacent equipment. Care should be taken in the use of water, as contraction may cause flanges and joints to leak, thereby adding more fuel to the fire. The water stream should be adjusted where necessary to very fine spray to lessen this danger.

Tower structures, such as fractionating towers, which form part of process units are often difficult to deal with on account of their height. The first step is always to get the feedstock shut off and the system taken out of service and depressurised. Water from spray branches may not have sufficient trajectory to reach fire at the top, and it may be necessary to use large solid jets which can be trained either to impinge on each other so that the spray is carried on to the structure, or so that they break up near the top of the structure and the wind or convection currents carry the spray to the tower. The jets must not be played directly on to the structure. If quantities of oil are flashed to lower levels and continue to burn in pools, foam or dry powder should be applied. Large fire areas should be covered with water spray so as to protect supporting structures, especially while operatives attempt to control the supply of fuel.

It should be remembered, however, that water streams used on surrounding risks will soon flood the area and may float the contents of oily water drainage systems to the surface in a short time. To prevent flash over and immediate danger to personnel, a foam blanket should be laid down quickly and maintained even after extinguishment until all possible sources of re-ignition have been checked.

It should be remembered that where large quantities of water are being used, much of it will run to waste. It may be possible to recycle the water, *i.e.*, to use pumps at suitable places where their suctions can be set in to the waste water, which can be directed back on to the fire.

(b) Fixed roof tank fires

On tanks from which the roof has blown or on which a seam has opened, foam should be used. Where fixed foam facilities exist, these should be used in the first instance if possible, but if foam cannot be applied immediately, the tank shell should be protected, particularly near the fixed foam chambers and risers, with cooling water until foam is ready to be used through this equipment. If there are no fixed chambers or risers, but portable towers are available, foam should be applied through these and discharged over the rim of the tank in sufficient quantity to maintain the recommended delivery rate, *i.e.*, at least 1 gallon of foam per square foot (50 l/m²) of surface area per minute. Advantage can also be taken of fixed equipment to apply foam to adjacent tanks if necessary, and to effect a seal on top of the contents.

Foam towers should not be erected and placed over burning tanks until such time as the equipment necessary to produce foam is ready. Without the cooling effect of the foam passing through the towers, they will be liable to rapid overheating and collapse. With some types of tower, foam should not be pumped through them until they are resting against the tank shell, as they are not designed to handle the hydraulic load without the support from the shell. Normally, however, portable towers are only supplied at a refinery to replace fixed chambers that may be damaged in an initial explosion, so there may not be sufficient available to give the required rate of foam application. If portable towers are not available in sufficient number, foam monitors should be used.

Fires burning outside the tank should be extinguished to avoid heat being applied to the tank shell. Fires in bunded areas, however, associated with tank fires are infrequent.

Cooling water should be applied to the tank shell *above* the liquid level and to any intact portion of the roof of the burning tank, provided that the water running off does not enter the tank. Water streams should on no account be directed into the tank as this will destroy the foam blanket and possibly cause a slop-over or a boil-over (*see* par. (i) and (ii) below).

Any tanks within 150 ft (45 m) downwind of the tank on fire should be cooled with water streams. Cooling a tank, the contents of which have not ignited but which is exposed to the heat of an adjacent fire, by means of water applied to the roof and/or shell, will prevent excessive evaporation and will lessen the danger of fire spread. Alternatively, screens of water can perhaps be projected downwind between tanks at risk (Fig. 5-26). The spray must be angled as wide as possible and should be at a height sufficient to prevent flames passing over the top of the spray curtain.

If the tank contains asphalt or other heavy stock and the roof has blown clear, one method of extinguishment which is suggested by some refinery personnel is that water streams should be directed high into the air upwind so that the spray will fall through the flames into the burning oil. This will cause foaming and may extinguish the flames. Such an application of water, however, must be done very carefully in intermittent waves to avoid an extensive slop-over. If foam is used in attempting extinguishment, it should be introduced at one point only and must be shut off immediately if a slop-over occurs.

(i) *Slop-overs.* The probability of slop-overs should be reckoned with under the conditions conducive to producing them. Sometimes when the tank is almost full and has little outage at the beginning of a fire, the thermal expansion of the oil or violent boiling on top of the cool oil due to the presence of a little water may cause sufficient increase in the volume of the oil so that the contents overflow. These preliminary overflows are referred to as '*slop-overs*' and although they may look serious (Plate 110), they are usually small in extent.

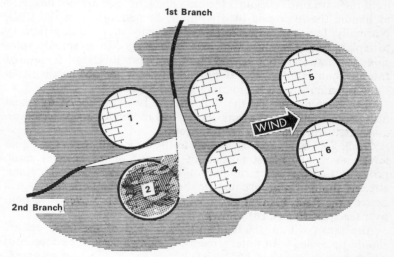

Fig. 5–26. Diagram showing how water sprays can be projected downwind between tanks so as to protect tanks which are not on fire.

Slop-overs may occur at almost any time during the fire. They may occur spontaneously with 'wet' oil (*i.e.* oil containing a percentage of water); they may occur from the sudden application of foam; from rain or sprays from branches, or they may result from the thermal expansion of the oil as it heats or from boiling of the surface.

Warning of a slop-over is given by the lighter colour of the smoke at the top of the tank on the windward side owing to the formation of steam, while a sizzling sound indicates wetness in the oil. If conditions are such that a slop-over is likely, preparations should be made to extinguish any burning oil which may reach the bunded area by water from hose lines equipped with fine spray nozzles. All fire-fighting personnel should be withdrawn to outside the bund wall whilst such conditions prevail.

(ii) *Boil-overs.* Some crudes and unrefined oils when burning develop a 'heat wave' that travels downward from the burning surface at a rate of from 15 to 20 in. (380 to 1,270 mm) per hour. The temperature of the oil in this heat wave may reach 250° to 300°C, that is, well above the boiling temperature of water. When this heat wave reaches the bottom water or reaches the bottom oil in which sufficient water is suspended, a violent *'boil-over'* will occur. A boil-over is a sudden eruption under the liquid whereby some of the liquid is carried out with the generated steam.

Since water flashed into steam increases in volume 1,700 times, if the steam be entirely held by the oil, one gallon of water would produce 1,700 gallons of froth. Unless this frothy steam can break out on the surface in large bubbles, it becomes entrained in the oil and a wave of burning oil which may amount to several hundred tons is thrown out. The burning oil first erupts and then falls, possibly spreading beyond the bund walls of the tank.

Three conditions must exist simultaneously if a boil-over is to occur, namely:

A.   water must be present;

B.   the oil must produce a heat wave;

C.   the oil must be viscous enough to form a froth when the heat wave hits the water and turns it into steam.

An oil containing fractions of widely differing gravities and boiling points can be expected to cause a heat wave as it burns, and the production of this heat wave and its rate of travel is mainly caused by the impurities and free carbon in it. Distilled oils, such as petrol, kerosene, diesel and lubricating oils with their narrower boiling ranges and lack of impurities *do not* produce a heat wave. The daily oil inventory which is maintained at each refinery should be consulted to determine the product in the tank, and bottom water gauges will confirm if and when a boil-over is expected.

A boil-over is usually preceded by a marked heightening and brightening of the flames for a period of a few minutes, and the officer in charge should always be on the lookout (or should delegate an officer for this purpose) for these warnings, so that positions of safety can be sought (*see* par. 7, 'Safety of personnel'). The signs of warning of a boil-over are somewhat similar to those for a 'slop-over'. A vertical stripe of temperature paint can be used on tanks to indicate the progress of the heat wave. Where no indicator paint is available, water thrown on the side of the tank will indicate the bottom of the hot layer. The location of the heat wave can also be determined from the wavy appearance of the air adjacent to the shell of the tank at the depth to which the hot oil has reached. If extinguishment has failed by the time the heat wave has reached a point 5 ft (1·5 m) above a known bottom water level, all personnel should be immediately withdrawn from the area.

It may be possible to use the draining pipes at the base of the tank to remove water, and so reduce the chances of a boil-over. There is a danger in using this procedure as it may not be possible to close the drain cocks once they have been opened, with the result that oil could escape into the bund and possibly ignite. Any action decided in this connection should only be taken after close consultation with the refinery officials.

After a boil-over has occurred, the oil at the base of the tank will have been cooled, but subsequently it will again be heated by conduction from above. A second heat wave may occur and if there is any water at the bottom, a second boil-over will occur. This sequence can continue so long as there is any water in the tank. Officers in charge should therefore continually be on their guard against the possibility of successive boil-overs.

Exact figures for the rate of expansion of the heat wave cannot be given, but the figures shown in Table VII give some guidance in estimating the time in which a boil-over may be expected. Also given are the burning rates for oil in a tank burning at the surface only; they are not applicable for oil in a tank involved in a bund fire.

TABLE VII

Rates of expansion of 'heat wave' and of burning rates

Type of oil	Rate of expansion of 'heat wave' per hour		Burning rate per hour	
	in.	mm	in.	mm
Light oils . .	—	—	6–12	152–305
Medium oils . .	—	—	5–8	127–203
Heavy oils . .	3–20	76–508	3–5	76–127
Light crude . .	15–35	381–889	4–18	102–457
Heavy crude . .	3–20	76–508	3–5	76–127

(c) Floating roof tanks

Because there is no vapour space beneath the roof of a floating roof tank, there should be no danger of explosion. A certain leakage of vapour will occur through the seal where the roof meets the shell, and this may become ignited, causing the seal to burn. Fire can also occur through dipholes, if they are left open. However, a floating roof tank is vulnerable to fire and/or explosion when the roof is standing on the jacks and there is a vapour space beneath it.

Small seal fires are generally extinguished by refinery personnel with portable dry powder equipment, but reflash due to the heated metal or smouldering seal fabric may occur. Foam can be applied from small portable foam branches on to the seal area. When foam is applied by refinery personnel, it is normally done from the wind girder or top gantry, as application from the ground is difficult and possibly ineffective. Very fine water spray can be used to cool the exposed metal to avoid reflash, and possibly to extinguish the fire itself. If the fire extends over a larger portion around the rim, the task of extinguishment can be speeded by applying two foam streams working from opposite directions around the wind girder.

Cooling water should be applied to the shell of any hot spot which will be indicated by blistered paint. It can be applied to the outside of the shell, or, if care is used, to the inside of the shell, but care should be taken to avoid directing heavy water streams into the flammable material at the roof edge, as this may splash the burning product on to the roof and increase the seriousness of the fire.

The same precautions should be taken for possible, but improbable, fires outside the tank, and the necessity for cooling adjacent tanks if the heat of the tank on fire is of such a magnitude to affect other tanks. Floating roof tank fires are not, however, usually of great magnitude.

Should the floating roof have been displaced by explosion or fire, the fire should be tackled with foam as for a fire in an open tank.

(d) Tank vent fires

Fire at a tank vent that is burning with a yellow-orange flame emitting black smoke indicates a vapour-rich condition within the tank that is above the flammable or explosive limits. This type of fire is usually dealt with by refinery personnel by smothering with steam, dry powder, carbon dioxide or wet blankets. Danger of an explosion is not indicated under these conditions.

Fire at a tank vent which burns with a snapping blue-red nearly smokeless flame indicates a vapour-air mixture within the tank that is within the flammable range. There is danger of an explosion should the flame reach the inside of the tank and no one should go on to the roof while this condition exists. The vapour space of the tank might be converted into a vapour-rich condition by refinery operatives pumping liquid into the tank, thereby maintaining a positive pressure, or by the introduction of fuel gas or other light flammable products. When a vapour-rich condition is indicated by a change in the flame character to a smoky or yellow-orange flame, danger of an explosion has subsided. Extinguishment can then be attempted by smothering with steam, water spray, dry powder or wet blankets.

Any action to convert the vapour space within the tank into a vapour-rich condition should not be attempted by firemen without prior consultation and agreement with responsible officials at the refinery, and then every precaution must be taken to prevent exposure of men to the danger of explosion.

(e) Fires in tanks under repair or demolition

Although for the sake of convenience, this section is included in this chapter on oil refineries, it should be borne in mind that there are many wharves or industrial concerns where flammable liquids are stored in tanks, and it is generally in these smaller establishments where the greatest risk arises as they do not always maintain the high standards of safety and efficiency which are to be found at the major refineries. The fire-fighting techniques which are suggested for dealing with fires in tanks under repair or demolition should be taken as applying to all establishments where such work is carried out.

Information which will be of value to the fire brigade officer will include:

A. the name of the Safety Officer or other person with whom contact should be made on arrival;

B. the types, general condition, history of previous uses of the tanks and any special features including properties, hazards and appropriate extinguishing methods for the substances concerned. If required, advice on the properties, etc. of any particular substances can be obtained from H.M. Chief Inspector of Explosives;

C. potential hazards which may arise at other points as a consequence of demolition or repair work being undertaken.

(i) *Hazards*. It is a requirement of Section 31(4) of the Factories Act 1961 that any tank or vessel which contains or has contained any explosive or flammable substance must be rendered inert before any welding, brazing or soldering or any cutting operation which involves the application of heat is started. The reason for this requirement is, of course, the very high risk of fire or explosion occurring where partially-closed vessels which might contain flammable materials are subject to such operations. In demolition work the more general requirements of regulation 40 of the Construction (General Provisions) Regulations 1961 apply.

Solid deposits tend to accumulate on the inside surfaces of tanks, or sludge forms in the base of a tank, and this can be as hazardous as the original contents. Furthermore, this may not necessarily be removed by normal processes of cleaning. In consequence, the demolition or repair of tanks is always a hazardous operation. It must be borne in mind that substances not normally regarded as presenting an explosion hazard can give off flammable vapours when heated or as a result of reaction with other substances, and these flammable vapours can form an explosive or combustible mixture when mixed with air. It is not practicable to give an extensive list, but examples are oils, paints, and even the less volatile solvents etc. In some cases old deposits adhering to the internal surfaces or sludge at the base of a tank may in this way be more hazardous than the original contents.

For small vessels, such as motor car fuel tanks, and tanks up to about 6,000 gallons (27 276 litres), both vapours and residues can usually be readily removed by steaming out. (Whenever steaming out is attempted, the steam nozzle should be bonded to the tank to dissipate the generation of electrostatic charges.) With larger tanks, the problem is somewhat different. Owing to the high heat capacity of the tank, steaming out cannot be relied upon to volatilise all residues unless very large quantities of steam are readily available. However, explosive concentrations of vapour in the tank can usually be eliminated either by forced ventilation using a blower or eductor system or, for vertical tanks, by natural ventilation by removing top and bottom manholes. Ventilation by itself, however, will ultimately only remove the volatile materials present in the tank and will never remove the heavy ends or solid residues and tars. These types of residue themselves can contain considerable quantities of volatiles and unless they are removed, can and do give rise to a very high fire risk.

The types of storage tank likely to be encountered are vertical cylindrical tanks, usually with a roof of light construction, either fixed or floating, or horizontal tanks of uniform construction without lightweight sections. These latter tanks generally present the greater hazard.

(ii) *General precautions.* If the fire brigade is called to a fire which has broken out when a tank is being demolished or repaired it will be clear that the proper safety procedure has not been observed. (Although it is less likely, fire may occur in any empty storage tank not under demolition or repair; but the advice in the following paragraphs is equally relevant.) The situation should be treated as potentially extremely hazardous. Normally for a fire to be sustained in a tank there must be openings in the tank to admit air. If these openings are limited the fire is likely to have extinguished itself before the brigade arrives. But even if the fire has apparently gone out, the vapour mixture in the tank may still be highly dangerous because the fire may have caused decomposition or vaporisation of residues which may produce a flammable or explosive mixture, probably with toxic hazards as well. It should *always* be assumed that there is a risk of a violent explosion except when the top or end of the tank has been previously removed.

In no circumstances should men go on top of or inside a tank in which there is a fire or in which one has recently occurred unless it is essential for rescue purposes. If it is essential to enter a tank, the probability of toxic hazards should be borne in mind and breathing apparatus should be worn. If anyone is on top of a tank, he should be told to come down. Nor should anyone go on top of an adjacent tank unless it is essential for operational reasons. No attempt should be made to open or close manholes or other fitments, because this may adversely affect the atmosphere in a tank. If forced ventilation is being used, for example by means of a blower or eductor, it should be switched off if this can be done remotely.

(iii) *Fire-fighting techniques.* Neither water jets nor high or low pressure sprays must be directed into a tank in which there is fire (or a fire is suspected) because entrainment of flammable materials— *i.e.*, gases or vapours—by the water can cause rapid mixing to give a potentially explosive mixture. Similarly, the cooling of the outside of a tank in which vapour has been ignited should be avoided, because of the danger of an intake of air following condensation of the vapours inside the tank.

The following paragraphs describe alternative situations in which either fire-fighting procedures are recommended (differing according to the system of venting or inerting in use during demolition or repair, the nature and location of the fire, or the size of the tank), or it is suggested that the fire should be allowed to burn out. The advice should be regarded as no more than a general guide, because the action to be taken must in the final analysis depend upon the circumstances of each case.

In addition to deciding whether the situation is one in which one of the recommended fire-fighting procedures is appropriate, fire brigade officers should bear in mind that any attempt to tackle a fire will possibly involve some degree of risk to their men, and they must judge whether the need to save lives and/or to prevent further damage to the tank itself or the spread of fire to surrounding property justifies taking that risk. In any event, whether the fire is fought or allowed to burn out, action should be taken to protect persons in the area from the effects of a possible explosion and to minimise the effect of radiant heat on adjacent property and installations.

(iv) *Fire in a tank being steamed.* If a fire occurs in a tank which is being steamed, the supply of steam should at least be maintained and if possible increased as a means of both inerting the tank and purging it of hazardous vapours. If this is unsuccessful, the fire should be allowed to burn out, notwithstanding the possibility of explosion. Water should under no circumstances be used in or on the tank, for the reasons given in par. (iii) above.

(v) *Fire in a tank not being steamed.* If a fire occurs in a tank not being steamed, then, unless it is clear when the brigade arrives that the fire has gone out, one of the following procedures may be appropriate:

A. *If there is a gas or vapour flame burning outside an opening on the top of the tank,* an attempt should be made to achieve quick extinction by means of a high pressure jet from a distance in order to remove the risk of a flash-back. The jet should be swept quickly across the aperture, care being taken to avoid as far as possible large quantities of water either entering the tank or cooling the outside surfaces, for the reasons given in par. (iii). If the attempt shows no sign of immediate success, or after initial success the flame reappears, the attempt should be discontinued since the implication is that the primary source of the fire is inside the tank, and in these circumstances the fire should be allowed to burn out notwithstanding the possibility of an explosion.

B. *If there are signs of fire but no external flames are visible,* the fire may have to be allowed to burn out notwithstanding the possibility of explosion. If, however, *a bottom manhole is open,* and it is felt that, for example because of surrounding risks, the fire must be tackled, this may be practicable in the following circumstances. Although assessment of the location of the fire within the tank will be difficult because only a very restricted view of the inside of the tank can be obtained from a distance, and even this is likely to be obscured by smoke, it is still possible that the source of the fire inside the tank may either be visible or can be confidently estimated from a safe distance. If so, and if the fire is at the base of the tank, low expansion foam may be introduced. If, however, the fire is higher up and high expansion foam is available, it can be used provided its application does not entail undue risk to personnel and is operationally feasible. If available, the use of carbon dioxide may be considered as an alternative to foam, *but only if the tank is known to be on fire,* because of possible static hazards during discharge operations which may themselves give rise to fire or explosion. Even if the foam or carbon dioxide does not succeed in extinguishing the fire it should have the effect of restricting it. Whatever extinguishing agent is used, it must be introduced only at points that are already open at the base of the tank.

(vi) *Fire in a small tank.* If a fire occurs in a small tank (which as a general rule should be regarded as one having a maximum capacity of approximately 2,000 cubic feet (about 60 m³) or 12,500 gallons (about 56 800 litres)) which has only one manhole open, the fire can only be attacked by playing a low expansion foam jet through the manhole from a distance. It should be appreciated that this is a difficult operation to carry out.

(vii) *Fire in a tank with the top or end off.* If the top or end of the tank has been completely removed, normal fire-fighting procedure with low expansion foam or water spray should be effective and there should be no risk of disruptive explosion. Water should not be used if light residues are likely to float out.

(viii) *Subsequent action.* In all cases the situation should be treated as hazardous. The period of danger must be regarded as lasting until the whole of the tank and its contents are cold—24 hours should be sufficient for this. It will not always be easy to tell whether the fire has in fact been extinguished. It must also be remembered that the atmosphere in a tank in which a fire has occurred may still be both explosive and toxic and strict precautions must be observed before such tanks are entered. If the owner of the tank is a small operator (*i.e.,* the tank is not at a major refinery), the operator should be warned that it is essential that all materials involved in a fire should be removed from the tank or other positions before demolition or repair work is resumed. He should also be advised to get expert guidance on what to do next, and to consult the District Inspector of Factories as to sources of advice. He should be particularly warned against further use of any heating device until expert advice has been obtained.

(f) Spill fires

This type of fire is most difficult to deal with especially if it is flowing, and is being fed by a tank or pressurised pipeline. The source of the leak should be immediately found and stopped if possible. If it is a continuous leak which cannot be stopped, the refinery personnel will endeavour to take the equipment out of service, de-pressurise it and steam it out if necessary.

Small fires can be blanketed with steam or dry powder, but care should be taken to avoid scattering the burning material. Large fire areas should be attacked with fine water spray in order to protect supporting structures, and the water spray should be maintained until refinery personnel can control the flow of fuel, but the danger of a flash-back should be remembered. If quantities of oil are flashed down to lower levels and continue to burn in pools, foam or dry powder should be applied.

One of the difficulties in applying foam is that most spill fires soon cover a large area, and there is no surface against which to break the velocity of the foam stream. A spray-stream is the most effective, but lacking such a nozzle, the foam branch should be held almost parallel with the ground so that the jet strikes between the operator and the fire and the foam carries forward to fall gently on the fire without undue disturbance of the liquid.

It is generally best at a flowing spill fire to start at the farthest point of the fire and work towards the source of the spill. Using either method of foam spray stream or bouncing, it is best to form a heavy blanket beyond the farthest point of the fire at the lowest level so that when burning liquid reaches this blanket, it will flow beneath it and be extinguished.

Sometimes it may be necessary to dig a trench or hole, or to erect an earthen dyke to collect burning liquid that is threatening structures or other plant in its path. When the liquid is contained, foam can be applied to it and to the path leading to the basin.

When a spill fire threatens buildings or property in its path, a thick blanket of foam should be applied to the exposed structure to act as an insulating medium. A straight foam stream is generally best for this purpose.

(g) Road tankers and rail cars

Fires involving road tankers or rail cars at refineries usually occur whilst filling operations are in progress. Pumping operations should be stopped immediately and the valves in the fuel lines to the tanks should be closed. Water from spray branches should be used to cool the tankers, and should be maintained after flame extinguishment until all danger of re-igniting from hot steel has been eliminated. Road tankers or rail cars in the vicinity of the fire should be removed if possible and adjacent refinery equipment and other tankers should also be protected by cooling with water spray. Fires in road tankers and rail cars whilst outside refineries are dealt with in Part 6C of the _Manual_, Chapter 5, 'Fires in Fuels'.

(h) Marine terminals or jetties

Here the chief danger is when oil tankers are discharging their cargo of crude oil and the first action is to get the fuel lines shut off if this is not automatic in action. If the fire involves the tankers themselves, foam will be required in large quantities, and if the refinery has fire-fighting tugs at hand, these should be brought into action immediately.

The action is similar to fighting a crude oil fire in a tank, but there is the added complication that there is also a danger of oil being discharged into the water and either causing oil contamination, or burning oil on the water can be a danger to other vessels or jetties.

Details of fighting tanker fires are contained in Part 7 of the *Manual*, Chapter 3, 'Fires in Ships'.

5. LIQUEFIED PETROLEUM GAS FIRES

Because the storage in bulk of liquefied petroleum gases occurs not only at oil refineries and distributing depots, but also at producer and holder stations of the Gas Boards, as well as at a number of large industrial premises, the subject of risks, types of container, fire protection and fire-fighting techniques is dealt with in detail in Part 6C of the *Manual*, Chapter 5, 'Fires in Fuels'.

6. PIPELINE FIRES

The routing, marking and legal aspects of pipelines as well as fire fighting, are also dealt within Chapter 5 of Part 6C of the *Manual*, but because most pipelines originate from the major oil refineries, the fire fighting and other aspects at a refinery are discussed in greater detail below.

(a) Operating pressures

Operating pressures in a pipeline may vary from several hundreds of pounds per square inch near the pumps to nominal pressures at the receiving terminals. Therefore, in the event of a fracture of a pipe within the refinery near the pumps, large quantities of highly flammable liquid may be discharged at considerable velocity; if this catches fire it may involve plant and equipment nearby. There is a better prospect, however, of the pumps being shut down more quickly than would be the case if the fracture occurred at a distance many miles away from the refinery.

(b) Diameter of pipelines

Pipeline diameters vary from a few inches to a number of feet, and Table VIII shows the approximate capacity per yard (metre) and the approximate length of pipe to contain 4,000 gallons (or 20 000 litres).

TABLE VIII

Diameter of pipe (in.)	Capacity Gals. per yard	Length to contain 4,000 gals. (yards)	Diameter of pipe (mm)	Capacity Litres per metre	Length to contain 20,000 litres (metres)
3	0·92	4,348	10	3·8	5 196
4	1·63	2,454	100	7·8	2 546
6	3·66	1,093	150	17·6	1 132
8	6·51	614	200	31·4	637
9	8·23	486	300	70·7	283
10	10·18	393	500	196·3	102
12	14·64	273	600	282·8	71
15	22·9	174			
20	40·7	98			
24	58·61	67			

(c) Isolating valves

Isolating valves, which are suitably indicated, are provided at intervals in the pipeline. They should only be operated under direction from refinery officials. Two types are found:

(i) *Underground.* These are contained in a concrete chamber beneath a metal cover. The spindle rotation direction is indicated and they can be operated by a standard hydrant key.

(ii) *Above ground.* These are situated in a padlocked wire compound. Control is by a wheel valve, also indicated with the direction of rotation. The location of control valves outside refineries is notified to the brigades through whose areas they pass.

(d) Contents of pipelines

The contents of a pipeline can be liquid or gas. Ethylene is conveyed as a gas to chemical works for the manufacture of ethylene glycol, ethylene oxide, polythene and terylene. Butane and propane are sent by pipeline to Gas Boards. Some pipelines are multiproducts; for example, petrol, jet fuel or other white oils are conveyed from Fawley to London Airport. Other pipelines are at present in use from the refineries on the north bank of the River Thames to Coventry, and these will eventually be extended to Ellesmere Port on the River Mersey in Lancashire. Brigades generally are advised of the contents of pipelines passing through their territory. Fires involving various flammable liquids or gases are discussed below.

(e) Fires involving ethylene pipelines

The fire should not be extinguished while the gas is escaping under pressure, but should be treated in the same way as a gas main fire, *i.e.*, surrounding risks should be covered with cooling spray whilst waiting for the appropriate valves to be turned off, or whilst permission to shut down is awaited, if away from the refinery. Water in the form of spray can be used to control an ethylene vapour fire, but water should never be used on liquid ethylene. If possible, the fire should be allowed to burn itself out. When the flame diminishes, it should be snuffed out to prevent the entry of air into the pipeline. Breathing apparatus may be required if there is a concentration of heavy vapour.

(f) Fires involving LPG pipelines

The liquid, due to the absorption of heat to cause vaporisation, will be very cold, and the gas will freeze the moisture in the atmosphere giving the appearance of a white fog; this would be flammable at the outer edges. To prevent ignition, consideration should be given to:

(i) the direction in which the gas will flow;

(ii) the strength of the wind;

(iii) weather conditions, *i.e.*, sunshine, dampness or fog.

Fire fighting of LPG pipelines is similar to that for bulk storage tanks (*see* Part 6C, Chapter 5). Protein foam can be used to limit the flame area on a spill which has ignited, applying gently from the edges and working progressively from the sides so as to avoid the conditions likely to lead to a flash-over. *Water jets should not be used* on liquid gas fires as this will cause very rapid vaporisation leading to a very hot, large burning cloud of gas (Plate 111).

Should pipelines containing LPG become exposed to radiated heat, or the discharge from the pipeline noticeably increase in volume, or become noisy, it should be taken as a DANGER sign. If additional cooling does not have the effect of reducing the pressure, hoses should be lashed and personnel withdrawn.

When the line has been isolated by closing the necessary valves, the pressure in the line will drop as escaping liquid is burned. Extinguishment should only be undertaken after consultation with an official of the oil company. Extinction can be achieved with water spray, dry powder or vaporising liquid.

(g) Fires involving multi-product pipelines

Escaping liquid should be contained in as small an area as possible, and action taken to avoid the liquid entering drains, ditches, streams or confined spaces. Until the liquid has been identified, it should be treated as for petrol and normal stand-by procedure adopted. It should be assumed that the liquid will vaporise, and so the necessary steps should be taken to guard against re-ignition, and to safeguard people downwind or at lower levels.

If the product has ignited, water spray should be used to protect adjacent equipment, pipelines or other exposed hazards, especially if the liquid contents of pipelines are known to have stopped flowing. When foam compound is available, the fire should be extinguished by a determined foam attack.

7. SAFETY OF PERSONNEL

There are many hazards in an oil refinery, especially so when a fire occurs, and the following are rules which should be observed by officers and men in the interests of general safety.

(a) Any crew of fire-fighting personnel stationed in a hazardous position should have an observer attached to it whose task is to warn the men when danger is imminent, and a pre-arranged signal for this purpose should be agreed upon. Often this observer could be an officer of the refinery, such as the Safety Officer, whose technical knowledge is such that he will be intimate with the main dangers, and a fire brigade officer should act as a liaison officer.

A path of retreat should be planned if necessary and kept clear of all obstructions. The path should be illuminated if necessary by night.

(b) Men should not work inside a bund wall if there is any danger of a boil-over or a slop-over, or if the work can be done adequately from outside. When it is necessary to work within a bund, points of egress should be agreed upon.

(c) Where necessary, men should be protected from radiated heat by improvised shields, and reliefs should be arranged at frequent intervals. This protection should be given even if the heat does not make it immediately necessary, as a change of wind may easily increase the heat. Men working in extreme heat may be kept cool by water spray.

(d) Men should *NOT* be allowed on tank roofs unless absolutely necessary, and *NEVER* on empty tanks which are on fire (*see* also page 326). If men have to go on to a tank roof (*e.g.* for a vent fire), they should take lines with them in case they are cut off from the ladder.

(e) When a boil-over is probable, no one should be allowed within a considerable distance of the tank. Men should not take shelter behind tanks or buildings if there is any danger of their being trapped by an oil wave. Direct flames from a boil-over may extend several tank-diameters away from the fire.

(f) The possibility of filled pipelines or drums of oil which are involved in the fire splitting or exploding must not be overlooked. When oil is held between two closed valves, a relatively small amount of heat will cause a considerable pressure rise with the possibility of fracture.

(g) Breathing apparatus should be worn when necessary to protect against toxic or asphyxiating vapours or gases.

(h) Personnel should *NOT* be allowed to smoke. It may not be dangerous in the vicinity of the fire, yet highly so if the men move within the range of vapour elsewhere in the refinery.

Printed in England for Her Majesty's Stationery Office by The Hillingdon Press, Uxbridge, Middlesex.
Dd 289177 K 104 8/75.